WRITINGS OF
LEON TROTSKY
[1934-35]

Writings of Leon Trotsky

is a collection, in eleven volumes, of pamphlets, articles, letters, and interviews written during Trotsky's third and final exile (1929-1940). They include many articles translated into English for the first time. They do not include the books and pamphlets from this period that are permanently in print, nor unpublished material in the Trotsky Archives at Harvard University Library.

WRITINGS OF LEON TROTSKY

[1934-35]

PATHFINDER PRESS, INC.
NEW YORK 1971

This volume is dedicated to the memory of
ART PREIS (1911-1964),
labor editor of *The Militant* and
author of *Labor's Giant Step.*

Edited by George Breitman and Bev Scott

First edition, 1971

PATHFINDER PRESS, INC.
410 West Street
New York, N. Y. 10014

CONTENTS

PREFACE

After four-and-a-half years in Turkey, Leon and Natalia Trotsky were permitted to move to France, where they lived for two years. This volume covers the second of those years: June 1934-June 1935.

Trotsky turned fifty-five during this year, and before it was over he wrote in his diary, "Old age is the most unexpected of all the things that happen to a man." Between recurring bouts of illness, he was still strong, vigorous, combative and productive. But his personal situation was extremely insecure.

His expulsion from the country was being demanded by the French fascists and the French Stalinists, and from both these quarters there was the possibility of physical assault. In April 1934 the Doumergue government had ordered him deported, but was unable to carry out the order because no country would accept him. Trotsky's friends feared that the government might at any time send him off to one of its penal colonies in Africa. Under severe restrictions from the police — he had to remain incognito, he could not stay in or near Paris or in any of the departments bordering other countries, etc. — Trotsky was forced to leave Barbizon, where he had settled in 1933, and spent most of the spring moving from one hotel and *pension* to another, trying to find a place to live and work. In July he finally found refuge in the home of a schoolteacher in Domene, a tiny Alpine village near Grenoble in the Department of Isere, with Natalia but without secretaries or bodyguards. Here he remained until he left the country in June 1935. In addition to constant uncertainty about their own future, the Trotskys were also beset at the end of 1934, during the Soviet purge that followed the assassination of Kirov, by worry about the fate of their relatives still living in the Soviet Union, including their younger son Sergei.

The year 1933 had been the political turning point of Trotsky's third exile and of the movement he led. Hitler came to power, thanks in great part to the Communist International's ultraleft policy of opposing an antifascist united front with the Social Democrats, whom the Stalinists dubbed "social fascists," that is, a variety of fascism. In addition, the Stalinists capitulated to Hitler without firing a single shot, and the Comintern expressed approval for its German party's policy from beginning to end.

These events led Trotsky in mid-1933, as he was leaving Turkey for France, to propose a fundamental change in the strategy of the International Left Opposition (Bolshevik-Leninists). Up to then the Left Opposition had been committed to the policy of working to reform the Comintern and its affiliated parties; the Opposition considered and called itself a faction of the Comintern even though its members had been expelled. Trotsky now asserted that this approach, while correct up until the Comintern's capitulation to Hitler, was outmoded; the Comintern and its parties were too corrupted to be regenerated along Leninist lines; it was necessary now to abandon the perspective of reform and proclaim the need for a new International and new Leninist parties throughout the world. The leadership of the Left Opposition adopted this new perspective in August 1933 and in that same month persuaded three independent groups attending an international conference in Paris — the Socialist Workers Party (SAP) of Germany, the Independent Socialist Party (OSP) and the Revolutionary Socialist Party (RSP), both of Holland — to join it in a "Declaration of Four," calling for the formation of a new International.

Trotsky's energies were focused in 1934-35 on the complex political and organizational tasks involved in taking the next steps toward the building of the new International. The context in which these tasks presented themselves included the following features:

1. Hitler's victory had produced a deep ferment in the European working-class movement, and especially in the ranks of the Social Democracy, among whom leftward-moving tendencies began to grow (as Trotsky had predicted in 1933). In 1934 the Social Democratic workers of two countries — Austria in February, Spain in October — fought heroic though unsuccessful armed struggles against reactionary governments. In France, Spain, Belgium and Switzerland, sections of the Socialist youth became sympathetic to Trotsky's ideas, but did not want to leave their own organizations to join the small band of Bolshevik-Leninists (now renamed the International Communist League). Some suggested that the ICL members

join them in fighting for revolutionary positions inside the Social Democratic organizations.

2. The French fascists made a bid for power through an armed demonstration against the Chamber of Deputies in February 1934. Although they failed in this bid, the axis of the government was turned toward the right and the danger of fascism coming to France became real. Trotsky saw France now entering a prerevolutionary period and concluded that it had become the key to the international situation, as Germany had been the key in 1930-33. (The second selection in this volume, "A Program of Action for France," printed in June 1934, presents his analysis of the demands the French revolutionaries should raise in this situation.)

3. The French Socialist Party (SFIO) had experienced a split at the end of 1933, with the right wing of the party (the Neo-Socialists, or Neos) breaking away to form their own organization. This shifted the equilibrium in the SFIO to the left, strengthening the revolutionary tendencies there, especially among the youth. The SFIO at this time was the biggest working-class party in France. The ICL's French section, the Communist League, was very small and largely isolated from the mass movement.

4. Until 1934 the Communist International clung to the "third period" policy which had led to disaster in Germany. When a prominent French CP leader, Jacques Doriot, of Saint-Denis, proposed a change of policy and support for a united front against fascism, he was rebuked and later expelled. But after the February 1934 events, the Stalinists began to move away from ultraleftism — only to head quickly, as they had done in past zigzags, for the abyss of opportunism. In July 1934 the French Stalinist and SFIO leaders signed a pact for united action against fascism, and for a time there was talk of "organic unity," that is, a merger of the two parties. Such a unification of the two large parties would inevitably increase the isolation of the Communist League and hamper the development of the leftward-moving tendencies inside the SFIO.

5. The Stalinists were not really interested in a *working-class* (that is, anticapitalist) united front against fascism. In accord with a new rightward trend emanating from Moscow and soon to be made the rule internationally, the French Stalinist leaders appealed in October to the capitalist Radical (or Radical Socialist) Party to join the CP and SFIO in a class-collaborationist front of working-class and liberal-capitalist parties to oppose reaction and fascism. The Radicals accepted the bid, thus giving birth to the People's Front in 1935. This development, sanctioned by Moscow in the name of Leninism,

strengthened the authority of the reformist leaders of the SFIO
and hampered or disoriented oppositional tendencies in the
ranks.

6. Internationally, also, the Stalinists went further to the
right than ever before. As Trotsky noted in the first selection
in this volume, printed in June 1934, the Soviet bureaucracy,
then preparing to enter the League of Nations, was jettisoning
the Leninist analysis of that predecessor of the United Nations.
But that was only the beginning. In May 1935 the Soviet
Union and France signed a nonaggression pact, and Stalin,
quickly followed by the French Stalinists, endorsed the rearmament program of French imperialism. Social patriotism was
strongly reinforced at the expense of revolutionaries both inside and outside the SFIO.

7. Another factor of concern to Trotsky was the backsliding
in 1934-35 by the leaders of the German Socialist Workers
Party (SAP), who had signed the declaration for a new International in 1933 but now began obstructing all positive
moves to follow through.

How Trotsky intervened to cope with these problems — starting with his proposal in July 1934 for the Communist League
to join the SFIO (the so-called French turn) — is the main
content of this volume, along with his responses to the monstrous frame-up charges leveled against him by Moscow after
the Kirov assassination.

Many of the articles here are translated into English for the
first time, and until now many others had been printed only
in internal bulletins restricted to members of the ICL. Other
articles by Trotsky included here were unsigned when first
published or were signed by pen names, usually for security
reasons. Translations originally done in the 1930s have been
revised slightly to correct obvious errors and to achieve uni-
formity in spelling of names, punctuation, etc. Acknowledg-
ments about the articles and translations, and explanatory
material about the persons and events mentioned in them,
will be found in the section entitled "Notes and Acknowledg-
ments." "Other Writings of 1934-35" lists the books, pamphlets
and articles from that period which are not included in this
volume because they are in print and available. The date
preceding each article indicates when it was completed; if that
is not known, the date in parentheses indicates when it was
published.

The Editors
February 1971

CHRONOLOGY

1934

June — Trotsky, ordered to leave France in April but unable to go because no government will accept him, continues his search for a place to live in France.

June 20 — Moscow announces that the Revolutionary War Council, created during the civil war as the Red Army's top military, political and educational organization, has been abolished and its duties transferred to the military command headed by Commissar of War Voroshilov.

June 27 — Jacques Doriot is expelled from the French Communist Party.

June 30 — Hitler launches the "blood purge" that wipes out potentially oppositional elements among the Nazis and other bourgeois groups in Germany.

July — Trotsky finds a temporary home in Domene, an Alpine village, and returns to work on his biography of Lenin.

July 2 — French Socialist and Communist party leaders meet to discuss the possibility of a united front.

July 10 — Moscow announces the abolition of the secret political police (GPU) and its replacement by another body headed by Henry Yagoda.

July — The Communist League of France begins to discuss a proposal (known as "the French turn") that its members join the Socialist Party.

July 25 — Pro-German Austrian fascists assassinate Chancellor Dollfuss and try to overthrow his pro-Italian fascist regime. The uprising is defeated in four days.

July 27 — A united-front pact against fascism is signed by the French Socialist and Communist party leaders.

August 8 — Trotsky meets with three left-wing union leaders and discusses tactics of the teachers union.

August 29 — The Communist League votes at its national conference in favor of the French turn. Its members begin to
join the Socialist Party, within which they form the Bolshevik-Leninist Group.

September 18 — The Assembly of the League of Nations at
Geneva votes to admit the Soviet Union and give it a permanent seat on the Council.

October 5 — A revolutionary general strike begins in Spain under the leadership of the Socialist Party. It is crushed by
October 11.

October 9 — French foreign affairs minister Barthou and Yugo-
slav King Alexander I are assassinated at Marseilles.

October — Trotsky completes the pamphlet *Whither France?*

October — Maurice Thorez expresses the French Communist
Party's eagerness to make an alliance with the bourgeois
Radical Party.

November 8-9 — The Radicals withdraw their support from
the Doumergue government of France, which falls and is
replaced by one headed by another right-winger, Flandin.

November 12 — Moscow announces that 130,000 members of
the Soviet Communist Party have been expelled and 90,000
others put on probation.

November 30 — Conventions of the Communist League of
America and the American Workers Party vote to form the
Workers Party of the United States.

December 1 — Sergei Kirov, Stalinist leader in Leningrad, is
assassinated. Execution of 117 people accused of complicity
is announced in a few weeks. Zinoviev, Kamenev and others
are arrested on December 16.

December 28 — Trotsky writes pamphlet on Kirov assassination.

December — Spanish Young Socialists call for the formation
of a new International.

1935

January — Sergei Sedov, Trotsky's nonpolitical son, is arrested in the Soviet Union.

January 13 — The Saar votes overwhelmingly in a plebiscite
to be reunited with Germany.

January 15-17 — Zinoviev, Kamenev and seventeen others are
convicted of plotting to kill Soviet leaders. Zinoviev gets
ten-year sentence, others lesser terms. Seventy-eight are exiled.

February 1 — Trotsky completes pamphlet changing his position on the "Thermidorean analogy."

February 7 — Trotsky begins entries in journal later published as *Trotsky's Diary in Exile, 1935.*

February 15 — Several centrist organizations at a conference in Paris sponsored by the IAG (International Labor Community) reject a Dutch proposal to work for a new International.

March 3 — Two Dutch parties merge to form the Revolutionary Socialist Workers Party of Holland (RSAP).

March 18-19 — A young Bolshevik-Leninist delegate to a CGT conference delivers a speech prepared by Trotsky.

March 20 — The Norwegian Labor Party (NAP) takes over the government when the Agrarians support its move to oust the Liberal cabinet.

March — Trotsky meets with Marceau Pivert, leader of one of the left-wing groups in the French Socialist Party.

April — Trotsky warns that the Stalinists are preparing a further shift to the right in foreign policy.

May 2 — A Franco-Soviet nonaggression pact is announced in Moscow.

May 15 — Stalin announces that he "understands and fully approves" the French government's rearmament policy.

May — Socialist and Communist parties make gains in French local elections, convincing a section of the Radical leadership that it should join them in the People's Front, which comes into being soon after.

May 25 — Trotsky learns the Norwegian government has decided to grant him a visa.

May 31 — Flandin cabinet resigns. Bouisson forms a new cabinet, which lasts only four days.

May — Mussolini gets approval of French government to speed up preparations for invasion of Ethiopia.

June — British government prepares pact with Hitler, approving expansion of German fleet.

June — Moscow announces the Communist International will soon hold its Seventh World Congress, the first in seven years.

June 7 — New French government is formed, headed by Pierre Laval.

June 9 — The French Socialist Party opens its national congress at Mulhouse, after which the reformist leadership begins to expel the Bolshevik-Leninists.

June 10 — Trotsky writes of the need for another turn in France, to expedite the building of an independent revolutionary party.

June 13 — Trotsky leaves France, arriving in Norway June 18.

THE FOREIGN POLICY OF THE SOVIET UNION[1]

(Published June 16, 1934)

Soviet foreign policy has taken a decidedly anti-Leninist turn particularly since the recognition of the Soviet Union by the United States.

In the first place, this recognition was granted only after American capitalism had been fully convinced that the Third International[2] would no longer serve as an instrument of world revolution in general nor as a revolutionary incitement and inspiration to the American laboring masses in particular. Secondly, in order to emphasize their good faith, the Stalinist bureaucracy officially declared that President Roosevelt represented peaceful American capitalism, which was honestly seeking a democratic and pacifistic solution to present-day imperialist contradictions and conflicts.

Recently Alexander A. Troyanovsky,[3] the Soviet ambassador to Washington, stated that the USSR and the United States should be able to find a "common ground" in an endeavor "to secure complete or partial disarmament." "The foreign policy of the Soviet Union," he continued, "shows an increasing activity for peace. . . . We greeted the resumption of normal relations with the United States from this point of view. Not material gains for our country, but the gain for international peace was regarded in our country as the important thing in friendly relations with the United States."

One can hardly doubt Troyanovsky's love for peace, especially if we take some of his other statements into account. "The cause of peace," he declared, "was so great that it must prevail over all other problems." And among these problems he cited the most important economic contradictions of our epoch. "All secondary [!?] problems, such as those of debts, of commercial competition, of tariffs, and so on," he explained, "must be settled as soon as possible by mutual agreements and to mutual satisfaction, for these relatively small [!?] questions spoil the international atmosphere and prevent friendly efforts to consolidate peace."

Can the worthy Stalinist ambassador really mean this? Has he completely forgotten Lenin's teachings regarding the economic causes of war? Troyanovsky should be reminded that in *Imperialism: The Last Stage of Capitalism* Lenin actually proves that the "secondary" and "small" questions he mentions are at the very root of imperialist war in particular and all war in general. Or is this counterrevolutionary Trotskyism, Monsieur l'Ambassadeur?

In line with this trend, the Stalinists have published abroad a brand new interpretation of capitalism and imperialism. They have divided the capitalist nations into two categories: one the peaceful, democratic and pacifist; the other the warlike, fascist and aggressive. (This is precisely the theory of the Second International.[4]) Under the former category are listed America, France, the Little Entente[5] and possibly England; under the latter are listed especially Germany and Japan.

Following through this anti-Marxist political philosophy, Litvinov[6] is now engaged in discussions for an "understanding" with imperialist France. Frederick T. Birchall, *New York Times* correspondent in Berlin, says that ". . . accompanying and alongside the military agreement, it is understood a thorough understanding has now been arrived at regarding Russia's entry into the League of Nations. It is to take place as soon as possible with the enthusiastic support of France, which, with the disarmament negotiations as an excuse [mark well!], will send to Geneva in the near future an impressive delegation. . . . The stage is all set in France to hail the Russian understanding . . . as a further guarantee of European peace and French security. Then France will be ready to talk about disarmament."

This maneuver is made in the name of Marx and Lenin, explain the Stalinists, in order to secure allies (?!) against a probable attack on the USSR from the side of fascist and warlike capitalism, namely, Germany and Japan. Also the entry of the Soviet Union into the capitalist League of Nations, characterized by the Third World Congress of the Communist International as "the international trust of the victorious states for the exploitation of their vanquished competitors and the colonial peoples," has been facilitated.

Today *Pravda*,[7] the official organ of the Stalinist bureaucracy, explains the politics of the League of Nations as follows: "As a matter of fact, the withdrawal from the League of Japan and Germany[8] — these countries which do not even try to conceal their determination to fulfill their imperialistic ambitions by the means of further armaments, encroachments and wars — has brought up the question whether the League could not to a certain degree [how cautious!] become the center of united forces that are ready to delay the bloody settlement of disputes and bring about at least some strengthening of peace." And Karl Radek[9] adds: "The danger of war against the USSR does not come from the League but from open opponents of the League and English diehards."

The Theses and Resolutions of the Third World Congress of the Communist International support this conclusion: "The new international labor organization is established for the purpose of organizing united action of the world proletariat, aspiring toward the same goal: the overthrow of capitalism, the establishment of the dictatorship of the proletariat, and of an International Soviet Republic, for the complete elimination of classes and the realization of socialism, the first step toward the Communist commonwealth."

Stalinism has eliminated all this. It has substituted in its place military alliances with capitalist countries and the insane theory of socialism in one country. [10] The Marxism-Leninism of the Third World Congress is now called counterrevolutionary Trotskyism. And in support of this thesis the French imperialist government is now persecuting Comrade Trotsky as a counterrevolutionist![11]

This new Stalinist policy will endanger not only the Soviet Union but also the prospects of a world revolution should an imperialist war break out. If the USSR is maneuvered into the League of Nations and thereby tied to the imperialist chariot of France and the Little Entente, or if it becomes a member of the permanent peace conference, it will have been demonstrated in either case that the Soviet Union is on the side of the strongest capitalist bandits. Thus, the emancipation of the oppressed by proletarian revolution is renounced, and the Soviet Union becomes a pawn (and ultimately a victim) in the imperialist game.

This policy, now aimed chiefly against Germany, is an inevitable consequence of the dastardly betrayal of the German workers and semiproletarian masses by the German Communist Party under the direct command of Stalin. At first the German revolution was sabotaged in the interest of peace and credits. Now, with the threat of Hitler before their eyes, Stalin and Co. veer towards imperialist France in order to stay Hitler's hand, that is, to checkmate his *Drang nach Osten* [eastern expansion] policy.

As usual, the Stalinist bureaucracy does not calculate the

effect of this course on the German masses. Having lost faith
in the world revolution and, more particularly, disdaining
the revolutionary aid of the German masses in case of a fascist
attack, Stalin once more plays into Hitler's hands. Goebbels
has already broadcast throughout bleeding Germany that the
Soviet Union has formed a technical military alliance with
the thoroughly hated France against the German people. And
thus the last drop of revolutionary blood is drained from
the veins of the German workers. This is the final stab in the
back.

The impending failure of the disarmament conference opens
up a dangerous prospect for the Soviet Union. England cannot afford to have France increase its power on the Continent.
It will not allow Germany to be further humiliated and crushed.
It also supports the German rearmament proposals. [12] It continues on friendly terms with Japan. For England needs both
Germany and Japan, at least as potential allies, to maintain
its far-flung empire.

The current policy of the Soviet Union, if carried through
to the bitter end, leads to imperialist entanglements and aims
a deathblow at the world proletarian movement.

It is obvious that such a situation calls for a new party
and a new (Fourth) International. [13]

A PROGRAM OF ACTION FOR FRANCE[14]

(Published June 1934)

1. Fascism and War Are Threatening!

TO ALL THE TOILERS OF FRANCE!

Led by the big bourgeoisie, France is foundering in the disintegration of the capitalist world. In the ruling circles of society, in all the institutions of the regime, scandals are multiplying; the corrupting influence of the rich is spreading.

For the workers, growing unemployment; for the small peasants, ruin; for all the exploited, misery is increasing.

Dying capitalism is bankrupt. And the ruling class has only one plan for trying to get out of this historical bankruptcy: still more misery for the laboring masses! Suppression of all reforms, even the most trifling! Suppression of the democratic regime!

Throughout the entire world, the iron heel of fascism is becoming the last resort of desperate capitalism.

Imperialism, given a deathblow by the Russian Revolution of October 1917, was able to maintain its domination over society because of the defeat of the proletarian parties in the two periods of the postwar epoch: the general betrayal by the Social Democracy and the degeneration of the Communist International following these defeats. The defeat of the German Revolution in 1923, of the Chinese Revolution in 1927 and of the German and Austrian proletariat[15] in 1933 and 1934 mark the decisive moments when capitalism succeeded in stabilizing itself.

However, these precarious victories, obtained without the former ruling class in Soviet Russia having been able to reestablish itself, only served to sharpen the universal crisis. More violently and anarchistically than ever, the pressure of the monopolies on the world market clashes with national boundaries and the principle of private property.

Benefiting from the reverses of the proletariat in its revolu-

tionary march towards socialism, the world bourgeoisie is
using its last resort, fascism, by means of which it is making
desperate efforts to clear the organized working class from its
road.

Such is the international situation that is pushing the French
bourgeoisie towards fascism.

But fascism alone is still not the last word of disintegrating
capitalism. When it has fought its internal enemy, each imperialism must expand externally. This is the source of a new
world war. Fifty million men perished in the atrocious suffering of the last war and its aftermath. Workers all over the
world will be massacred by the hundreds of millions in the
next war. France, whose population is stationary, will escape
this less than any other country.

The workers must oppose these criminal plans of the bourgeoisie with all their might!

2. The Plan of the French Bourgeoisie

To try to emerge from the chaos in which it has plunged
the country, the French bourgeoisie must first resolve the monetary problem. One section wants to do this by *inflation,* i.e.,
the issuing of paper money, the depreciation of wages, the
raising of the cost of living, the expropriation of the petty
bourgeoisie; the other by *deflation,* i.e., retrenchment on the
backs of the workers (lowering of salaries and wages), extension of unemployment, ruin of the small peasant producers
and the petty bourgeoisie of the towns.

Either alternative means increased misery for the exploited.
To choose between these two capitalist methods would be to
choose between two instruments with which the exploiters are
preparing to cut the throats of the workers.

Brutal deflation is the first step in the plan of the French
capitalists. The workers are being deprived of unemployment
relief; social insurance is being menaced; wages are being
reduced. Government employees are already being affected;
the small peasants are next.

This will not prevent the bourgeoisie from passing to the
other method of inflation tomorrow, if it is expedient. Hitlerite
Germany is an example. The exploited must vigorously oppose
this plan of the bourgeoisie!

To the program of deflation, of the reduction of their means
of existence, the workers must counterpose their own program
of fundamentally transforming social relations by the complete
"deflation" of the privileges and profits of the band of Oustrics
and Staviskys who exploit the country! [16] This is the only
road to salvation.

3. Abolition of "Business Secrets"

To find a solution favorable to the toiling masses, we must draw up, without delay, the pitiless balance sheet of capitalist bankruptcy, conduct an inventory of the receipts and expenditures of all classes, of all social groups.

For the proletarians, the exploited of all categories, this is not difficult. The workers' wages are recorded in capitalist account books. As for expenditures, small businessmen register them from week to week. The income and expenditures of the peasants, artisans, small businessmen, petty functionaries are a secret to no one. The rapacious banks estimate precisely by mortgages the rate of increase of ruin of the peasants!

But the capitalists, the great exploiters, jealously guard their secrets. The trusts, the monopolies, the large companies, which dominate the total production of the country by directly possessing nine-tenths of it, never give an accounting of their larceny.

This exploiting mafia covers itself with the sanctity of "business secrets."

Business secrets are but a device for controlling the life of the poor, disguising all the banking, industrial and commercial affairs of the rich, the Staviskys and the de Wendels, who hide under the cloak of "general welfare" and "national economy."

Down with business secrets: Those who demand sacrifices must start by presenting their account books. Thus will their crookedness be unveiled!

4. Workers' and Peasants' Control over Banks, Industry and Commerce

Bourgeois democracy accorded the laboring masses a semblance of political control over their leaders by the ballot box. As long as this did it no harm, the bourgeoisie permitted such democracy. But it never permitted even a shadow of control over its economic administration, over the basis of its exploitation, which ends in anarchy, bankruptcy and destitution of the masses.

The parasitic shareholder has the right to know how the business that enriches him functions. The worker, the exploited producer, has only to obey and keep his mouth shut; he is merely a part of the machinery.

But the workers want to know all parts of the machine. They alone can judge its functioning. Over the capitalist rule of management let us set up the implacable control of the laboring people.

Factory committees, peasant committees, committees of small functionaries, of employees could very easily, with the help of honest technicians, engineers, accountants loyal to the working people, do away with the "business secrets" of the exploiters. It is by this method that we must establish *public control over banks, industry and commerce.*

5. To the Workers!

Under this general appeal, the Communist League fights for the following measures in behalf of the workers:

1. *Forty-hour week, wage increases.* Workers' control will demonstrate that the level of productive forces permits the reduction of the working day. Wage increases at the expense of the magnates of the Comite des Forges, of the Comite des Houilleres, of the Finalys, the Schneiders and the Staviskys, and to the material and moral advantage of the laboring people.

2. *Real social security* and, first of all, unemployment insurance. Annual vacation of at least one month. Retirement pensions permitting one to live after fifty years of age.

3. *Equal wages for equal work.* Abolition of the superexploitation imposed on women, young people, aliens and colonials.

4. *For working women, the same wages and same rights as for working men.* Maternity protection with supplementary leaves of absence.

5. *For young people, wages equal to adults.* Extension of study and apprenticeship at the collective expense. Special hygienic measures.

6. *Suppression of all special legislation over foreign and colonial workers.*

6. Nationalization of Banks, Key Industries, Insurance Companies and Transportation

At the present time, it is the banks that direct and actually control the whole economy of the country. But if the working people seize the banks and through their medium start to manage industry, transportation and commerce, the general standard of living could be raised immediately.

The nationalization of banks, big industry, transportation and insurance companies is the preliminary condition for an economy directed toward the welfare of the great laboring masses, of the whole people.

This nationalization must allow no indemnity for the big capitalists who have enriched themselves by bleeding the proletarians for years and years and who were able to offer only wretchedness and economic anarchy.

The nationalization of the great means of production and exchange absolutely does not mean the crushing of the small peasant, commercial and artisan enterprises. On the contrary, the great privileged monopolies are the ones who strangle the small concerns.

The small concerns must be left free and then the workers, having nationalized the large enterprises, could come to their aid. Planned economy, based on the immense riches accumulated by the banks, trusts, corporations, etc., would permit the establishment of a plan of production and distribution that offers the small producers direct orders from the state, raw materials and credits under entirely favorable conditions. Thus the peasantry would receive agricultural machinery and fertilizer at low prices.

Nationalization by the workers means the destruction of the great private monopolies, support of small enterprises, redistribution of products for the benefit of the great mass of producers.

7. Monopoly of Foreign Trade

All foreign trade must pass through the hands of the state. Thus trade would no longer be controlled by private monopolies that regulate imports and exports with no care for the consumers' interests. Invaluable advantages for the great masses would arise from this intervention between national production and the world market. Thus only the state, ruled by the workers, would really control all foreign commerce for the benefit of the collectivity.

8. The Alliance of the Workers and the Peasants

The peasantry constitutes nearly half the French population. The proletarian state must rest on the exploited peasants as well as on the workers of town and country. Our program answers the needs of the great rural masses as well as those of the working class.

We affirm that our final aim, as a higher form of progress, is the *collectivization* of agriculture as well as of industry. But the proletariat cannot force this aim on the peasantry. It can only facilitate the evolution toward this goal. The proletariat can only make proposals in this direction, which must then be completed, corrected and broadened through the common experience of the two classes equally oppressed by the capitalist exploiters. We must first secure for the peasants a real opportunity to determine their own fate, to decide the use of their forces and their property, to express their preferences in methods of farming, to choose by their own judgment the moment to pass from private to collective economy.

The rural population is far from being homogeneous. The ruling class and its servile professors carefully hide the fact that a small minority has monopolized a great part of landed property and has concentrated in its hands the best means of agricultural production (machines, tractors, cattle, etc.), not to mention sources of credit.

We propose the struggle for immediately putting into effect the following measures:

1. *The same rights for agricultural workers as for those of the towns.* General laws bearing on contracts, the workday and the weekly day of rest, social security (including unemployment insurance). Labor legislation must be applied in its entirety to agricultural workers.

2. *Expropriation of the large properties, estates and model farms* on behalf of collective and cooperative farming and small peasant farming.

3. *Abolition of sharecropping slavery.* Revision of current leases by committees of peasant laborers elected by departments.

4. *Revision of mortgages.* Moratorium. Stop all suits and foreclosures.

9. Social Services for the Collectivity!

The great institutions of the state (post office, customs, education, etc.), which exploit several million toilers, function for the benefit of capitalism. The recent scandals have shown the corruption that reigns among the higher functionaries.

The small government employees are exploited by the corrupt and venal officials who utilize their office to permit the possessing class to crush the laborers still more.

We must make a clean sweep. With the collaboration of all the exploited, committees and unions of small government employees will make the necessary changes to establish real social services that function by and for the laboring masses.

10. Disbanding of the Police, Political Rights for Soldiers

The government extorts billions of francs from the poor, from the exploited, from people of all conditions, to develop and arm its police, its *gardes mobiles* and its army — in a word, not only to develop the *civil war* but also to prepare the *imperialist war*. Young workers mobilized by the hundreds of thousands into the armed forces of land and sea are deprived of all rights.

We demand the dismissal of the reactionary and fascist officers and noncommissioned officers, instruments of coup d'etat. On the other hand, the workers under arms must retain all political rights and should be represented by soldier committees elected in special assemblies. Thus they will remain closely linked to the great mass of toilers and will unite their forces with the people organized and armed against reaction and fascism.

All the police executors of the capitalist will, of the bourgeois state, and its cliques of corrupt politicians must be disbanded. Execution of police duties by the workers' militia. Abolition of class courts, election of all judges, extension of the jury for all crimes and misdemeanors; the people will render justice themselves.

11. Right of Self-Determination of Nationalities, Including Separation

The robber Treaty of Versailles is a source of atrocious evils not only for the workers of all Europe but also for those of the "victorious" country, France. Defense of the international relations issuing from this treaty, by which the bourgeoisie annexed Alsace-Lorraine[17] without even a plebiscite like that it demands for the Saar,[18] *today leads to war.*

The French bourgeoisie not only oppresses indirectly a whole section of Europe but also lays waste and crushes immense colonies. For all the peoples oppressed by the big French capitalists — by the de Wendels and the Michelins, the banks of Paris and others — for the people of Alsace-Lorraine as well as of Indochina, Morocco and Madagascar, *we demand the right of complete self-determination, up to and including separation if they desire it.*

The toiling masses of this country have *no* interest in helping the French banks maintain their domination over other peoples. On the contrary, by winning allies and supporters for their own struggle, the toilers are helping the fight for liberation.

12. Against the War, For the Socialist United States of Europe!

In order to transform society and lift it out of chaos, we must first save it from the war in which the bourgeoisie would plunge it anew.

Against the moves of German fascism, the French capitalists have set up a policy of blocs of states bearing allegiance to the criminal Treaty of Versailles. France uses the League of Nations, the gathering of the rapacious bourgeoisie, to cover

its actions with a veil of pacifism while it places the burden
of the crushing cost of the armaments race on the laboring
people. And the "defensive" lie of "security" allows chauvinistic
frenzy to do its work, to hurl the country towards the monstrous massacres of tomorrow.

Proletarians, peasants, tradesmen, artisans and government
employees can avoid this future only by establishing all forms
of their control, by unmasking secret diplomacy, by opposing
with every means the preparations for the war, by wresting
the government from the hands of imperialism.

Only the victory of the revolutionary toilers of France can
eliminate all possibility of imperialist war and arouse the enslaved peoples of Europe and the colonies. Pacts and treaties
would then turn to dust; the only possible solution, which
was seen as early as 1919, would then be: *The Socialist United
States of Europe.*

Against the politics of imperialist blocs, against the pacifist
lie of the League of Nations, against the secret diplomacy
of the war and the madness of armaments! Throughout the
aged European continent, divided, militarized, bloodstained,
threatened with total destruction by a new war, we raise the
only banner of liberation, that of *the Workers' and Peasants'
United States of Europe, the fraternal Federation of Soviet
States!*

13. For the Defense of the Soviet Union

For every proletarian, the first step in this direction is the
unconditional defense of the Soviet Union, where the October
Revolution of 1917 created the great foundations of the first
experience of proletarian dictatorship based on the abolition of
private property of the big capitalists.

The struggle against the Soviet Union still remains the
fundamental objective of world imperialist reaction.

The toilers of France will fight for the defense of the Soviet
Union by unmasking the "pacifist" plans of the bourgeoisie.
Pacts and treaties will not effectively defend the Soviet proletariat, but revolutionary struggle for the overthrow of the
bourgeoisie in other countries will.

The union of the Socialist Republics of France and Russia
will broaden international proletarian solidarity; compromises
with Barthou, Tardieu, Herriot[19] and their imperialist gangs
will not.

Only these broad measures can save the masses from misery
and lead them to socialism. From today on, all the toilers
must vigorously struggle for their fulfillment.

Moreover, not through individual action, not through activity of one grouping or another, can these measures be fully applied; it can be done only through the state power that is at the helm of the economy, of the politics and the culture of the whole country. In whose hands is the helm? That is the whole question!

14. Down with the Bourgeois "Authoritative State"! For Workers' and Peasants' Power

The bourgeoisie is starting to carry out its plan of the transformation of state power, to eliminate once and for all the resistance of the workers: decreasing the rights of elected democratic institutions (parliament and the communes), and even complete suppression of these rights, for the proletarian pressure is felt there even though in a perverted way.

The bourgeoisie is trying to concentrate the executive power in the hands of a few men who impose their decisions by means of an administrative, military and police apparatus, which is brutal, uncontrolled, costly.

The bourgeois plan of the "authoritative state," directed against the exploited, must be ruthlessly attacked by the toiling masses.

Only the laboring masses, taking their future into their own hands, in one powerful revolutionary thrust, can energetically and with iron will create the necessary great power to save society from the capitalist oligarchy that corrupts it and leads it to ruin.

The task is to replace the *capitalist state,* which functions for the profit of the big exploiters, by the workers' and peasants' *proletarian state.* The task is to establish in this country the rule of the working people. To all we declare that it is not a matter of secondary "modification," but rather that the domination of the small minority of the bourgeois class must be replaced by the leadership and power of the immense majority of the laboring people.

The alliance of the peasants and the workers is necessary for this. Reaction tries to frighten the peasants with the specter of a proletarian dictatorship that subjugates the peasants to the workers. But in reality the proletarian state cannot be achieved as long as the proletariat is isolated from the peasantry.

The example of the October Revolution, of Soviet Russia, helps us. However, in France we can do better than our Russian brothers and avoid some of their mistakes. France's economic level is higher, and we intend to act in conformity with the actual conditions of our country. It is on the basis of a clear and precise program and a close understanding between the proletariat and the exploited peasants that the dictatorship of the proletariat can be established.

The peasantry is scattered. This is one of the reasons for its political impotence, in spite of its numbers and its importance in production. The peasants can only gain power by making common cause with the workers against the bourgeoisie.

15. The Struggle for the Workers' and Peasants' Commune

The alliance of the peasantry and the workers will be achieved only if the working class shows its strength, its decided initiative and its ability to carry out this program. This is why we must, above all, create conditions for unity of action.

The *workers' alliance of parties and trade unions* must be organized, uniting all the forces of the laboring people without exception.

A national committee of the workers' alliance, regional committees, local committees, should be organized. Creation of shop committees elected by the workers.

The impulse given by these workers' alliance committees, their authority among the masses, will inspire the laboring people of the countryside to organize themselves into *peasant committees*.

In the struggle against fascism, reaction and war, the proletariat accepts the aid of petty-bourgeois groupings (pacifists, League for the Rights of Man, the Common Front, etc.), but such alliances can be only of secondary importance. *Above all, the task is to secure the united action of the working class itself in the factories and the workers' neighborhoods of industrial centers.* The alliance of the important workers' organizations (Communist Party, Socialist Party, CGT, CGTU,[20] Communist League) will have no revolutionary value unless it is oriented toward the creation of:

1. Committees of struggle representing the mass itself (embryo soviets);

2. Workers' militia, always united in action, even though organized by various parties and organizations.

To reinforce the struggle of both the workers and peasants, the workers' committees should establish close collaboration with the peasant committees. Constituted as organs of popular defense against fascism, these workers' alliance committees and these peasant committees must become, during the course of the struggle, organisms directly elected by the masses, organs of power of the workers and peasants. On this basis the proletarian power will be erected in opposition to the capitalist power, and the Workers' and Peasants' Commune will triumph.

16. For a Single Assembly

We are thus firm partisans of a Workers' and Peasants' State, which will take the power from the exploiters. To win the majority of our working-class allies to this program is our primary aim.

Meanwhile, as long as the majority of the working class continues on the basis of bourgeois democracy, we are ready to defend it with all our forces against violent attacks from the Bonapartist[21] and fascist bourgeoisie.

However, we demand from our class brothers who adhere to "democratic" socialism that they be faithful to their ideas, that they draw inspiration from the ideas and methods not of the Third Republic but of the Convention of 1793.[22]

Down with the Senate, which is elected by limited suffrage and which renders the power of universal suffrage a mere illusion!

Down with the presidency of the republic, which serves as a hidden point of concentration for the forces of militarism and reaction!

A single assembly must combine the legislative and executive powers. Members would be elected for two years, by universal suffrage at eighteen years of age, with no discrimination of sex or nationality. Deputies would be elected on the basis of local assemblies, constantly revocable by their constituents, and would receive the salary of a skilled worker.

This is the only measure that would lead the masses forward instead of pushing them backward. A more generous democracy would facilitate the struggle for workers' power.

If, during the course of the implacable struggle against the enemy, the party of "democratic" socialism (SFIO),[23] from which we are separated by irreconcilable differences in doctrine and method, were to gain the confidence of the majority, we are and always will be ready to defend an SFIO government against the bourgeoisie.

We want to attain our objective not by armed conflicts between the various groups of toilers but by real workers' democracy, by propaganda and loyal criticism, by the voluntary regrouping of the great majority of the proletariat under the flag of true communism.

Workers adhering to democratic socialism must further understand that it is not enough to defend democracy; democracy must be regained. The moving of the political center of gravity from parliament towards the cabinet, from the cabinet towards the oligarchy of finance capital, generals, police, is an accomplished fact. Neither the present parliament nor the new elections can change this. We can defend the sorry remains of democracy, and especially we can enlarge the democratic arena for the activity of the masses only by annihilating the armed fascist forces that, on February 6, 1934, started moving the axis of the state and are still doing so.

17. The Bourgeoisie Will Never Give Up Voluntarily

The bourgeoisie will never willingly consent to measures that can pull society out of chaos. It wants to perpetuate all its privileges, and in order to protect them it is starting to use fascist gangs.

Our slogan is not the disarming of the fascist gangs of finance capital by finance capital's own police. We refuse to spread the criminal illusion that a capitalist government can actually proceed to the disarming of the capitalist bands. The exploited must defend themselves against the capitalists.

Arming of the proletariat, arming of the poor peasants!
People's Antifascist Militia!

The exploiters, who are but a tiny minority, will recoil before the unleashing of civil war; the fascist and reactionary bands will lose their audacity *only* if the workers are armed and lead the masses.

Only if the workers proceed in this way will the greater part of the soldiers and sailors, children of laboring people to whom our propaganda must unceasingly recall their origins and their class duty, be won to the cause of the workers and take the side of the working masses against the reactionary and fascist officers who would use them against their class.

The task is enormous, but it is the only road to salvation! The Communist League shows the way.

Society, which can only exist by your labor, is rotting away because the ruling bourgeoisie will not give up a single one of its odious privileges. To retain them, the bourgeoisie is preparing fascist bands which threaten your existence.

On February 12 [24] you displayed your power and your determination not to submit to this violence. But on that day your leaders betrayed you; they outlined no concrete slogan, no serious perspective of struggle for you. To attain your strength, to defend your right to live, to work no more for the enrichment of a minority of shameless exploiters — prepare your revolution, join the action of the Communist League!

THE LEAGUE FACED WITH A TURN[25]

(July 1934)

1. It is not enough for a revolutionist to have correct ideas. Let us not forget that correct ideas have already been set down in *Capital* and in *The Communist Manifesto*. But that has not prevented false ideas from being broadcast. It is the task of the revolutionary party to weld together the correct ideas with the mass labor movement. Only in this manner can an idea become a driving force.

2. A revolutionary organization does not mean a paper and its readers. One can write and read revolutionary articles day in and day out and still remain in reality outside of the revolutionary movement. One can give the labor organizations good advice—from the sidelines. That is something. But that still does not make a revolutionary organization.

3. Although the living conditions inside the Comintern are hardly normal, the Left Opposition as a faction would have developed in constant contact with the mass movement. But the Stalinist apparatus isolated the Opposition mechanically from the very first steps of its existence. Two aims were achieved by this: (1) the internal life of the Comintern was choked off and (2) the Opposition was deprived of the necessary sphere of political action.

4. The League (like other sections) was forced to develop as an isolated propaganda group. This determined both its positive sides (an honest and serious attachment to the principles) and its negative sides (observing the labor movement from the outside). In the course of the elaboration of the principles and methods of the Left Opposition, the positive sides of the League carried the day. At present, when it becomes necessary to circulate the accumulated capital, the negative sides are threatening to get the upper hand.

5. The leadership of the League has entrusted the circulation end [of the paper] to a capitalist concern. For a group of

literati the circulation end is an unpleasant burden. For a
revolutionary organization it is an important lever. How can
one entrust such an important lever to the enemy when one
is seriously preparing for the struggle? The revolutionary
movement is composed of dozens and hundreds of different
sorts of just such "uninteresting," "technical" labors. Without
detailed and assiduous preparatory work it is impossible to
begin with a militia or a strike, and even less so with the
general strike or the insurrection. A revolutionary organization that is incapable (or more clearly, unwilling) of taking
care of the circulation end thereby forgoes in advance leadership in the execution of more complicated labors.

6. In relation to the Socialist Party, the League has shown
not only insufficient initiative but also a hidebound sectarianism. Instead of taking for its task the creation of a faction
inside the SFIO just as soon as the crisis in the latter became
obvious, the League demanded that every Socialist become
convinced of the correctness of our ideas and leave his mass
organization to join the group of *La Verite* readers. In order
to create an internal faction, it was necessary to pursue the
mass movement, to adapt oneself to the environment, to carry
on menial daily work. Precisely in this very decisive field the
League has not been able to make any progress up to the
present—with very few exceptions. A great deal of valuable
time was allowed to be lost. After a delay of a whole year,
the Political Bureau now poses the task: "to create an internal
faction." No—that is no longer sufficient. The situation requires more decisive measures.

7. The criticism, the ideas, the slogans of the League are
in general correct, but in this present period particularly inadequate. The revolutionary ideas must be transformed into
life itself every day through the experience of the masses themselves. But how can the League explain this to them when it
is itself cut off from the experience of the masses? It is necessary to add: several comrades do not even see the need of
this experience. It seems to them to be sufficient to form an
opinion on the basis of newspaper accounts they read and
then to give it expression in an article or in a talk. Yet if the
most correct ideas do not reflect directly the ideas and actions
of the mass, they will escape the attention of the masses altogether.

8. In that case the League is bankrupt, is it not?—An absolutely false conclusion. The successes of the League are obviously much smaller than many of us had hoped—much
smaller than they could have been if there were not the fetters
of an abstract conservatism. But despite the immense obstacles,

there have been undoubtedly some successes. The League has exercised certain influence on the ideas and slogans of the labor movement in its entirety (united front, the workers' militia, trade-union unity). But it is exactly these successes, when taken into consideration together with the whole situation and particularly with the changed tactics of the bureaucratic apparatuses, that demand on the part of the League a new and decisive turn. Whither? To the masses.

9. The general situation in France puts the entire conscious labor movement before a task of short perspective: either the proletariat will in the course of six months, a year or perhaps the coming two years, destroy fascism and take a tremendous step forward all the way to the struggle for power, or it will itself be destroyed and all of Europe will become the arena for fascist tyranny and war. The pressure of this terrible alternative has forced both of the labor parties to strike out on the road of the united front. But in an exact sense this great victory poses the question before the League in all its amplitude: to be or not to be.

10. The joint meeting of July 2 gives a remarkably clear picture of the situation created. Just as the League has so often predicted, the very first step of the united front has aroused an extraordinary enthusiasm among the masses. The *possibility* of victory along this road is beyond all doubt. And yet neither the Stalinists nor the Socialists utilized the unification in order to advance aims of struggle but, on the contrary, directed their energy towards having the mass find satisfaction in the fact of unification itself. Yesterday the greatest danger was the *sabotage* of the united front. Today the greatest danger lies in the *illusions* of the united front, very closely related to the parliamentary illusions: the diplomatic notes, the pathetic speeches, the handshaking, the bloc without revolutionary content — and the betrayal of the masses. At this symbolic gathering, the League did not get the floor. And this is no accident: we face the program of action of both these bureaucracies for the whole coming period.

11. This program can be realized practically only because the League remains isolated from the masses. The attempt to skim over this isolation through an exchange of diplomatic notes with the Central Committee or through attendance at the sessions of the Socialist National Council is nothing but diplomatic horseplay that aims to conceal the unfavorable relationship of forces. That is not at all worthy of us. The relationship of forces has to be changed, not concealed. It is necessary to go to the masses. It is necessary to find a place

for oneself within the framework of the united front, i.e., within the framework of one of the two parties of which it is composed. In actual practice, that means within the framework of the SFIO.

12. Is that not a capitulation before the Second International? Such a complaint can be lodged with much more justice against the Stalinists. It was they who renounced, inside of twenty-four hours and on command from Litvinov, the theory of social fascism [26] when they realized that democracy is to be preferred. And they even gave up all criticism of their new friends. But we have nothing to renounce. We merely admit honestly that our organization is too weak to establish for itself a practical independent role in the struggles that are looming ahead of us. At the same time, as good revolutionists, we do not want to stand on the sidelines. In 1848 Marx and his weak Communist organization entered the democratic party. In order not to stand on the sidelines, Plekhanov [27] attempted to join his group "Emancipation of Labor" to that of the "People's Will" (Narodnaya Volya), with which he had broken on principled grounds only five years before. For different reasons and in a different situation, Lenin advised the Communist Party of England to join the Labour Party. [28] We, on our part, have been ready to form a new International together with the SAP [29] and OSP. [30] We urgently advised our British comrades to enter the ILP [31] and some of them took our advice. Was that capitulation? Not at all. We are now concerned with applying and developing the same policy in France.

13. Nevertheless — have we not proclaimed the necessity of creating a new party and a new International? This program remains in force in its entirety. But we have never promised to stop and ruminate until such a time as the Fourth International gathers about us. We have always declared that the means for its creation are complex and not of the same character in the different countries, just as was the case with the Third International. Comrade Trotsky reminded us a year ago particularly of the French example. There, in spite of the break of the Bolsheviks with the Second International, the whole section was won over to the Third International. We know of no law that says that a repetition of the Tours Congress [32] is impossible. On the contrary, many of the prevailing conditions speak for such a possibility.

14. But in that case the SFIO will not accept us! — It is quite possible that the big shots will refuse. But the local organizations, on the other hand, will for the most part go with us. Inside of the party, the struggle of the tendencies continues

to pursue its course. The left wing will be for us. Our ties with the left wing will be strengthened. And the developments themselves appear to work for the left wing.

15. And we are to agree to maintain discipline? To be sure, we shall work in the membership and maintain discipline. We shall develop into a faction. In return for that, we shall be in constant contact with tens of thousands of workers, and we shall receive the right to participate in the struggle and in the discussion — and we shall have the opportunity, particularly indispensable for us, of controlling our ideas and slogans daily in the actions of the masses.

16. But does not entry into the SFIO imply the danger of opportunist adaptation or of degeneration? Undoubtedly. Yet it would be naive to think that one can escape this danger through self-isolation. The League is at present independent. But unfortunately its position on the SFIO policy contains elements of an impermissible adaptation. It is not necessary to use strong words against the leaders, but it is absolutely necessary to expose the danger of such a purely decorative attitude toward the "struggle against fascism" as has been expressed in the columns of *Le Populaire* (or *l'Humanite*).[33] The proletariat is facing a deadly enemy who is prepared for all events and who will be armed to the teeth if necessary. The proletarian vanguard should develop in its own ranks and among the broad masses an unshakable preparedness for struggle, an iron will, a revolutionary spirit of discipline, a military pugnacity. Parades at given times, demonstrations with permission of the police and other such symbolic actions tend only to lull the watchfulness and the willpower of the workers. A fighting organization is necessary; steel battalions are necessary; instructors and officers are necessary. It is necessary to disarm the enemy, to sweep him off the streets, to terrorize him. The task of the League — whether it remains independent or joins one of the parties of the united front — demands imperiously an explanation to the workers as frank, as clear, as honest as the seriousness of the situation and the tasks flowing from it require.

17. In that case, what will be our position as regards the Communist Party? We shall come more closely in contact with it than before — through the united front. We must clearly bear in mind that the CP is capable only of such a dissolution of the SFIO as will be of no advantage whatever to the revolution. It is notoriously true that this has been the result of the coalition between the CP of England and the ILP. But if we can intervene effectively, we will have a new and invaluable opportunity to influence the proletarian core of the CP. In such

a manner, a powerful section of the Fourth International may evolve.

18. But the proletarian party must be independent. Quite so. But the League is not yet a party. It is an embryo, and an embryo needs covering and nourishment in order to develop.

19. But if . . . and then . . . and if? To foresee everything and to provide for everything in advance is impossible. It is necessary to understand the situation clearly, to determine the tasks and to proceed with their fulfillment. In six months we can lose forever that opportunity that we are offered now. We must look at things from the short perspective.

20. To conclude: the Koran says that the mountain came to the prophet. Marxism counsels the prophet to go to the mountain.

THE LEAGUE FACED WITH A DECISIVE TURN[34]

(July 1934)

For several years the most active fighting slogan of the League was "The United Front." Without a doubt this slogan was, in spite of its "abstract" character for two or three years, the key to the situation in Germany, then in France. The defeat of the German proletariat, the Austrian catastrophe, the growth of fascism in France and other countries were necessary before the Comintern bureaucracy took a radical turn in the question of the united front. The examples of earlier turns have only proven to us all too well that without a critical *overhauling* of the old position and without a theoretical foundation for the new one a turn even formally progressive offers no guarantee for a correct policy. On the contrary, it unavoidably bears within it a chain of new vacillations and mistakes. Eloquent signs of the new dangers are already there: the ultimatists become opportunists. For this reason our whole struggle transfers itself to a new, higher plane.

Social Democracy on its part has trod the path of the united front with the definite purpose of breaking off its revolutionary head. In the field of the united front, the fight against the reformist[35] bureaucracy must be carried on less noisily in form but in a more systematic and concentrated way than ever.

Both bureaucracies are united by their common interest against the growing opposition that brings to expression or tries to express the tasks of the hour. On the other hand, both bureaucracies inimically oppose each other in a competition sharper than ever. For this reason, one can differentiate in the policy of both bureaucracies: the conspiracy against all who aim to encroach on their rule and the fear of each of them becoming a victim of the ally. The result is the readiness to break the united front at any time.

Only a short time ago the lessons of the events, Marxist analysis, the criticism of the Bolshevik-Leninists spoke for the policy of the united front. Now in France a mighty factor has added itself, *the active pressure of the masses themselves.* Now this factor is decisive. It expresses itself directly in the militant demonstrations on the street and indirectly in the political turn of both apparatuses. That is a tremendous step forward. But just because the step is tremendous, *it changes the political situation* from top to bottom.

Only yesterday the slogan of the united front was the sole monopoly of the Bolshevik-Leninists. Today this monopoly has been taken from us. The slogan has become common property. It expresses the deep, passionate, but politically very nebulous longing of the masses to oppose the forward march of reaction with the united forces of all the oppressed. The presence of this longing creates the most important condition, if not for a directly revolutionary situation, at least for a pre-revolutionary one. But, unfortunately, the existing organizations see very poorly the real *changes* in the mood of the working masses. To have an ear for the average worker in the factory, on the street, in the streetcar, in the cafe, in the family in order to know how he sees the situation, what hopes he cherishes, what he believes in — to listen attentively to such a worker — that is the first duty of a revolutionary organization, above all in a critical period such as the present when the consciousness of the masses literally changes every day. At the moment one can judge the depth and the acuteness of the turn in the consciousness of the masses, above all, by their sympathetic expression, especially by the events that are taking place within both parties (crystallization of a left wing within the Social Democracy, the split of Saint-Denis, the turn of both bureaucracies to the united front, etc.). The character of such symptomatic expressions has certainly remained backward and is distorted; nevertheless they allow the following conclusion: (1) the workers see not only the danger but also the possibility of resistance; (2) they see their salvation in the united front; (3) with a halfway correct policy that reinforces the confidence of the workers in themselves, the active defense can in a short time go over to a general attack.

The task of the Bolshevik-Leninists does not now consist in the repetition of abstract formulas on the united front (workers' alliances, etc.) but in the formulation of definite slogans, concrete activity and the perspective of the struggle on the basis of the policy of a mass united front. It is the task of the defense to set up soviets and to hasten their transformation into organs of the struggle for power. The task of the League according to the present situation does not diminish but, on the contrary, grows, shifts to another plane and takes on another character. Not to understand that, to occupy oneself with the reflection of what has already been learned, would mean to lose the game.

Of decisive significance for the fate of the League will be from now on its relation to the united front, not as an abstract slogan, but as the living reality of a mass struggle. The new situation expresses itself most clearly in the example of Saint-Denis. Only yesterday Doriot[36] was the leader in the fight for the united front, which he, in his own way, made a reality in Saint-Denis. Tomorrow, in case of an agreement between the two bureaucracies, the masses will see in Doriot an obstacle, a splitter, a saboteur of the united front. The Stalinist bureaucracy will either press Saint-Denis to return to the ranks of its old party (with or without Doriot?) or will smash Saint-Denis.

The policy of the League is naturally not exhausted with the abstract idea of the united front, for this reason — *historically seen,* the course of the Bolshevik-Leninists cannot be liquidated by the agreement of both bureaucracies. Should the League remain passive, however, unable to adjust itself courageously and rapidly to the new situation, the League can be for a long period cast back into the void.

One can object: the united front demands the participation of all proletarian groupings and organizations, consequently the participation of Saint-Denis as well as that of the League. But this objection is only of formal significance. Decisive is the relation of forces. If the League had been able at the proper time to take deeper roots in the masses, if Saint-Denis had joined the League, if . . . etc., then there would have been a third *force* alongside of both bureaucracies whose participation in the united front would have been necessitated by the situation itself. In the field of the united front, this third force would have become decisive. But that is not the situation. The League is organizationally weak; Saint-Denis and other groups are politically exceptionally weak. For this reason they are all, including the League, threatened with the danger of actually having to remain outside of the united front, in spite of the fact that it is the tremendous merit of the League to have set it in motion.

If the League remains on the outside and concentrates its efforts upon criticism *from without,* it risks the danger of creating anger among the workers instead of attention. Let us once more recapitulate: in the unity of the ranks, the masses now see their only means of salvation. Everyone who remains outside the common ranks, everyone who criticizes from the sidelines, the masses look upon as an obstacle. Not to take

this mighty and, at bottom, healthy mood of the masses into
consideration, to work against it, that would be death. With
the rise of a movement, the task of the Marxists consists in,
supported by the wave, bringing in the necessary clarity of
thought and method.

The League must take an organic place in the ranks of the
united front. It is too weak to claim an *independent* place.
That is as much to say that it must immediately take a place
in one of the two parties that have negotiated the agreement.
For us there is no principled difference between the two parties,
or almost none. Practically, however, only the entry into the
Social Democratic party is possible.

What? At once we hear a hail of objections, the League
should go into Leon Blum's party? It should capitulate before
reformism? But we are for a new party? We are for the Fourth
International? How can we join the Second? What will the
Stalinists say? What will the workers say? etc., etc. All of these
arguments look very mighty, but in reality they are superficial, for they make a leap over reality. They are based on
that which *would be desirable*, not on that which *is*.

Of course, we are against reformism — in the present situation more adamantly than ever. But one must know how
to come nearer the goal in the given, concrete situation. To
renounce the principles or to "provisionally" relinquish the
struggle for them would be open treason. But to bring the
methods of struggle in congruence with the situation and our
own forces is an elementary demand of realism. Bolshevism, [37]
represented by the Leninist leadership, did not betray and renounce itself, but in 1905-06 the Bolsheviks were forced by the
pressure of the masses that longed for unity to coalesce themselves with the Mensheviks. This coalition led progressively
to a new split. But in 1910 Lenin, under the pressure of the
sentiment in his own ranks, was himself forced to undertake
an attempt at unity that was in two years to lead to a final
split. Irreconcilableness of principle has nothing in common
with sectarian ossification, which heedlessly passes over the
changes in the situation and the mood of the masses. From
the thesis that the proletarian party must be independent at
all costs, our English comrades concluded that it would be impermissible to go into the ILP. Alas! They only forgot that
they were far from being a party, but were only a propaganda
circle, that a party does not fall from heaven, that the propaganda circle must pass through a period of embryonic existence before it can become a party. Our English comrades
(the majority) doubtlessly paid dearly for their mistake in perspective, and we with them. Let us here recall the following:

at the time we did not reproach Walcher [38] and Co. for entering the SAP, but, in doing so, for sheathing the banner of Marxism. We will not do this.

Naturally the League cannot enter the Socialist Party other than as a Bolshevik-Leninist faction. It will maintain *La Verite*, which will transform itself into a factional organ with the same rights as *Action Socialiste*, [39] etc. Openly posing the question of admission, the League will say: "Our views have completely vindicated themselves. The united front is getting under way on the rails of the masses. We want to participate actively. The sole possibility for our organization to participate in the mass united front under the given circumstances is by entering the Socialist Party. Now as before we consider it to be more necessary than ever to fight for the principles of Bolshevism, for the creation of a truly revolutionary party of the proletarian vanguard and for the Fourth International. We hope to convince the majority of the Socialist as well as the Communist workers of this. We will bind ourselves to pursue this task within the framework of the party, to subject ourselves to its discipline and to preserve the unity of action."

Naturally the Stalinists will fly up in a furious howl or attempt to fly up. But, in the first place, they themselves have undertaken a sharp turn by their entry into a bloc with the "social fascists." Secondly, in their campaign against us, they will encounter the indignation of the Socialist workers. Thirdly, and that is at bottom the only important consideration, it is not a question of what the Stalinists will say but of how the League can become a serious force in the labor movement. If it succeeds, by its entry into the Socialist Party, in the course of a year or even in six months (all processes evolve very quickly today) in rallying to its banner several thousand workers, it will never occur to anyone to remember the campaign of the Stalinists.

Several comrades, I among them, accused the leadership of the League and *La Verite* of insufficiency in the struggle against the Social Democratic leadership. At first glance it might seem as though there lay an irreconcilable contradiction between this criticism, which I still maintain today in its full extent, and the proposal to enter the Social Democratic party. In reality, that is not the case. To exist as an independent organization and thereby not to demarcate oneself sharply from the Social Democrats means to risk becoming an appendage of Social Democracy. To enter openly (*under the given concrete conditions*) the Social Democratic party in order to develop an inexorable struggle against the reformist leadership means to perform a revolutionary act. The critical examination of the policy of Blum[40] and Co. must be the same in both cases.

One can make still another objection: Why begin with the Socialist Party? Would it not be more correct to address oneself first to the Communist Party? At any rate the question cannot become the object of serious differences of opinion; it is clear that the appeal to the Stalinists can only have the character of a demonstration. Is it necessary? It is possible that it would be useful as regards a definite section of Communist workers. The declaration of the League could then have the following content: "We have fought against the theory of social fascism, for the united front, etc. The latest steps of the party are evidence of a certain turn in this direction. For this reason we are ready to make a loyal attempt to work within the party, naturally under the condition that it be possible for us to fight for our ideas on the basis of party democracy." After the inevitable refusal, the League would have to address itself to the Socialist Party. If the leadership of the Socialist Party refuses to admit the League (and that is very well possible), then a broad field would be opened for the fight against the leadership in the lower bodies. The sympathies of the Socialist workers would in this case undoubtedly be on the side of the League.

The League is faced with the most serious turn in its whole history. The success of this turn will only be ensured by *boldness, quickness and unanimity.* Loss of time, endless discussions and internal strife would mean destruction.

First the Central Committee, beginning with the Politburo, must establish its position, naturally hand in hand with the International Secretariat.[41] Then the members of the Politburo must, on the spot, prepare the opinion of the members. Because of the extraordinary significance of the question, it would be necessary to summon a *conference* in order to pass a final resolution. In the face of this rapid course of events, the conference should convene not later than the middle of July, for example on the fourteenth of July. Only by observing this tempo in deeds and by the character of the turn itself can one firmly count not only on the League not running along behind the events but also on it making a great stride forward on the road to the creation of a really revolutionary party of the proletariat and the building of the Fourth International.

GREETINGS TO
THE NEW INTERNATIONAL [42]

(July 1934)

Editorial Board
The New International

Dear Comrades:

The fact that you have established a theoretical organ, I consider as a festival occasion. Its name, *The New International,* is a program of an entire epoch. I am convinced that your magazine will serve as an invaluable weapon in the establishment of the new International on the foundations laid by the great masons of the future: Marx, Engels, Lenin.

With communist greetings,

L. Trotsky

THE EVOLUTION OF THE SFIO[43]

(July 10, 1934)

The crisis of the democratic state of the bourgeoisie necessarily also signifies a crisis of the Social Democratic party.
This interdependence must be pondered and thoroughly analyzed. The passage of the bourgeoisie from the parliamentary
to the Bonapartist regime does not yet finally exclude the Social
Democracy from the legal combination of forces upon which
the government of capital reposes. As is known, Schleicher,[44]
in his time, sought the support of the trade unions. Through
the medium of his Marquet, Doumergue naturally negotiates
with Jouhaux and Co.[45] Langeron,[46] white baton in hand,
indicates the road to both fascists and Socialists. To the extent
that the Socialist Party is aware of the dependence of the Bonapartist equilibrium upon its own existence, it too still relies,
so far as its leadership goes, upon this equilibrium; it pro-
nounces itself against revolutionary fighting methods; it stig-
matizes Marxism with the sobriquet of "Blanquism";[47] it preach-
es the almost Tolstoyan doctrine of "Resist not evil with violence." Only, this policy is just as unstable as the Bonapartist
regime itself, with whose aid the bourgeoisie seeks to ward off
more radical solutions.

The essence of the democratic state consists, as is known,
in that everybody has the right to say and to write what he
will, but that in all important questions the final word rests
with the big property owners. This result is attained by means
of a complex system of partial concessions ("reforms"), illusions,
corruption, deceit and intimidation. When the economic possibility of partial concessions ("reforms") has been exhausted,
the Social Democracy ceases to be the "main political support
of the bourgeoisie." This means capital can then no longer
rest upon a domesticated "public opinion"; it requires a (Bonapartist) state apparatus independent of the masses.

Paralleling this shift in the state system, important shifts take place within the Social Democracy. With the decline of the epoch of reformism (especially during the postwar decade), the internal regime of the Social Democracy is a reproduction of the regime of bourgeois democracy: every party member can say and think what he will, but the decisions are made by the summits of the apparatus closely bound up with the state. To the extent that the bourgeoisie loses the possibility of ruling with the support of the public opinion of the exploited, the Social Democratic leaders lose the possibility of directing the public opinion of their own party. But the reformist leaders, unlike the leaders of the bourgeoisie, have no coercive apparatus at their disposal. To the extent, therefore, that parliamentary democracy is exhausted, the internal democracy of the Socialist Party, contrariwise, becomes more and more of a reality.

The crisis of the democratic state and the crisis of the Social Democratic party develop in parallel, but opposite, directions. Whereas the state marches towards fascism across the Bonapartist stage, the Socialist Party approaches a life-and-death struggle with fascism across a "loyal," quasi-parliamentary opposition to the Bonapartist state. An understanding of this dialectic of the reciprocal relations between bourgeois state and Social Democracy is an indisputable prerequisite for the correct revolutionary policy; this is just the question on which the Stalinists broke their necks.

In the Bonapartist stage through which France is at present passing, the leaders of the Social Democratic party are endeavoring with all their might to remain within the limits of (Bonapartist!) legality. They do not give up the hope that an improvement of the economic conjuncture and other favorable circumstances will lead to the restoration of the parliamentary state. Just the same, the experience of Italy, Germany and Austria compels them to count upon the other, less alluring perspective against which they would like to insure themselves. They are afraid of detaching themselves from the masses who demand a fight against fascism and await guidance. Thus the Socialist apparatus gets caught in the vise of a violent contradiction. On the one hand, it proceeds in its struggle against the radicalization of the masses to the downright preaching of Tolstoyanism: "Violence only begets violence; against brass knuckles and revolvers we must counterpose . . . wisdom and prudence." On the other hand, it talks about dictatorship of the proletariat, general strike, etc., and betakes itself to the road of the united-front policy. In the apparatus itself, a stratification takes place at the same time. The "left-wingers" acquire an ever-greater popularity. The official leaders

are compelled to rest their right arm on Doumergue ("legality"
at all costs!) and the left on Marceau Pivert, Just, etc. [48] But
the objective situation is not likely to preserve such an equilibrium. Let us repeat: *the present condition of the Socialist Party
is still more unstable than the preventive-Bonapartist state
regime.*

There can be no more devastating mistake in politics than
to operate with ready-made conceptions that relate to yesterday
and to yesterday's relationship of forces. When, for example,
the leadership of the Socialist Party reduces its task to the
demand for parliamentary elections, it is transferring politics
from the realm of reality to the realm of shadows. "Parliament,"
"government," "elections" today no longer have any of the content they possessed before the capitulation of the parliamentary
regime on February 6. Elections by themselves cannot produce
a shift in the center of gravity of power; for this is required
a leftward shift of the masses, capable of completely abrogating
and effacing the results of the rightward shift of February 6.

But a mistake of exactly the same kind is made by those
comrades who, in appraising the Socialist Party, themselves
operate with the ready-made formulas of yesterday: "reformism,"
"Second International," "political support of the bourgeoisie."
Are these definitions correct? Yes and no. More no than yes.
The old definition of the Social Democracy corresponds still
less to the facts than the definition of the present state as a
"parliamentary democratic republic." It would be false to con-
tend that there is "nothing" left of parliamentarism in France.
Under certain conditions, even a temporary relapse into parliamentarism is possible (just as a man in death agony usually
still retains a glimmer of consciousness). However, the general
evolution as a whole is already proceeding *away from* parliamentarism. Were we to give a definition of the present French
state that more closely approximates reality, we should have
to say: "a preventive-Bonapartist regime, garbed in the deso-
lated form of the parliamentary state and veering between the
not-yet-strong-enough camp of the fascist regime and the insufficiently conscious camp of the proletarian state." Only such
a *dialectical* definition can offer the basis for a correct policy.

But the same laws of dialectical thinking hold also for the
Socialist Party, which, as has already been said, shares the
fate of the democratic state, only in the reverse direction. To
which should be added that, to a substantial degree, thanks
to the experience of Germany and Austria, the evolution of the
Socialist Party even outstrips the evolution of the state to a certain extent; thus the split with the Neos preceded the coup

d'etat of February 6 by several months. Naturally it would be a crude mistake to assert that "nothing" has remained of reformism and patriotism in the party since this split. But it is no less a mistake to talk about it as about the *Social Democracy* in the old sense of the word. The impossibility of employing henceforward a simple, customary, fixed definition is precisely the flawless expression of the fact that what we have here is a *centrist*[49] party, which, by virtue of a long protracted evolution of the country, still unites extreme polar contradictions. One must be a hopeless scholastic not to discern what is going on in reality under the label "Second International." Only a dialectical definition of the Socialist Party, that is, primarily, the concrete evaluation of its internal dynamics, can permit the Bolshevik-Leninists to outline the correct perspective and to adopt an active, and not a waiting, position.

Without the revolutionary impulsion of the masses, which could shift the political center of gravity sharply to the left — or better yet, *before* such an impulsion — the state power must identify itself more openly and brutally with the military and police apparatus, fascism must become stronger and more insolent. Parallel to this, the antagonisms within the Socialist Party must come to the fore, that is, the incompatibility of the Tolstoyan preaching of "Resist not evil with violence" with the revolutionary tasks dictated by the class foe. Simultaneous with the Bonapartization of the state and the approach of the fascist danger, the party majority must inevitably become radicalized; the internal differentiation, which is far from being completed, must enter a new phase.

The Bolshevik-Leninists are duty bound to say all this openly. They have always rejected the theory of "social fascism" and hooligan methods in polemic, in which theoretical impotence unites with lie and calumny. They have no cause to stand themselves on their heads and to call black white. We advocated the united front at a time when it was rejected both by the Socialists and the Stalinists. That is just why we remain, even today, with a critical, realistic attitude towards the abstraction of "unity." In the history of the labor movement, demarcation is often the premise of unity. In order to take the first step towards the united front, the Socialist Party was compelled first to split away from the Neos. This ought not to be forgotten for an instant. The Socialist Party can take a leading part in a genuine mass and fighting united front only in the event that it sets out its tasks clearly and purges its ranks of the right wing and masked opponents of revolutionary struggle. It is not a question here of any abstract "principle," but of an iron necessity resulting from the logic of the struggle. The problem is not one that can be solved by any diplomatic turn of the phrase, as is believed by Zyromsky,[50] who endeavors to find the formula that will reconcile social patriotism with internationalism. The march of the class struggle, in its present stage, will pitilessly explode and tear down all tergiversation, deception and dissimulation. The workers in general and the Socialists in particular need the truth, the naked truth and nothing but the truth.

The Bolshevik-Leninists correctly formulated what is and what is to be. But they have not been able — it must be openly avowed — to fulfill the task that they set themselves a year ago: *more deeply to penetrate the ranks of the Socialist workers,* not in order to "lecture" down to them from above as learned specialists in strategy, but in order to learn together with the advanced workers, shoulder to shoulder, on the basis of actual mass experience, which will inevitably lead the French proletariat on the road of revolutionary struggle.

In order the better to illuminate the tasks lying before us on this field, one must, however, dwell upon the evolution of the so-called Communist Party.

BONAPARTISM AND FASCISM[51]

(July 15, 1934)

The vast practical importance of a correct theoretical orientation is most strikingly manifested in a period of acute social conflict, of rapid political shifts, of abrupt changes in the situation. In such periods, political *conceptions* and *generalizations* are rapidly used up and require either a complete replacement (which is easier) or their concretization, precision or partial rectification (which is harder). It is in just such periods that all sorts of *transitional, intermediate* situations and combinations arise, as a matter of necessity, which upset the customary patterns and doubly require a sustained theoretical attention. In a word, if in the pacific and "organic" period (before the war) one could still live on the revenue from a few ready-made abstractions, in our time each new event forcefully brings home the most important law of the dialectic: *the truth is always concrete.*

The Stalinist theory of fascism indubitably represents one of the most tragic examples of the injurious practical consequences that can follow from the substitution of the dialectical analysis of reality, in its every concrete phase, in all its transitional stages, that is, in its gradual changes as well as in its revolutionary (or counterrevolutionary) leaps, by abstract categories formulated upon the basis of a partial and insufficient historical experience (or a narrow and insufficient view of the whole). The Stalinists adopted the idea that in the contemporary period, finance capital cannot accommodate itself to parliamentary democracy and is obliged to resort to fascism. From this idea, absolutely correct within certain limits, they draw in a purely deductive, formally logical manner the same conclusions for all the countries and for all stages of development. To them, Primo de Rivera, Mussolini, Chiang Kai-shek, Masaryk, Bruening, Dollfuss, Pilsudski, the Serbian King Alexander, Severing, MacDonald, etc., were the repre-

sentatives of fascism.[52] In doing this, they forgot: (*a*) that
in the past, too, capitalism never accommodated itself to "pure"
democracy, now supplementing it with a regime of open repression, now substituting one for it; (*b*) that "pure" finance capitalism nowhere exists; (*c*) that even while occupying a dominant position, finance capital does not act within a void and
is obliged to reckon with the other strata of the bourgeoisie
and with the resistance of the oppressed classes; (*d*) that, finally, between parliamentary democracy and the fascist regime a series of transitional forms, one after another, inevitably interposes itself, now "peaceably," now by civil war. And
each one of these transitional forms, if we want to go forward
and not be flung to the rear, demands a correct theoretical
appraisal and a corresponding policy of the proletariat.

On the basis of the German experience, the Bolshevik-Leninists recorded for the first time the transitional governmental
form (even though it could and should already have been
established on the basis of Italy) that we called Bonapartism
(the Bruening, Papen, Schleicher governments). In a more
precise and more developed form, we subsequently observed
the Bonapartist regime in Austria. The determinism of this
transitional form has become patent, naturally not in the fa-
talistic but in the dialectical sense, that is, for the countries
and periods where fascism, with growing success, without en-
countering a victorious resistance of the proletariat, attacked
the positions of parliamentary democracy in order thereupon
to strangle the proletariat.

During the period of Bruening-Schleicher, Manuilsky-Kuusi-
nen[53] proclaimed: "Fascism is already here"; the theory of
the intermediate, Bonapartist stage they declared to be an attempt to paint over and mask fascism in order to make easier
for the Social Democracy the policy of the "lesser evil." At
that time the Social Democrats were called social fascists, and
the "left" Social Democrats of the Zyromsky-Marceau Pivert-
Just type passed — after the "Trotskyists" — for the most dangerous social fascists. All this has changed now. With regard to
present-day France, the Stalinists do not dare to repeat: "Fascism is already here"; on the contrary, they have accepted the
policy of the united front, which they rejected yesterday, in order to prevent the victory of fascism in France. They have
found themselves compelled to distinguish the Doumergue regime from the fascist regime. But they have arrived at this
distinction as empiricists and not as Marxists. They do not
even attempt to give a scientific definition of the Doumergue
regime. He who operates in the domain of theory with abstract
categories is condemned to capitulate blindly to facts.

And yet it is precisely in France that the passage from parliamentarism to Bonapartism (or more exactly, the first stage of this passage) has taken on a particularly striking and demonstrative character. It suffices to recall that the Doumergue government appeared on the scene between the rehearsal of the civil war by the fascists (February 6) and the general strike of the proletariat (February 12). As soon as the irreconcilable camps had taken up their fighting positions at the poles of capitalist society, it wasn't long before it became clear that the adding machine of parliamentarism lost all importance. It is true that the Doumergue government, like the Bruening-Schleicher governments in their day, appears at first glance to govern with the assent of parliament. But it is a parliament that has abdicated, a parliament that knows that in case of resistance the government would dispense with it. Thanks to the relative equilibrium between the camp of counterrevolution that attacks and the camp of the revolution that defends itself, thanks to their temporary mutual neutralization, the axis of power has been raised above the classes and above their parliamentary representation. It was necessary to seek the head of the government outside of parliament and "outside the parties." The head of the government has called two generals to his aid. This trinity has supported itself on its right and its left by symmetrically arranged parliamentary hostages. The government appears not as an executive organ of the parliamentary majority, but as a judge-arbiter between two camps in struggle.

A government that raises itself above the nation is not, however, suspended in air. The true axis of the present government passes through the police, the bureaucracy, the military clique. It is a military-police dictatorship with which we are confronted, barely concealed with the decorations of parliamentarism. But a government of the saber as the judge-arbiter of the nation — that's just what *Bonapartism* is.

The saber by itself has no independent program. It is the instrument of "order." It is summoned to safeguard what exists. Raising itself *politically* above the classes, Bonapartism, like its predecessor Caesarism, for that matter, represents *in the social sense*, always and at all epochs, the government of the strongest and firmest part of the exploiters; consequently, present-day Bonapartism can be nothing else than the government of finance capital, which directs, inspires and corrupts the summits of the bureaucracy, the police, the officers' caste and the press.

The "constitutional reform," about which so much has been said in the course of recent months, has as its sole task the adaptation of the state institutions to the exigencies and conveniences of the Bonapartist government. Finance capital is seeking legal paths that would give it the possibility of each time imposing upon the nation the most suitable judge-arbiter with the forced assent of the quasi-parliament. It is evident that the Doumergue government is not the ideal of a "strong government." More suitable candidates for a Bonaparte exist in reserve. New experiences and combinations are possible in this domain if the future course of the class struggle is to leave them enough time.

In prognosticating, we are obliged to repeat what the Bolshevik-Leninists said at one time about Germany: the political chances of present French Bonapartism are not great; its stability is determined by the temporary and, at bottom, unsteady equilibrium between the camps of the proletariat and fascism. The relation of forces of these two camps must change rapidly, in part under the influence of the economic conjuncture, principally in dependence upon the quality of the proletarian vanguard's policy. The collision between these two camps is inevitable. The measuring time of the process will be calculated in months and not in years. A stable regime could be established only after the collision, depending upon the results.

Fascism in power, like Bonapartism, can only be the government of finance capital. In this *social* sense, it is indistinguishable not only from Bonapartism but even from parliamentary democracy. Each time, the Stalinists made this discovery all over again, forgetting that *social* questions resolve themselves in the domain of the *political.* The strength of finance capital does not reside in its ability to establish a government of any kind and at any time, according to its wish; it does not possess this faculty. Its strength resides in the fact that every nonproletarian government is forced to serve finance capital, or better yet, that finance capital possesses the possibility of substituting for each one of its systems of domination that decays, another system corresponding better to the changed conditions. However, the passage from one system to another signifies the *political crisis* that, with the concourse of the activity of the revolutionary proletariat, may be transformed into a social danger to the bourgeoisie. The passage of parliamentary democracy to Bonapartism itself was accompanied in France by an effervescence of civil war. The perspective of the passage from Bonapartism to fascism is pregnant with infinitely more formidable disturbances and consequently also revolutionary possibilities.

Up to yesterday, the Stalinists considered that our "main mistake" was to see in fascism the petty bourgeoisie and not finance capital. In this case too they put abstract categories in place of the dialectics of the classes. Fascism is a specific means of mobilizing and organizing the petty bourgeoisie in the social interests of finance capital. During the democratic regime, capital inevitably attempted to inoculate the workers with confidence in the reformist and pacifist petty bourgeoisie. The passage to fascism, on the contrary, is inconceivable without the preceding permeation of the petty bourgeoisie with hatred of the proletariat. The domination of one and the same superclass, finance capital, rests in these two systems upon directly opposite relations of oppressed classes.

The political mobilization of the petty bourgeoisie against the proletariat, however, is inconceivable without that social demagogy, which means playing with fire for the big bourgeoisie. The danger to "order" of the unleashed petty-bourgeois reaction has just been confirmed by the recent events in Germany.[54] That is why, while supporting and actively financing reactionary banditry, in the form of one of its wings, the French bourgeoisie seeks not to push matters to the point of the political victory of fascism, but rather only to establish a "strong" power, which, in the last analysis, is to discipline the two extreme camps.

What has been said sufficiently demonstrates how important it is to distinguish the Bonapartist form of power from the fascist form. Yet, it would be unpardonable to fall into the opposite extreme, that is, to convert Bonapartism and fascism into two logically incompatible categories. Just as Bonapartism begins by combining the parliamentary regime with fascism, so triumphant fascism finds itself forced not only to enter into a bloc with the Bonapartists but, what is more, to draw closer internally to the Bonapartist system. The prolonged domination of finance capital by means of reactionary social demagogy and petty-bourgeois terror is impossible. Having arrived in power, the fascist chiefs are forced to muzzle the masses who follow them by means of the state apparatus. By the same token, they lose the support of broad masses of the petty bourgeoisie. A small part of it is assimilated by the bureaucratic apparatus. Another sinks into indifference. A third, under various banners, passes into opposition. But while losing its social mass base, by resting upon the bureaucratic apparatus and oscillating between the classes, fascism is regenerated into Bonapartism. Here, too, the gradual evolution is cut into by violent and sanguinary episodes. Differing from prefascist or *preventive Bonapartism* (Giolitti,[55] Bruening-Schleicher, Doumergue, etc.), which reflects the extremely unstable and short-lived equilibrium between the belligerent camps, *Bonapartism of fascist origin* (Mussolini, Hitler, etc.), which grew out of the destruction, the disillusionment and the demoralization of the two camps of the masses, distinguishes itself by its much greater stability.

The question "fascism or Bonapartism?" has engendered certain differences on the subject of the Pilsudski regime among our Polish comrades.[56] The very possibility of such differences testifies best to the fact that we are dealing not with inflexible logical categories but with living social formations that represent extremely pronounced peculiarities in different countries and at different stages.

Pilsudski came to power at the end of an insurrection based upon a mass movement of the petty bourgeoisie and aimed *directly* at the domination of the traditional bourgeois parties in the name of the "strong state"; this is a fascist trait characteristic of the movement and of the regime. But the specific political weight, that is, the mass of Polish fascism, was much weaker than that of Italian fascism in its time and still more so than that of German fascism; to a much greater degree, Pilsudski had to make use of the methods of military conspiracy and to put the question of the workers' organizations in a much more circumspect manner. It suffices to recall that Pilsudski's coup d'etat took place with the sympathy and the support of the Polish party of the Stalinists. The growing hostility of the Ukrainian and Jewish petty bourgeoisie towards the Pilsudski regime made it, in turn, more difficult for him to launch a general attack upon the working class.

As a result of such a situation, the oscillation between the classes and the national parts of the classes occupied and still occupies with Pilsudski a much greater place, and mass terror a much smaller place, than in the corresponding periods with Mussolini or Hitler; there is the Bonapartist element in the Pilsudski regime. Nevertheless, it would be patently false to compare Pilsudski to Giolitti or to Schleicher and to look forward to his being relieved by a new Polish Mussolini or Hitler. It is methodologically false to form an image of some "ideal" fascism and to oppose it to this real fascist regime that has grown up, with all its peculiarities and contradictions, upon the terrain of the relationship of classes and nationalities in the Polish state. Will Pilsudski be able to lead the action of destruction of the proletarian organizations to the very end? The logic of the situation drives him inevitably on this path, but the answer depends not upon the formal definition of "fascism" as such but upon the true relationship of forces, the dynamics of the political processes taking place in the masses, the strategy of the proletarian vanguard and, finally, the course of events in Western Europe and, above all, in France.

History may successfully inscribe the fact that Polish fascism was overthrown and reduced to dust before it succeeded in finding for itself a "totalitarian" form of expression.

We said above that Bonapartism of fascist origin is incomparably more stable than the preventive-Bonapartist experiments to which the big bourgeoisie resorts in the hope of avoiding fascist bloodletting. Nevertheless, it is still more important—from the theoretical and practical point of view—to emphasize that *the very fact of the regeneration of fascism into Bonapartism signifies the beginning of its end.* How long a time the withering away of fascism will last, and at what moment its malady will turn into agony, depends upon many internal and external causes. But the fact that the counterrevolutionary activity of the petty bourgeoisie is quenched, that it is disillusioned, that it is disintegrating, and that its attack upon the proletariat is weakening opens up new revolutionary possibilities. All history shows that it is impossible to keep the proletariat enchained with the aid merely of the police apparatus. It is true that the experience of Italy shows that the psychological heritage of the enormous catastrophe experienced maintains itself among the working class much longer than the relationship between the forces that engendered the catastrophe. But the psychological inertia of the defeat is but a precarious prop. It can crumble at a single blow under the impact of a powerful convulsion. Such a convulsion—for Italy, Germany, Austria and other countries—could be the success of the struggle of the French proletariat.

The revolutionary key to the situation in Europe and in the entire world is now, above all, in France!

SUMMARY OF THE DISCUSSION[57]

(August 6, 1934)

Our group has appointed me to formulate certain general conclusions that we have arrived at on the basis of the information in the internal bulletin of the League and other documents.

1. Are the divergences ones of principle or of a purely practical nature? In this general form, the question is put incorrectly. The divergences have arisen over a very important question of tactics, but they have different roots in different comrades, springing from different ideological premises. Thus, for example, we maintain that the differences with Comrade Georges (to the extent that there are differences) are of a purely practical character and should be verified in the process of applying the common policy. The differences with Comrade P. N.[58] are differences of principle.

2. Comrade Georges has undoubtedly presented the best paper on the question. Nine-tenths of his letter consists of facts throwing light on the real situation and not of general formulas that might be applied equally well to Paris or Honolulu. Nevertheless, we feel that in Comrade Georges's letter there is a grave error in evaluating the dynamics and rhythm of the development. On the basis of a very interesting analysis of the National Council of the SFIO, G. shows that the majority of the Socialist Party is still reformist, that a significant leftward trend may be found only in Paris and in the Young Socialists and, therefore, that it would be "premature" to enter the SFIO. In answer to these claims, we wish to say briefly:

a. Paris and the Young Socialists are today going through the stage that the provinces will pass through tomorrow. There is no need for us to guide ourselves by the situation in the provinces.

b. Paris and the Young Socialists are *decisive fields* for the League.

c. The party machine in the provinces (as in Paris) is the old one, i.e., reformist. Still, the machine found itself forced to break with Renaudel [59] and accept the united front with Moscow. It is precisely the opportunist character of the SFIO apparatus that best indicates the power of the pressure from below, that is, the dynamics of the development. Comrade Georges is right when he says that entering the party six days too soon would mean mishandling the situation. We must merely add that entering six days too late would mean ruining it entirely.

3. How shall we determine the right moment for entry and the most reasonable form? By political reconnoitering and by actively establishing tie-ups with the Socialists, discussing political questions with them, etc.

A year has passed since we took the turn for a *new party.* One of the principal tasks assigned to the League was work on the inside of the SFIO. What has been accomplished during the year in Paris? Nothing. The comrades in charge of this work have not set up any relationships, have made no preparations. On the contrary, *they have opposed the creation of a faction in the SFIO.* This fact is of major importance for an understanding of the present difficulties, including even difficulties of discussion. These same comrades who, during the past year, have opposed working inside the SFIO are now opposed to our entering that body. In both cases they repeat the same general talk about "independence." For them the fundamental thing seems to be to remain independent of the working class, the masses, the changes in the state of affairs, of the whole reality. These comrades substitute a monologue for actual political work among the masses. Their politics follows the line of least resistance; it is politics of self-complacency disguised by formulas of imaginary intransigence.

We must demand that these comrades give an accounting of the work they were entrusted with doing in the SFIO and the results of this work. The League and these comrades themselves need such a report, and not general slogans! The report will show that these comrades are afraid of the masses, are afraid of the difficulties connected with working among the masses, that they want to preserve their "purity" by a kind of self-isolation. That is why they remain unchanged through all the changes in the political situation. The psychology of passive waiting that existed before the proposal of entry into the SFIO was a powerful brake on the development of the League, especially during the past year. This psychology is now in glaring contradiction to the whole situation in this country and in the working class.

4. The only differences that are serious, important and fruitful are those that arise from the pressure of major events and changes in the state of mind of the masses. The same traits of abstract propagandism, which were to a *certain extent* inevitable in the initial period of the League's development (before the German catastrophe) and which have more and more checked the work during these last years, have now definitely taken on a reactionary character and in the present turmoil of events threaten to lead the League to total ruin. It is particularly now that we must put up a pitiless fight against abstract, passive propagandism, against a policy of waiting. Along this line, the differences are certainly differences of principle, although the exponents of the conservative tendency have not yet drawn the necessary ideological conclusions from their position.

5. Comrades P. N., Bauer [60] and certain others who think as they do assume the cloak of "ideological intransigence." However in actuality, in the present policy, things are quite different. Let us consider the stand taken by *La Verite* after February 6. During this entire time, *La Verite* adapted itself politically to the SFIO. In his letter P. N. says: "Several documents sent to the Central Committee indicate that for the past six months we have been following a semisocialist line. . . . But here is the conclusion: since you have 'adapted' yourselves so well to the SFIO, why not enter that group?"

Remarkable logic!

This declaration is the crux of P. N.'s letter. It throws a brilliant light on the real progress of the preparation of the divergences and, at the same time, reveals the nondialectical, abstract, journalistic thinking of Comrade P. N. Yes, in a whole series of letters and conversations we did accuse Comrade P. N. and others of obscuring (toning down, blurring) the differences with the SFIO, of not openly stating the fundamental questions of the revolutionary struggle, of risking the transformation of the League into a left wing of the SFIO. We stand by this criticism without modification, even today. Members who insist upon *formal* independence are always inclined to capitulate before the reality when it treads upon their toes. The adaptation of the League to the SFIO has found symbolic expression in very recent happenings: in reply to the proposal that we enter the SFIO, the Political Bureau decided to make do by obtaining the floor for a representative of the League at the National Council of the SFIO!! Here again they displayed their penchant for purely diplomatic negotiations with the heads of the SFIO, without any serious attempt to penetrate the mass base of the organization. (We are not speaking of the Young Socialists; among them real work has been done.) We must carefully consider what the intransigence of Comrade P. N. and the others has consisted of during the past six months:

a. external weakening of criticism of the SFIO,

b. diplomatic maneuvers with the SFIO bureaucrats,

c. refusal to create a faction inside the SFIO (because they did not want to spoil their relations with the bureaucrats?).

There you have the real picture of the relations of the "intransigents" with the SFIO during the past six months, so crowded with events. No general slogan, no gesture can change the political meaning of this picture, which demonstrates the emptiness of an intransigence that is factional or, worse still, literary. Until Comrade P. N. and the others arrive at an understanding of their own history during the last six months, they will not move one step forward in their development.

6. When we analyzed the rotten policy of the Anglo-Russian Committee, [61] the Stalinists said: "You are opposed to working in the unions!" We replied: "We are opposed to adventurous maneuvering with the leaderships, but in favor of working with the membership." There, it is true, we were concerned with unions. But we can give a similar illustration with regard to parties. We denounced Walcher for his political complicity in the Tranmael [62] case. At the same time, we said: "If any revolutionary group can enter the NAP [63] for revolutionary work among the masses, it is the duty of that group to do so, and they will have our support."

We have criticized passive adaptation to the official policy of the SFIO and, at the same time, we have upheld active participation in the internal life of that body, the building of an internal faction. In principle that does not differ at all from entry into the SFIO. Comrade P. N. sees a contradiction here. Isn't that absurd? Under the influence of that false position he has taken, the perspectives and retrospect are distorted for him, just as they always are in such cases.

7. It would, of course, be incorrect to attribute the "soft" diplomatic line of *La Verite* during the last six months of the year to an error on the part of a few comrades. The truth of the matter is that the League has suddenly come under the great pressure of events. The same causes that forced the SFIO bureaucracy and the Stalinists to accept the slogan of the united front have suggested to the leadership of the League, consciously or unconsciously, the fear that they would find themselves left quite outside of things, and since there was

the chance of getting the floor and selling their publications through the SFIO, there arose the hope of managing the latter, of adapting themselves to that body. The League's place in the working-class movement was more clearly and seriously decided by this policy of *La Verite* than by all the talk of imaginary intransigence. The unfortunate thing is that the leadership yielded unconsciously to the events and only gropingly adapted itself to the new situation. This experience has clearly and forcefully shown up the fiction of organizational independence and verbal intransigence in the face of great historic developments, when the masses begin stirring.

8. When we criticized Comrade P. N. and others for their adaptation to the SFIO, we did not at all consider that we were confronted with irreconcilable contradictions threatening a split. We do not think so now, either. But the situation becomes tremendously more dangerous inasmuch as Comrade P. N., growing convinced of the total failure of *passive adaptation from without,* wishes at all costs to *prevent revolutionary work from within.* The progress of events now permits no delay to any of us, and particularly not to Comrade P. N. We must boldly and resolutely judge what our previous course was and start moving on the new road.

9. It is true that now Comrade P. N. and others generously offer to create a faction inside the SFIO while preserving their own "independence." That means letting everything go on as before. It means continuing to swim on the sand instead of venturing into the water. There is only one way to save the "intransigents" for the revolutionary movement: force them to get into the water up to their necks.

10. Is there not a danger that the comrades adapting themselves from the outside to the SFIO policy will completely lose their political identity if they enter the SFIO? The question cannot be put in that general form. A certain differentiation will inevitably be produced; a certain number of the comrades may abandon our ideas. The experience of all countries shows that the ones who are most prone to lose their identity in the opportunistic milieu are yesterday's ultimatists. But it would be absolutely incorrect to extend this fear to the League in its entirety or even to all our present opponents in the League.

To our mind, the very possibility of bringing up the question of entry into the SFIO springs from the fact that in the body of the League we have serious cadres. If we delay too long in applying the yeast to the dough, it will go sour on us and be wasted. That is the danger threatening the League.

Look at the Bordigists[64] with their famous *Bilan* (Balance), which should really be named "Balance: Zero."

11. Certain comrades are inclined to shift the center of gravity to the question of the "declaration."[65] Some of them have in mind a declaration that would make entry into the SFIO impossible. Others are inclined to see in the declaration a talisman that will protect them from all dangers. In reality, the role of the declaration is very modest. It must show:

a. that we are not giving up our ideas,

b. that we are ready to learn from joint activity,

c. that we will fight for our ideas on the basis of democracy of the party,

d. that we will maintain discipline.

The declaration must be drawn up so as to win the confidence of Socialist workers and make it very difficult for the reactionary SFIO bureaucracy to decide on nonadmission of the League.

12. Aside from retaining our ideology, the only way we can keep the Bolshevik-Leninists from dissolution once they are inside the SFIO is by means of great cohesion, creation of a factional body, adaptation to new working conditions and international control. We must direct all our efforts to that end.

13. International control must be understood in its broad sense, without limiting it to the International Secretariat. The exchange of publications and information, international discussion, should be not weakened but developed and reinforced. It is true that Comrade P. N. presents the matter as if the international organization had prevented (!) the League from working, particularly during the elaboration of the program of action. Comrade P. N. does not and cannot bring forth the slightest proof of his assertion. We propose to Comrade P. N. that he publish (only in the *International Bulletin,* if need be) all the correspondence devoted to the elaboration of the program of action as well as the general policy of the League during the last six months. A piece of work of this kind done in good faith would show the enormous importance of our international organization as such, and would, incidentally, refute the definitely incorrect and prejudiced assertions of Comrade P. N.

14. The lack of a real ideological position on the part of Comrades Bauer and P. N. appears most plainly on the question of the ILP.[66] Bauer was in favor of the entry of the British section into the ILP from its beginning. P. N. was against this, but after his trip to England, having become aware of the actual situation at first hand, he recognized the incorrect-

ness of his original position. To set up an ideological difference between the ILP and the SFIO, especially the latter's Parisian organization and the Young Socialists, is simply ridiculous. Neither P. N. nor Bauer has made any attempt to explain the difference in their ideological stand with regard to England and France.

However, the experience of the British section, on a small scale, is highly instructive. The "majority" maintaining its "organizational autonomy" actually finds itself in a state of constant internal strife and division. Certain leaders have left the organization altogether. On the other hand, the "minority" that entered the ILP has maintained its internal solidarity and its connection with the international Bolshevik-Leninists, has made large use of the publications of the League in America and has had a series of successes inside the ILP. We must learn from the example.

15. Certain comrades threaten a split in case the new line is adopted. That shows their lack of seriousness with regard to the things that unite us, the ideas and tactics we have in common, elaborated in the course of eleven years of a great collective work on an international scale. We must, of course, do everything possible to avoid a split, even the withdrawal of a single group. Every comrade is valuable to us, for he can and should become an officer in the proletarian army. But it would be ridiculous and unworthy of us to be afraid of threats of withdrawal. We have seen withdrawals of this kind before, and we know how they have ended up. Dear as our comrades are to us, the development of the organization is immeasurably dearer to us. There is no room for hesitation![67]

THE TASK OF
REVOLUTIONARY TEACHERS[68]

A Letter to Maurice Dommanget

(August 10, 1934)

Dear Comrade,

In this letter I shall attempt to summarize the discussion we had a few days ago on questions concerning French teachers in general, and the Federation Unitaire in particular.

I cannot refrain from repeating: Monmousseau,[69] this tightrope artist without scruples or conscience, set a trap for us on the question of merging the two federations, sacrificing union and revolutionary considerations to the ruling CGTU bureaucrats' considerations of prestige and "pie-card" jobs. Their turn has nothing in common with an honest acceptance of the revolutionary united front. As far as we can make out, two maneuvers are entangled in their obscure game: a wider one, corresponding to the aims of Soviet diplomacy, and a narrower, subordinate one, which is supposed to "satisfy" the adventurist bankrupts of the Comintern. The semiofficial doctrine of the ruling bureaucracy in the USSR seeks to explain the failure of the Comintern — incontestable for them as well — by the conservative qualities of the proletariat in the West. If the reformists used to say that Bolshevism was no good for Europe, the Comintern bankrupts now declare that the European proletariat is not good enough for Bolshevism. On this issue, as on many others [three illegible words] Western communism only represent two sides of the same coin.

Having thus transformed the failure of the Comintern into a failure of the Western proletariat, the ruling bureaucrats draw the conclusion: "For the security of the USSR, we have to look elsewhere for help. Since the conservative proletariat is attached to democracy, nothing remains but for us to attach ourselves to it, to support and preserve democracy." We revolutionaries say, "To the extent that the workers retain their confidence in democracy, we are prepared to defend democracy with them against the fascist danger; but we can never forgo our criticism of democratic illusions." The Stalinists easily waive the right to criticize, since for them (the Soviet bureaucracy) it is a question not of leading the proletariat through the democratic stage towards the conquest of power but of ensuring themselves international democratic support, as the only realizable goal. French "democracy" is embodied in the Radical Party,[70] which cannot rule without the support of the Socialist Party; but this party, in turn, can lend its support to the Radical government only on condition that the Communists "shut up." The overriding plan of the Soviet bureaucracy is to reestablish the regime of Herriot, the "friend of the USSR," aided by Leon Blum, freed from Thorez's[71] criticism by the mechanism of the so-called united front. That is the principal incentive of the great turn dictated by the telegraph.

To calm the left wing of the Comintern, the Bela Kun[72] types, they say: "All this is only a trick; hold your tongue and wait; the right moment will come when we'll break open the united front, catching the Socialist leaders asleep and unawares, and bring their workers with us."

These are the two entangled maneuvers. For the moment it is the first that is operative. But if the democratic perspective leads nowhere, the big bureaucrats can always squirm out of it by allowing the worst Bela Kun adventurists to utilize the united front in their own fashion.

What is Monmousseau's place in this double and perhaps triple deal? I know nothing about that, and Monmousseau himself knows no more than I. Nevertheless, he is sufficiently versed in Stalinist stage management not to fear that the delicate structure propping up the turn will collapse upon his own head. That is why, while carrying out orders, he would really like to drag out matters, to dodge and slow things down. Thus he was able to impose on the Montpellier congress[73] an evasive and dangerous decision dodging the immediate merger of the two federations. To put off the decision until January 1935 is not to take the world and oneself seriously, since the coming months must bring decisions that are all the more serious.

Let one thing be well understood: the fascist danger is not an agitational formula; it is an ominous reality that can soon assert itself. The claims of *Popu* and *l'Huma* that "the united front has already made the fascists pull back" are nothing but naive or dishonest bravado.

The rise of fascism, like all historic processes of this type, is accomplished by spasmodic leaps and twists. We are between two spasms; that is the real key to the present situation.

And it won't be Monmousseau who will succeed in "putting off" the second leap until after January 1, 1935.

The triumph of fascism would signify, in the first place, the crushing of the cadre of revolutionary teachers. Even before it takes on the workers' organizations, the fascist reaction will have to club its way through the brain of the resisting civil servants and teachers. Idle chatterboxes tell us: "The danger is far from imminent; France is not Germany; the temperament of the French does not lend itself to fascism." It is not our role to take such foolishness seriously. Fascism is a product not of national temperament but of social struggle. It becomes an unavoidable necessity for French capitalism when its back is against the wall. And to the extent that the national temperament opposes fascism, a fascist regime in France will claim two or ten times the number of victims it claims elsewhere. It is not accidental that all stages of French history have witnessed the bloodiest of repressions.

Our Federation Unitaire, with its 3,000 members, would be the first mouthful for triumphant reaction. Physical self-defense alone forces us to end our isolation and merge with the Syndicat National. Each day we lose is an irreparable loss. Yes, I know, we are on vacation, and many of us are enjoying it blissfully. When we look around us, we almost have the impression of watching peasants, oblivious to danger, tilling the slopes of Vesuvius a few moments before the fatal eruption that will sweep away their property, their work and the peasants themselves.

Whatever the cost, we must find some means of overturning the dangerous decision that the CGTU imposed upon the Montpellier congress. It is wartime; formalities, even the most respectable ones, must yield to supreme necessities. For my part, I am sure that a bold initiative on the part of the federation leadership — which enjoys the full confidence of the rank and file — would be supported by an overwhelming majority of the federation. And merger of the two federations — and here I agree with Delmas[74] — would provide a vigorous thrust for unification of the entire union movement, shattering the bad will of the Jouhaux and Monmousseaus.

Naturally, we can merge with the Confederes [CGTers] only to promote the revolutionary mobilization of the teachers. That is why we must work out an action program that is precise, vigorous and adapted to the situation. Witness the spectacle of Paul Faure,[75] leader of the SFIO, who, before the revolvers, clubs and machine guns of fascism, develops Buddhist and Tolstoyan theories of not opposing evil by violence! For him, the task is still to win the confidence of the majority (51 percent) in order to bring about the socialist ideal. But Austrian Social Democracy had its throat slit with 44 percent. We doubt Paul Faure's ability to beat their record. For even if one is totally and exclusively committed to a democratic basis of winning power with 51 percent of the votes, that possibility must be ensured through armed defense against the fascist bands, just as workers are obliged to defend the most modest of strikes by picketing. The bourgeoisie says hypocritically: "The security of the nation requires the arming of the nation." With utmost confidence we can say, "The security of the pro- letariat's democratic rise to power requires, above all, the *arming of the workers* and, in the first place, the creation of *workers' militias.*"

Yet here we see the Thorezes, Cachins[76] and Monmousseaus rushing to the defense of Paul Faure's Tolstoyan theories; it seems that only "Trotskyist provocateurs" would oppose the armed reaction with an armed proletariat. Shameful, imbecilic sophistry! All the more so coming from the lips of people who only yesterday still depicted all of France (at least *l'Humanite's* France) as a land of barricades and revolution- ary battles. On this question the turn demonstrates most clearly the slavish dependence of the CP and CGTU bureaucrats on Soviet diplomacy. The Thorezes want to replace armed militias with "self-defense of the entire proletariat." You bet! And what becomes of the *vanguard* role of the proletariat in this scheme? Without the support of the working class, the militias are noth- ing, but without the militia, and exposed to the blows of fas- cism, the class is very little. The militia is the active army; the class is its great reserve. This ABC of Marxism is aban- doned, trampled upon and sullied as "Blanquism." A teacher's self-defense — of this I am absolutely convinced — must trans- form teachers into fierce propagandists and tireless organizers of the *workers' and peasants' militias.* The aim of such a militia is *defense* of the exploited masses, of their organiza- tions, meetings, press, of their democratic rights and social conquests.

What I have said in this letter is not at all sufficient. It is, I hope, the beginning of an exchange of views on burning issues that directly concern our federation, but whose impli- cations go much further. Very much interested in the opinions of you and other comrades, I am ready to reply in turn. The vacation must not put us to sleep. Senator Gautherot from Loire-Inferieure, as well as Fougeres, deputy from Indre, have already submitted questions concerning the teachers. The reac- tion does not waste its time; let us not waste ours.

Fraternally,

TO THE BOLSHEVIK-LENINISTS IN THE USSR[77]

(Published August 17, 1934)

Dear Comrades,

For a long time the Stalinists prepared Rakovsky's[78] capitulation as a decisive blow. And now, only several months later, it is proved that the blow has miscarried: among the thousands in the USSR who are imprisoned, exiled, expelled from the party and deprived of bread, two or three tired veterans followed Rakovsky; in the rest of the world — not a single man. And that despite the extraordinarily difficult situation of the Bolshevik-Leninists against whom the Stalinists unite with world reaction in order to pursue and hound them.

The principal argument of the capitulation is, at the same time, the principal proof of the political inconsistency of the capitulators. The victorious offensive of fascism requires, according to Rakovsky, the unity of "all forces" for the defense of the Soviet power. But the question is: how to resist the victorious offensive of the reaction and *how* to safeguard the Soviet power? Stalin declared that Social Democracy and fascism were Siamese twins. On this basis the united front was irrevocably condemned. Two days before the victory of Hitler, the Comintern stated that the proletarian revolution in Germany was traveling full steam ahead to victory. It presented the uncontested establishment of the fascist dictatorship in the most industrialized nation of Europe as "the acceleration of the proletarian revolution." The policy of the German Communist Party before, during and after the fascist coup d'etat was declared beyond reproach. By means of such deception and such crimes, a situation chock full of revolutionary possibilities was lost in Germany. During the years 1929-33, the Comintern prepared and struck such a blow to Soviet power and to the world revolution that in comparison the economic successes of the USSR are relegated to second and third place. Rakovsky did not even attempt to answer the question: was the policy of Stalin-Thaelmann[79] in the great class battles correct or fatal? Whoever substitutes fawning before the bureaucracy, its errors and crimes, for the defense of the historic interests of the revolution can hope for nothing from the Bolshevik-Leninists but well-deserved scorn.

When the waters of fascism rose up to the Comintern's neck in France, frightened, it accomplished in several days, if not in several hours, a turn unprecedented in political history; it cast off the theory of social fascism like a dirty rag, recognized —and in what a vulgar Menshevik form! — the defense of democracy and proclaimed the united front with the Social Democracy not only a superior but also a unique precept, by which they tacitly sacrifice the revolutionary tasks and the criticism of reformism. With an appalling cynical attitude toward ideas, these gentlemen no longer accuse us of advocating the "counterrevolutionary united front with the leaders" but of lacking a "loyal" regard for the leadership by attempting to utilize the united front in order to strengthen the revolutionary wing at the expense of the Social Democracy. What can this "plunge into the void" signify?

Moscow understands, it seems, that the increase of tractors alone not only does not solve the problems of socialism but does not even assure the existence of the Soviet state. Even if one were to believe for a moment that a complete socialist society will be built in the USSR in the next four or five years, it is still impossible to close one's eyes to the fact that fascism obtains its cannibal victories in increasingly shorter intervals. It is unnecessary to explain the consequences that the fascistization of all Europe would have on "socialism in one country" during the next twelve or twenty-four months. Hence the panic among the leaders of the bureaucracy. Hence the telegraphic order: perform a 180-degree turn and camouflage it with a new barrage of slander-gas against the "Trotskyists"!

By means of such procedure, the bureaucracy now has an unlimited domination of the Comintern, but at the same time the Comintern is losing the esteem and confidence of the working masses. The turn in France was accomplished without a semblance of discussion or criticism. The members of the French party simply awoke to find out that today it was necessary to call the truth that which had yesterday been called a lie. Such a regime, declare the Rakovskys and the Sosnovskys,[80] is to the "credit" of Stalin! We think that such a regime is the misfortune of the revolution. In any case, the capitulators should, at least, make clear to what extent they have capitulated: to yesterday's policy of Stalin-Thaelmann, which brought such happy results? Or to the directly opposite policy of Stalin-Cachin in France today? But the capitulators do not dare make a choice. They have capitulated not to a policy but to a bureaucracy!

In the last ten years, the policy of the Comintern has permitted the Second International to retrieve its dominant position in the working class. Of course, the crisis, misery, reactionary gangsterism and the approach of a new war violently push different groups of workers towards the sections of the Comintern. But these superficial and ephemeral "successes" caused by the situation do not at all correspond to the political situation and to its gigantic tasks. The German Communist Party had incomparably greater "successes" up to the end of its legal existence, but that did not save it from an ignominious collapse.

Within the parties of the Second International, whose leadership is a reflection of its miserable and infamous orientation, there is at this moment a process of radicalization of the masses. The regime of the Comintern, the "somersaults" of the Stalinist bureaucracy and the cynicism of its means and methods constitute now the principal obstacle on the road to the revolutionary education and solidification of the proletarian vanguard. However, without the mobilization of the workers — not only for parades and meetings but also for decisive struggle — without correct leadership, fusing revolutionary intransigence with Leninist realism, the victory of fascism will come in France with the same inevitability as in Germany. What will remain then of the theory of "socialism in one country"? No more than remains today of the theory of "social fascism."

The Bolshevik-Leninists will not capitulate but, on the contrary, will redouble their efforts. The Socialist workers ought now to become the principal arena of their activity. It is necessary to explain the issues to them, more precisely, to find side by side with them a road to the revolution. It is only thus that the Communist workers can be torn from the vise of the bureaucracy; it is only thus that unity of action in the struggle against fascism can be assured as well as the creation of a truly revolutionary party of the masses, a section of the Fourth International that will lead the proletariat to the conquest of power.

Dear Friends! Your comrades-in-arms in all the countries of the world know the difficult inhuman conditions you endure under the Stalinist bureaucracy. They have only respect for the firmness that the majority of you have shown in the face of new repressions, new calumnies, new betrayals. No, you have not capitulated in spite of everything. On the contrary, you have before you a grand revolutionary mission to perform. You have a duty to place, insofar as possible, before the advanced workers of the USSR the problems of the international revolution now monopolized by the Manuilskys, the Kuusinens, the Piatnitskys, the Lozovskys[81] and the other third- and fifth-rate irresponsible functionaries.

Bolshevik-Leninists! The development of Europe and the entire world is now entering a critical stage, in which the fate of Europe and the international revolution will be decided for a whole historical epoch. We will now bring to the masses the revolutionary lessons that we assimilated in a dozen years of struggle against the centrist bureaucracy (Stalinism). Step by step, we will point the way to them.

For the defense of the USSR!
For the world proletarian revolution!
For the Fourth International!

Foreign Representatives of the
Russian Bolshevik-Leninists

IF AMERICA SHOULD GO COMMUNIST[82]

(August 17, 1934)

Should America go communist as a result of the difficulties and problems that your capitalist social order is unable to solve, it will discover that communism, far from being an intolerable bureaucratic tyranny and individual regimentation, will be the means of greater individual liberty and shared abundance.

At present most Americans regard communism solely in the light of the experience of the Soviet Union. They fear lest Sovietism in America would produce the same material result as it has brought for the culturally backward peoples of the Soviet Union.

They fear lest communism should try to fit them to a bed of Procrustes, and they point to the bulwark of Anglo-Saxon conservatism as an insuperable obstacle even to possibly desirable reforms. They argue that Great Britain and Japan would undertake military intervention against the American soviets. They shudder lest Americans be regimented in their habits of dress and diet, be compelled to subsist on famine rations, be forced to read stereotyped official propaganda in the newspapers, be coerced to serve as rubber stamps for decisions arrived at without their active participation or be required to keep their thoughts to themselves and loudly praise their soviet leaders in public, through fear of imprisonment and exile.

They fear monetary inflation, bureaucratic tyranny and intolerable red tape in obtaining the necessities of life. They fear soulless standardization in the arts and sciences, as well as in the daily necessities of life. They fear that all political spontaneity and the presumed freedom of the press will be destroyed by the dictatorship of a monstrous bureaucracy. And they shudder at the thought of being forced into an uncomprehended glibness in Marxist dialectic and disciplined social philosophies. They fear, in a word, that Soviet America will become the counterpart of what they have been told Soviet Russia looks like.

Actually American soviets will be as different from the Russian soviets as the United States of President Roosevelt differs from the Russian Empire of Czar Nicholas II. Yet communism can come in America only through revolution, just as independence and democracy came in America. The American temperament is energetic and violent, and it will insist on breaking a good many dishes and upsetting a good many apple carts before communism is firmly established. Americans are enthusiasts and sportsmen before they are specialists and statesmen, and it would be contrary to the American tradition to make a major change without choosing sides and cracking heads.

However, the American communist revolution will be insignificant compared to the Bolshevik Revolution in Russia, in terms of your national wealth and population, no matter how great its comparative cost. That is because civil war of a revolutionary nature isn't fought by the handful of men at the top — the 5 or 10 percent who own nine-tenths of American wealth; this handful could recruit its counterrevolutionary armies only from among the lower middle classes. Even so, the revolution could easily attract them to its banner by showing that support of the soviets alone offers them the prospect of salvation.

Everybody below this group is already economically prepared for communism. The depression has ravaged your working class and has dealt a crushing blow to the farmers, who had already been injured by the long agricultural decline of the postwar decade. There is no reason why these groups should counterpose determined resistance to the revolution; they have nothing to lose, providing, of course, that the revolutionary leaders adopt a farsighted and moderate policy toward them.

Who else will fight against communism? Your corporal's guard of billionaires and multimillionaires? Your Mellons, Morgans, Fords and Rockefellers? They will cease struggling as soon as they fail to find other people to fight for them.

The American soviet government will take firm possession of the commanding heights of your business system: the banks, the key industries and the transportation and communication systems. It will then give the farmers, the small tradespeople and businessmen a good long time to think things over and see how well the nationalized section of industry is working. Here is where the American soviets can produce real miracles.

"Technocracy"[83] can come true only under communism, when the dead hands of private property rights and private profits are lifted from your industrial system. The most daring proposals of the Hoover[84] commission on standardization and rationalization will seem childish compared to the new possibilities let loose by American communism.

National industry will be organized along the line of the conveyor belt in your modern continuous-production automotive factories. Scientific planning can be lifted out of the individual factory and applied to your entire economic system. The results will be stupendous.

Costs of production will be cut to 20 percent, or less, of their present figure. This, in turn, would rapidly increase your farmers' purchasing power.

To be sure, the American soviets would establish their own gigantic farm enterprises, as schools of voluntary collectivization. Your farmers could easily calculate whether it was to their individual advantage to remain as isolated links or to join the public chain.

The same method would be used to draw small businesses and industries into the national organization of industry. By soviet control of raw materials, credits and quotas of orders, these secondary industries could be kept solvent until they were gradually and without compulsion sucked into the socialized business system.

Without compulsion! The American soviets would not need to resort to the drastic measures that circumstances have often imposed upon the Russians. In the United States, through the science of publicity and advertising, you have means for winning the support of your middle class that were beyond the reach of the soviets of backward Russia with its vast majority of pauperized and illiterate peasants. This, in addition to your technical equipment and your wealth, is the greatest asset of your coming communist revolution. Your revolution will be smoother in character than ours; you will not waste your energies and resources in costly social conflicts after the main issues have been decided; and you will move ahead so much more rapidly in consequence.

Even the intensity and devotion of religious sentiment in America will not prove an obstacle to the revolution. If one assumes the perspective of soviets in America, none of the psychological brakes will prove firm enough to retard the pressure of the social crisis. This has been demonstrated more than once in history. Besides, it should not be forgotten that the Gospels themselves contain some pretty explosive aphorisms.

As to the comparatively few opponents of the soviet rev-

olution, one can trust to American inventive genius. It may
well be that you will take your unconvinced millionaires and
send them to some picturesque island, rent-free for life, where
they can do as they please.

You can do this safely, for you will not need to fear foreign
interventions. Japan, Great Britain and the other capitalistic
countries that intervened in Russia couldn't do anything but
take American communism lying down. As a matter of fact,
the victory of communism in America — the stronghold of capitalism — will cause communism to spread to other countries.
Japan will probably have joined the communistic ranks even
before the establishment of the American soviets. The same
is true of Great Britain.

In any case, it would be a crazy idea to send His Britannic
Majesty's fleet against Soviet America, even as a raid against
the southern and more conservative half of your continent.
It would be hopeless and would never get any farther than
a second-rate military escapade.

Within a few weeks or months of the establishment of the
American soviets, Pan-Americanism would be a political reality.

The governments of Central and South America would be
pulled into your federation like iron filings to a magnet. So
would Canada. The popular movements in these countries
would be so strong that they would force this great unifying
process within a short period and at insignificant costs. I am
ready to bet that the first anniversary of the American soviets
would find the Western Hemisphere transformed into the Soviet
United States of North, Central and South America, with its
capital at Panama. Thus for the first time the Monroe Doctrine
would have a complete and positive meaning in world affairs,
although not the one foreseen by its author.

In spite of the complaints of some of your arch-conserva-
tives, Roosevelt is not preparing for a soviet transformation
of the United States.

The NRA[85] aims not to destroy but to strengthen the foundations of American capitalism by overcoming your business
difficulties. Not the Blue Eagle but the difficulties that the Blue
Eagle is powerless to overcome will bring about communism
in America. The "radical" professors of your Brain Trust[86] are
not revolutionists: they are only frightened conservatives. Your
president abhors "systems" and "generalities." But a soviet government is the greatest of all possible systems, a gigantic gen-
erality in action.

The average man doesn't like systems or generalities either.
It is the task of your communist statesmen to make the system deliver the concrete goods that the average man desires:

his food, cigars, amusements, his freedom to choose his own neckties, his own house and his own automobile. It will be easy to give him these comforts in Soviet America.

Most Americans have been misled by the fact that in the USSR we had to build whole new basic industries from the ground up. Such a thing could not happen in America, where you are already compelled to cut down on your farm area and to reduce your industrial production. As a matter of fact, your tremendous technological equipment has been paralyzed by the crisis and already clamors to be put to use. You will be able to make a rapid step-up of consumption by your people the starting point of your economic revival.

You are prepared to do this as is no other country. Nowhere else has the study of the internal market reached such intensity as in the United States. It has been done by your banks, trusts, individual businessmen, merchants, traveling salesmen and farmers as part of their stock-in-trade. Your soviet government will simply abolish all trade secrets, will combine all the findings of these researches for individual profit and will transform them into a scientific system of economic planning. In this your government will be helped by the existence of a large class of cultured and critical consumers. By combining the nationalized key industries, your private businesses and democratic consumer cooperation, you will quickly develop a highly flexible system for serving the needs of your population.

This system will be made to work not by bureaucracy and not by policemen but by cold, hard cash.

Your almighty dollar will play a principal part in making your new soviet system work. It is a great mistake to try to mix a "planned economy" with a "managed currency." Your money must act as regulator with which to measure the success or failure of your planning.

Your "radical" professors are dead wrong in their devotion to "managed money." It is an academic idea that could easily wreck your entire system of distribution and production. That is the great lesson to be derived from the Soviet Union, where bitter necessity has been converted into official virtue in the monetary realm.

There the lack of a stable gold ruble is one of the main causes of our many economic troubles and catastrophes. It is impossible to regulate wages, prices and quality of goods without a firm monetary system. An unstable ruble in a Soviet system is like having variable molds in a conveyor-belt factory. It won't work.

Only when socialism succeeds in substituting administrative

control for money will it be possible to abandon a stable gold
currency. Then money will become ordinary paper slips, like
trolley or theater tickets. As socialism advances, these slips
will also disappear, and control over individual consumption—
whether by money or administration—will no longer be necessary when there is more than enough of everything for everybody!

Such a time has not yet come, though America will certainly
reach it before any other country. Until then, the only way
to reach such a state of development is to retain an effective
regulator and measure for the working of your system. As
a matter of fact, during the first few years a planned economy
needs sound money even more than did old-fashioned capitalism. The professor who regulates the monetary unit with
the aim of regulating the whole business system is like the
man who tried to lift both his feet off the ground at the same
time.

Soviet America will possess supplies of gold big enough
to stabilize the dollar—a priceless asset. In Russia we have
been expanding our industrial plant by 20 and 30 percent
a year; but—owing to a weak ruble—we have not been able
to distribute this increase effectively. This is partly because
we have allowed our bureaucracy to subject our monetary
system to administrative one-sidedness. You will be spared
this evil. As a result you will greatly surpass us in both increased production and distribution, leading to a rapid advance in the comfort and welfare of your population.

In all this, you will not need to imitate our standardized
production for our pitiable mass consumers. We have taken
over from czarist Russia a pauper's heritage, a culturally
undeveloped peasantry with a low standard of living. We had
to build our factories and dams at the expense of our consumers. We have had continual monetary inflation and a monstrous bureaucracy.

Soviet America will not have to imitate our bureaucratic
methods. Among us the lack of the bare necessities has caused
an intense scramble for an extra loaf of bread, an extra yard
of cloth by everyone. In this struggle our bureaucracy steps
forward as a conciliator, as an all-powerful court of arbitration. You, on the other hand, are much wealthier and would
have little difficulty in supplying all of your people with all
of the necessities of life. Moreover, your needs, tastes and habits would never permit your bureaucracy to divide the national income. Instead, when you organize your society to
produce for human needs rather than private profits, your
entire population will group itself around new trends and

groups, which will struggle with one another and prevent an overweening bureaucracy from imposing itself upon them.

You can thus avoid growth of bureaucratism by the practice of soviets, that is to say, democracy — the most flexible form of government yet developed. Soviet organization cannot achieve miracles but must simply reflect the will of the people. With us the soviets have been bureaucratized as a result of the political monopoly of a single party, which has itself become a bureaucracy. This situation resulted from the exceptional difficulties of socialist pioneering in a poor and backward country.

The American soviets will be full-blooded and vigorous, without need or opportunity for such measures as circumstances imposed upon Russia. Your unregenerate capitalists will, of course, find no place for themselves in the new setup. It is hard to imagine Henry Ford as the head of the Detroit Soviet.

Yet a wide struggle between interests, groups and ideas is not only conceivable — it is inevitable. One-year, five-year, ten-year plans of business development; schemes for national education; construction of new basic lines of transportation; the transformation of the farms; the program for improving the technological and cultural equipment of Latin America; a program for stratosphere communication; eugenics — all of these will arouse controversy, vigorous electoral struggle and passionate debate in the newspapers and at public meetings.

For Soviet America will not imitate the monopoly of the press by the heads of Soviet Russia's bureaucracy. While Soviet America would nationalize all printing plants, paper mills and means of distribution, this would be a purely negative measure. It would simply mean that private capital will no longer be allowed to decide what publications should be established, whether they should be progressive or reactionary, "wet" or "dry,"[87] puritanical or pornographic. Soviet America will have to find a new solution for the question of how the power of the press is to function in a socialist regime. It might be done on the basis of proportional representation for the votes in each soviet election.

Thus the right of each group of citizens to use the power of the press would depend on their numerical strength — the same principle being applied to the use of meeting halls, allotment of time on the air and so forth.

Thus the management and policy of publications would be decided not by individual checkbooks but by group ideas. This may take little account of numerically small but important groups, but it simply means that each new idea will be compelled, as throughout history, to prove its right to existence.

Rich Soviet America can set aside vast funds for research and invention, discoveries and experiments in every field. You won't neglect your bold architects and sculptors, your unconventional poets and audacious philosophers.

In fact, the Soviet Yankees of the future will give a lead to Europe in those very fields where Europe has hitherto been your master. Europeans have little conception of the power of technology to influence human destiny and have adopted an attitude of sneering superiority toward "Americanism," particularly since the crisis. Yet Americanism marks the true dividing line between the Middle Ages and the modern world.

Hitherto America's conquest of nature has been so violent and passionate that you have had no time to modernize your philosophies or to develop your own artistic forms. Hence you have been hostile to the doctrines of Hegel, Marx and Darwin. The burning of Darwin's works by the Baptists of Tennessee[88] is only a clumsy reflection of the American dislike for the doctrines of evolution. This attitude is not confined to your pulpits. It is still part of your general mental makeup.

Your atheists as well as your Quakers are determined rationalists. And your rationalism itself is weakened by empiricism and moralism. It has none of the merciless vitality of the great European rationalists. So your philosophic method is even more antiquated than your economic system and your political institutions.

Today, quite unprepared, you are being forced to face those social contradictions that grow up unsuspected in every society. You have conquered nature by means of the tools that your inventive genius has created, only to find that your tools have all but destroyed you. Contrary to all your hopes and desires, your unheard-of wealth has produced unheard-of misfortunes. You have discovered that social development does not follow a simple formula. Hence you have been thrust into the school of the dialectic — to stay.

There is no turning back from it to the mode of thinking and acting prevalent in the seventeenth and eighteenth centuries.

While the romantic numskulls of Nazi Germany are dreaming of restoring the old race of Europe's Dark Forest to its original purity, or rather its original filth, you Americans, after taking a firm grip on your economic machinery and your culture, will apply genuine scientific methods to the problem of eugenics. Within a century, out of your melting pot of races there will come a new breed of men — the first worthy of the name of Man.

One final prophecy: In the third year of soviet rule in America, you will no longer chew gum!

THE WAY OUT[89]

(August 1934)

The Socialist Party in France, we have written, is developing
in a direction opposite to that of the state: whereas for parliamentarism has been substituted Bonapartism, which represents
an unstable stage on the road to fascism, the Social Democracy, on the contrary, has been moving towards a mortal conflict with fascism. However, can one invest this view, which at
present has an enormous importance for French politics, with
an absolute and, consequently, an international significance?

No, the truth is always concrete. When we speak of the di-
vergent paths of development of the Social Democracy and
the bourgeois state under the conditions of the present social
crisis, we have in mind only the general tendency of development and not a uniform and automatic process. For us,
the solution of the political problem depends upon the degree
of effective realization of the tendency itself. The contrary theo-
rem can also be advanced, which, let it be hoped, will not
encounter any objections among us, namely, the destiny of the
proletariat depends, in large measure, in our epoch, upon the
resolute manner with which the Social Democracy will succeed,
in the brief interval which is vouchsafed it by the march of
development, in breaking with the bourgeois state, in transforming itself and in preparing itself for the decisive struggle
against fascism. The very fact that the destiny of the proletariat can thus depend upon the destiny of the Social Democracy is the consequence of the bankruptcy of the Communist
International as the leading party of the international proletariat and also of the unusual acuteness of the class struggle.

The tendency for reformism to be pushed aside by centrism,
as well as the tendency toward the radicalization of centrism,
cannot help but have an international character, corresponding to the overall crisis of capitalism and the democratic state.
But what is of decisive importance for drawing practical and,
above all, organizational conclusions from this is the question

of knowing *how* this tendency is refracted — at the *given* stage of development — in the Social Democratic party of a *given* country. The general line of development defined by us should only guide our analysis, but it should by no means presage our deductions from it.

In prefascist Germany, the approach of the break between the bourgeois state and reformism found its expression in the constitution of the left wing within the Social Democracy. But the power of the bureaucratic apparatus, given the complete disorientation of the masses, proved sufficient to cut off in advance the still feeble left wing (SAP) and to keep the party on the rails of a conservative and expectant policy. At the same time, the German Communist Party, under the spell of the drugs of the "third period"[90] and "social fascism," substituted "Amsterdamian" parades[91] for the revolutionary mobilization of the masses, unrealizable under the actual relationship of forces without the policy of the united front. As a result, the powerful German proletariat proved incapable of offering the slightest resistance to the fascist coup d'etat. The Stalinists declared: it is the fault of the Social Democracy! But by that alone, they recognized that all their pretensions of being the leaders of the German proletariat were nothing but empty braggadocio. This tremendous political lesson shows us, above all, that even in the country where the Communist Party was the most imposing — in the absolute as well as in the relative sense — it was incapable, at the decisive moment, of lifting even its little finger while the Social Democracy retained the possibility of barring the road by virtue of its conservative resistance. Let us bear that firmly in mind!

The same fundamental historical tendency has been refracted in France in an essentially different manner. Under the influence of specific national conditions as well as of international lessons, the internal crisis of the French Social Democracy has experienced a much deeper evolution than that of the German Social Democracy in the corresponding period. The Socialist bureaucracy found itself forced to deliver a blow *at the right.* Instead of seeing a weak left wing expelled, as was the case in Germany, we have witnessed the break with the consistent *right* wing (in its quality as an agency of the bourgeoisie), the Neos. The essential difference existing between the evolution of the German and the French Social Democracies could not better be underscored than by the symmetry of these two splits, in spite of the presence in both parties of common historical tendencies: the crisis of capitalism and of democracy, the crumbling of reformism and the break between the bourgeois state and the Social Democracy.

What ought to be done is to gauge, from the indicated angle, the internal situation in the Socialist parties of all the capitalist countries passing through the various stages of the crisis. But this task goes beyond the framework of this article. Let us mention only Belgium, where the Social Democratic party, swathed throughout by a reactionary and corrupted bureaucracy — a parliamentary, municipal, trade-union, cooperative and banking bureaucracy — is at present engaged in a struggle against its *left* wing and trying not to remain behind its German prototype (Wels-Severing and Co.[92]). It is clear that the same practical deductions cannot be drawn for France and for Belgium.

Yet it would be erroneous to think that the policy of the German and Belgian Social Democracies, on one side, and of the French Social Democracy, on the other, represent, once for all, two incompatible types. In reality, these two types can and will more than once transform themselves into one another. One can support with certainty the idea that if, in its time, the German Communist Party had pursued a correct policy of united front, it would have given a powerful impulsion to the radicalization of the Social Democratic workers, and the whole political evolution of Germany would have acquired a revolutionary character. On the other hand, it cannot be considered excluded that the Social Democratic bureaucracy in France, with the active aid of the Stalinists, will isolate the left wing and give the evolution of the party a retrogressive direction; it is not difficult to foresee its consequences in advance: prostration in the proletariat and the victory of fascism. As for Belgium, where the Social Democracy retains virtually the monopoly as a party in the proletariat, one cannot, in general, imagine a victorious struggle against fascism without a decisive regrouping of forces and tendencies within the ranks of the Social Democracy. A hand must be kept on the pulse of the labor movement and the necessary conclusions must be drawn each time.

What has been said suffices, in any case, for an understanding of the enormous importance that the internal evolution of the Social Democratic parties has acquired for the destiny of the proletariat — at least in Europe and for the coming historical period. By recalling to mind that in 1925 the Communist International declared in a special manifesto that the French Socialist Party no longer existed at all, we will easily understand how great is the retreat made by the proletariat and, above all, by its vanguard during the years of the domination of the epigones![93]

It has already been said that with regard to Germany, the

Communist International has acknowledged — after the fact, it is true, and in a negative form — that it was totally incapable of fighting against fascism without the participation in the struggle of the Social Democracy. With regard to France, the Comintern has found itself forced to make the same avowal, but in advance and in a positive form. So much the worse for the Comintern, but so much the better for the cause of the revolution!

In abandoning, without explanation, the theory of social fascism, the Stalinists have at the same time thrown overboard the revolutionary program. "Your conditions shall be ours," they have declared to the leaders of the SFIO. They have renounced all criticism of their ally. They are quite simply paying for this alliance at the cost of their program and their tactics. And yet, when it is a question of the defensive against the common mortal enemy — defensive, in which each of the allies pursues his vital interests — nobody needs to pay anybody for this alliance, and each has the right to remain what he is. The whole conduct of the Stalinists has such a character that they seem to want to whisper to the Socialist leaders: "Demand still more; squeeze harder; don't stand on ceremony; help us rid ourselves as rapidly as possible of those coarse slogans that inconvenience our Moscow masters in the present international situation."

They have thrown overboard the slogan of the workers' militia. They have declared the struggle for the arming of the proletariat a "provocation." It is better, isn't it, to parcel out "spheres of influence" with the fascists, with the "honorable" prefects of police as arbitrators? This combination between wholes is by far most advantageous to the fascists: while the workers, lulled by general phrases on the united front, will occupy themselves with parades, the fascists will multiply their cadres and their arms supplies, will attract new contingents of masses and, at the suitable hour chosen by them, will launch the offensive.

The united front, for the French Stalinists, has thus been a form of their capitulation to the Social Democracy. The slogans and the methods of the united front express the capitulation to the Bonapartist state which, in turn, blazes the trail for fascism. By the intermediary of the united front, the two bureaucracies defend themselves not unsuccessfully against any interference by a "third force." That is the political situation of the French proletariat, which can very speedily find itself faced by decisive events. This situation might be fatal were it not for the existence of the pressure of the masses and the struggle of tendencies.

He who asserts, "the Second as well as the Third Internationalals are condemned; the future belongs to the Fourth International," is expressing a thought whose correctness has been confirmed anew by the present situation in France. But this thought, correct in itself, does not yet disclose how, under what circumstances and within what intervals the Fourth International will be constituted. It may be born — theoretically it is not excluded — out of the unification of the Second International with the Third, by means of a regrouping of the elements, by the purging and tempering of their ranks in the fire of the struggle. It may be formed also by means of the radicalization of the proletarian kernel of the Socialist Party and the decomposition of the Stalinist organization. It may be constituted in the process of the struggle against fascism and the victory gained over it. But it may also be formed considerably later, in a number of years, in the midst of the ruins and the accumulation of debris following upon the victory of fascism and war. For all sorts of Bordigists, all these variants, perspectives and stages have no importance. The sectarians live beyond time and space. They ignore the living historical process, which pays them back in the same coin. That is why their "balance" is always the same: zero. The Marxists can have nothing in common with this caricature of politics.

It goes without saying that if there existed in France a strong organization of Bolshevik-Leninists, it could and should have become, under present conditions, the independent axis around which the proletarian vanguard would crystallize. But the Communist League of France has not succeeded in becoming such an organization. Without in any way shading off the faults of the leadership, it must be admitted that the fundamental reason for the slow development of the League is conditioned by the march of the world labor movement, which, for the last decade, has known nothing but defeats and setbacks. The *ideas* and the *methods* of the Bolshevik-Leninists are confirmed at each new stage of development. But can it be anticipated that the League, *as an organization,* will show itself capable, in the interval that remains until the approaching denouement, of occupying an influential, if not a leading, place in the labor movement? To answer this question today in the affirmative would mean either to set back in one's mind the denouement for several years, which is confuted by the whole situation, or just simply to hope for miracles.

It is absolutely clear that the victory of fascism would mark the crumpling up of all the labor organizations. A new historic chapter would open up in which the Bolshevik-Leninists would have to seek a new organizational form for themselves. The task of today should be formulated concretely in indissoluble connection with the character of the epoch in which we are living: how to prevent, with the greatest probability of success, the victory of fascism, taking into account the existing groupings of the proletariat and the relationship of forces existing between these groupings? In particular, what place should be taken by the League, a small organization that cannot lay claim to an independent role in the combat that is unfolding before us, but that is armed with a correct doctrine and a precious political experience? What place should it occupy in order to impregnate the united front with a revolutionary content? To put this question clearly is, at bottom, to give the answer. The League must immediately take its place *on the inside of the united front,* in order to contribute actively to the revolutionary regrouping and to the concentration of the forces of this regrouping. It can occupy such a place under present conditions in no other way than by entering the Socialist Party.

But the Communist Party, object certain comrades, is nevertheless more revolutionary. Assuming that we give up our organizational independence, can we adhere to the less revolutionary party?

This main objection — more exactly, the only one made by our opponents — rests upon political reminiscences and psychological appreciations, and not upon the living dynamics of development. The two parties represent *centrist* organizations, with this difference: the centrism of the Stalinists is the product of the decomposition of Bolshevism, whereas the centrism of the Socialist Party is born out of the decomposition of reformism. There exists another, no-less-essential difference between them. Stalinist centrism, despite its convulsive zigzags, represents a very *stable* political system that is indissolubly bound up with the position and the interests of the powerful bureaucratic stratum. The centrism of the Socialist Party reflects the *transitional* state of the workers, who are seeking a way out on the road of the revolution.

In the Communist Party, there are undoubtedly thousands of militant workers. But they are hopelessly confused. Yesterday, they were ready to fight on the barricades by the side of genuine fascists against the Daladier government.[94] Today, they capitulate silently to the slogans of the Social Democracy. The proletarian organization of Saint-Denis, educated by the Stalinists, capitulates resignedly to PUPism.[95] Ten years of attempts and efforts aimed at regenerating the Comintern have yielded no results. The bureaucracy has showed itself powerful enough to carry out its devastating work to the very end.

In giving the united front a purely decorative character, in consecrating with the name of "Leninism" the renunciation of elementary revolutionary slogans, the Stalinists are retarding the revolutionary development of the Socialist Party. By that they continue to play their role as a brake, even now, after their acrobatic flip-flop. The internal regime of the party excludes, still more decisively today than it did yesterday, any idea of the possibility of its renaissance.

The French sections of the Second and Third Internationals cannot be compared in the same way as two pieces of cloth: which fabric is the best, which the best woven? Each party must be considered in its development, and the dynamics of their mutual relations in the present epoch must be taken into account. It is only thus that we shall find for our lever the most advantageous fulcrum.

The adherence of the League to the Socialist Party can play a great political role. There are tens of thousands of revolutionary workers in France who belong to no party. Many of them have passed through the CP; they left it with indignation or else they have been expelled. They retained their old opinion about the Socialist Party, that is, they turn their backs to it. They sympathize wholly or in part with the ideas of the League, but they do not join it because they do not believe that a third party can develop under present conditions. These tens of thousands of revolutionary workers remain outside of a party, and in the trade unions they remain outside of a fraction.

To this must be added the hundreds and the thousands of revolutionary teachers not only of the Federation Unitaire but also of the Syndicat National who could serve as a link between the proletariat and peasantry. They remain outside of a party, equally hostile to Stalinism and reformism. Yet, the struggle of the masses in the coming period will seek for itself, more than ever before, the bed of a party. The establishment of soviets would not weaken but, on the contrary, would strengthen the role of the workers' parties, for the masses, united by millions in the soviets, need a leadership that only a party can give.

There is no need to idealize the SFIO, that is, to pass it off, with all its present contradictions, as the revolutionary party of the proletariat. But the internal contradictions of the party can and should be pointed out as a warranty of its further evolution and, consequently, as a fulcrum for the Marxist lever. The League can and should show an example to these thousands and tens of thousands of revolutionary workers, teachers, etc., who run the risk, under present conditions, of remaining outside the current of the struggle. In entering the Socialist

Party, they will immensely reinforce the left wing; they will fecundate the whole evolution of the party; they will constitute a powerful center of attraction for the revolutionary elements in the "Communist" Party and will thus immeasurably facilitate the emergence of the proletariat on the road of revolution.

Without renouncing its past and its ideas, but also without any mental reservations from the days of small-circle existence, while saying what is, it is necessary to enter the Socialist Party, not for exhibitions, not for experiments, but for serious revolutionary work under the banner of Marxism.

ON THE THESES
"UNITY AND THE YOUTH"[96]

(Summer 1934)

The aim of this text is to correct the slogan of organic unity, which is not our slogan. The formula of organic unity — without a program, without concretization — is hollow. And as physical nature abhors a vacuum, this formula fills itself with an increasingly ambiguous and even reactionary content. All the leaders of the Socialist Party, beginning with Just and Marceau Pivert and ending with Frossard,[97] declare themselves partisans of organic unity. The most fervent protagonist of this slogan is Lebas,[98] whose antirevolutionary tendencies are well enough known. The Communist Party leaders are manipulating the same slogan with increasing willingness. Is it our task to help them amuse the workers by an enticing and hollow formula?

The exchange of open letters of the two leaderships on the program of action is the promising beginning of a discussion on the aims and the methods of the workers' party. It is here that we should intervene vigorously. Unity and split are two methods subordinated to program and political tasks. Since the discussion has happily begun, we should tactfully destroy the illusory hopes in organic unity as a panacea. Our thesis is that the unity of the working class can be realized only on a revolutionary basis. This basis is our own program.

If fusion takes place tomorrow between the two parties, we place ourselves on the basis of the united party in order to continue our work. In this case the fusion may have a progressive significance. But if we continue to sow the illusion that organic unity is of value as such — and it is thus that the masses understand this slogan and not as a more ample and more convenient audience for the Leninist agitators — we shall be doing nothing but making it easier for the two conjoined bureaucracies to present us, Bolshevik-Leninists, to the masses as the great obstacle on the road of organic unity. In these conditions, unity might well take place on our backs and become a reactionary factor. We must never play with slogans that are not revolutionary by their own content but that can play a quite different role according to the political conjuncture, the relationship of forces, etc. . . . We are not afraid of organic unity. We state openly that the fusion *may* play a progressive role. But our own role is to point out to the masses the conditions under which this role would be genuinely progressive. In sum, we do not set ourselves against the current toward organic unity, which the two bureaucracies have already cornered. But while supporting ourselves on this current, which is honest among the masses, we introduce into it the critical note, the criterion of demarcation, programmatic definitions, etc.

"Nothing would be more dangerous," say the theses of Comrades Craipeau[99]-Kamoun, "than to get hypnotized over this single perspective and to consider all work useless so long as unity is not accomplished." This is right, but it is not sufficient. It is necessary to understand clearly that this perspective of organic unity detached from the revolutionary tasks can serve for nothing else than to hypnotize the workers by reconciling them with the passivity of the two parties.

In order to parry the sterilizing hypnotism of the slogan of organic unity, the theses propose a "minimum of elementary Marxist principles as the charter of this unity." The formula is almost classic as the beginning of a downsliding on the opportunist incline. One begins by dosing up the Marxist principles for the delicate stomachs of the Social Democrats and the Stalinists. If it is a question only of enlarging the audience and of opening up to oneself an access to the Communist workers, why put conditions in the guise of "elementary principles" (very elementary, alas!)? And if it is a question of something else, that is to say, of the party and the proletariat, how could a minimum of principles and, what is more, of "elementary principles" suffice?

Immediately after this, the theses demand that it be explained to the workers "that there cannot be a genuine revolutionary unity except that which makes out of the Marxist party a coherent and disciplined organism." So? So? So?

We do not know if the very next stage of development will be an attempt at fusion or, on the contrary, a series of new splits in the two parties. We do not engage ourselves on the road of abstract formulas.

Since February 6, *La Verite* has spent its time repeating the formula of the united front (which was moreover much richer in content at that epoch than the formula of organic unity is *today*). We criticized Naville for not concretizing the revolutionary content of the united front, thus permitting the two bureaucracies to seize upon this slogan without great risk. The same mistake must not be repeated under aggravated circumstances.

And for the youth? The same thing. There are not two policies: one for the youth, the other for the adults. Insofar as the youth carry on politics — and that is their duty — their policy must be adult. There are too many factors that are driving the revolutionary and inexperienced youth towards the Stalinists. The formula of unity facilitates this tendency and augments the dangers. Our weapon, which coincides with the superior interests of the proletarian vanguard, is the *content* of the unity. While basing ourselves on the currents toward unity, we develop the discussion; we deepen it; we group the best elements of the two camps around the "maximum" of our not-at-all-"elementary" principles; we reinforce our tendency. And then, come what may, the revolutionary vanguard will profit by the fusion as by the split.

Let us look at the theses: "The united youth (Jeunesse Unique) cannot have the Leninist principles as its basis." Who says that? The reformists? The Stalinists? No, it is the Leninists of the generous type themselves. Every worker who reflects and who takes things in their totality will reply: "If your principles are not good for making the revolutionary unity, they are good for nothing." "We will retreat," continue our generous Leninists, "on certain points if the agreement is impossible otherwise." Precisely why do the Leninists need to retreat on certain of their principles, of which they already possess only a minimum? It's absolutely incomprehensible.

We will be told: "But we are only a small minority!" Good. Then the two majorities — or better yet, the two bureaucracies supporting themselves on the two majorities — will make (or will not make) their fusion without our retreat. They have no need of it since they are the majority. The authors of the theses stand up not as propagandists of Leninism but as benefactors of the human race. They want to reconcile the reformists with the Stalinists, even at their own expense. Still worse, they say so in advance, before being compelled to do so by the situation. They capitulate in anticipation. They retreat out of platonic generosity. All this contradictory reasoning, in which the authors feel themselves simultaneously the representatives of a small minority and the inspectors general of history, is the unhappy result of the trap that they set for themselves with the slogan of organic unity detached from all content or charged with a "minimum" content.

The authors of the theses obligate themselves, even in case the Socialists should not want to accept the soviet form of power, to intervene among the Stalinists (in the given case, the Leninists are the most logical intermediaries!) in order to persuade them to withdraw the slogan that the Leninists themselves find correct. Isn't that absurd, dear comrades? If you defend before the Socialists the slogan of soviets (with *our* interpretation), you can win over a part of the Socialists and the sympathy of a part of the Stalinists. At the same time, you remain faithful to yourselves, meanwhile assuring your future. But that does not suffice for you, because you are the courtiers of unity. If this unity is realized thanks to your mediating intervention, the Stalinists will treat you like traitors — and this time not without reason — whereas the revolutionary socialists will pass over to the left by the Stalinist path. Nobody will take kindly to you. That's the fate of all political courtiers.

I want to draw the attention of the comrades to paragraph 2, which speaks of the necessity of reconstructing the revolutionary party "over the innumerable obstacles produced by the ruins of the Third International and the attraction *still exercised* by the Soviet Union." This formula must be characterized as criminal. The attraction "still exercised" by the Soviet Union is treated as an obstacle to the creation of the revolutionary party. Wherein consists this attraction for the broad masses, who receive neither a subsidy from the bureaucracy nor free tickets for trips to anniversary celebrations, nor any of the other gratuities well known by several "friends of the USSR"? The masses say to themselves: It is the only state that has come out of the workers' revolution. This sentiment is profoundly revolutionary. It is now reinforced all over again thanks to the fascist danger. To appraise this attachment to the proletarian revolution and its acquisitions as an obstacle is criminal towards the Soviet Union, as well as to the workers of the West.

It may be objected: "It's only a question of an unhappy expression; the authors mean to speak of the injurious result of the Soviet bureaucracy's imprint upon a part of the world proletariat." If it were only a question of a poorly chosen formula, it would not be worth discussing. Unfortunately this is not the case. In the ranks of the youth, and especially the nonproletarian, a display of cheap radicalism is often made by sowing doubts about the proletarian character of the Soviet state, by identifying the Comintern with the Soviet bureaucracy and, above all, the latter with the entire workers' state. This mistake is ten times more grievous than, for example, to identify Jouhaux with the trade-union organizations, or Blum with the entire SFIO. Whoever does not have a clear and clean-cut point of view on this fundamental question does not have the right to speak before the workers because he can only sow confusion and skepticism, repulsing the young workers towards Stalinism.

Whence come these artificial and even ambiguous constructions? They proceed from the bad social composition of the Socialist youth. Too many students. Too few workers. The students are occupied too much with themselves, too little with the workers' movement. A worker-environment disciplines a young intellectual. The worker wants to learn the fundamental and solid things. He asks for clear-cut replies. He does not like these factitious witticisms.

Salvation for the Seine district lies in mobilizing the students for the hard labor of recruiting workers. Whoever does not want to occupy himself with that has nothing to look for in the socialist organization. The proletarian organization needs intellectuals, but only as aids for the rise of the working masses. On the other hand, the sincerely revolutionary and socialist intellectuals must learn a good deal from the workers. The internal regime of the youth must be adapted to this task; a division of labor must be organized; their exact tasks must be given to the students or groups of students in the workers' quarters, etc. Ideological oscillations will become all the less frequent, the solider the proletarian base of the organization will become.

AN ADVOCATE TAKES UP A POSITION
ON THE FRENCH SITUATION[100]

(September 22, 1934)

1. The turn in France has aroused passionate and prolonged discussion. Nothing could be more natural. We learn by experience and we analyze our experience by the Marxist method. Only the International Bolshevik-Leninists can allow themselves such a discussion.

The little fainthearts of the SAP, who yesterday were making common cause against us with the miserable de Kadt,[101] are talking today of our "annihilation."

We have an ideological tradition. We have a clear-cut program. We give a clear-cut answer to every question. Answers from our sections agree in the main, without being arranged in advance. That means that we have trained cadres. If we form blocs with other organizations or if one of our sections even enters the Socialist Party, we do this always in the name of our principles, which prove incontrovertible and which we are learning and shall learn to apply to the conditions of each country.

2. Our internal discussion must now pass from the stage of perspectives, hypotheses and proposals into the stage of analyzing application. We must study the most recent experience of our French section. The experience is still very short, but very important. The first step along the new path already shows the complete incorrectness of the objections raised by the opponents of the entry. It is precisely for this reason that they have to change their arguments daily and even shift the field of discussion, to say nothing of the "intransigents" who have already entered the Socialist Party so as to fight us there.

3. What did the opponents who were guided only by ideological and political considerations say? Let us take the document that contains the position of the majority of the Belgian section. In it we read: "How are we to conceive that we enter the SFIO *as an independent political faction, retaining its own*

banner and its organ? Is this not to be premature and to leave the strength of the SFIO bureaucracy out of account? The history of left socialist groups teaches us that the Social Democratic parties can no longer afford to let revolutionary factions grow within them." We ask the Belgian comrades: Have you read the special issue (Number 4) of *Combat des Jeunes* and Number 220 of *La Verite?* If the expression "entry with banner unfurled" has a meaning, *Combat des Jeunes* and *La Verite* are that unfurled banner, and nevertheless *Le Populaire* has published advertisements for *La Verite* four times, and it has already been possible for our comrades to be taken into the SFIO. Such a fact would be impossible in Belgium, Holland or many other countries. It can be explained by the present situation of the Socialist Party in France. The basic error of the Belgian document consists in the fact that it treats Social Democracy as an abstraction, independent of time and place, instead of analyzing what the real state of affairs is with the SFIO. Read the passage quoted above again, and you will be convinced of this. In the whole document devoted to the entry into the SFIO there is not a word of the peculiarities of this party or its state at the moment in comparison with, say, the Belgian Labor Party (POB). [102]

4. The opponents said, "The entry into the SFIO means almost automatically the abandonment of the slogan of the Fourth International." Read *Combat des Jeunes* and *La Verite.* Our section entered the SFIO to fight *for* the Fourth International there.

5. Not the slightest reconciliation with Social Democracy *as a system of ideas and actions* is possible for us. But this system of ideas is represented in different ways in living bodies. In certain circumstances they begin to fall apart. The system as such collapses. It is replaced by a struggle of different tendencies, and this struggle can create a situation that demands our immediate and direct intervention and even organizational entry into the Socialist Party.

6. The Belgian document sees only "the system of ideas" and not the living body of the workers' organizations. This basic error is also shown in the way the document brings up the Russian experience: "The supporters of entry into the SFIO seem to forget that the break between the two basic tendencies of the workers' movement took place in 1903 in the Russian Social Democracy." This view is mechanical in method and incorrect in content. For the authors of the document, it seems that after the 1903 split there were two absolute entities, Bolshevism and Menshevism, which developed in two different parts of the universe. That is pure metaphysics. The history

of the struggle of Bolshevism against Menshevism is in fact
rich in lessons. It is a pity the document makes use of it in
a one-sided, abstract, formalistic manner.

7. History did not stop in 1903. The split turned out to
have been too early, that is, not in tune with the objective
situation and the mentality of the masses, and the Bolsheviks
had to reunite with the Mensheviks at the end of 1906. But
here the document interrupts us: "It is admittedly true that
under the pressure of the masses toward unity there came
about a link between the Bolsheviks and the Mensheviks in
1906. In our opinion, an *alliance* of two factions of the workers' movement is to be equated with a united front. Hence
the historical reference is no more relevant than the first one
(to Marx)." I am very sorry to have to say that this is turning the Russian experience upside down. It was a case not of
an *alliance* or a united front but of a *fusion of the two parties,* confirmed by the Stockholm congress of 1906, and this
united party, though split by factional struggle, existed till
1912, i.e., six years. What does this error arise from? From
the fact that the authors of the document are not even able
to conceive that the two absolutely irreconcilable "essences"
(after the 1903 split) could come closer again and find ac-
commodation together in a single party. The historical error is the product of the metaphysical method.

8. The attempt has been made to scare us with the prediction that the entry "would be exploited to the full by the Stalinists" (document of the Belgian majority). We replied, "The
Stalinists, who are fraternizing with the Socialist bureaucracy,
will not be able to accuse us of betrayal, of capitulation to
reformism, etc., at least not before new orders."

The facts have proved us right. Of course the Stalinists are
attacking us, but not as abettors of reformism but, on the
contrary, as destroyers of the Socialist Party. They warn the
Young Socialists "fraternally" of our diabolical tricks (*L'Avant-
garde*). That means that it is the Stalinists who are appearing as helpers, indeed as lackeys, of the reformist bureaucracy
against us, and not as revolutionary accusers. If one still
required this confirmation of the correctness of our turn, it
is to be found in the columns of the Stalinist press. '

9. Who is playing revolutionary accuser? The Bordigists
and Co. With them it is very simple. They speak only in the
name of eternity. They still regard themselves, if I am not
wrong, as a faction of the Third International. What does
that mean? Nothing. They might as well regard themselves
as a faction of the Salvation Army.

It would really be wasted effort to pay even the slightest

attention to these premature corpses. The ideas, wants and criticism of a simple member of the Young Socialist Guard [JGS][103] of Belgium are a hundred times more important for our orientation and our methods than the learned nonsense of *Bilan*.

10. What is important is to study experience. The Socialist youth of France has received our comrades and their *Combat des Jeunes* with open arms. They have guaranteed them the organizational seniority rights on the basis of their connection with the Leninist youth. The bureaucratic apparatus declared this decision invalid as being in conflict with the statutes. The sections of the Socialist youth had to make do with a protest resolution. This significant fact shows that the view the majority of the League had of the relations between the base and apparatus is confirmed by the facts, at least as far as the youth is concerned.

11. Does this mean that everything is assured? Far from it. Not a few difficulties are caused by the intrigues and calumnies of the unrestrained elements of the minority who try to blacken the League in the eyes of the Socialists. But that is not the problem. These people, who go from one extreme to the other, only show their emptiness and liquidate themselves.

There are more important factors that can turn against us. The situation in and around the SFIO may change. The bureaucracy may set about radically getting rid of us. Even if that should occur tomorrow, we can already register considerable gains: the League is oriented toward the masses; the prejudices of a self-satisfied and barren sectarianism are uncovered; the connections with the best Socialist elements are established; our publications have undergone an unprecedented increase in circulation and in entirely new circles. Even more, our youth as Socialists have for the first time had the opportunity of approaching the Stalinists "to discuss with them in comradely fashion." And all this despite the indisputable fact that the "substances" Bolshevism and Menshevism are more irreconcilable than ever.

12. However, expulsion does not stand on the agenda. We must work and root ourselves. To that end we must not turn to the ultraleft conservatives, must not justify ourselves before the shrill accusation of people who lost all balance and all sense of responsibility (Bauer and others), but rather speak in language understandable by Socialist and nonparty workers who seek a way out of the impasse.

13. Our Swiss section writes that, after negotiations and political as well as theoretical discussion, the four hundred members of the Zurich Socialist youth proposed to our comrades

to enter into their organization as a Bolshevik-Leninist faction, guaranteeing them in advance full freedom of action and a place in the leadership and on the editorial board. Can we accept these conditions? Yes or no? If the conditions are correctly represented, the only answer is: We must enter into the Socialist youth. It would be a mistake, more, a crime, even worse, sectarian stupidity, not to enter.

All our sections must study not only the far-removed experience of the struggle between Bolshevism and Menshevism in Russia but also the living experience of our French League as well as the claims and forecasts of both sides through their confirmation by reality. Each section will draw precious lessons from it. It is a question not of applying the same procedure under different conditions but of learning how to proceed suitably in a national and even local situation. Each section must make a survey of all organizations, groups and strata of the proletariat in order to understand how to intervene in time and how to propagate ideas by realistic means.

TO THE UKRAINIAN COMRADES IN CANADA[104]

(October 20, 1934)

To the Editors of *Robitnichi Visti*

Dear Friends:

It is with great interest and warm sympathy that I follow your efforts to extend the ideas and methods of unfalsified Marxism (Leninism) among the Ukrainian proletarians in Canada.

The theory and practice of "socialism in one country" stand in particularly sharp contradiction to the interests of the Ukrainian proletariat. The principal factor holding back the development of the highly talented Ukrainian people is its national dismemberment, which has been accompanied, and is now being accompanied, by cruel national oppression in the capitalist countries. The October Revolution unquestionably gave a mighty impetus to the development of Ukrainian culture. However, while the toiling masses of the entire Soviet Union are suffering many losses in their development under the present Soviet bureaucracy, the Ukrainian workers and peasants are in addition suffering the consequences of their national dismemberment. What a magnificent achievement it would be if the Ukrainian people could be reunited in its entirety in a Soviet Ukraine! What a far-reaching development would be in store for Ukrainian culture then!

Only the European and international revolution, starting with Poland, could bring to the Ukrainian people its complete national unification and liberation.

Advanced Ukrainian workers have less reason than any other workers to be satisfied with the theory of "socialism in one country." This conservative theory does not open up before them even the perspective of national liberation, which is an elementary prerequisite of socialist society. That is why I follow with great pleasure your efforts to explain to the Ukrainian workers that their fate, as well as the fate of the entire toiling Ukrainian people, is intimately and indissolubly linked not only to the fate of the Soviet Union but also to the fate of the international proletarian revolution.

I regret very much that I am not able to write you this letter in Ukrainian.[105] Even though I have known the Ukrainian language since my childhood and have been inspired by the lines of the great Shevchenko,[106] learning his verses by heart, and although I am able to follow your newspaper, my own Ukrainian vocabulary is a bit too meager to permit me to express myself in writing directly in Ukrainian. But I hope that these lines will reach you in a competent Ukrainian translation.

Fraternal greetings,
L. Trotsky

AUSTRIA, SPAIN, BELGIUM AND THE TURN[107]

(November 1, 1934)

To the International Secretariat and
the Leadership of the Belgian Section

Dear Comrades:

I have had an opportunity to peruse the minutes of the Viennese Schutzbund conference at which Otto Bauer and Julius Deutsch participated (June 1934).[108] This document is full of lessons. It gives an authentic picture not only of what Austro-Marxism[109] was but also of the unexpected and unhoped for gains of the Austrian Stalinists. After breaking with the Social Democracy, the most militant workers sought support in the Comintern. The minutes show that events have in all seriousness vaccinated the advanced workers against reformism, but have left them almost entirely defenseless against Stalinism. This means that the best elements in the proletariat have as yet to pass through other tragic experiences before they finally find their way.

These same minutes, ample enough and detailed though they are, do not make any mention whatsoever of the various groupings of the Left Opposition. It was in Austria that sectarianism, as exemplified by Landau[110] and by Frey, raged altogether unhampered. And the results? The most formidable of crises came and passed entirely over the heads of these grouplets, despite the fact that there had always been broad sympathies for our ideas in Vienna. It is a very sad but, nevertheless, invaluable lesson. It must be said now openly: ever since the beginning of the crisis in the Austrian party, it was a supreme duty of our friends to enter the Austro-Marxist party, to prepare within it the revolutionary current. One cannot avow that on that condition events would have taken a different path of development. But it is absolutely certain that no matter what development events would have produced, our tendency would have come out of it ten times, a hundred times stronger than it is now. The objection may be raised that entry into a Social Democratic party a year and a half ago would have been psychologically impossible, since the evolution of the reformist and Stalinist parties was not then advanced sufficiently to impose on us our new orientation. This objection would be quite correct. But in this letter we are not concerned with finding an explanation or a justification for the shortcomings of this or that section at one moment or another. We are concerned here with taking inventory of the fundamental tendencies arising in the labor movement since the defeat in Germany, which imposes upon us a much more daring turn towards the masses. Without this, entirely fresh layers of the proletariat will be pushed into the arms of Stalinism, and another whole period will be lost for the revolution.

The recent, as yet brief, experience of our French section already enables us to adduce a positive confirmation of the negative lessons of the Austrian experience. It is becoming self-evident that the French section has made a great step forward, which may have some genuinely salutary consequences . . . always on the condition, however, that the Bolshevik-Leninist Group learns to rid itself of propagandistic narrowness and, without losing sight for a moment of its clear ideas and slogans, shows an ability to adapt itself to the milieu of the masses in order to fuse our program with their experiences and their struggles. It may be said now almost with certainty that, if we had been able to bring about entry into the SFIO right after the departure of the Neos and, in any case, before the conclusion of the united front, we should already at the present be able to show considerable successes to our credit. All this is said not in order to deplore things that are past but in order that we may learn — and we must all learn without any exceptions — to orient ourselves on a national scale more rapidly and more courageously.

I have not as yet received any documents on the recent events in Spain,[111] generally, and on the role played by our section. But the general line of development suffices to draw the conclusion that our Spanish comrades should have joined the Socialist Party there at the very outset of the internal differentiation that began to prepare that party for the armed struggle. Our position in the Spanish situation would today be more favorable.[112]

One of our Belgian comrades who plays quite a part in the youth movement has sent me some documents that describe the relationship existing among the Young Socialist Guard [JGS], the Stalinists and ourselves, and also a little about the internal life of the JGS. The conclusion that I have drawn from these documents is that our young comrades should *immediately* join the JGS. With this declaration, I will perhaps run headlong up against the impassioned objections of several dozen comrades. But I firmly hope that the French experience will be convincing enough for those of our friends who are more inclined to stress the dangers than the advantages of the new orientation. In any case, the question appears to me to be most urgent, a burning question even, and I pose it before the international as well as the national leadership.

The united front of the three youth organizations in Belgium was naturally an important principled acquisition. The fact alone that the question of so-called Trotskyism is posed before the Belgian Young Socialists is itself a step forward. But I do not believe that the triangular united front can last very long. Even if it does last, I do not believe that it can bring us any additional important gains. We are strong as a revolutionary tendency, but weak as an organization. Accordingly, the united front, not only in the hands of the opponents, but in those of the well-intentioned allies as well, becomes an instrument to paralyze the development of our ideological expansion through the very statutes of the united front. The speeches of our comrades at the negotiations between the three organizations show the firm desire of our comrades to do their best and make the most of it. But it is also apparent how they are hampered, if we wish to avoid saying chained down, by the *diplomacy* of the united front. The disproportion between our forces and those of the Socialists imposes upon our comrades, as a matter of fact, a very modest attitude, and even too modest an attitude that corresponds to the relationship of the numerical forces, but not at all to the ideological role that we can and must play within the working-class youth.

The united front, as it is proceeding in France and elsewhere at present, is poisoned by the diplomatic hypocrisy that is a means of self-defense for the two bureaucracies. By placing ourselves on the level of the united front as a weak organization, we are condemned in the long run to play the part of a poor relation who must not raise his voice too high so as not to incur the displeasure of his host. In this manner, our organizational independence avenges itself upon our political and ideological independence. We have witnessed the same phenomenon in France after the events of February 6, and especially after the realization of the united front. *La Verite* today is much more independent in its criticism than it was before the entry into the SFIO. That is not an accident. The criticism that was banished from the domain of interorganizational relations can only find its place in an intraorganizational form, not at all times and not in every place, but in any case inside of the SFIO and, as far as I am able to judge, inside of the JGS. In such a case, organizational independence must give the right of way to political independence. Inside the JGS, our comrades will be able to carry on much more systematic work and much more fruitful work than from the outside. I have become definitely convinced of the necessity of entry there, ever since I heard that the JGS members with whom our comrades are in contact insisted that we come in and join them in their organization.

To postpone the decision would be a great mistake. The crisis in the POB, and especially between the youth and the party leadership, may become brusquely sharpened and lead to a split. In that case, the JGS would unquestionably look to the Stalinists for attachment, in the manner of the Austrian left. That would mean a whole series of demoralizing experiences with the bureaucracy, an unfavorable "purge," that is, a selection of docile camp followers and careerists, the expulsion of the embattled and independent characters. In order not to perish, the JGS requires an anti-Stalinist vaccination. Only our comrades can provide it for them. But in order to fill this sanitary requirement, our comrades must be entirely free from the embarrassment imposed upon them by the statutes of the united front. It is necessary to go along with the JGS, to partake of their experiences, to inculcate them with our ideas and methods on the basis of these experiences.

I have not yet received any documents on the last congress of the POB. The question of the attitude of the left — including the *Action Socialiste*[113] — is of extreme importance to the development of the proletarian vanguard in Belgium. But it seems to me that entry into the JGS is just as necessary, in case of an accentuation of the struggle inside the party as well as in the case of a momentary lapse. I shall await with the greatest impatience the opinions of the Belgian comrades.

Crux [Leon Trotsky]

P. S. The SFIO is, in a certain sense, a petty-bourgeois organization not only because of its dominant tendency but also because of its social composition: the liberal professions, municipal functionaries, labor aristocracy, teachers, white-collar workers, etc. This fact naturally limits the possibilities created by the entry itself. The POB, on the other hand, embraces the working class, and the composition of the JGS is proletarian in its overwhelming majority. That means that adherence to the JGS would open up even more favorable opportunities for us.

ON BONAPARTISM
(MARXISM IS SUPERIOR)[114]

(Published December 1, 1934)

In the single but extremely important question of present-day Bonapartism is to be found fresh confirmation of the superiority of Marxist analysis over all forms of political empiricism. More than three years ago, we set forth in these columns the idea that, as it disappeared from the scene, bourgeois democracy, fully in accordance with the laws of history, gives way to the Bonapartism of a capitalism on the decline. Let us recall the course of the analysis of democracy; it is primarily a committee of conciliation organized between two classes; it is maintained for as long as class contradictions allow conciliation. The explosion in democracy is provoked by the tension of class contradictions. Democracy can give place either to the fascist dictatorship of monopoly capital or to the dictatorship of the proletariat. But before one of these two warring sides can gain victory over the other, of necessity inside the society is established a transitional regime of unstable equilibrium between the two extreme wings, the proletariat and fascism, which paralyze each other and thus allow the bureaucratic apparatus to acquire exceptional independence and force in its capacity of arbiter and savior of the nation. A supraparliamentary government of the big bourgeoisie that creates an equilibrium between the two warring sides, basing itself on the police and the army, is precisely a government of the Bonapartist type. That was the character of the governments of Giolitti in Italy, of Bruening-Papen-Schleicher in Germany, of Dollfuss in Austria.[115] To this same type belong the governments of Doumergue and today of Flandin in France, Colijn in Holland, etc.[116] To understand the essence of neo-Bonapartism is to understand the character of the last period of time still left the proletariat to prepare itself for decisive battle.

Writings of Leon Trotsky, 1934-35

When we first made this analysis, the Stalinists were more than a little proud of the aphorism of their science, "Social Democracy and fascism are twins." They announced, "Fascism is here now." They accused us — neither more nor less — of having deliberately given the name Bonapartist to the fascist regime in order to reconcile (!) the proletariat to it. Who does not know that the Stalinist arguments are always distinguished by their theoretical profundity and political honesty?!

However, the Stalinists were not alone. Political invalids Thalheimer and Brandler[117] more than once exercised their great irony on the subject of Bonapartism; in this way they were hoping to find the shortest road to the Communist International's trough.

Final proof in the debate was brought by France, classic country of Bonapartism. In a series of articles, Leon Blum has recently shown that the proposal to reform the constitution was completely impregnated with the spirit of Bonapartism. The Antifascist Committee of Left Intellectuals[118] (Langevin and others) showed in its appeal the truly astounding analogy between the latest speeches of Doumergue and the manifestos of Louis Napoleon[119] in 1850. The subject of Bonapartism is no longer absent from today's agenda. People who did not want any talk about Bonapartism when the social and political conditions for it were being prepared have recognized it now by its juridical formulas and its blackmailing rhetoric.

The Marxist method has once more shown its superiority. It was that precisely that allowed us to recognize the new state form when it was only beginning to take shape; we had established it not by its juridical and rhetorical flowerings but by its social roots. This method also allows us to understand better the direction of the neo-Bonapartism that has taken form in our country. Its essence is not at all in the formal revision of the constitution, as Leon Blum thinks. It is only the juridical tradition of French political thought that has driven Doumergue on the road to Versailles. The real revision of the constitution has in fact already been made. It was a question not of three or four paragraphs but of three or four score thousand fascist revolvers. Long ago, Engels said the state was a detachment of armed men with material attributes, like prisons. For aged, simple-minded democrats of the Renaudel type, this definition was almost always a blasphemy. Now the state stands before us in all its cynical nudity. With the help of some thousands of revolvers, the fascists, watchdogs of finance capital, have matched and neutralized millions of unarmed workers and peasants; it is this material fact alone that has made possible the appearance of the Bonapartist regime. To overthrow the Bonapartist government we must before all else crush its armed auxiliary detachments. For that we must arm the proletarian vanguard by creating a workers' militia.

That is the lesson of historical experience and Marxist analysis.

ON THE SAP'S PROPOSALS[120]

(December 1934)

To the International Secretariat
For All Sections

From the formal point of view, the SAP proposal can be considered a certain step forward. The most important gain is that the SAP for the first time characterizes Comintern policy not as ultraleft but as a continuous oscillation between ultraleft and right. But even this concession to our criticism is not drawn out to the necessary consequences. What is the significance theoretically and politically of a tendency — or, to say it better, of a world organization — that oscillates between two extremes? These oscillations should have a social body and a political physiognomy. Long ago we defined it as bureaucratic centrism. The SAP leaders have fought against this definition. They propose no other for it. The oscillations remain enigmatic. The necessity to liberate the world proletarian vanguard from the grip of the Soviet bureaucracy thus remains unmotivated. The first theoretical concession, stopping halfway, remains worthless. (See page 7 of the theses.)

Page 5 defines fascism and page 6 reformism tied to bourgeois democracy. But the theses do not breathe one word on the transitional stage between the reformist democratic epoch and the fascist epoch. The SAP omits completely the question of Bonapartism, which for a large number of countries is the most burning actuality. How can one orient oneself in the present political situation in France, Belgium, Holland, etc., without having given a definition and explanation of neo-Bonapartism?

In the *theses on war*, it is surprising to find nothing about the role of the national state in the present crisis of the capitalist system. The fundamental contradiction is between the productive forces of capitalism and the level of consumption of the masses. But this contradiction does not present itself in an arena of capitalism that is one and indivisible. The national state delimits the framework within which this contradiction comes to light. That is how the contradiction between the productive forces of capitalism and the national state becomes the immediate cause of wars. Without characterizing the economically reactionary role of the national state, one cannot refute the idea of national defense. That is why the theses are very weak on this major point.

But even more important than these theoretical and political mistakes and omissions (there are still more) is the main equivocation on which is based the whole organization of the IAG.[121] This equivocation is inherent in a policy that substitutes the diplomacy of apparatuses for frank explanation and reciprocal Marxist criticism.

We read, "The IAG is not an International. Between its members there is as yet no such solidarity in theory and practice that it allows them to bear responsibility for the totality of the policy of each of the organizations." The equivocation is based on the words *"die gesamte Politik"* ("the totality of the policy"). The question is whether the SAP bears responsibility not for all the actions of the NAP but for its general orientation, its guiding line. The same question with respect to the ILP, etc. . . .

For us, the NAP policy is oriented in a direction diametrically opposed to our policy. In the sessions of the IAG, no trace can be found of an explanation of the general direction of the activity of the member parties. Under these conditions, the conference and theses of the IAG lose all revolutionary value. Worse than that, with suitably drawn-up theses they mask an activity that is directed in a contrary direction.

Sometimes we are answered with the objection, "But your French section has gone back into the Social Democratic party. The Belgian Leninist youth is preparing to adhere to the JGS. How can you, you Bolshevik-Leninists, under these conditions upbraid us bitterly for the lack of cohesion in the IAG?!"

This argument is absolutely false. Our French section is not keeping a double set of books. It does not separate its principles from its actions. It does not substitute diplomacy for revolutionary criticism. Sometimes it is compelled to limit the form in which it expresses its ideas. But it is never silent on the essentials, including the mistakes and crimes of the SFIO leaders. In contrast, the IAG is stubbornly silent on all questions that have real importance and, above all, on the policy of the NAP leadership that is preparing the ground for fascism in Norway.

It is true that page 8 of the theses on tasks "obliges"

(*verpflichtet*) the member organizations to orient their policies toward the conquest of power, etc. . . . It obliges (*verpflichtet*) them to elaborate programs of action, etc. . . . These "obligations" should give the IAG the appearance of wishing to take a step forward toward theoretical and political cohesion. But in reality this is no more than a purely formal procedural matter. How can one "oblige" what-you-will organizations that never give any account of their activity and that cannot even tolerate any criticism by other organizations? To *"oblige,"* it is necessary to be able to *control.* And to *control,* it is necessary to have the right to *criticize.*

De Man,[122] Jouhaux and others want to "oblige" capitalist economy to be directed. But they reject the slogan of control of production, beginning with the abolition of commercial secrets — and for a reason! The plan of directed economy separated from real activity is nothing but a witticism to distract or to mock at the naive while the abolition of commercial secrets, a much more modest slogan, demands implacable struggle against the bourgeoisie. The SAP theses represent a directed political plan. But the commercial secrets of Tranmael and Co. remain intact. The whole misfortune lies there. And this misfortune totally annihilates the little progress in the theoretical formulas.

The equivocation continues, naturally, in the question of the new International. The theses recognize that "the two great Internationals have increasingly become brakes on the proletarian struggle," but at the same time they abstain from advancing the slogan of the new International (the Fourth). Why? Because Tranmael and people like him proclaim with that air of fictitious wisdom peculiar to them that there is already one International too many. Imagine for a moment an agitator who declares at workers' meetings that the Second and Third Internationals are putting the brakes on and handicapping the proletarian revolution. The audience can agree or not, but they expect the speaker to say to them, "We must create on such-and-such a base a new International." But the speaker from the SAP does not have the right to say it. He is disarmed. His criticism of the two Internationals is only a blank shot. That is why the SAP like the IAG is marking time.

The final slogan of the theses is the calling of a congress of all proletarian organizations against war. This slogan is a fiction from every point of view. Even if the most important organizations, like the trade unions, were to be prepared to sit with the Russian Bolsheviks if they found themselves the government to authorize such a congress, this result for the struggle against war would be altogether unofficial. It could even encourage bourgeois imperialism by the sight of our impotence. If the trade union, Social Democratic and Stalinist bureaucracies found themselves forced to convene such a congress, we would have to participate in it in order to struggle for our ideas and methods. But to make this congress our slogan and to proclaim it in advance as an instrument of struggle against war means sowing one illusion more. The workers are being saturated today with abstractions of the united front, the common front and organic unity. The "world congress" belongs to the same category of comforting fictions.

To sum up:

If the IAG wishes to stop being a dead weight, it should place at the head of the agenda for its February conference the reports of the member organizations (beginning with the NAP as the most important) on their activities in their own countries. Discussion, frank and without reticence, on the basis of the report should end up in the elaboration of theses on the general policy of the proletariat and of each member organization in particular. These theses can only begin with a merciless condemnation of Tranmaelism and of every policy that flirts with it.

In a word, we must say openly what is. That is the true beginning of wisdom.

Crux [Leon Trotsky]

THE STALINIST BUREAUCRACY
AND THE KIROV ASSASSINATION[123]

A Reply to Friends in America

(December 28, 1934)

1. A Grandiose "Amalgam"[124]

The assassination of Kirov has remained a complete mystery for several weeks. At first the official dispatch referred only to the execution — as an immediate repressive measure — of some scores of terrorists from among White[125] emigres arriving via Poland, Romania and other border states. The conclusion one naturally drew was that the assassin of Kirov belonged to the same counterrevolutionary terrorist organization.

On December 17, a dispatch was issued stating for the first time that Nikolaev had previously belonged to the Opposition group of Zinoviev in Leningrad in 1926. The dispatch itself revealed very little. The entire Leningrad organization of the party, with only a few exceptions, was part of the Zinoviev Opposition in 1926 and was represented at the Fourteenth Party Congress by a delegation consisting entirely or almost entirely of erstwhile Zinovievists who are today under arrest. Subsequently they all capitulated with their leader at the head; then they repeated their capitulation in a much more decisive and humiliating manner. They were all reinstated into the Soviet apparatus. The information that Nikolaev — whose name reveals nothing to anyone — had at one time taken part in the Zinoviev group implies hardly more than the fact that Nikolaev in 1926 was a member of the Leningrad organization of the party.

It was clear, however, that this information relating to the "Zinoviev group" was not issued by accident; it could imply nothing else but the preparation of a juridical "amalgam," that is to say, a consciously false attempt to implicate in the assassination of Kirov individuals and groups who did not and could not have anything in common with the terrorist act. This is no new method. Let us recall that as early as 1927 the GPU[126] sent one of its official agents who had formerly fought in the Wrangel army[127] to a young man, unknown to everybody, who was distributing the documents of the Opposition. And then the GPU accused the entire Opposition of maintaining relations . . . not with the GPU agent, but with a "Wrangel officer." Hired journalists immediately transmitted this amalgam to the Western press. At the present time, the same procedure is being employed, only on an infinitely larger scale.

On December 27, TASS [telegraphic agency of the Soviet Union] opened wide the parentheses of the amalgam by transmitting facts of a particularly sensational character. Aside from the unknown individuals brought to justice in Leningrad for the act of the terrorist Nikolaev, fifteen members of the old "anti-Soviet" group of Zinoviev were arrested in Moscow in connection with this same affair. TASS even here states, it is true, that concerning seven of the arrested there are not "sufficient facts to hand them over to justice," wherefore they were handed over to the Commissariat of Internal Affairs for the purpose of administrative repression. Let us enumerate the fifteen party members who, according to TASS, were arrested in Moscow, in connection with the Nikolaev affair:

1. Zinoviev — Lenin's collaborator for many years in exile, former member of the Central Committee and the Political Bureau, former chairman of the Communist International and of the Leningrad Soviet;

2. Kamenev — Lenin's collaborator in exile for many years, former member of the Central Committee and the Political Bureau, vice-chairman of the Council of People's Commissars, chairman of the Council of Labor and Defense and of the Moscow Soviet. These two men together with Stalin composed the governing *troika* [triumvirate] during 1923-25;

3. Zalutsky, one of the oldest worker-Bolsheviks, former member of the Central Committee, former secretary of the Leningrad Committee, chairman of the first Central Commission for the purging of the party;

4. Yevdokimov, one of the oldest worker-Bolsheviks, former member of the Central Committee and the Organization Bureau, one of the leaders of the Leningrad Soviet;

5. Feodorov, one of the oldest worker-Bolsheviks, former member of the Central Committee, chairman of the workers' section of the soviet during the October Revolution;

6. Safarov, one of the oldest members of the party, arrived with Lenin in the "sealed" train,[128] former member of the Central Committee, editor-in-chief of the Leningrad *Pravda*;

7. Kuklin, one of the oldest worker-Bolsheviks, former member of the Central Committee and the Leningrad Committee;

8. Bakaev, one of the oldest worker-Bolsheviks, former member of the Central Control Commission, one of the outstanding participants in the civil war;

9-15. Sharov, Faivilovich, Vardin, Gorchenin, Boulak, Guertik and Kostina — all of them old party members, militants during the period of illegality, participants in the civil war, who occupied the most responsible posts in the party and the soviets — these fifteen individuals are implicated, no more, no less, in the assassination of Kirov and, according to explanations given by *Pravda,* they had as their aim the seizure of power, beginning with Leningrad, "with the secret intention of reestablishing the capitalist regime." Subsequent dispatches that have appeared in the Soviet press added to the fifteen arrested "Zinovievists" several more individuals of the same importance in the party.

Thus collapsed the first version according to which Nikolaev was presented to the reading public as connected with the organization of White Guard emigres who are sending in terrorists by way of Poland and Romania. Nikolaev becomes the *terrorist agent of an internal opposition in the party,* at the head of which there were to be found the former chairman of the Communist International, Zinoviev, and the former chairman of the Political Bureau, Kamenev, both of them Stalin's colleagues in the *troika.* It is clearly to be seen why we have called the dispatch of TASS a colossal sensation. We can now also call it a colossal lie.

2. Are Zinoviev and Kamenev Terrorists?

There is not the slightest reason or motive for us to defend the policies or the personal reputations of Zinoviev, Kamenev and their friends. They were at the head of that faction that inaugurated the struggle against Marxist internationalism under the name of "Trotskyism"; they were subsequently driven against the bureaucratic wall raised with their own efforts and under their own leadership; having taken fright at their own handiwork, they joined the Left Opposition for a brief period and revealed the frauds and falsehoods utilized in the struggle against "Trotskyism"; frightened by the difficulties of the struggle against the usurping bureaucracy, they capitulated; reinstated to the party, they substituted for principled opposition, sniping, secret machinations; they were again expelled — they capitulated for the second time.

They disavowed the banner of Marxism and camouflaged themselves, hoping to gain a place in the party that had been corrupted and strangled by the apparatus. Having generally lost esteem and confidence, and even the possibility of waging a struggle, they found themselves, in the end, cruelly punished. It is not our task to defend them!

But the Stalinist bureaucracy is not judging them for their real crimes against the revolution and the proletariat, because its own ranks consist to a large degree of abject turncoats, camouflaged individuals and careerists ready for anything. Once again the bureaucracy wishes to turn its deposed chiefs into scapegoats for its own transgressions. Zinoviev and Kamenev were lacking in character, but no one considered them fools or ignorant buffoons. The other thirteen above-named Bolsheviks lived through the experiences of the Bolshevik Party for twenty-five or thirty and more years. They could not suddenly turn to a belief in the utility of individual terror for changing the social regime, even were one to admit for a single moment the absurdity that they might have actually aspired to "reestablish the capitalist regime." Similarly, they could not have possibly thought that the assassination of Kirov, who, besides, played no independent role, could lead them to power. The American workers may more easily understand how insane is such an idea if they imagine for a moment the left-wing opposition in the trade unions deciding to assassinate some right-hand man of Green, [129] with the aim of . . . seizing the leadership of the trade unions!

The dispatch of TASS itself admits, at least as regards seven of those arrested — Zinoviev, Kamenev, Zalutsky, Yevdokimov, Feodorov, Safarov and Vardin — that they really had no connection with the Nikolaev affair. But this admission is made in such a way that one can call it nothing but brazen. The dispatch speaks of "lack of proof" — as if there could generally be any proof of an accusation intentionally so false and improbable as is this accusation by its very essence. By making an artificial division into two groups of the Old Bolsheviks arrested in Moscow and by declaring that for one of them there are insufficient proofs, the Stalinist clique seeks by this very thing to color its so-called investigation with a tinge of "objectivity" in order to hold in reserve the subsequent possibility for replacing the juridical amalgam by an administrative amalgam.

As regards the real motives and circumstances of Nikolaev's crime, we now learn from the dispatch of TASS as little as we knew before. The implication that Kirov may have been the victim of vengeance for depriving Zinoviev of leading posts in Leningrad is manifestly absurd. Eight years have since gone by. Zinoviev himself and his friends have had time enough to repent twice; the "grievances" of 1926 have long ago paled in the face of events of infinitely greater importance. It is clear that there must have been much more recent circumstances that drove Nikolaev onto the road of terrorism, and that there must have been very serious reasons that impelled Stalin to venture on a monstrous amalgam that—regardless of whether or not it succeeds immediately in attaining its practical goal—cruelly compromises the Soviet group in power.

3. Was the Purpose to Restore Capitalism?

The first question that must inevitably arise in the minds of all thinking workers is the following: how could it come to pass that at a time like this, after all the economic successes, after the "abolition"—according to official assurances—of classes in the USSR and the "construction" of the socialist society, how could it come to pass that Old Bolsheviks, the most intimate collaborators of Lenin, those who shared power with Stalin, members of the "Old Guard," could have posed for their task the *restoration of capitalism?* Do Zinoviev, Kamenev and the others consider that the socialist regime is no boon to the masses? Or, on the contrary, do they expect from capitalism personal advantages both for themselves and their descendants? And what sort of advantages?

Only utter imbeciles would be capable of thinking that capitalist relations, that is to say, the private ownership of the means of production, including the land, can be reestablished in the USSR by peaceful methods and lead to the regime of bourgeois democracy. As a matter of fact, even if it were possible *in general,* capitalism could not be regenerated in Russia except as the result of a savage counterrevolutionary coup d'etat that would cost ten times as many victims as the October Revolution and the civil war. In the event of the overthrow of the Soviets, their place could only be taken by a distinctly Russian fascism, so ferocious that in comparison to it the ferocity of the Mussolini regime and that of Hitler would appear like philanthropic institutions. Zinoviev and Kamenev are no fools. They cannot but understand that the restoration of capitalism would first of all signify the total extermination of the revolutionary generation, themselves, of course, included. Consequently, there cannot be the slightest doubt here that the accusation concocted by Stalin against the Zinoviev group is fraudulent from top to bottom, both as regards the *goal* specified, restoration of capitalism, and as regards the *means,* terrorist acts.

4. Nikolaev's Crime Is No Accidental Event

In any case, the fact remains that the leading bureaucratic group is not at all inclined to estimate Nikolaev's crime as an isolated and accidental phenomenon, as a tragic episode; on the contrary, it is investing this act with a political importance so exceptional that it does not stop at constructing an amalgam that compromises itself, nor even at placing all types of opposition, discontent and criticism on the same plane with terrorist acts. The goal of the maneuver is quite evident: to terrorize completely all critics and oppositionists, and this time not by expulsion from the party, nor by depriving them of their daily bread, nor even by imprisonment or exile, but by the firing squad. *To the terrorist act of Nikolaev, Stalin replies by redoubling the terror against the party.*

The thinking workers of the entire world should ask themselves with the greatest anxiety the following question: is it possible that the Soviet power is in so difficult a position that the leading stratum is compelled to resort to such monstrous machinations in order to maintain its equilibrium? This question leads us to a second one that we have posed time and again but to which we have never received the semblance of a reply. If it is correct that the dictatorship of the proletariat has for its task the crushing of the resistance on the part of the exploiting classes — and this is correct — then the weakening of the former ruling classes and, so much more so, their "liquidation" concurrently with the economic successes of the new society must necessarily lead to the mitigation and the withering away of the dictatorship. Why isn't this so? Why is there to be observed a process of a directly opposite character? Why have we seen during the period of the two five-year plans the monstrous growth of the omnipotence of the bureaucracy, which has led the party, the soviets and the trade unions to complete submission and humiliation?

If one were to judge *solely* on the basis of the party and the political regime, one would have to say that the position of the Soviets grows manifestly worse, that the ever-increasing pressure of bureaucratic absolutism expresses the growth of the internal contradictions that sooner or later must lead to an explosion with the danger of the downfall of the whole system. Such a conclusion would be, however, one-sided and, consequently, incorrect.

5. Socialism Has Not Yet Been Built; the Roots of the Classes Have Not Yet Been Extirpated

If we want to understand what is occurring, we must, above all, reject the official theory according to which a classless socialist society is already established in the USSR. In fact, why was it necessary for the bureaucracy to have complete power? Against whom? In reality, the "abolition" of classes

by administrative decree does not suffice; it still remains necessary to overcome them economically. So long as the overwhelming majority of the population has not yet emerged
from actual want, the urge for individual appropriation and
for the accumulation of goods retains a mass character and
comes into continual collision with the collectivist tendencies
of the economic life. It is true that essentially this accumulation
has consumption for its immediate goal; but if no vigilance
is exercised, if the accumulation is permitted to exceed certain
limits, it will transform itself into primitive capitalist accumulation and can result in overthrowing the *kolkhozes* [collective
farms], and after them the trusts as well. "Abolition of classes,"
in a socialist sense, means the guaranteeing to all members
of society such living conditions as will kill the stimulus for
individual accumulation. We are still very far from that. Were
one to compute the national income per capita, especially that
part of the national income that goes for consumption, the
Soviet Union, despite the technological successes it has
achieved, would still find itself at the tail end of capitalist
countries. The satisfaction of the essential elementary needs
is always bound up with a bitter struggle of each against
all, illegal appropriation, evasion of laws, cheating of the
state, favoritism and thievery on a mass scale. In this struggle,
the role of controller, judge and executioner is assumed by the
bureaucracy. It uses administrative pressure to compensate
for the deficiency in economic power.

It is infantile to think that the omnipotence of the Soviet
bureaucracy was necessitated by the struggle with the "remnants" of the exploiting classes in the socialist society. Indeed,
the historical justification for the very existence of the bureaucracy is lodged in the fact that we are still very far removed
from socialist society, in the fact that the present transitional
society is full of contradictions, which in the sphere of consumption, the most immediate and vital sphere for everyone, bears
a character of extreme tension and always threatens to cause
an explosion in the sphere of production. The collectivization
of peasant economy has tapped new and colossal sources of
power for the bureaucracy. It is precisely in rural economy
that questions of consumption are bound up most intimately
with questions of production. That is why collectivization has
led, in the village, to the need of guarding by the severest methods of repression the property of the collectives against the
peasants themselves.

This entire intense struggle does not have a clear-cut and open
class character. But potentially, as regards the possibilities
and dangers latent in it, it is a class struggle. The regime

of the dictatorship is therefore not only the heritage of previous class struggles (with the feudal landlords and the capitalists), as the Stalinists would have it, a struggle that has been basically consummated, but also the instrument for preventing a new class struggle that is looming from out of the fierce competition between the interests involved in the sphere of consumption, on the basis of a still lagging and unharmonious economy. In this and in this alone rests the historical justification for the existence of the present Soviet dictatorship.

6. The Dual Role of the Bureaucracy

The Soviet bureaucracy, however, in the interests of its own domination and welfare, ruthlessly exploits its role of controller and regulator of the social contradictions and its function of waging a preventive struggle against the regeneration of classes. It not only concentrates in its own hands the entire power but also consumes by hook and crook an enormous share of the national income. In this way it has succeeded in removing itself so far away from the masses of the population as to make it impossible any longer to permit any control whatever over its actions and its income.

Certain observers and superficial critics have declared the Soviet bureaucracy to be a new ruling class. The falsity of this definition from the Marxist standpoint has been amply clarified by us. [130] A ruling economic class presupposes a system of production and of property that is peculiarly its own. The Soviet bureaucracy is but a reflection of the transitional stage between two systems of production and of property, between the capitalist system and the socialist system. There can be no question of an independent development of this transitional regime.

The role of the Soviet bureaucracy remains a dual one. Its own interests constrain it to safeguard the new economic regime created by the October Revolution against the enemies at home and abroad. This work remains historically necessary and progressive. In this work the world proletariat support the Soviet bureaucracy without closing their eyes to its national conservatism, its appropriative instincts and its spirit of caste privilege. But it is precisely these traits that are increasingly paralyzing its progressive work. The growth of industry and the drawing of agriculture into the sphere of state planning complicate extraordinarily the tasks of the economic leadership.

An equilibrium between the various branches of production and, above all, a correct balance between national accumulation and consumption can be achieved only with the active participation of the entire toiling population in the elaboration of the plans, the necessary freedom to criticize the plans and the opportunity to fix the responsibility and to recall the bureaucracy from top to bottom. Unrestricted domination over the economy of 170 million people implies the inevitable accumulation of contradictions and crises. The bureaucracy extricates itself from difficulties arising from its mistakes by loading their consequences onto the shoulders of the toilers. The partial crises converge towards the general crisis that is creeping onward and that expresses itself in the fact that, despite the titanic expenditure of energy by the masses and the greatest technological successes, the economic achievements keep lagging far behind, and the overwhelming majority of the population continues to lead a poverty-stricken existence.

Thus *the singular position of the bureaucracy,* which is the result of definite social causes, *leads to an increasingly more profound and irreconcilable contradiction with the fundamental needs of Soviet economy and culture.* Under these conditions, the dictatorship of the bureaucracy, although it remains a distorted expression of the dictatorship of the proletariat, translates itself into a permanent political crisis. The Stalinist faction is compelled ever anew to destroy "completely" the "remnants" of old and new oppositions, to resort to ever more violent methods and to place in circulation amalgams that become more and more envenomed. At the same time, this very faction raises itself above the party and even above the bureaucracy itself. It openly proclaims the purely Bonapartist principle of the infallibility of a lifetime leader. The sole virtue of a revolutionist to be recognized hereafter is fidelity to the leader. This demoralizing slavish philosophy of the bureaucracy is carried by the agents of the Comintern into its foreign sections.

7. The Two Series of Difficulties

Thus we see that in the evolution of the Soviet Union up to the present stage, we must sharply differentiate between two series of difficulties, one of which flows from the contradictions of the transitional period, aggravated by the diseases of bureaucratism. These are the *fundamental* difficulties from which the entire Soviet organism suffers. The other series of difficulties has a *derivative* character and represents a danger not to the Soviet regime but to the dominant position of the bureaucracy and the personal rule of Stalin.

These two series of difficulties are, of course, interrelated, but they are not at all identical. They are in a large measure opposed to one another, and the degree of their opposition is in a process of continual growth. The economic successes and the cultural progress of the population that were determined by the October Revolution turn more and more against bureaucratic conservatism, bureaucratic license and bureaucratic rapacity. Analogous processes are to be observed in the history of the development of various ruling classes in the past. The czarist bureaucracy aided in the development of capitalist relations only to come subsequently into conflict with the needs of bourgeois society. The domination of the Soviet bureaucracy costs the country too dearly. The progress in technology and culture, the increasingly exacting demands and the increasingly critical attitude of the people automatically turn against the bureaucracy. The young generation begins to sense in a particularly painful manner the yoke of "enlightened absolutism" that, besides, increasingly reveals the incapacity of its "shining lights." Thus conditions are created that clearly menace the rule of the bureaucracy, which has outlived itself.

8. Individual Terrorism, a Product of Bureaucratic Decay

The foregoing enables us to reply to the question we posed at the beginning of the article. Is it possible that the situation in the Soviets is so bad that the governing group is forced to resort to machinations, dirty tricks and criminal amalgams that profoundly compromise it in the eyes of the world proletariat? We can now reply with a feeling of relief that it is a question not of the difficult position of the Soviets themselves but of the position of the bureaucracy that is growing worse within the Soviets. Obviously the position of the Soviets is neither so rosy nor so magnificent as it is depicted by those false "friends" who are not disinterested and who — let us keep it in mind — will betray the Soviet Union at the first sign of serious danger. But it is far from being so bad as might be concluded on the basis of those acts of shameful panic by the bureaucracy. The ruling group would never have consented to connecting the terrorist crime of Nikolaev with the Zinoviev-Kamenev group if the Stalinists had not felt the ground slipping from under their feet.

Nikolaev is depicted by the Soviet press as a participant in a *terrorist organization made up of members of the party.* If the dispatch is true — and we see no reason to consider it an invention, because the bureaucracy has not confessed it with an easy heart — we have before us a new fact that must be considered of great *symptomatic* significance. There is always the possibility that it was a chance shot fired by a man for personal reasons. But a terrorist act prepared beforehand and committed by order of a definite organization is, as the whole history of revolutions and counterrevolutions teaches us, inconceivable unless there exists a political atmosphere favorable to it. The hostility to the leaders in power must have been widespread and must have assumed the sharpest forms for a terrorist group to crystallize out within the ranks of the party youth or, more properly speaking, within its upper stratum, which is intimately connected with the lower and middle circles of the bureaucracy.

Essentially this fact not only is admitted but also is stressed in the official statements. We learn from the Soviet press that the blind hatred of the "children" was nourished by the criticism of the oppositionist fathers. The explanations of Radek and Co. sound like plagiarisms of the czarist publicist, Katkov, who used to accuse the cowardly liberal fathers of provoking, voluntarily or involuntarily, the young generation to commit terrorist acts. It is true that the leaders in power have this particular time chosen only the Zinoviev group from among the generation of fathers. But this is the line of least resistance for Stalin. In repressing the compromised groups, Stalin wants to discipline the bureaucratic ranks, which are disintegrating and which have lost their internal cohesion.

When a bureaucracy comes into contradiction with the necessities of development and with the consciousness of the class that has raised it to power, it begins to decompose and to lose faith in itself. The function of the leadership is concentrated in the hands of an ever-narrowing circle. The others work by inertia, negligently; they think more of their personal affairs; they express themselves disdainfully within their own circles about the high authorities; they harbor liberal thoughts; and they grumble. Thus they indubitably undermine among their own youth the confidence in and the respect for the official leaders. If, at the same time, discontent is spreading within the masses of the people, for which the means of proper expression and an outlet are lacking, but which isolates the bureaucracy as a whole; if the youth itself feels that it is spurned, oppressed and deprived of the chance for independent development, the atmosphere for terroristic groupings is created.

Hypothetically, but with complete verisimilitude, we can reestablish, from what has been said, the role of the Zinoviev group. What depths of infamous stupidity are reached by the statement that it might have had any direct or indirect connection with the bloody deed of Smolny, [131] with its preparation and its political justification! Zinoviev and Kamenev returned to the party with the firm intention of winning the confidence of those at the top and rising again into their ranks. But the general condition of the lower and middle bureaucracy with which they were joined prevented them from realizing their intentions. While in official declarations they paid their tribute to the "greatness" of Stalin in which they, less than anyone else, could believe, they became infected in their daily surroundings by the generally prevailing spirit, that is to say, they cracked jokes, retailed stories about Stalin's ignorance, etc. . . . The general secretary did not remain ignorant, indeed, of all this. Could Stalin have chosen a better victim than this group when the shots at Smolny impelled him to teach the vacillating and decomposing bureaucracy a lesson?

9. Marxism, Terrorism and Bureaucracy

The negative attitude of Marxism towards the tactic of individual terror is known to every worker able to read and write. A great deal has been written on this question. I take the liberty of quoting here from an article of mine published in 1911, in German, in the Austrian periodical *Kampf*. Needless to say, it was then a question of the capitalist regime. In this article I wrote:

"Whether or not the terrorist act, even if 'successful,' throws the ruling circles into turmoil depends upon the concrete political circumstances. In any case such turmoil can only be of short duration; the capitalist state is not founded upon ministers and cannot be destroyed with them. The classes it serves will always find new men; the mechanism remains whole and continues its work.

"But the turmoil that the terrorist act introduces into the ranks of the toiling masses themselves is far more profound. If it is enough to arm oneself with a revolver to reach the goal, what need is there for the strivings of the class struggle? If people in high positions can be intimidated by the noise of an explosion, what need is there then for a party?"

To this article that counterposed to terrorist adventurism the method of preparing the proletariat for the socialist revolution, I can add nothing today, twenty-three years later. But if Marxists categorically condemned individual terrorism, obviously for political and not mystical reasons, even when the shots were directed against the agents of the czarist government and of capitalist exploitation, they will even more relentlessly condemn and reject the criminal adventurism of terrorist acts directed against the bureaucratic representatives of the first workers' state in history. The subjective motivations of Nikolaev and his partisans are a matter of indifference to us. The road to Hell itself is paved with the best of intentions. So long as the Soviet bureaucracy has not been removed by the proletariat, a task that will eventually be accomplished, it fulfills a necessary function in the defense of the workers' state. Should terrorism of the Nikolaev type spread, it could, aided by new, unfavorable conditions, render service only to the fascist counterrevolution.

Only political fakers who bank on imbeciles would endeavor to link Nikolaev with the Left Opposition, even if only in the guise of the Zinoviev group as it existed in 1926-27. The terrorist organization of the Communist youth was fostered not by the Left Opposition but by the bureaucracy, by its internal corruption.

Individual terrorism is in its very essence bureaucratism turned inside out. For Marxists this law was not discovered yesterday. Bureaucratism has no confidence in the masses and endeavors to substitute itself for the masses. Terrorism works in the same manner; it seeks to make the masses happy without asking their participation. The Stalinist bureaucracy has created a vile leader-cult, attributing to leaders divine qualities. "Hero" worship is also the religion of terrorism, only with a minus sign. The Nikolaevs imagine that all that is necessary is to remove a few leaders by means of a revolver in order for history to take another course. Communist terrorists, as an ideological grouping, are of the same flesh and blood as the Stalinist bureaucracy.

10. Bureaucratic Centrism, the Cause of the Collapse of the Comintern

By dealing this blow to the Zinoviev group, Stalin, as we said, aimed at consolidating the ranks of the bureaucracy. But that is only one aspect of the matter. There is another, and no less important, side: *Using the Zinovievist group as a footstool, Stalin is aiming to strike a blow at Trotskyism.* And cost what it may, he must strike that blow. In order to understand the goal and the direction of this new stage of the struggle against "Trotskyism," it is necessary to consider — even though briefly — the international work of the Stalinist faction.

As regards the USSR, the role of the bureaucracy, as has already been said, is a dual one: on the one hand, it protects the workers' state with its own peculiar methods; on the other hand, it disorganizes and checks the development of economic and cultural life by repressing the creative activity of the masses. It is otherwise *in the sphere of the international working-class movement,* where not a trace remains of this dualism; here *the Stalinist bureaucracy plays a disorganizing, demoralizing and fatal role from beginning to end.* Irrefutable evidence of this is the history of the Comintern during the last eleven years. We have made a study of this history in a series of writings. To our analysis there has not come a single word in answer from the Stalinists. Generally speaking, they do not care to learn their own history. They have not a single book nor a single article that makes an attempt to draw the balance of the policies of the Comintern in China, India, England, Germany, Austria and Spain during events of worldwide scope and importance.

No attempt has been made to explain why, under conditions of capitalist decay and of an entire series of revolutionary situations, the Comintern, during the last eleven years, has known nothing save shameful defeats, political disgrace and the atomization of its organization. Finally, why has it not dared during the past seven years to convoke a single world congress?

What is the balance sheet of the "workers' and peasants' parties" in the Orient?[132] What were the fruits of the Anglo-Russian Committee? What has become of the celebrated Peasant International?[133] What about the theory of the "third period"? What has become of the program of "national liberation" for Germany?[134] What was the fate of the great theory of "social fascism"? And so forth and so on. . . . Each of these questions is bound up with a definite zigzag in the policies of the Comintern; each of these zigzags has ended in an inevitable catastrophe. The chain of these catastrophes makes up the history of the Stalinist Comintern. Its most recent zigzag, particularly in France, is a deplorable and fatal opportunist convulsion. It is obvious that such a chain of mistakes, confusion and crimes can be the result not of individual or fortuitous causes, but rather of general causes. These causes are lodged in the social and ideological qualities of the Stalinist bureaucracy as the leading stratum. *Bureaucratic centrism* brought the Comintern to collapse. The Third International, like the Second, is doomed. No force can any longer save it.

Fundamentally, the Stalinist ruling group has given up the Comintern a long time ago. A most obvious proof of this is Stalin's refusal to convoke the world congress. Why bother? Nothing will come of it anyhow. Among themselves the Moscow bureaucrats explain the bankruptcy of the Comintern by the "nonrevolutionary character" of the Western working class and by the incapacity of the Western leaders. There is no need whatever to give the lie to this calumny of the world proletariat, especially after the recent events in Spain and Austria. As for the leaders of the Communist Parties abroad, Lenin as early as 1921 warned Zinoviev and Bukharin by letter: If you demand nothing but approbation in the Comintern, you will surround yourselves exclusively with "docile imbeciles."

Lenin liked to call a spade a spade. During the past eleven years, the selection of "dolts" has attained a colossal success. As a necessary corollary to this, the political level of the leadership has fallen below zero.

11. The Worldwide Growth of Genuine Leninism Is a Dreadful Danger to Stalin

As already stated, the Kremlin has reconciled itself to the Comintern as a nonentity, by means of the theory of socialism in one country. The hopes based on the world proletarian revolution it has swapped for hopes in the League of Nations. Command has been issued to the Communist Parties abroad to conduct "realistic" policies that would succeed in destroying, in a very short period of time, whatever still remains of the Comintern. Stalin is already reconciled to all this. But it is impossible for him to become reconciled to *the regeneration of the world revolutionary movement under an independent banner.* Criticism of reformism may be renounced; blocs may be concluded with Radicals; the workers may be poisoned with the venom of nationalism and pacifism; but under no condition is it permissible for the international proletarian vanguard to obtain the opportunity to verify freely and critically the ideas of Leninism through its own experience and to juxtapose Stalinism and so-called Trotskyism in the broad light of day.

Since 1923, the entire ideology of the Soviet bureaucracy has been formed via the ever increasingly hostile repulsion from "Trotskyism." The starting point for each new zigzag was Trotskyism. And now that the terrorist blow of Nikolaev is posing anew before the bureaucracy those very important political questions that it used to consider as solved once for all, it is trying once again to find, by means of the Zinoviev group, the culprit in the guise of Trotskyism, which is—as is very well known—the vanguard of the bourgeois counterrevolution, the ally of fascism and so on. Within the USSR, the bureaucracy has succeeded in establishing this version to the extent that the masses are deprived of the possibility of verifying things for themselves, and those who know the truth are reduced to silence. Precisely out of this stifled condition of the party there has originated the monstrous phenomenon of terrorism within the party. But danger is approaching stealthily; it has already drawn near, arriving from without, from the international arena. Those very ideas of Marx and Lenin, which as "counterrevolutionary Trotskyism" within the USSR meet with the penalties of imprisonment, exile and even the firing squad, are now becoming recognized on an increasingly wider scale and with increasing clarity by the most conscious, active and devoted elements of the vanguard of the world proletariat. The vile calumnies that paid journalists, without honor or conscience, continue to repeat even now in the rags of the Comintern, are provoking ever-increasing indignation in the very ranks of the Communist Parties and are, at the same time, isolating the sections of the Comintern from broad strata of the workers.

This prospect, let us repeat, no longer frightens Moscow. But another danger exists that is beginning to weigh like a nightmare on the Stalinist faction. The growing influence of the unfalsified ideas of Leninism in the working-class movement of Europe and America cannot long remain a mystery to the workers in the USSR. It is possible to keep quiet, even if this is not easy, about the participation of the former Communist League of America in the Minneapolis strike; it is possible, although difficult, to maintain silence about the merger of the League with the American Workers Party;[135] but when the confluence of events will take on a broader sweep and the revolutionary Marxists, the Leninists, will take a leading part therein, it will no longer be possible to keep quiet about these facts. The enormous danger that flows from this for the Stalinist faction is obvious. The entire structure of lies, calumnies, persecutions, falsifications and amalgams — the structure that has been uninterruptedly rising since Lenin's illness and death — will crumble upon the very heads of the engineers, that is to say, the calumniators and forgers. The Stalinists are blind and deaf to the perspectives of the world proletarian movement, but they have a very keen nose for the dangers that menace their prestige, their interests and their bureaucratic privileges.

12. The Inevitability of New Amalgams Had Been Foretold

In my isolation, following in the press the gradual successes, slow but sure, of the ideas of genuine Leninism in America and Europe, I often remarked to friends that the moment is approaching when the principled "quality" of this international current will begin to transform itself into a mass "quantity"; this moment will ring in the ears of the Stalinists like a sound of mortal danger. It is one thing to crush the revolutionary Marxist grouping by the sheer weight of the bureaucratic apparatus during a period of revolutionary ebb, fatigue, disillusion and disintegration of the masses; it is another thing to free the world proletarian vanguard from the Stalinist quack-substitute for Bolshevism by the force of Marxist criticism.

But that is precisely why — that is exactly the way we have expressed it more than once in conversations and letters — the Stalinist leaders cannot passively await the victory of Leninism. They must resort to "their measures," certainly not measures of an ideological character, for here their impotence is so obvious that Stalin within these last few years has, generally speaking, stopped making pronunciamentos upon questions pertaining to the world workers' movement. "His" measures, for Stalin, mean increasing repressions, new amalgams of an increasingly monstrous kind and, finally, an alliance with bourgeois police against the Leninists on the basis of mutual rendering of services.

Already, immediately after Kirov's assassination, when the whole world was still convinced that it was a matter of a White Guard crime, one of my friends sent me from Geneva the circular letter devoted to the bloody deed of Smolny, issued by the International Secretariat of the International Communist League. Referring to the protracted methods of the inquest and to the extremely ambiguous tenor of the first communications from the Kremlin, the International Secretariat suggested in the postscript the following possibility: is there perchance being prepared a colossal amalgam of some sort against the "Trotskyists" by the GPU? The circular letter of the International Secretariat is dated December 10 and has undoubtedly circulated the world over. It is true that the International Secretariat itself made a reservation in the sense that the amalgam, although possible, was "somewhat improbable." Nevertheless, the "improbable" has come to pass. When the first dispatch appeared in which Nikolaev was said to have been a member of the Leningrad Opposition in 1926, there was no further room for doubt. The new campaign against Zinoviev and Kamenev was not long in following. At that moment, in a conversation with a friend (I apologize for these personal details, but they are necessary for the understanding of the psychological undercurrents in the case), I said, "The matter will not rest long on this plane. Tomorrow they will bring Trotskyism to the fore." To be able to make such a prediction, it was really not necessary to be a prophet. The December 25 issue of *Le Temps,*[136] which I received two or three days later, contained in a telegraphic dispatch from Moscow the following item: "We must point out . . . that as the days go by, Trotsky's name is being mentioned more and more often alongside Zinoviev's."* Kirov's corpse and the Zinoviev group

---

* *Le Temps,* which is very friendly to Stalin, even emphasizes that among the arrested Zinovievists there is a known "Trotskyist,"

thus become preparatory steps for a much wider and bolder scheme: to deal a blow at international Leninism.

What must be the character of the *next* blow? This question has not been definitely decided, perhaps not even within the most intimate circle of the conspirators (Stalin-Yagoda-Yaroslavsky [137] and Co.). That largely depends upon the subsequent development of events. But one thing is clear: the conspirators lack neither the malevolent will nor the material means. The growth of international Leninism daily prods on their malevolent will; that is why it is impossible to exclude in advance *a single one of those hypotheses that flow from the very soil of the situation that has been created.* Whatever the course may be that will be drummed up by the march of events and by the creative imagination of Stalin and Yagoda, the preparation of "public opinion" will proceed along the line of a campaign concerning terrorist dangers on the part of the "Trotskyists" that menace the peace and order of Europe. *L'Humanite* has already made mention of a "terrorist group of — Trotskyists" in Leningrad. Lackeys always run ahead of their masters.

There is only one way to forestall en route the amalgams that are in preparation: *expose the scheme in advance.* The Stalinists are trying to mold the public opinion of the world police towards expulsions, extraditions, arrests and other more decisive measures. The Leninists must prepare the public opinion of the world proletariat for these possible events. In this case, as in others, it is necessary to speak out openly about what is; that is also the aim of the present article.

13. Several Conclusions

Given the abominable manner in which the Soviet leaders are acting, can one unconditionally recognize the USSR as a workers' state? This is probably the way that certain idealists, certain moralists or merely ultraleft confusionists express themselves. Instead of analyzing the concrete forms and stages of the development of the workers' state such as are created by the conjuncture of historical conditions, these wiseacres (Treint [138] in France is their inimitable "theoretician") "recognize" or refuse to "recognize" the workers' state, depending on whether the acts of the Soviet bureaucracy please them or not. We could indeed with equal justification refuse to recog-

---

Yevdokimov. As a matter of fact, Yevdokimov is one of the original members of the Zinoviev group. He never was a "Trotskyist." Naturally, this does not change matters any, but we cannot avoid pointing out the petty falsifications of this type appearing in the friendly press. They are innumerable.

nize the American working class as a working class on the
grounds that at its head there were and are to be found such
gentry as Gompers,[139]   Green and Co. The working class
needs a bureaucracy, and so much the more so does the workers' state. But the bureaucracy cannot be identified with the
class. The workers' state, like the working class as a whole,
passes through different stages of upswing as well as decline.
The Stalinist faction won its hegemony during the period of
the defeats of the world proletariat, during the fatigue and
apathy of the Russian proletariat and the rapid formation
of a privileged leading stratum. He who sees only the victories and the defeats of personalities understands nothing
in the struggle between factions in the USSR.

In 1926, N. K. Krupskaya,[140]   who along with Zinoviev
and Kamenev then adhered to the Left Opposition, said, "Were
Lenin alive, he would most assuredly be in a GPU prison."
That would certainly not be because Stalin would prove himself stronger than Lenin; it would be absurd even to compare
these two figures: Lenin, the genius and innovator, and Stalin,
the solid and consummate incarnation of bureaucratic medioc-
rity. But the revolution is a dialectical process that knows its
high upswings and its sharp declines. During the last two years
of his life, Lenin saw in the bureaucracy the principal danger
to the revolution and in Stalin the most consummate representative of this danger. Lenin fell ill and died during a feverish
preparation of the struggle against the Stalinist apparatus.

It would be criminal to deny the progressive work accomplished by the Soviet bureaucracy. With no initiative, with no
horizons, with no understanding of the historical dynamic
forces, the bureaucracy, after a stubborn resistance, found
itself compelled by the *logic of its own interests* to adopt the
program of industrialization and collectivization. By its general
level, by the character of its interests, the Stalinist bureaucracy
is hardly superior to the bureaucracy of the American trade
unions but, in contradistinction to the latter, its roots are im-
bedded in the nationalized means of production and it is compelled to safeguard and develop them. It has accomplished
this task bureaucratically, that is to say, badly, but the work
itself bears a progressive character. The initial, major successes along this road, which were not foreseen by the bureaucracy itself, have augmented its self-esteem and consolidated
it around the leader who incarnates in the most complete fashion the positive and negative traits of the bureaucratic stratum.

This "heroic" epoch of the bureaucracy is coming to a close.
The bureaucracy has exhausted the internal resources of "enlightened absolutism." Further development of economic and

cultural life demands the destruction of the bureaucracy by way of the regeneration of Soviet democracy. The bureaucracy resists desperately. In the struggle against the progressive needs of the new society, it must inevitably decompose. After the bureaucracy had strangled the internal life of the party, the Stalinist leaders strangled the internal life of the bureaucracy itself. Henceforth only one thing is permissible: to glorify the "Great Leader," the "Beloved Chief." Out of this tissue of contradictions is emerging the "communist" terror against the bureaucratic leadership.

The "internal" terror indicates in what a blind alley bureaucratism finds itself, but it does not at all show the way out of this impasse. No way out can be found except through the *regeneration of the Bolshevik Party.* This problem can only be solved on an international scale. In order for the Russian workers to reject the opium of "socialism in one country" and to turn en masse toward the world socialist revolution, the world proletarian vanguard must consolidate itself around the banner of the Leninist party. The struggle against reformism, more intransigent than ever, must be supplemented by the struggle against the paralyzing and demoralizing influence of the Stalinist bureaucracy upon the international working-class movement. The defense of the Soviet Union is inconceivable without the struggle for the *Fourth International.*

THE INDICTMENT[141]

(December 30, 1934)

After the inevitable day's delay, I received the Paris newspaper *l'Humanite* of December 28, containing extracts from the indictment, with a statement by one Duclos.[142] As both the extracts and the statement originate from the GPU, there is no need to enter into a discussion with hired lackeys. It will suffice for us to disclose the plans of their masters.

Just as one could have expected, the indictment doesn't mention the Zinoviev-Kamenev group by so much as a word. In other words, the initial amalgam fell apart into dust. However, concurrently it has fulfilled its task by psychologically preparing for another amalgam; in the indictment there emerges suddenly — suddenly for naive people — the name of Trotsky. Nikolaev, the murderer of Kirov, was — according to his confession — in contact with a consul of a foreign power.[143] During one of Nikolaev's visits to the consulate, the consul gave him 5,000 rubles for expenses. Nikolaev adds, "He told me that he can establish contact with Trotsky, if I give him a letter to Trotsky from the group." And that is all. *Period!* The indictment does not subsequently return to this episode.

It must also be remarked that Nikolaev made his first avowal concerning the foreign consul and his offer to transmit a letter to Trotsky only on the twentieth day after his arrest. Manifestly, the examining magistrate was compelled to assist the terrorist's memory in the course of twenty days in order to extract from him such precious evidence! But let us skip that. Let us allow that the evidence is authentic. Let us, moreover, allow that the consul in question does actually exist in the flesh. Let us allow that he established contact with a terrorist group (there have been such instances in history). But how and why does my name suddenly appear here? Is it, perhaps, because the terrorist group was seeking contact with Trotsky? No, even the GPU does not dare to assert this. Perhaps Trotsky was seeking contact with the terrorist group? No, the indictment does not dare say this either. The consul himself was the one to assume the initiative and, while giving Nikolaev *5,000 rubles on the eve of the terrorist act that was being prepared, he requested a letter addressed to Trotsky.* This is the sole deposition — a truly astounding piece of evidence made by Nikolaev. The personality of the "consul" at once stands revealed in glaring light. The "consul" is wide-awake! The "consul" is at his post! The "consul" requires a tiny document, a letter from the terrorists financed by him to — Trotsky.

Did the consul obtain this letter? One should imagine that this question would be of paramount importance. But it is precisely on this score that we cannot gather a single word from the indictment as it is printed in *l'Humanite.* Is it conceivable that neither the examining magistrate nor the prosecutor became at all interested in this fact? For, of interest are not the exploits of a consul unknown to anybody but the question of the *relations between the terrorists and Trotsky. Were* there such relations or *not?* Was the letter *written* and *transmitted?* Was a reply received? To these unavoidable questions we get no answer. Is that surprising? Only to naive people. The GPU could not permit the prosecutor any indiscretion within that sphere over which it has been compelled to draw the curtain of silence.

One need not doubt for a moment that the letter was never written, because if the terrorists knew anything at all about Trotsky — and they couldn't but know — it was no secret to them that running like a red thread through my thirty-seven years of revolutionary and literary activity (see several articles in my *Collected Works,* published by the State Publishing House) is my irreconcilable attitude towards the adventurism of individual terror. However, an admission that the terrorists could not have the slightest reason for seeking contact with Trotsky, and for this reason did not respond to the kind offer of the "consul," would be tantamount to the immediate bungling of the entire amalgam. Best keep quiet about it. Let us, nevertheless, make momentarily an entirely improbable supposition; the eloquent provocateur did actually succeed in obtaining the letter that so interested him. But what happened to it? Of course, the temptation would have been great to transmit such a letter to Trotsky and . . . to receive from him some sort of an encouraging answer for the Leningrad "supporters," even if without any reference to terror. But his inspirers, if not the consul himself, understood only too well the risk of such an enterprise; the previous attempts at provocation, which, it is true, were on a smaller scale, ended in an inevitable fiasco. The letter — if it had been written, we repeat, contrary to all likelihood — would have to simply remain in the archives of the GPU as a weapon unsuitable for its purposes. But this cannot be said aloud without confessing by this very fact that the consul is a second cousin to the Wrangel officer [144] (see below).

Is it possible, however, to conceive of a consul in a role of an agent provocateur? We have no means at all of knowing whether a real or a fake consul is here concerned; the resources for fraud in the given instance are illimitable. But even genuine consuls bear very little resemblance to saints. Some of them engage in smuggling and illicit deals in currency and fall into the hands of the police (not only of the GPU, of course). Such a compromised consul may be offered not only forgiveness for his sins but also some entirely legal coin in addition, should he be so obliging as to perform a few trifling and innocent services. There were, there are and there will be such cases . . . as long as there exist consuls, customs, currencies, intermediaries, male and female, and police.

The version we have adduced, which unfailingly flows from the indictment itself, if one is able to read it, *presupposes consequently that the GPU itself, through the medium of an actual or fake consul, was financing Nikolaev and was attempting to link him up with Trotsky.* This version finds its indirect but very actual confirmation in the fact that all the responsible representatives of the GPU in Leningrad were kicked out immediately after the assassination, and the investigation subsequently kept marking time for a protracted period, faced with the obvious difficulty of what variant to choose in order to explain what had happened.

We do not mean to say that the GPU, in the person of its Leningrad agents, premeditated the murder of Kirov; we have no facts for such a supposition. But the agents of the GPU knew about the terrorist act that was in preparation; they kept Nikolaev under surveillance; they established contacts with him through the medium of trumped-up consuls for the double purpose of capturing as many persons as possible involved in the matter and, at the same time, of attempting to compromise the political opponents of Stalin by means of a complex amalgam. Alas, an amalgam much too complex, as the subsequent course of events proved; before the "consul" had succeeded in preparing the political blast against Trotsky, Nikolaev fired the shot at Kirov. After this, the organizers of the surveillance and the provocation were thrown headlong from their posts. And in writing the indictment, it became necessary to steer painstakingly around the sandbars and the submarine reefs, to leave the "consul" in the shade, to wipe away all traces of the activities of the GPU and, at the same time, to save as much as possible of the shattered amalgam. The mysterious delay in the investigation thus finds an entirely natural explanation.

But why was the consul necessary? There was no getting along without the consul. The consul symbolizes the link between the terrorists, Trotsky and world imperialism (although the consul represented, one should imagine, some very petty and god-forsaken state; that is the least dangerous way). The consul is serviceable in another connection; out of "considerations of diplomacy," he cannot be named in the indictment nor consequently called as a witness. Thus, the mainspring of the combination remains behind the scenes. Finally, the consul himself — if he really exists in the flesh — runs no special risk, even if recalled by his government. Out of considerations of diplomatic politeness, he returns home as a distinguished hero who suffered in the service of his passionately loved fatherland; moreover, a certain supplementary sum to his modest salary would be found in his pocket for a rainy day, and there is no harm in that either.

The character of the machination is easiest understood if one is in the least bit acquainted with the preceding history of the behind-the-scenes struggle of Stalin against "Trotskyism." I shall mention only three instances. As early as 1927, hired journalists broadcast through the entire world the report that the Left Opposition had been implicated in relations with . . . White Guards. We were bewildered. It turned out that the GPU had sent one of its official agents to an eighteen-year-old youth, unknown to anybody, and sympathetic to the Opposition, with an offer to assist in spreading Opposition literature. Some six to seven years previously, the GPU agent, it appears, served in the army of Wrangel (which, incidentally, was never verified). On this basis, Stalin publicly accused the Opposition of making a bloc with . . . not an agent of the GPU but White Guards.

On the eve of my exile to Central Asia (January 1928), a foreign journalist made me an offer, through Radek, to transmit secretly, if need be, a letter to my friends abroad. I expressed to Radek my conviction that the journalist was an agent of the GPU. However, I wrote the letter, because I had nothing to say to my friends abroad that I could not repeat openly. The very next morning my letter was published in *Pravda* as proof of my secret connections "with foreign countries."

On July 20, 1931, the yellow sheet, *Kurjer Codzienny,* of Krakow published a gross forgery under the signature of

Trotsky. Despite the fact that my literary works are banned
on the pain of severest penalty in the USSR (Blumkin[145] was
shot for attempting to bring in the *Biulletin Oppozitsii* [146]),
the article from the *Kurjer* was reprinted in the Moscow *Pravda*— in facsimile. The most elementary analysis proves that
it was manufactured by the GPU, with the assistance of the
well-known Yaroslavsky, and printed in the *Kurjer* (one should
imagine at the regular advertising rates) only in order to be
reproduced by *Pravda.*

I am compelled to leave aside a number of other combinations and amalgams that are more clarifying in order not
to cause harm, by premature revelations, to other people involved. In any case, the type of this creative effort is clear
from what has been said above. The triangle composed of
Nikolaev, the "consul" and Trotsky is not new. It resembles
a dozen similar triangles and differs from them only by being on a much bigger scale.

It is necessary, however, to point out that the Soviet press,
as is evident from the cable extracts in the same issue of
l'Humanite [December 28], makes very circumspect use of the
latest amalgam in relation to Trotsky and does not go beyond
inferences concerning "the ideological inspirers." In return, however, *l'Humanite* broadcasts my participation in the murder
of Kirov with almost the same assurance with which *Le Matin*
recently wrote concerning my participation in the assassination of King Alexander and Barthou.

The difference in the conclusions drawn by *l'Humanite* and
Pravda is to be explained not only by the fact that the idiocy
of the Nikolaev-"consul"-Trotsky amalgam is much more obvious in Moscow than in Paris but also because, by its very
essence, this part of the amalgam is destined for foreign consumption, primarily for France. Its direct aim is to exert an
influence of the necessary kind on the French workers through
the medium of the united front and to exert pressure upon the
French authorities. Hence, the unbelievable tone of *l'Humanite!*
The Soviet authorities were compelled to admit openly that the
participation of Zinoviev, Kamenev and others "was not
proved." The official dispatches generally made no mention
of me at all. The indictment refers only to the anxiety of the
"consul" to obtain a letter to Trotsky — without drawing any
conclusions. The lackeys of *l'Humanite* write that Trotsky's
participation in the murder of Kirov was "proved."

This article, as I have already said, is addressed not to
the lackeys but to their masters. However, I cannot leave un-
mentioned here the fact that one of my first sharp conflicts
with the *troika* (Stalin, Zinoviev and Kamenev) came as a
result of my protest against their busy efforts, during the time

of Lenin's illness, to corrupt the more pliant "leaders" of the labor movement in the West, particularly by means of bribes. Stalin and Zinoviev replied in rebuttal, "Doesn't the bourgeoisie buy the leaders of trade unions, members of parliament and journalists — why shouldn't we do likewise?" My answer was that by means of bribes one could disintegrate the workers' movement but not create revolutionary leaders. Lenin used to warn against selecting "docile imbeciles" for the Comintern. But the selection has been extended to include cynics who are ready for anything. Ready for anything? Up to the first serious danger. People who have neither honor nor conscience cannot be trustworthy revolutionists. In the moment of difficulty, they will inevitably betray the proletariat. My only counsel to workers is that they remember well the names of these shameless vilifiers in order that they may verify this forecast.

STATEMENT TO THE PRESS[147]

(December 30, 1934)

Sir:

I request you not to refuse publication of the following lines.

In the indictment connected with the assassination of Kirov, mention is to be found of my name. This circumstance has provided certain organs of the press with the pretext for speaking of my implication in the terrorist act at Smolny. One of the newspapers, which I see no need to name and characterize, asserts that my participation in the affair is "proved."

The truth is that even if every word of the indictment is taken at its face value it is only stated that a certain "consul" proposed to Nikolaev to transmit a letter to Trotsky. Testimony of such exceptional importance was only given by Nikolaev twenty days after his arrest. The indictment makes absolutely no mention of how Nikolaev reacted to the unknown consul's initiative and whether the letter was written and transmitted. One would indeed think that if, in the material of the preliminary investigation, there had been found something worthwhile, if not for juridical attention, then at least for propaganda purposes, the indictment would not have been silent about it.

As to what concerns me, I can only add:

1. In the circle of my acquaintances, the only consuls I know are those who refused me visas.

2. If the mysterious consul in Leningrad knows my address, he has completely forgotten to let me have his.

It is hardly necessary, after what has been said, to stress the fact that during nearly forty years of my revolutionary activity I have always, as a Marxist, opposed, from the point of view of the interests of the workers' movement, any recourse to individual terrorism — against czarism as well as against the workers' state. Dozens of my articles, published in different languages, are devoted to implacable criticism of individual terrorism. I see no reason to change this opinion today.

Within the limits of this brief letter, for which I ask your hospitality, I cannot dwell either upon an analysis of the political conditions that led to the appearance of Nikolaev's terrorist group or upon bringing to light the purpose of the attempt to mix my name into this mad and criminal act. To these questions I am devoting a special pamphlet, which will appear in the next few days.

L. Trotsky

SOME RESULTS OF THE STALIN AMALGAM[148]

(January 12, 1935)

Conditions now permit us to elucidate briefly the latest episodes of the investigation relating to the assassination of Kirov
as well as the amalgams (or more exactly, series of amalgams)
interwoven with this affair.

1. The mysterious consul has now turned out to be a Latvian
consul; our supposition that a petty consul of a tiny nation
would be chosen for the amalgam has been fully confirmed.
However, it became necessary to name the consul—obviously
because of diplomatic pressure—and this necessity threatened
to blast the amalgam, for who would believe that a consul of
Latvia is the organizer of world intervention against the USSR?
A new version had to be found; the Latvian consul was, as a
matter of fact, the agent of Hitler. Quite possible. But how
then to connect Trotsky with Hitler? Stalin did not even attempt to provide an explanation. He left his hirelings abroad
to extricate themselves as best they could. But the hirelings are
incapable of giving more than nature has endowed them with.

2. The Zinoviev group was arrested in connection with the
Kirov assassination. Yet the indictment does not so much as
let out a peep concerning a single one of the Zinovievists arrested in Moscow. But why then are they arrested? The foreign
lackeys now besmirch Zinoviev with mud as shamelessly as
in 1923-25 they crawled on their bellies before him.

3. What charge, *politically*, may be brought against Zinoviev, Kamenev and their friends? Their capitulation. By this
act of political cowardice, they drove the revolutionary youth
into a blind alley. The youth has been left without perspectives. At the same time, under the ponderous lid of bureaucratism, the youth is not permitted to think, live or breathe.
Under precisely such conditions are terrorist moods bred. Only
the growth of genuine Bolshevism on a world scale can instill
new hopes into the Soviet revolutionary youth and safeguard
it from taking the road of despair and adventurism.

4. The gap between the terrorist group and Zinoviev and his friends was to be bridged by the "platform of the Left Opposition" of the year 1926.[149] Citing one of the accused, who obviously mouths the formula of the GPU examining magistrate, the indictment proclaims the "ideological" succession from the "new opposition" of 1926 (the Zinoviev faction) to the Nikolaev group. But how to link this up with the consul's intervention and the terrorist act?

The "platform" of 1926 has been published in every language. The attitude towards the USSR was there set forth with exhaustive clarity. The lackeys, it is true, do not have to bother pondering over this. But class-conscious workers, even at this date, can profit much by acquainting themselves with the 1926 document. Upon acquainting themselves with it, they will draw the specific conclusion that while the bureaucracy did appropriate the most progressive measures from the program it had vilified, the Leningrad terrorists could never derive from this Marxist document any justification for senseless adventurism.

5. There is a specific historical stench to this attempt at connecting the Left Opposition with the idea of intervention. In 1917, Miliukov, Kerensky[150] and Co. accused Lenin, Trotsky and other Bolsheviks of being agents of the German general staff and of serving the interventionist plans of the Hohenzollern. In its time, this moronic calumny made a tour of the entire world. Stalin has been unable to think up a single new word. He slavishly repeats the hoary calumny about the leaders of Bolshevism. He is only the pupil of Miliukov and Kerensky.

6. When, in March 1917, I was arrested by the British naval authorities and incarcerated in a concentration camp in Canada, Lenin wrote in *Pravda* (No. 34, April 1917): "Can one for a moment believe in the veracity of the dispatch that the British government has received, which purports that Trotsky, the former chairman of the Petersburg Soviet of Workers' Deputies in 1905, a revolutionist who has unselfishly devoted himself for decades to the service of the revolution — that this man is involved in a plan subsidized by the German government? This is indeed a deliberate and unheard-of and unconscionable vilification of a revolutionist!"

These words were written before I joined with Lenin, prior to my election as chairman of the Bolshevik Soviet in 1917, prior to the October Revolution, the civil war, the creation of the Third International and the founding of the Soviet state. Today, after a lapse of eighteen years, not agents of British counterespionage but rather Stalinists are repeating this very same "deliberate and unheard-of and unconscionable vilification

of a revolutionist"! This simple juxtaposition reveals best of
all the poison of lies, vilification and fraud that the Stalinist
bureaucracy is pouring into the world working-class movement!

7. The fourteen who were accused in connection with the
Kirov assassination were all shot. Did they all participate in
the terrorist act? The indictment answers this question in the
affirmative, but it does not adduce even the semblance of proof.
We do not believe the indictment. We have seen with what
brazen and cowardly tendentiousness it has injected the name
of Trotsky into its text and how deliberately it passes in silence
over what happened to the consul's provocation regarding
the "letter."

It is much easier to implicate in the affair a dozen or so
Leningrad YCLers[151] than to implicate Trotsky. Who are
these YCLers? We do not know. There is not much difficulty
in executing unknown YCLers. Among the number there must
have also been GPU agents, the very ones who had arranged
to bring Nikolaev together with the "consul" and who had
prepared the amalgam, but who, at the last moment, proved
negligent and allowed Nikolaev to fire the fatal shot. The
physical elimination of these agents became necessary in order
to remove embarrassing participants in and witnesses of the
amalgam. But among those shot there may also have been
YCLers who were simply critically minded. The task of the
amalgam was to terrorize completely the youth, which was
thirsting for independence, by showing it that the slightest
doubt about the divine blessings that flow from Stalin or about
the immaculate conception of Kaganovich[152] would meet,
hereafter, with the same penalty as terrorist acts.

8. The foreign agents of the GPU, who pass themselves off
as friends of the USSR and who compromise the real friends
of the USSR, accuse everyone who has a critical attitude towards the repressions that have taken place of being in sympathy with (!) the terrorists. A revolutionist can feel nothing
but contempt for these toadying methods. It is indubitable that
the enemies and stealthy opponents of the October Revolution
utilize to the utmost, for their own aims, the confused and
contradictory statements as well as the summary measures of
repression. But this circumstance should not at all impel us to
blind ourselves to the dual role of the Soviet bureaucracy,
which, on the one hand, guards (in its own fashion) the conquests of the October Revolution against the class enemies and
which, on the other hand, tigerishly defends its own economic
and political privileges against criticisms and protests by the
advanced workers.

As a tool of the bureaucracy, the GPU directs the weapon

of terror both against the counterrevolutionists who threaten the workers' state and against the YCLers who are dissatisfied with the absolutism of the uncontrolled bureaucracy. Identifying itself with the workers' state — in accordance with the ancient formula, "I am the state!" — the bureaucratic upper crust portrays the terror against the party and the YCL as terror against the counterrevolution. This is the very goal that the venomous amalgams are intended to achieve.

9. What is here involved is not so much the struggle of the Soviet bureaucracy against Trotsky and the "Trotskyists" but the question of the moral atmosphere of the world working-class movement. The vile amalgam constructed around the "consul," who apparently was in the simultaneous employ of three governments, stands today as one of a number of ordinary and normal measures utilized by the Stalinist bureaucracy in the struggle for its caste positions. In 1921, warning his most intimate comrades against electing Stalin as general secretary, Lenin said, "This cook will prepare only peppery dishes." At that time there could, of course, be no reference as yet to the poisoned dishes of the amalgams. To whom are they being offered today? To the workers. The Stalinists are systematically poisoning the world proletarian vanguard with lies. Can the interests of the workers' state possibly demand this? Never! But this is demanded by the rapacious interests of the uncontrolled bureaucracy, which seeks to guard at all costs its prestige, its power and its privileges, by means of terror against everyone in the ranks of the proletariat who thinks and criticizes.

10. However passionate may be one's devotion to the Soviet Union, it must not be blind, or else it is worthless. The development of the workers' state proceeds through contradictions, internal and external. The forms and the methods of the workers' state have already changed several times, and they will continue to change in the future. The bureaucratic stage, for which there were objective causes, is exhausted.

The absolutism of the bureaucracy has become the greatest brake upon the further cultural and economic growth of the Soviets. The lackeys of the bureaucracy who deify its regime play a reactionary role. The Marxist revolutionists set as their task the freeing of the world proletarian vanguard from the fatal influence of the uncontrolled bureaucratic clique, in order subsequently to aid the workers in the USSR to regenerate the party and the soviets, not by means of terrorist adventures that are doomed beforehand, but by means of the class-conscious mass movement against bureaucratic absolutism.

THE CASE OF ZINOVIEV, KAMENEV AND OTHERS[153]

(January 16-18, 1935)

January 16, 8 P.M.

I have just learned the news over the radio that Zinoviev and Kamenev have been brought before a military tribunal "in connection with the case of the Kirov assassination." With that, the amalgam enters a new phase.

Let us recall the most important stages: Zinoviev, Kamenev and their Moscow friends had been arrested "in connection" with the Kirov assassination. During the preliminary investigation, however, an unexpected snag occurs.

The Central Executive Committee is compelled to extend the time allotted to the preliminary investigation by setting aside the law recently promulgated. Nevertheless, it emerges that sufficient facts are still lacking to have Zinoviev and the others brought to trial. Why were they arrested? The conclusion is clear: they were arrested *not for some reason* but *for some purpose.*

They were arrested with a view to an amalgam, that is to say, in order to establish a connection between the terrorist assassination and the Opposition, *all* opposition, all criticism in general, past, present or future. It was decided to arrest them when everything seemed to have been already settled. The GPU was conversant with the preparations for the Leningrad terrorist act. The "consul" had carried out the task assigned to him; he was the link in the amalgam. The real terrorist, Nikolaev, however, it appears, at the last moment — for conspiratorial reasons — detached himself from his own group, including the agents of the GPU who were playing a part in it. The fatal shot rang out. It wasn't in Stalin's program. But that was the risk in the enterprise. Kirov fell victim. The GPU agents paid for it: the higher officials were dismissed, the lower ones were shot together with the terrorists. The unexpected shot brought confusion into the amalgam.

The "consul" and his masters had no time to prepare anything. It was necessary to leave out from the trial the case of Zinoviev, Kamenev and their friends. The indictment in the Nikolaev case said not one word about them; the government communique said they would be subjected by the administration to deportation. For what reason? It is not known! The fourteen Leningrad accused were tried; all were shot. It appeared that the case was closed. But it could appear so only to those who had forgotten the main aim of the whole business: *the amalgam.*

"Hindsight prophecy," an opponent might say.

Fortunately, I am able to cite a whole series of documents, some of which have been published.

Shortly after my arrival in Turkey, on March 4, 1929, in very concrete fashion, I explained in the Russian *Biulletin Oppozitsii* the aims Stalin pursued in having me expelled. Showing the continuing vitality of the Opposition's ideas in the party, I wrote: "There remains only one thing for Stalin: to try to draw a line of blood between the official party and the Opposition. He absolutely must *connect the Opposition with terrorist crimes, preparation of armed insurrection, etc.* . . . (emphasis in the *Biulletin*).

"But precisely on that road," I continued, "stands the leadership of the Opposition. As has been shown by the shameful incident of 'the Wrangel officer' whom Stalin tried to plant on the Opposition in the autumn of 1927, it was sufficient for one of the Opposition to make a statement for Stalin's trick to rebound on his own head.

"Hence Stalin's plan [was] . . . to exile on this pretext the Opposition [still other expulsions were considered at the time — L. T.] and thereby free his own hands for criminal work against young and rank-and-file Oppositionists whose names are still not known to the masses, especially abroad. . . .

"That is why after the exile of the leaders of the Opposition we must expect with certainty an attempt by the Stalin clique in one way or another to provoke one or another so-called oppositional group to an adventure, in the case of failure, to fabricate or plant on the Opposition 'a terrorist act' or 'a military plot.' . . ."

These lines written, as has been said, on March 4, 1929, were published in the Russian *Biulletin Oppozitsii*, Number 1-2, July 1929 (p. 2). And barely a few months later, Stalin had Blumkin shot for having had an interview with me in Constantinople and for having carried a letter from me to comrades in Moscow. This letter, strictly principled in character, was of so little use for an amalgam that it has not even been used in the Soviet press, which, moreover, has likewise said not a word about Blumkin's execution.

On January 4, 1930, I wrote about this:

"Blumkin was shot — by decision of the GPU. This could have happened only because *the GPU has become Stalin's personal instrument.* During the years of the civil war, the Cheka[154] carried out grim work. But this was done under the control of the party. . . . Now the party is strangled. . . . In the GPU the chief role is taken by Yagoda, a despicable careerist who has tied his fortune to Stalin's and who is ready to perform anything he is told to do, without thinking and without questions. . . . Bukharin[155] has already stated that Stalin holds the members of the so-called Political Bureau in his hands by means of documents collected by the GPU. Under these conditions, the shooting of Blumkin was Stalin's personal affair" (*Biulletin,* No. 9, February-March 1930, p. 8).

The article quoted shows, for the first time, the new, extremely important factor which drives Stalin along the road of bloody amalgams. "By shooting Blumkin, Stalin wishes to signify to the *International* Opposition of Bolshevik-Leninists that he has inside the country hundreds and thousands of hostages who will pay with their heads for the successes of genuine Bolshevism in the world arena" (Ibid.).

The Moscow correspondent of the *Biulletin* communicated (on p. 10) that a proposal was made to the imprisoned Blumkin that he could save his head by his participation, as a provocateur, in an amalgam against the Opposition; Blumkin's refusal was his death sentence.

That is how we warned our friends beforehand, six years ago, of the inevitability of "attempts by the Stalin clique to draw one way or another into an adventure some or other so-called oppositionist group and, in the event of failure, to fabricate or attribute to the Opposition 'a terrorist act.' . . ." For six years, despite all the efforts of the GPU, these attempts have brought no results. Meantime, the regimes of the party and the soviets have gradually worsened. Among the new generation, feelings of despair have been compressed to the point of explosion into a terrorist adventure. Under these conditions, could not Stalin have seized on the Kirov assassination to carry out through the amalgam the idea which he has cherished for so long?

January 17

The morning newspaper dispatches have brought some explanations: the declarations of the accused Bakaev, in connection with other matters, have made it possible, according to the official communique, "to establish the participation of Zinoviev, Yevdokimov, Kamenev and Feodorov,[156] members of the Moscow Center, in counterrevolutionary activity." Nineteen people, the four named among them, have been brought to court before a military tribunal. In the communique, as transmitted by the French press, the Kirov case is not even mentioned. It speaks of "counterrevolutionary activity" in general. What that means we know very well; everything that is not in accord with the interests, ideas, zigzags and prejudices of the head of the bureaucracy is taxed with counterrevolution. So, it follows from the communique that when Zinoviev, Kamenev and their friends were arrested, there were no facts as to either their participation in Kirov's murder — these facts evidently don't exist now either — or their participation in some kind of oppositional grouping. Only now, on the basis of Bakaev's declarations, about which we know nothing (he must have been threatened for this purpose with seeing himself brought to trial for the Nikolaev affair, that is to say, threatened with being shot), only now have they managed, it appears, to *prove* the participation of Zinoviev and the others in "counterrevolutionary activity." How that expressed itself we shall certainly not know. What is most probable is that in a closed circle they complained about Stalin, recalled Lenin's "Testament," listened to the rumors circulating in the bureaucracy and dreamed of a "genuine" party congress that would remove Stalin. Very likely there was nothing more serious. But they in themselves represented this danger — that they could become an axis for the lower and middle bureaucracy, which is discontented with Stalin. Now, in this sphere, the chief does not joke.

But in spite of everything, it is not understandable, at first sight, why a military tribunal was necessary this time. Even for the most corrupt of Stalin's international lackeys, it will not be easy to explain to workers why and wherefore, that is to say, for precisely what "counterrevolutionary activity," there have been brought before a military tribunal nineteen Old Bolsheviks who, for the most part, have been in the party since its inception. Stalin cannot be unaware that he is pulling too hard on the rope. Is it possible that there has been no purpose, that it is a kind of blind vengeance? No, we don't think so.

The Moscow correspondent of *Le Temps* emphasizes that despite the whole campaign of accusations and incitements, "Zinoviev and Kamenev are not yet excluded from the party." The newspapers were still talking of their deportation. Suddenly, yesterday, the papers announced that they are to be brought

before a military tribunal. It would seem that Zinoviev and
Kamenev have been made to undergo the torture of the unknown: "We can leave you in the party, but we can also shoot
you." It seems Stalin wants to get something from Zinoviev
and Kamenev, which is why he is playing on their nerves
that are not very strong. What can he want? Probably some
"suitable," "necessary," or "useful" declarations. Zinoviev, Kamenev and their friends, held under threat of execution, have
to help Stalin repair and perfect the amalgam that a too-hesi-
tant consul has cruelly compromised. I can find no other explanation for the military tribunal.

In 1928, when I was in Central Asia, the GPU arrested my
closest collaborator, G. V. Butov, director of Military and Ma-
rine Supply Commissariats, and enjoined him to furnish proofs
of my "counterrevolutionary" preparations. Butov answered
with a hunger strike in the GPU prison; the strike went on for
fifty days and ended with his death. With pistol threatening,
they demanded from Blumkin that he give himself over to
provocation; he refused; they pulled the trigger. From Bakaev
and others they demanded testimonies against Zinoviev and
Kamenev. If we are to believe the official communique, they
got such testimonies.* Why then not admit they demanded,
likewise, testimonies from Zinoviev, Kamenev and the others
by threatening them with a military trial and, not getting them,
they passed the case over to the military tribunal?

                                                    January 18
L'Humanite of January 17 has given extracts from the indictment of Zinoviev and the others. If that is an "indictment,"
it is of the Stalin regime.

Let me present the chief deductions on the basis of the Stalin
communiques:

1. The Moscow group of the accused had no connection with
the terrorist act in Leningrad. Stalin is charging Zinoviev,
former leader of the *former* Leningrad Opposition, with *political* responsibility for terrorist tendencies. But these tendencies originated inside the Bolshevik Party. The leadership of
the party is responsible for them. In that sense, it is absolutely correct to say: Stalin and his regime are politically responsible for the Kirov assassination.

2. The chief witness for the prosecution, Safarov,[157] whose

---

* Very probably in denying the charges against him, Bakaev declared, "Yes, we met; we criticized the Central Committee, but there
was no question of terror." The words, "We met; we criticized the
Central Committee" would thus be made the basis of the accusation.
Obviously, this is only a hypothesis on our part.

case—we don't know why—was examined separately (the role of this individual in the affair appears most enigmatic), shows that the "counterrevolutionary" activity of Zinoviev, Kamenev and the others was particularly intense in 1932! Yet it was precisely for this activity that in 1932 they were expelled from the party and deported. This happened at the time when the excessive collectivization, following the overlong friendship with the kulaks [rich peasants], had caused immense sacrifices and had literally gambled with the fate of the Soviet regime. Everything was boiling up in the country, and the entire bureaucracy, perplexed and terrified, was muttering. What did the Central Control Commission charge Zinoviev and Kamenev with in 1932? With having had relations with the Right Oppositionists (Riutin[158] and others). Here is the literal text of the indictment: "Knowing that counterrevolutionary documents were being disseminated, they preferred to discuss (!) these (?) documents and, instead of unmasking immediately (!) this agency of the kulak, thus show themselves to be direct accomplices of the counterrevolutionary, antiparty group." Consequently, Zinoviev and Kamenev were accused of having "discussed" the platform of the Right before denouncing it. For this reason they were expelled.

But thereafter they recanted (and how!) and were readmitted into the party. What does their most recent counterrevolutionary activity consist of? On this subject we learn not a word. The indictment speaks of the hostility of the Zinoviev group to the leaders, of the political directives they gave (which? when? and to whom?) and so on, but it carefully avoids clarification, facts and dates. It emerges clearly that we are dealing with the same year, 1932. And the accused Safarov, who preferred to change over into a witness for the prosecution, confesses that after the debacle of the Riutin group, Zinoviev's "counterrevolution" assumed a "groveling" character, in other words, it disappeared from the scene.

3. It is true, the "indictment" says, that Kuklin, Guertik, Yevdokimov and Sharov,[159] who maintained relations with the Leningrad counterrevolutionary group, "scorned no means in their struggle against the Soviet power." Unfortunately, not one of these means is mentioned! Similarly, it is not shown when these relations were maintained. From all the evidence, it was in 1932! The indictment does not mention by a single word the connection of the accused with Nikolaev. The only political conclusion that can be drawn from the indictment's cheating is the following: the second capitulation by Zinoviev and Kamenev left the Zinovievist youth without a leadership and without perspectives; life in the party was becoming increasingly stifling. The Communist International was piling

up crimes and defeats. To examine them or openly ask for an
explanation was equivalent to being immediately arrested. In
this atmosphere, the most extreme, most excited (and incited by
GPU agents) conceived this senseless idea of assassinating
Kirov.

4. The indictment in the Nikolaev case tried, as we recall,
to connect the terrorists with the "platform" of the 1926 Opposition. Against that, the indictment openly admits that the
Zinoviev group "had no definite program." It couldn't be otherwise. The Zinoviev group had disavowed the platform of 1926;
what is more—and this is more important—the 1926 platform gives no answer to the questions of our epoch. Thus
the last "ideological" thread connecting the Leningrad group
with the former Left Opposition is broken.

5. But, someone will say, didn't Zinoviev and Kamenev
themselves "confess" their fault? Precisely here is contained the
most dishonorable part of the trial. According to the basis
of the accusations, Zinoviev and Kamenev had confessed nothing, could not confess to anything at all since there was no
material element of a crime. But, under the hatchet of the military tribunal, they agreed to assume "political" responsibility
so as to escape execution for a terrorist act. Zinoviev testifies
to nothing, tells nothing; he only argues placidly on the theme
that the "earlier activity" of "the *former* Opposition"—by the very
force of *"the objective course of events"*—"could not but contribute . . . to degeneration into crime." Zinoviev agrees to
recognize not the juridical amalgam of the Stalin press but the
"philosophical" amalgam: if opposition and criticism did not
exist, there would be no harmful straying; the young people
would be obedient; and terrorist acts would be impossible.
That is the meaning of Zinoviev's declarations in reply to the
indictment.

What is particularly remarkable is Kamenev's recantation:
"He confirmed that before 1932 he participated in illegal counterrevolutionary activity and was a member of the 'Moscow
Center' and that, right up to the last moment, he had not
stopped having relations with Zinoviev!" Nothing more!!!
However, what we are dealing with is not the oppositional
criticism of 1932, for which Kamenev had been expelled, but
the assassination of 1934. Of course, of course; but Kamenev
"had not stopped having relations with Zinoviev" (after their
joint recantation!) and though Zinoviev had stopped "counterrevolutionary activity" it was from the circle of his adherents that there emerged by *"the objective course of events"* (that
is to say, completely without the will of Zinoviev) the terrorist
Nikolaev.

The meaning of this repugnant, deliberately conceived confusion is absolutely clear. Stalin put an ultimatum to Zinoviev and Kamenev: they must themselves supply him with such a formula as would justify repression against themselves; then he would clear them of the organization of the Kirov assassination. Zinoviev's formula must have passed back and forward a dozen times from the prison to Stalin's desk until, after the necessary corrections, it could be found acceptable. Thereafter the military tribunal came on the scene. That is how Stalin, by the threat of still greater repression, extorts confessions that justify lesser repression.

6. Did Stalin try to complete the consul's work by means of the military tribunal in order to extract declarations against Trotsky? I don't doubt it. In any case, he didn't succeed. The constant principle of the Bolshevik-Leninist faction is: break irreconcilably with capitulators. We do not allow double book-keeping — not out of loyalty to the disloyal bureaucracy but out of loyalty to the masses. Since the usurping and thoroughly conservative bureaucracy has stifled any movement of thought in the party, revolutionary Marxists can act in no other way but secretly. That is their right; that is their duty. But they must never renounce their ideas and spit on the flag as do the capitulators. We broke in the past with the Zinovievists as resolutely as last year we broke with Rakovsky. This complete rupture in personal and political relations has made impossible — despite the help of a consul and a military tribunal — future success in developing amalgams from the side of the Bolshevik-Leninists.

7. However, it would be criminal light-mindedness to think that Stalin has given up trying to frame us up in some new "case" cooked up by the GPU and its foreign agents. Stalin has no other method of struggle against us. The Zinoviev case has, besides its own significance, the importance of a warning. The struggle for the cleansing of the atmosphere of the world workers' movement demands a clear understanding of the mechanics of the Stalin amalgams.

EVERYTHING GRADUALLY
FALLS INTO PLACE[160]

(January 26, 1935)

I am very grateful to you, dear friends, for the request you sent me in December; it spurred me to give my evaluation of the Kirov affair at its most important stages. Every reader of good faith now has the possibility of comparing our a priori considerations and hypotheses with the official admissions made subsequently, and of drawing the necessary conclusions.

On December 30, 1934, I expressed the firm conviction that the GPU from the outset knew about the terrorist act that was being prepared. The participation of the "consul," who could only be an agent of the GPU, was the irrefutable evidence. Now we have the proof. On January 23, a military tribunal condemned twelve responsible representatives of the GPU in Leningrad, with, at their head, their chief, Medved, to hard labor: two to ten years' imprisonment! The sentence on them was for the charge that — no more, no less — *"they were aware of the attempt being prepared against Kirov* but showed criminal negligence (!) in not taking the necessary security measures." The admission of the real participation by the GPU in the crime is masked by a miserable phrase about "negligence." Can one admit for a single moment that such pillars of the GPU as Medved could show negligence when dealing with the preparation, known to them beforehand, of the assassination of Kirov? No, "negligence" doesn't come into it here. *Excessive zeal, taking a chance with Kirov's life,* that is the explanation that fits better the basis of the affair.

When the preparation of the terrorist act that the GPU knew about had begun, the task of Medved and his colleagues was not at all to stop the conspirators — that would have been all too easy; what they had to do was find a suitable consul, put him in touch with Nikolaev, inspire Nikolaev with confidence in the consul and so on; at the same time, they had to establish a connection between the Zinoviev-Kamenev group and the Leningrad terrorists. That was not easy. It needed time. And Nikolaev refused to wait. The difference in rhythms between Medved's work and Nikolaev's finished up in a bloody outcome, precisely!

The verdict of the tribunal states openly that Medved, Zaporozhets and the others "did not take measures to bring to light and to end" the activity of the terrorist group *"although they had every possibility of doing so."* It is impossible to be more explicit. They could have forestalled the attack, but didn't. Why? From negligence, the tribunal answers. Who will believe it? Medved and the others couldn't take steps to cut short the preparation of the assassination because they hadn't yet wound up a delicate affair entrusted to them; they hadn't yet any little note from Zinoviev that they could use (it is not for nothing that the first government communique complained of the lack of proofs regarding the Zinoviev-Kamenev group); they hadn't yet found the necessary agents linking Leningrad and Moscow; they hadn't yet been able to extort from Nikolaev a letter for Trotsky. In a word, what was most important was not yet ready. And Nikolaev didn't want any further postponement.

Medved "knew," the verdict tells us. We don't doubt it. From whom did he know? From his own agents participating in the preparation of the attack and who were keeping an eye, at the same time, on Nikolaev. What happened to these agents? At Medved's trial not a word about them. It's not surprising! This affair was settled with the Nikolaev affair; without a doubt GPU agents were among the fourteen conspirators shot. Some paid for the assassination of Kirov, others for the failure of their mission.

It is altogether clear, however, that Medved could not have taken all this gamble at his own risk and peril. The participation of a foreign consul in the assassination of Kirov could not have remained a secret to Medved alone. For an affair of such extraordinary importance, Medved could not but refer daily by telephone to Yagoda, and Yagoda to Stalin. We are dealing with the heads of people known throughout the world. Moreover, even in the case of the most "fortunate" outcome, the amalgam with the consul threatened diplomatic complications. *Without the direct agreement of Stalin* — more precisely, without his initiative — *neither Yagoda nor Medved would have decided to mount such a risky enterprise.*

No one, we hope, will now object to us, "But, look, Medved himself recognized the accusation as just." To be sure! What else was left him? The accused chose the lesser of two evils. They couldn't, in fact, say that they had participated in a

criminal provocation with the aim of an amalgam, directly
instructed by Yagoda; such a confession would have cost them
their heads. They preferred to be accused of "criminal negligence." It was more prudent. Besides, in a few months, they
could be needed again!

Everything gradually falls into place. The Medved affair
throws a gleam of light on the Zinoviev-Kamenev affair—on
its place in Stalin's strategy. Let us imagine for a moment that
before the people of the USSR and of the whole world there had
been only two trials: that of Nikolaev and that of Medved. The
unfinished amalgam would have come out into the light in all
its nakedness. Nikolaev with his revolver in Kirov's office; the
consul begging the day before for a letter from Nikolaev to
Trotsky; then Medved, who knew all about it beforehand but
hadn't taken the necessary measures. Everything is too clear;
the provocation breaks through brazenly. That is precisely why
it was impossible to mount the Nikolaev trial and the Medved
trial one after the other. It was necessary in the interval to
deafen the country with some sensational affair that would
push into the shadows Nikolaev and Medved, unknown by
everyone. The trials of the real participants in the assassination—Nikolaev and Medved—had to be separated by the trial
of the old revolutionaries, the companions of Lenin, the build-
ers of the party, accused of a crime with which—unlike Stalin
who criminally played with fire—they had absolutely nothing
to do. The Zinoviev affair is a gigantic smoke screen over
the Stalin-Yagoda affair.

The first government communique and official articles after
the arrest of the Moscow group of Old Bolsheviks said that
Zinoviev-Kamenev and their friends had taken as their aim
"the restoration of the capitalist system" and they were trying
to provoke "armed intervention" from abroad (by the inter-
mediacy of a consul—from Latvia!). No serious person could
believe it; that is understood.

Stalin's lackeys, who cover themselves with the name of
"leaders" of the Communist International, don't, however, recoil
at the assertion that Zinoviev, Kamenev and the others "have
themselves admitted their crimes."

Which ones? Preparation of the restoration of capitalism?
Preparation of armed intervention? Preparation of the assassination of Kirov and Stalin? No, not that at all. Under the
pistol they admitted: (1) they had a very critical attitude towards the methods of collectivization; (2) they had had no
sympathy for Stalin-Kaganovich; (3) they had not concealed

their thoughts and feelings from their close friends. Nothing more! All that was in 1932. For these grave crimes, especially for their lack of love for Stalin, they were in the past expelled from the party. But subsequently they recanted and were re-admitted into the party. So what crime is imputed to them since that recantation? From the mishmash of hollow and insulting lackey phrases, we can draw the only indication that is con-crete: in December 1934, Zinoviev said to his friends that the policy of the united front had not been conducted by the Com-munist International in the correct fashion, that in fact the ini-tiative had passed into the hands of the Social Democrats.

The very fact that this kind of critical appraisal of the latest policy of Stalin-Bela Kun[161] was brought before the tribunal as a criminal act and was officially quoted as proof of *counter-revolutionary* conspiracy shows to what vileness the party has been brought by the unbridled arbitrariness of the Thermi-dorean-Bonapartist bureaucracy!

Let us admit that Zinoviev's criticism was false. Let us even grant that the lackeys were right to judge criticism directed against them "criminal." But are we to see in that the "restora-tion of capitalism" and "armed intervention"? What connection is there between the demand for a more revolutionary policy against the bourgeoisie and a program for "the restoration of a bourgeois regime"? Where has common sense gone? It is completely buried beneath a monstrous defecation of infamy.

And what happened with the consul? That is a question to which we hear no answer. The consul from Latvia handed over 5,000 rubles for the organization of Kirov's assassination. This fact was officially established by the tribunal. And then? At the time of the verdict, the Latvian diplomat was on leave in Finland—not in the hated USSR, not in his native Latvia, but in "neutral" Finland. A consul with foresight who must have friends warning him! It is clear, in any case, it was not on his own initiative and at his own risk that the consul fi-nanced the assassination of Kirov. Such plans are beyond the scope of a petty functionary. If, as Stalin's lackeys would have us believe, the consul was not an agent of the GPU, he could have acted only by mandate of some foreign government, Latvian or German (as the Stalin press has suggested). Then why not bring to light the criminal band? For example, like the Yugoslavs, why not bring the question of diplomatic crim-inal terrorists before the League of Nations? The game is worth the candle, it would seem. However, Stalin has not shown the slightest interest in the terrorist diplomat and those who inspired him. Apropos the so-called recall of the consul, there hasn't been even a government communique. They simply moved on to the next business.

This enigma has another side: *Why is the consul himself silent?* He is now outside the USSR and can, it would appear, reveal the whole truth. If he financed the terrorists, that means he is a sworn enemy of the Soviets. Why then doesn't he make revelations about his enemies? Because the drilled consul knows very well the international proverb, "Revelations are silver, silence is golden."

Revolutionary terrorism does not need a mask because it finds its immediate justification in the consciousness of the popular masses. The need for amalgams emerges when a bureaucracy rises above the revolutionary class as a privileged caste, with its special interests, secrets and machinations. Fearing for its power and its privileges, the bureaucracy is compelled to deceive the people. The very need for recourse to amalgams pitilessly unmasks and condemns the bureaucratic regime.

As far as I can judge at a distance, as an isolated observer, the strategy developed around the corpse of Kirov has not brought Stalin any great laurels. But precisely for this reason he can neither stop nor retreat. *Stalin is forced to cover up the unsuccessful amalgams with new, broader . . . and more successful ones.* We must meet them well armed. The struggle against the ferocious repressions against the Marxist opposition in the USSR is inseparable from the struggle for the liberation of the world proletarian vanguard from the influence of Stalinist agents and Stalinist methods. Not one honest revolutionary proletarian ought to be silent. Of all political figures, the most despicable is Pontius Pilate.

WHERE IS THE STALIN BUREAUCRACY LEADING THE USSR?[162]

(January 30, 1935)

A new chapter is being opened in the history of the Soviet Union. To the majority, the shot that was fired at Kirov struck like thunder from a clear sky. Yet the sky was not at all clear. In Soviet economic life, despite its successes, to a large measure because of its successes, profound contradictions have accumulated that it is impossible not only to eliminate but even to mitigate by the sole means of issuing decrees and orders from above. At the same time, there has been an extreme sharpening of the contradiction between the bureaucratic methods of management and the needs of economic and cultural development as a whole. The unexpected terroristic act, and particularly the trials, the administrative reprisals and the new cleansing of the party that followed it, provided only an external and dramatic form to that general turn in Soviet policies that has been unfolding during the last year and a half. The general direction of this turn is to the *right, more to the right and still further to the right.*

The crushing of the German proletariat, which resulted from the fatal policies of the Communist International that supplemented the perfidious role of the Social Democracy, has led to the entry of the Soviet Union into the League of Nations. With its characteristic cynicism, the bureaucracy represented this action not as a forced retreat necessitated by the worsening of the international position of the Soviets but, on the contrary, as a supreme success. In Hitler's victory over the German proletariat, the Soviet workers and peasants are duty bound to see the victory of Stalin over the League of Nations. The essence of the turn is amply disclosed by the speeches, the votes at Geneva and the interviews by Litvinov: if Soviet diplomacy did score a victory over anything, it was, perhaps, only a victory over its last vestiges of restraint in the face of the public opinion of the proletariat. In international policies, all class and national-liberationist criteria have been entirely discarded. The sole, guiding principle is — the preservation of the status quo!

In harmony with this, the Communist International — without any discussion and without the promised congress, of course (after all, of what service are congresses in serious matters?) — has executed the most breakneck turnabout in its entire history. From the theory and practice of the "third period" and "social fascism," it has gone over to permanent coalitions not only with the Social Democracy but also with Radical Socialists, the main prop of the national government in France. The program of the struggle for power is today decreed to be counterrevolutionary provocation. The policies of the vassal "alliance" with the Kuomintang [163] (1925-27) are transferred without a hitch to the soil of Europe. The turn has the very same goal of — preserving the European status quo!

In the sphere of Soviet economic life, the turn is no less profound in its tendencies. The planned beginning has demonstrated what forces were latent in it. But, at the same time, it has also indicated the limits within which it can be applied. An a priori economic plan in general — all the more so, in a backward country with a population of 170 million and a profound contradiction between the city and the village — is not a military decree but a working hypothesis which must be painstakingly checked and recast in the process of fulfillment. Two levers must serve to regulate the plan, the financial and political levers: a stable monetary system and an active response on the part of the interested groups in the populace to the incompatibilities and gaps in the plan. But the political self-action on the part of the population has been stifled. And at the last party convention, Stalin proclaimed that the need for a stable currency was a "bourgeois superstition." This happy aphorism had to be revised together with another and no-less-famous one — about the "twins," fascism and Social Democracy.

How long ago was it that this very same Stalin promised to send the NEP, that is to say, the market, to "the devil"? How long ago was it that the entire press trumpeted that buying and selling were to be completely supplanted by "direct socialist distribution"? It was proclaimed that the consumers' card was the external symbol of this "distribution." According to this theory, the Soviet currency itself, by the close of the second five-year plan, was already to be transformed into mere consumers' tokens, like theater or streetcar tickets. Indeed, is there really room for money in a socialist society where no classes and no social contradictions exist and where products are distributed in accordance with a provided plan?

But all these promises grew dimmer as the second five-year

plan drew closer to its conclusion. Today the bureaucracy finds itself compelled to apply to "the devil" with a very humble request that the market given over to his safekeeping be returned. True, according to the blueprints, trading is to take place only through the organs of the state apparatus. The future will show to what extent it will be possible to adhere to this system. If the collective farm engages in trading, the collective farmer will also trade. It is not easy to fix the boundaries beyond which the trading collective farmer becomes transformed into a tradesman. The market has laws of its own.

The system of consumers' cards, beginning with bread cards, is being eliminated gradually. The relations between the city and the village are to be regulated in an increasing measure by monetary calculation. For this, a stable *chervonetz* [gold currency] is required. Colossal and not unsuccessful efforts are being made in the production of gold.

The translation of economic relations into the language of money is absolutely necessary at the given, initial stage of socialist development in order to have the basis for calculating the actual social usefulness and economic effectiveness of the labor energy expended by workers and peasants; only in this way is it possible to rationalize economic life by regulating the plans.

For the last few years we have dozens of times pointed out the need for a stable monetary unit, the purchasing power of which would not depend upon plans but which would be of assistance in checking them. The Soviet theoreticians saw in this proposal only our urge to "restore capitalism." Now they are compelled to reeducate themselves in a hurry. The ABC of Marxism has its superior points.

The transition to the system of monetary calculation implies inevitably and primarily the translation into the ringing language of gold of all the hidden and masked contradictions in the economic life. Someone, however, will have to pay for the accumulated miscalculations and disproportions. Will it be the bureaucracy? Of course not, for, indeed, the keeping of accounts and the treasury will remain in its hands. The peasantry? But the reform is taking place to a large measure under pressure of the peasantry and, at least during the period immediately ahead, it will prove most profitable for the top strata in the *village.* The workers are the ones who will have to pay; the mistakes of the bureaucracy will be corrected at the expense of the workers' vital needs. The repeal of the consumers' cards hits the workers directly and immediately, especially the lowest and most poorly paid sections, that is, the vast majority.

The primary aim of returning to the market and to the stable monetary system (the latter is still in project) consists in interesting the collective farmers directly in the results of their own labor and thus eliminating the most negative consequences of forced collectivization. This retreat is dictated unconditionally by the mistakes of preceding policies. We must not close our eyes, however, to the fact that the regeneration of market relations inevitably implies the strengthening of individualistic and centrifugal tendencies in rural economy and the growth of differentiation between the collective farms, as well as inside the collectives.

The political sections were instituted in the village, according to Stalin's report, as supraparty and suprasoviet militarized apparatuses to exercise ruthless control over the collective farms. The party press celebrated the political sections as the ripest product of the "Leader's genius mind." Today, after a year's labor, the political sections have been liquidated on the sly, almost without any obituaries; the bureaucracy is retreating before the *moujik* [peasant]; administrative pressure is being supplanted by a *"smychka"* [alliance] through the *chervonetz*; and because of this very fact, the forced leveling must give way to differentiation.

Thus, towards the conclusion of the second five-year plan, we have not the liquidation of the "last remnants" of class society, as the conceited and ignorant bureaucrats had promised, but, on the contrary, new processes of class stratification. The epic period of the *administrative* "liquidation of the kulak as a class" is followed by entry into the belt of *economic* concessions to the kulak tendencies of the "well-to-do collective farmer." In the very heat of 100 percent collectivization, the Bolshevik-Leninists forecast the inevitability of retreat. Zinoviev was sentenced to ten years of imprisonment for having dared to express doubts as to the possibility of realizing 100 percent collectivization (no other accusations are brought against him!). But what did experience prove? The retreat has begun. Where it will stop cannot be known as yet. Once again the Stalinist bureaucracy has shown that it is never able to foresee the day after tomorrow. Its shortsighted empiricism, the product of crushing all criticism and thought, plays dirty tricks upon its own self and, what is much worse, upon the country of socialist construction.

Even before the Neo-NEP, [164] which was unprovided for in any of the plans, has had a chance to manifest any economic results, it has called forth very acute political consequences. The turn to the *right* in foreign and domestic policies could not fail to arouse alarm among the more class-conscious ele-

ments of the proletariat. To alarm there was added dissatisfaction because of the considerable rise in the cost of living.
The mood of the peasantry remains unstable and tense. To
this must be added the dull rumbling among the youth, particularly among that section that, being close to the bureaucracy, observes its arbitrariness, its privileges and its abuses.
In this thick atmosphere, the shot of Nikolaev exploded.

The Stalinist press strives to deduce the terrorist act of 1934
from the Opposition platform of 1926. "Every opposition [we
are told] leads inevitably to counterrevolution." Should one
seek to locate here a political idea, it would turn out to be
approximately the following: although the platform as such
excludes the idea of individual terror, it, nevertheless, awakens
criticism and dissatisfaction; and since dissatisfaction can find
no normal outlet through party, soviet or trade-union channels,
it must, in the end, inevitably lead those who are unbalanced
to terroristic acts. There is a kernel of truth in such a supposition, only one must know how to husk it. As is well known,
criticism and dissatisfaction do not always lead to terroristic
attempts and to assassinations, which arise only under those
exceptional circumstances when the contradictions become
strained to the utmost, when the atmosphere is surcharged
electrically, when dissatisfaction is very widespread and when
the bureaucracy holds the advanced elements of the country
by the throat. In its aphorism: "every opposition leads inevitably to counterrevolution," the Stalinist press supplies the most
merciless and somber criticism possible of the Stalinist regime.
And this time it speaks the truth.

The bureaucracy's reply to the shot of Nikolaev was a ra-
bid attack against the left wing of the party and the working
class. It almost seems as if Stalin only awaited a pretext for
the onslaught upon Zinoviev, Kamenev and their friends. The
newspapers, just as in 1924-29, are waging an absolutely
inconceivable campaign against "Trotskyism." Enough to say
that Trotsky is now being depicted in *Pravda* as the planter
of "counterrevolutionary nests" within the Red Army during
the period of the civil war; and, of course, the salvaging of the
revolution from these "nests" is the heroic feat of Stalin. In
schools, universities, periodicals and commissariats are being
discovered ever new "Trotskyists," in many instances, back-
sliders. Arrests and exiles have once again assumed a mass
character. About 300,000 individuals, 15 to 20 percent, have
again been removed from the many-times-purged party. Does
this mean that the Bolshevik-Leninists have had such large
successes during the recent period? Such a conclusion would

be too premature. The dissatisfaction among workers has indubitably grown; there has also been a growth in sympathy toward the Left Opposition. But suspicion and fear of the bureaucracy have grown still greater. The bureaucracy is already incapable of assimilating even capitulators who are sincere. For its sharp turn to the right, it requires a massive amputation on the left. Nikolaev's shot served to provide the external justification for Stalin's political surgery.

Individual terror is adventuristic by its very essence; its political consequences cannot be foreseen, and they almost never serve its goals. What did Nikolaev want? This we do not know. Very likely he wished to protest against the party regime, the uncontrollability of the bureaucracy or the course to the right. But what were the results? The crushing of the lefts and semilefts by the bureaucracy, the intensification of the pressure and of uncontrollability, and a preventive terror against all those who might be dissatisfied with the turn to the right. In any case, the fact that Nikolaev's shot could have called forth such disproportionately great consequences is indubitable testimony that these "consequences" were already lodged in the political situation and were only awaiting a reason to break out into the open.

The bureaucracy is entering the period for checking the balance of the two five-year plans, and it hastens to insure itself beforehand. It is ready to make economic concessions to the peasantry, that is to say, to its petty-bourgeois interests and tendencies. But it does not want to make any concessions to the political interests of the proletarian vanguard. On the contrary, it begins its new turn towards the "well-to-do collective farmer" with a wild police raid against every living and thinking element in the working class and the student youth.

Today one can already forecast that, after the raid against the lefts, there will sooner or later follow a raid against the rights. Bureaucratic centrism, which has developed into the *Soviet form of Bonapartism,* would not be what it is, if it could maintain its equilibrium in any other manner save by continual attacks on "two fronts," i.e., in the last analysis, against proletarian internationalism and against the tendencies of capitalist restoration. The basic task of the bureaucracy is — to hold its own. The enemies and the opponents of the ruling clique, or merely those friends who are not quite reliable, are classified as left or right "agencies of the intervention," often depending only upon the technical conveniences of the amalgam. The expulsion of Smirnov, [165] the former people's commissar of agriculture, from the party is a subtle warning to the rights: "Don't bestir yourselves. Remember there is a tomorrow!" Today, at any rate, the blows are being directed entirely at the left.

The diplomatic retreat before the world bourgeoisie and before reformism; the economic retreat before the petty-bourgeois tendencies within the country; the political offensive against the vanguard of the proletariat—such is the tripartite formula of the new chapter in the development of Stalinist Bonapartism. With what does this chapter close? In any case, not with a classless society and the bureaucracy peacefully dissolving within it. On the contrary, the workers' state is again entering a period of open political crisis. What endows it with an unheard-of acuteness today is not the contradictions of the transitional economic system, however profound they may be in themselves, but the singular position of the bureaucracy that not only refuses but moreover can no longer make political concessions to the vanguard of the toilers. Having become itself the captive of the system it has erected, the Stalinist clique is now the main source of the political convulsions in the country.

How far-reaching will be the political, the Communist International and the economic turns to the right? To what new social consequences will they bring the USSR? Judgment on these questions can be passed only on the basis of carefully estimating all the stages of the development during the years immediately ahead. In any case, nothing can save the Comintern. Falling step by step, its completely demoralized bureaucracy literally betrays the most vital interests of the world proletariat in return for the favors of the Stalinist clique. But the state that was created by the October Revolution is virile. The years of forced industrialization and collectivization, under the lash and with all lights extinguished, have produced vast difficulties along with great successes. The present forced retreat secretes, as always, new difficulties, economic and political. It is possible, however, to state even at this moment with absolute certainty that the political crisis engendered by bureaucratic absolutism represents an immeasurably more immediate and acute danger to the Soviet Union than all the disproportions and contradictions of the transitional economy.

The bureaucracy not only has no desire to reform itself but also cannot reform itself. Only the vanguard of the proletariat could restore the Soviet state to health by ruthlessly cleansing the bureaucratic apparatus, beginning with the top. But in order to do so, it must set itself on its feet, close its ranks and reestablish or, more exactly, create anew the revolutionary party, the soviets and the trade unions. Has it sufficient forces to meet such a task?

The working class in the USSR has had an enormous numerical growth. Its productive role has grown even more immeasurably than its numbers. The social weight of the Soviet proletariat today is tremendous. Its political weakness is conditioned by the variegated nature of its social composition, the lack of revolutionary experience in the new generation, the decomposition of the party and the interminable and heavy defeats of the world proletariat.

At the given stage, the last reason is the decisive one. The absence of international perspectives constrains the Russian workers to enclose themselves within the national shell and to tolerate the theory of "socialism in one country," with the deification of the national bureaucracy flowing from this theory. In order to restore confidence in their own forces, the Soviet workers must once more regain faith in the forces of the world proletariat.

The struggle between the forces within the USSR as well as the zigzags of the Kremlin are, of course, of tremendous significance in respect to the hastening or, on the contrary, the retarding of consummation. But *the main key to the internal position of the Soviet Union is today already outside the Soviet Union.* Should the Western proletariat surrender the European continent to fascism, the isolated and profoundly degenerated workers' state will not maintain itself long, not, however, because it must inevitably fall under the blows of military intervention; under a different set of conditions Soviet intervention can lead, on the contrary, to the overturn of fascism. But right now the internal contradictions of the USSR have been brought to the point of extreme tension by the victories of the world counterrevolution. The further spread of fascism, by weakening still further the resisting force of the Soviet proletariat, would render impossible the supplanting of the degenerated Bonapartist system by a regenerated system of soviets. A political catastrophe would become inevitable, and in its wake would follow the restoration of private ownership of the means of production.

In the light of the present world situation, the theory of "socialism in one country," this gospel of the bureaucracy, stands before us in all its nationalistic limitation and its braggard falsity. We do not refer here, of course, to the purely abstract possibility or impossibility of building a socialist society within this or another geographic area — such a theme is for scholiasts; rather we have in mind the vastly more immediate and concrete, living and historical, not metaphysical, question: is it possible for an isolated Soviet state to maintain itself for an indeterminate period of time in an imperialist environment, within the constricting circle of fascist counterrevolutions? The answer of Marxism is No. The answer of the internal condition of the USSR is No. The imperialist pressure from without, the expenditure of forces and resources for defense, the impossibility of establishing correct economic ties — these obstacles by themselves are sufficiently profound and grave; but vastly more important than these is the fact that the defeats of the world revolution are inevitably disintegrating the living bearer of the Soviet system, the proletariat, compelling it to place its neck obediently under the yoke of the national bureaucracy, which, in turn, is being corroded by all the vices of Bonapartism. Outside of world revolution there is no salvation!

"Pessimism!" — the trained parrots of the so-called Comintern will say. And the hired charlatans, who have long since waved good-bye to revolution and Marxism will howl, "Defense of capitalism!" On our part, we really view with no "optimism" at all the Stalinist system of directing the workers' state, that is to say, of suppressing the workers' state. The collapse of this system is equally inevitable under all possible variations of the historical development. The Soviet bureaucracy, however, will fail to drag the workers' state down with itself into the abyss only in the event that the European and world proletariat takes to the road of offensive and victories. The first condition for success is the emancipation of the world vanguard from the deadly, numbing jaws of Stalinism. This task will be solved despite all the obstacles introduced by the powerful apparatus of lies and slanders. In the interests of the world proletariat and of the Soviet Union, onward!

THE WORKERS' STATE,
THERMIDOR AND BONAPARTISM[166]

(February 1, 1935)

The foreign policies of the Stalinist bureaucracy — within both its channels: the primary one of diplomacy and the subsidiary channel of the Comintern — have taken a sharp turn toward the League of Nations, toward the preservation of the status quo and toward alliances with reformists and bourgeois democracy. At the same time, the domestic policies have turned toward the market and the "well-to-do collective farmer." The latest drive against oppositionist and semioppositionist groups, as well as against isolated elements who are in the least critical, and the new mass purge of the party have as their object giving Stalin a free hand for the course to the right. Involved here is essentially the return to the old organic course[167] (staking all on the kulak, alliance with the Kuomintang, the Anglo-Russian Committee, etc.) but on a much larger scale and under immeasurably more onerous conditions. Where does this course lead? The word "Thermidor" is heard again on many lips. Unfortunately, this word has become worn from use; it has lost its concrete content and is obviously inadequate for the task of characterizing either that stage through which the Stalinist bureaucracy is passing or the catastrophe that it is preparing. We must, first of all, establish our terminology.

Controversies over "Thermidor" in the Past

The question of "Thermidor" is bound up closely with the history of the Left Opposition in the USSR. It would be no easy task today to establish who resorted first to the historical analogy of Thermidor. In any case, the positions on this issue in 1926 were approximately as follows: the group of "Democratic Centralism" (V. M. Smirnov, Sapronov and others who were hounded to death in exile by Stalin) declared, "Thermidor is an accomplished fact!" The adherents to the platform of

the Left Opposition, the Bolshevik-Leninists, categorically denied this assertion. And it was over this issue that a split occurred. Who has proved to be correct? To answer this question,
we must establish precisely what each group itself understood
"Thermidor" to mean; historical analogies allow of various
interpretations and may therefore be easily abused.

The late V. M. Smirnov—one of the finest representatives
of the Old Bolshevik school—held that the lag in industrialization, the growth of the kulak and of the Nepman (the new
bourgeois), the liaison between the latter and the bureaucracy
and, finally, the degeneration of the party had progressed so
far as to render impossible a return to the socialist road without a new revolution. The proletariat had already lost power.
With the crushing of the Left Opposition, the bureaucracy began
to express the interests of a regenerating bourgeois regime.
The fundamental conquests of the October Revolution had been
liquidated. Such was in its essentials the position of the group
of "Democratic Centralists."

The Left Opposition argued that although the elements of
dual power had indubitably begun to sprout within the country,
the transition from these elements to the hegemony of the bourgeoisie could not occur otherwise than by means of a counterrevolutionary overturn. The bureaucracy was already linked
to the Nepman and the kulak, but its main roots still extend
into the working class. In its struggle against the Left Opposition, the bureaucracy undoubtedly was dragging behind it
a heavy tail in the shape of Nepmen and kulaks. But on the
morrow this tail would strike a blow at the head, that is, at
the ruling bureaucracy. New splits within the bureaucratic
ranks were inevitable. Face to face with the direct danger of
a counterrevolutionary overturn, the basic core of the centrist
bureaucracy would lean upon the workers for support against
the growing rural bourgeoisie. The outcome of the conflict
was still far from having been decided. The burial of the October Revolution was premature. The crushing of the Left
Opposition facilitated the work of "Thermidor." But "Thermidor"
had not yet occurred.

We need only review accurately the *gist* of the controversies
of 1926-27 for the correctness of the position of the Bolshevik-
Leninists to emerge in all its obviousness, in the light of subsequent developments. As early as 1927, the kulaks struck a
blow at the bureaucracy, by refusing to supply it with bread,
which they had managed to concentrate in their hands. In
1928, an open split took place in the bureaucracy. The Right
was for further concessions to the kulak. The centrists, arming
themselves with the ideas of the Left Opposition whom they

had smashed conjointly with the Rights, found their support among the workers, routed the Rights and took to the road of industrialization and, subsequently, collectivization. The basic social conquests of the October Revolution were saved in the end at the cost of countless unnecessary sacrifices.

The prognosis of the Bolshevik-Leninists (more correctly, the "optimum variant" of their prognosis) was confirmed completely. Today there can be no controversy on this point. Development of the productive forces proceeded not by way of restoration of private property but on the basis of socialization, by way of planned management. The world-historical significance of this fact can remain hidden only to the politically blind.

The Real Meaning of Thermidor

Nevertheless, today we can and must admit that the analogy of Thermidor served to becloud rather than to clarify the question. Thermidor in 1794 produced a shift of power from certain groups in the Convention to other groups, from one section of the victorious "people" to other strata. Was Thermidor counterrevolutionary? The answer to this question depends upon how wide a significance we attach, in a given case, to the concept of "counterrevolution." The social overturn of 1789 to 1793 was bourgeois in character. In essence it reduced itself to the replacement of fixed feudal property by "free" bourgeois property. The counterrevolution "corresponding" to this revolution would have had to attain the reestablishment of feudal property. But Thermidor did not even make an attempt in this direction. Robespierre sought his support among the artisans, the Directory among the middle bourgeoisie. Bonaparte allied himself with the banks. All these shifts — which had, of course, not only a political but also a social significance — occurred, however, on the basis of the new bourgeois society and state.

Thermidor Was Reaction in Operation on the Social Foundation of the Revolution

Of the very same import was the Eighteenth Brumaire of Bonaparte, the next important stage on the road of reaction. In both instances, it was a question not of restoring either the old forms of property or the power of the former ruling estates but of dividing the gains of the new social regime among the different sections of the victorious "Third Estate." The bourgeoisie appropriated more and more property and power (either directly and immediately or through special agents like Bonaparte) but made no attempt whatever against the social conquests of the revolution; on the contrary, it solicitously sought to strengthen, organize and stabilize them. Napoleon guarded bourgeois property, including that of the peasant, against both the "rabble" and the claims of the expropriated proprietors. Feudal Europe hated Napoleon as the living embodiment of the revolution, and it was correct according to its standards.

The Marxist Evaluation of the USSR

There is no doubt that the USSR today bears very little resemblance to that type of Soviet republic that Lenin depicted in 1917 (no permanent bureaucracy or permanent army, the right of recalling all elected officials at any time and the active control over them by the masses "regardless of who the individual may be," etc.).[168] The domination of the bureaucracy over the country, as well as Stalin's domination over the bureaucracy, have well-nigh attained their absolute consummation. But what conclusions would follow from this? There are some who say that since the actual state that has emerged from the proletarian revolution does not correspond to ideal a priori norms, therefore they turn their backs on it. This is political snobbery, common to pacifist-democratic, libertarian, anarcho-syndicalist and, generally, ultraleft circles of petty-bourgeois intelligentsia. There are others who say that since this state has emerged from the proletarian revolution, therefore every criticism of it is sacrilege and counterrevolution. That is the voice of hypocrisy behind which lurk most often the immediate material interests of certain groups among this very same petty-bourgeois intelligentsia or among the workers' bureaucracy. These two types — the political snob and the political hypocrite — are readily interchangeable, depending upon personal circumstances. Let us pass them both by.

A Marxist would say that the present-day USSR obviously does not approximate the a priori norms of a Soviet state; let us discover, however, what we failed to foresee when working out the programmatic norms; let us, furthermore, analyze what social factors have distorted the workers' state; let us check once again if these distortions have extended to the economic foundations of the state, that is to say, if the basic social conquests of the proletarian revolution have been preserved; if these have been preserved, then let us find in what direction they are changing; and let us discover if there obtain in the USSR and on the world arena such factors as may facilitate and hasten the preponderance of progressive trends of development over those of reaction. Such an approach is complex. It brings with it no ready-made key for lazy minds, which the latter love so much. In return, however, it not only preserves one from the two plagues, snobbery and hypocrisy, but also presents the possibility of exerting an active influence upon the fate of the USSR.

When the group of "Democratic Centralism" declared in 1926 that the workers' state was liquidated, it was obviously burying the revolution while it was still alive. In contradistinction to this, the Left Opposition worked out a program of reforms for the Soviet regime. The Stalinist bureaucracy smashed the Left Opposition in order to safeguard and entrench itself as a privileged caste. But in the struggle for its own positions, it found itself compelled to take from the program of the Left Opposition all those measures that alone made it possible to save the social basis of the Soviet state. That is a priceless political lesson! It shows how specific historical conditions, the backwardness of the peasantry, the weariness of the proletariat, the lack of decisive support from the West, prepare for a "second chapter" in the revolution, which is characterized by the suppression of the proletarian vanguard and the smashing of revolutionary internationalists by the conservative national bureaucracy. But this very same example shows how a correct political line enables a Marxist grouping to fructify developments even when the victors of the "second chapter" run roughshod over the revolutionists of the "first chapter."

A superficial idealistic mode of thinking that operates with ready-made norms, mechanically fitting living processes of development to them, easily leads one from enthusiasm to prostration. Only dialectical materialism, which teaches us to view all existence in its process of development and in the conflict of internal forces, can impart the necessary stability to thought and action.

The Dictatorship of the Proletariat and the Dictatorship of the Bureaucracy

In a number of previous writings, we established the fact that despite its economic successes, which were determined by the nationalization of the means of production, *Soviet society* completely preserves a contradictory transitional character, and, measured by the inequality of living conditions and the privileges of the bureaucracy, it still stands much closer to the regime of capitalism than to future communism.

At the same time, we established the fact that despite monstrous bureaucratic degeneration, the *Soviet state* still remains the historical instrument of the working class insofar as it assures the development of economy and culture on the basis of nationalized means of production and, by virtue of this, prepares the conditions for a genuine emancipation of the toilers through the liquidation of the bureaucracy and of social inequality.

Whoever has not seriously pondered and accepted these two fundamental propositions, whoever in general has not studied the literature of the Bolshevik-Leninists on the question of the USSR from 1923 on runs the risk of losing the leading thread with every new event and of forsaking Marxist analysis for abject lamentations.

Soviet (it would be more correct to say, anti-Soviet) bureaucratism is the product of social contradictions between the city and the village, between the proletariat and the peasantry (these two kinds of contradictions are not identical), between the national republics and districts, between the different groups of peasantry, between the different layers of the working class, between the different groups of consumers and, finally, between the Soviet state as a whole and its capitalist environment. Today, when all relationships are being translated into the language of monetary calculation, the economic contradictions come to the forefront with exceptional sharpness.

Raising itself above the toiling masses, the bureaucracy regulates these contradictions. It uses this function in order to strengthen its own domination. By its uncontrolled and self-willed rule, subject to no appeal, the bureaucracy accumulates new contradictions. Exploiting the latter, it creates the regime of bureaucratic absolutism.

The contradictions within the bureaucracy itself have led to a system of handpicking the main commanding staff; the need for discipline within the select order has led to the rule of a single person and to the cult of the infallible leader. One and the same system prevails in factory, *kolkhoz,* university and the government: a leader stands at the head of his faithful troop; the rest follow the leader. Stalin never was and, by his nature, never could be a leader of masses; he is the leader of bureaucratic "leaders," their consummation, their personification.

The more complex the economic tasks become, the greater the demands and the interests of the population become, all the more sharp becomes the contradiction between the bureaucratic regime and the demands of socialist development, all the more coarsely does the bureaucracy struggle to preserve its positions, all the more cynically does it resort to violence, fraud and bribery.

The constant worsening of the political regime in face of the growth of the economy and culture — this crying fact finds its explanation in this, and this alone: that oppression, persecution and suppression serve today in a large measure not for the defense of the state but for the defense of the rule and

privileges of the bureaucracy. This is also the source of the
ever-increasing need to mask repressions by means of frauds
and amalgams.

"But can such a state be called a workers' state?" — thus
speak the indignant voices of moralists, idealists and "revolutionary" snobs. Others a bit more cautious express themselves
as follows, "Perhaps this is a workers' state, in the last analysis,
but there has not been left in it a vestige of the dictatorship
of the proletariat. We have here a degenerated workers' state
under the dictatorship of the bureaucracy."

We see no reason whatever to resume this argumentation
as a whole. All that has to be said on this score has been said
in the literature and in the official documents of our tendency.
No one has attempted to refute, correct or supplement the
position of the Bolshevik-Leninists on this most important
question.

We shall here limit ourselves solely to the question whether
the factual dictatorship of the bureaucracy may be called the
dictatorship of the proletariat.

The terminological difficulty here arises from the fact that
the term dictatorship is used sometimes in a restricted, political
sense and, at other times, in a more profound, sociological
sense. We speak of the "dictatorship of Mussolini" and, at the
same time, declare that fascism is only the instrument of finance capital. Which is correct? Both are correct, but on different planes. It is incontestable that the entire executive power
is concentrated in Mussolini's hands. But it is no less true that
the entire actual content of the state activity is dictated by the
interests of finance capital. The *social* domination of a class
(its dictatorship) may find extremely diverse *political* forms.
This is attested by the entire history of the bourgeoisie, from
the Middle Ages to the present day.

The experience of the Soviet Union is already adequate for
the extension of this very same sociological law — *with all
the necessary changes* — to the dictatorship of the proletariat
as well. In the interim between the conquest of power and
the dissolution of the workers' state within the socialist society,
the forms and methods of proletarian rule may change sharply,
depending upon the course of the class struggle, internally
and externally.

Thus, the present-day domination of Stalin in no way resembles the Soviet rule during the initial years of the revolution. The substitution of one regime for the other occurred
not at a single stroke but through a series of measures, by
means of a number of minor civil wars waged by the bureaucracy against the proletarian vanguard. In the last historical

analysis, Soviet democracy was blown up by the pressure of social contradictions. Exploiting the latter, the bureaucracy wrested the power from the hands of mass organizations. In this sense we may speak about the dictatorship of the bureaucracy and even about the personal dictatorship of Stalin. But this usurpation was made possible and can maintain itself only because the *social content of the dictatorship of the bureaucracy is determined by those productive relations that were created by the proletarian revolution.* In this sense we may say with complete justification that the dictatorship of the proletariat found its distorted but indubitable expression in the dictatorship of the bureaucracy.

The Historical Analogy Must Be Revised and Corrected

In the internal controversies of the Russian and the International Opposition, we conditionally understood by Thermidor the first stage of the bourgeois counterrevolution, aimed against the social basis of the workers' state.* Although the substance of the controversy, as we have seen, did not suffer by it in the past, nevertheless, the historical analogy became invested with a purely conditional and not a realistic character, and this conditional character comes into ever-increasing contradiction with the demands for an analysis of the most recent evolution of the Soviet state. Enough to mention the fact that we ourselves often speak — and with ample cause — of the plebiscitary or the Bonapartist regime of Stalin. But Bonapartism, in France, came after Thermidor. If we are to remain within the framework of the historical analogy, we must necessarily ask the question: Since there has been no Soviet "Thermidor" as yet, whence could Bonapartism have arisen? Without making any changes *in essence* in our former evaluations — there is no reason whatever to do so — we must radically revise the historical analogy. This will enable us to gain a closer view of certain old facts and to understand better certain new manifestations.

The overturn of the Ninth Thermidor did not liquidate the

---

* The Mensheviks also speak about Thermidorean degeneration. It is impossible to understand what they mean by this. The Mensheviks were opposed to the seizure of power by the proletariat. Even today, the Soviet state is nonproletarian, in their opinion (what it really is — remains a mystery). In the past they demanded the return to capitalism; today they demand the return to "democracy." If they themselves are not representatives of Thermidorean tendencies, then what does "Thermidor" mean at all? Self-evidently, it is merely a current literary expression.

basic conquests of the bourgeois revolution, but it did transfer
the power into the hands of the more moderate and conservative Jacobins, the better-to-do elements of bourgeois society.
Today it is impossible to overlook that in the Soviet revolution
also a shift to the right took place a long time ago, a shift
entirely analogous to Thermidor, although much slower in
tempo and more masked in form. The conspiracy of the Soviet
bureaucracy against the left wing could conserve its comparatively "dry" character during the initial stages only because
the conspiracy itself was executed much more systematically
and thoroughly than the improvisation of the Ninth Thermidor.

Socially the proletariat is more homogeneous than the bourgeoisie, but it contains within itself an entire series of strata
that become manifest with exceptional clarity following the conquest of power, during the period when the bureaucracy and
a workers' aristocracy connected with it begin to take form.
The smashing of the Left Opposition implied in the most direct
and immediate sense the transfer of power from the hands
of the revolutionary vanguard into the hands of the more conservative elements among the bureaucracy and the upper crust
of the working class. The year 1924 — that was the beginning of
the Soviet Thermidor.

Involved here, of course, is the question not of historical
identity but of historical analogy, which always has as its
limits the different social structures and epochs. But the given
analogy is neither superficial nor accidental: it is determined
by the extreme tension in the class struggle that prevails during
the period of revolution and counterrevolution. In both cases
the bureaucracy raised itself upon the backs of plebeian democracy that had assured the victory for the new regime. The
Jacobin clubs were strangled gradually. The revolutionists
of 1793 died on the battlefields; they became diplomats and
generals; they fell under the blows of repression . . . or went
underground. Subsequently, other Jacobins successfully transformed themselves into Napoleon's prefects. Their ranks were
swelled in ever-increasing numbers by turncoats from old parties, by former aristocrats and by crass careerists. And in
Russia? The very same picture of degeneration, but on a much
more gigantic arena and a much more mature background,
is reproduced some 130 to 140 years later by the gradual
transition from soviets and party clubs seething with life to
the commandeering of secretaries who depend solely upon
the "passionately beloved leader."

In France, the prolonged stabilization of the Thermidorean-
Bonapartist regime was made possible only thanks to the
development of the productive forces that had been freed from

the fetters of feudalism. The lucky ones, the plunderers, the relatives and the allies of the bureaucracy enriched themselves. The disillusioned masses fell into prostration.

The upsurge of the nationalized productive forces, which began in 1923 and which came unexpectedly to the Soviet bureaucracy itself, created the necessary economic prerequisites for the stabilization of the latter. The upbuilding of the economic life provided an outlet for the energies of active and capable organizers, administrators and technicians. Their material and moral position improved rapidly. A broad, privileged stratum was created, closely linked to the ruling upper crust. The toiling masses lived on hopes or fell into apathy.

It would be banal pedantry to attempt to fit the different stages of the Russian Revolution to analogous events in France that occurred towards the close of the eighteenth century. But one is literally hit between the eyes by the resemblance between the present Soviet political regime and the regime of the First Consul, particularly at the end of the Consulate when the period of the empire was nigh. While Stalin lacks the luster of victories, at any rate, he surpasses Bonaparte the First in the regime of organized cringing. Such power could be obtained only by strangling the party, the soviets, the working class as a whole. The bureaucracy upon which Stalin leans is materially bound up with the results of the consummated national revolution, but it has no point of contact with the developing international revolution. In their manner of living, their interests and psychology, the present-day Soviet functionaries differ no less from the revolutionary Bolsheviks than the generals and prefects of Napoleon differed from the revolutionary Jacobins.

Thermidoreans and Jacobins

The Soviet ambassador to London, Maisky, recently explained to a delegation of British trade unionists how necessary and justifiable was the Stalinist trial of the "counterrevolutionary" Zinovievists. This striking episode — one from among thousands — immediately brings us to the heart of the question. We know who the Zinovievists are. Whatever their mistakes and vacillations, one thing is certain: they are representatives of the "professional revolutionist" type. The questions of the world workers' movement — these have entered into their blood. Who is Maisky? A right-wing Menshevik who broke with his own party in 1918, going to the right in order to avail himself of the opportunity to enter as a minister into the Trans-Ural White government, under the protection of Kolchak. [169] Only after Kolchak was annihilated did Maisky consider the time ripe for turning his face towards the Soviets. Lenin — and I along with him — had the greatest distrust, to say nothing of contempt, for such types. Today Maisky, in the rank of ambassador, accuses "Zinovievists" and "Trotskyists" of striving to provoke military intervention in order to restore capitalism — the very same capitalism that Maisky had defended against us by means of civil war.

The present ambassador to the United States, A. Troyanovsky, joined the Bolsheviks in his youth; shortly afterwards he left the party; during the war he was a patriot; in 1917, a Menshevik. The October Revolution found him a member of the Menshevik Central Committee, in addition to which, during the next few years, Troyanovsky carried on an illegal struggle against the dictatorship of the proletariat; he entered the Stalinist party, more correctly, the diplomatic service, after the Left Opposition was crushed.

The ambassador to Paris, Potemkin, was a bourgeois professor of history during the period of the October Revolution; he joined the Bolsheviks after the victory. The former ambassador to Berlin, Khinchuk, participated, as a Menshevik, during the days of the October overturn, in the counterrevolutionary Moscow Committee for the Salvation of the Fatherland and the Revolution, together with Grinko, a right-wing Social Revolutionary, the present people's commissar of finance. Suritz, who replaced Khinchuk in Berlin, was the political secretary of the Menshevik Chkheidze, the first chairman of the Soviets; he joined the Bolsheviks after the victory. Almost all other diplomats are of the same type; and in the meantime there are being appointed abroad — especially after the experience with Bessedovsky, Dimitrievsky, Agabekov[170] and others — only the most dependable people.

Not so long ago dispatches appeared in the world press relating to the major successes of the Soviet gold-mining industry, with comments concerning its organizer, the engineer Serebrovsky. The Moscow correspondent of *Le Temps*, who is today successfully competing with Duranty and Louis Fischer[171] as the official spokesman for the bureaucratic upper crust, took particular pains to stress the fact that Serebrovsky is a Bolshevik from 1903, a member of the "Old Guard." That is what Serebrovsky's party card actually states. As a matter of fact, he participated in the 1905 Revolution as a young student and Menshevik and then went over to the camp of the bourgeoisie for many long years. The February 1917 revolution found him holding the post of government director of two munitions plants, a member of the Board of Trade and an active participant in the struggle against the metal workers' union. In May 1917, Serebrovsky declared that Lenin was a "German spy"! After the victory of the Bolsheviks, Sere-brovsky along with other *spetzes* [technical experts, specialists] was drawn into technical work by myself. Lenin did not trust him at all; I had hardly any faith in him myself. Today, Serebrovsky is a member of the Central Committee of the party!

The theoretical journal of the Central Committee, *Bolshevik* (December 31, 1934), carries an article by Serebrovsky, "On the Gold-Mining Industry of the USSR." We turn to the first page: ". . . under the leadership of the beloved leader of the party and the working class, Comrade Stalin . . ."; three lines down: ". . . Comrade Stalin in a conversation with the Amer-ican correspondent, Mr. Duranty . . ."; five lines further down: ". . . the concise and precise reply of Comrade Stalin . . ."; at the bottom of the page: "that's what it means to fight for gold in the Stalinist way." Page two: ". . . as our great leader, Comrade Stalin, teaches us . . ."; four lines down: ". . . reply-ing to their (the Bolsheviks') report, Comrade Stalin wrote: 'Congratulations on your success'. . ."; further down on the same page: "inspired by the guidance of Comrade Stalin . . ."; one line below: ". . . the party with Comrade Stalin at the head . . ."; two lines following: ". . . the guidance of our party and (!!) Comrade Stalin." Let us now turn to the conclusion of the article. In the course of half a page we read: ". . . the guidance of the genius leader of the party and the working class, Comrade Stalin . . ."; and three lines later: ". . . the words of our beloved leader, Comrade Stalin. . . ."

Satire itself stands disarmed in the face of such a flood of sycophancy! "Beloved leaders," one should imagine, are never in need of having declarations of love made to them five times on each page and, besides, in an article devoted not to the leader's anniversary but to . . . the mining of gold. On the other hand, the author of an article with a capacity for such fawning obviously cannot have anything in him of a revolu-tionist. Of such caliber is this former czarist director of large factories, bourgeois and patriot, who waged a struggle against the workers and who is today a bulwark of the regime, mem-ber of the Central Committee and 100 percent Stalinist!

Another specimen. One of the pillars of the present-day *Pravda*, Zaslavsky, propounded in January of this year that it was just as impermissible to publish the reactionary novels of Dostoyevsky as the "counterrevolutionary works of Trotsky, Zinoviev and Kamenev." Who is this Zaslavsky? In the dim past — a right-wing Bundist [Menshevik of the Jewish Bund], later a bourgeois journalist who carried on a most contempt-ible campaign in 1917 against Lenin and Trotsky as agents of Germany. In Lenin's articles for 1917 there is to be found,

as a refrain, the phrase, "Zaslavsky and other scoundrels like
him." Thus has Zaslavsky entered into the literature of the
party as the consummate type of venal bourgeois calumniator.
During the civil-war period, he was, while in hiding in Kiev,
a journalist for White Guard publications. Only in 1923 did he
go over to the side of the Soviet power. Today he defends
Stalinism from the counterrevolutionists Trotsky, Zinoviev and
Kamenev! In the USSR as well as abroad, Stalin's press is
crammed with such individuals.

The old cadres of Bolshevism have been smashed. Revolutionists have been smashed. Revolutionists have been supplanted by functionaries with supple spines. Marxist thinking
has been driven out by fear, flattery and intrigue. Of Lenin's
Political Bureau, only Stalin has remained: two members of
the Political Bureau are broken politically and grovel in the
dust (Rykov and Tomsky); two members are in prison (Zinoviev and Kamenev); one is exiled abroad and deprived of his
citizenship (Trotsky). Lenin, as Krupskaya herself expressed
it, was spared only by death from the repressions of the bureaucracy; failing the opportunity to put him in prison, the
epigones shut him up in a mausoleum. The entire warp of
the ruling layer has degenerated. The Jacobins have been
pushed out by the Thermidoreans and Bonapartists; Bolsheviks have been supplanted by Stalinists.

To the broad stratum of the conservative and in-no-way-
disinterested Maiskys, Serebrovskys and Zaslavskys, large,
medium and petty, Stalin is the judge-arbiter, the fountain of
all boons and the defender from all possible oppositions. In
return for this, the bureaucracy, from time to time, presents
Stalin with the sanction of a national plebiscite. Party congresses, like Soviet congresses, are organized upon a sole
criterion: *for* or *against* Stalin? Only "counterrevolutionists"
can be *against,* and they are dealt with as they deserve. Such
is the present-day mechanism of rule. This is a *Bonapartist*
mechanism. No other definition for it can be found as yet in
a political dictionary.

The Difference Between the Roles of a Bourgeois and a Workers' State

Without historical analogies we cannot learn from history.
But the analogy must be concrete; behind the traits of resemblance, we must not overlook the traits of dissimilarity. Both
revolutions put an end to feudalism and serfdom. But one of
them, in the shape of its extreme wing, could only strive in
vain to pass beyond the limits of bourgeois society; the other
actually overthrew the bourgeoisie and created the workers'

state. This fundamental class distinction, which introduces the necessary material limits to the analogy, bears a decisive significance for the prognosis.

After the profound democratic revolution, which liberates the peasants from serfdom and gives them land, the feudal counterrevolution is generally impossible. The overthrown monarchy may reestablish itself in power and surround itself with medieval phantoms. But it is already powerless to reestablish the economy of feudalism. Once liberated from the fetters of feudalism, bourgeois relations develop automatically. They can be checked by no external force; they must themselves dig their own grave, having previously created their own gravedigger.

It is altogether otherwise with the development of socialist relations. The proletarian revolution not only frees the productive forces from the fetters of private ownership but also transfers them to the direct disposal of the state that it itself creates. While the bourgeois state, after the revolution, confines itself to a police role, leaving the market to its own laws, the workers' state assumes the direct role of economist and organizer. The replacement of one political regime by another exerts only an indirect and superficial influence upon market economy. On the contrary, the replacement of a workers' government by a bourgeois or petty-bourgeois government would inevitably lead to the liquidation of the planned beginnings and, subsequently, to the restoration of private property. *In contradistinction to capitalism, socialism is built not automatically but consciously.* Progress towards socialism is inseparable from that state power that is desirous of socialism or that is constrained to desire it. Socialism can acquire an immutable character only at a very high stage of its development, when its productive forces have far transcended those of capitalism, when the human wants of each and all can obtain bounteous satisfaction and when the state will have completely withered away, dissolving in society. But all this is still in the distant future. At the given stage of development, the socialist construction stands and falls with the workers' state. Only after thoroughly pondering the difference between the laws of the formation of bourgeois ("anarchistic") and socialist ("planned") economy is it possible to understand those limits beyond which the analogy with the Great French Revolution cannot pass.

October 1917 completed the democratic revolution and initiated the socialist revolution. No force in the world can turn back the agrarian-democratic overturn in Russia; in this we have a complete analogy with the Jacobin revolution. But a *kolkhoz* overturn is a threat that retains its full force, and with it is threatened the nationalization of the means of production. Political counterrevolution, even were it to recede back to the Romanov dynasty,[172] could not reestablish feudal ownership of land. But the restoration to power of a Menshevik and Social Revolutionary bloc would suffice to obliterate the socialist construction.

A Hypertrophy of Bureaucratic Centrism Into Bonapartism

The fundamental difference between the two revolutions and, consequently, between the counterrevolutions "corresponding" to them is of utmost importance for understanding the significance of those *reactionary political shifts that compose the essence of Stalin's regime.* The peasant revolution, as well as the bourgeoisie that leaned upon it, was very well able to make its peace with the regime of Napoleon, and it was even able to maintain itself under Louis XVIII. The proletarian revolution is already exposed to mortal danger under the present regime of Stalin; it will be unable to withstand a further shift to the right.

The Soviet bureaucracy—"Bolshevist" in its traditions but in reality having long since renounced its traditions, petty bourgeois in its composition and spirit—was summoned to regulate the antagonism between the proletariat and the peasantry, between the workers' state and world imperialism; such is the social base of *bureaucratic centrism,* of its zigzags, its power, its weakness and its influence on the world proletarian movement that has been so fatal.* As the bureaucracy becomes more independent, as more and more power is concentrated in the hands of a single person, the more does *bureaucratic centrism* turn into Bonapartism.

The concept of Bonapartism, being too broad, demands concretization. During the last few years we have applied this term to those capitalist governments that, by exploiting the

---

* The Brandlerites, including the leaders of the SAP, remaining even today the theoretical pupils of Thalheimer, saw only "ultra-leftism" in the policies of the Comintern and denied (and continue to deny) the very meaning of bureaucratic centrism. The present "fourth period" when Stalin is pulling the European workers' movement on the hook of the Comintern to the *right* of official reformism demonstrates how shallow and opportunistic is the political philosophy of Thalheimer-Walcher and Co. These people are incapable of thinking a single question out to its conclusion. Precisely for this reason have they such a revulsion for the principle of *saying what is,* i.e., the highest principle of every scientific analysis and every revolutionary policy.

antagonisms between the proletarian and fascist camps and by leaning directly upon the military-police apparatus, raise themselves above parliament and democracy, as the saviors of "national unity." We always strictly differentiated between this Bonapartism of decay and the young, advancing Bonapartism that was not only the gravedigger of the political principles of the bourgeois revolution but also the defender of its social conquests. We apply a common name to these two manifestations because they have common traits; it is always possible to discern the youth in the octogenarian despite the merciless ravages of time.

The present-day Kremlin Bonapartism we juxtapose, of course, to the Bonapartism of bourgeois rise and not decay: with the Consulate and the First Empire and not with Napoleon III and, all the more so, not with Schleicher or Doumergue. For the purposes of such an analogy, there is no need to ascribe to Stalin the traits of Napoleon I; whenever the social conditions demand it, Bonapartism can consolidate itself around axes of the most diverse caliber.

From the standpoint that interests us, the difference in the social basis of the two Bonapartisms, of Jacobin and of Soviet origin, is much more important. In the former case, the question involved was the consolidation of the bourgeois revolution through the liquidation of its principles and political institutions. In the latter case, the question involved is the consolidation of the worker-peasant revolution through the smashing of its international program, its leading party, its soviets. Carrying the policies of Thermidor further, Napoleon waged a struggle not only against the feudal world but also against the "rabble" and the democratic circles of the petty and middle bourgeoisie; in this way he concentrated the fruits of the regime born out of the revolution in the hands of the new bourgeois aristocracy. Stalin guards the conquests of the October Revolution not only against the feudal-bourgeois counterrevolution but also against the claims of the toilers, their impatience and their dissatisfaction; he crushes the left wing that expresses the ordered historical and progressive tendencies of the unprivileged working masses; he creates a new aristocracy by means of an extreme differentiation in wages, privileges, ranks, etc. Leaning for support upon the topmost layer of the new social hierarchy against the lowest—sometimes vice versa—Stalin has attained the complete concentration of power in his own hands. What else should this regime be called if not Soviet Bonapartism?

Bonapartism, by its very essence, cannot long maintain itself; a sphere balanced on the point of a pyramid must invariably roll down on one side or the other. But it is precisely at this point, as we have already seen, that the historical analogy runs up against its limits. Napoleon's downfall did not, of course, leave untouched the relations between the classes; but in its essence the social pyramid of France retained its bourgeois character. The inevitable collapse of Stalinist Bonapartism would immediately call into question the character of the USSR as a workers' state. A socialist economy cannot be constructed without a socialist power. The fate of the USSR as a *socialist* state depends upon that *political* regime that will arise to replace Stalinist Bonapartism. Only the revolutionary vanguard of the proletariat can regenerate the soviet system, if it is again able to mobilize around itself the toilers of the city and the village.

Conclusion

From our analysis there follows a number of conclusions that we set down briefly below:

1. The Thermidor of the Great Russian Revolution is not before us but already far behind. The Thermidoreans can celebrate, approximately, the tenth anniversary of their victory.

2. The present political regime in the USSR is the regime of "Soviet" (or anti-Soviet) Bonapartism, closer in type to the empire than the Consulate.

3. In its social foundation and economic tendencies, the USSR still remains a workers' state.

4. The contradiction between the political regime of Bonapartism and the demands of socialist development represents the most important source of the internal crises and is a direct danger to the very existence of the USSR as a workers' state.

5. Due to the still low level of productive forces and to the capitalist environment, classes and class contradictions, now weakening, now sharpening, will still continue to exist within the USSR for an indeterminately long period of time, in any case, up to the complete victory of the proletariat in the important capitalist nations of the world.

6. The existence of the proletarian dictatorship also remains for the future the necessary condition for the development of economy and culture in the USSR. Therefore the Bonapartist degeneration of the dictatorship represents the direct and immediate threat to all the social conquests of the proletariat.

7. The terrorist tendencies within the ranks of the Communist youth are one of the most virulent symptoms of the fact that Bonapartism has exhausted its political possibilities and has entered the period of the most ruthless struggle for its existence.

8. The inevitable collapse of the Stalinist political regime

will lead to the establishment of Soviet democracy only in the event that the removal of Bonapartism comes as the conscious act of the proletarian vanguard. In all other cases, in place of Stalinism there could only come the fascist-capitalist counter-revolution.

9. The tactic of individual terrorism, no matter under what banner it proceeds, can, under the given conditions, play only into the hands of the worst enemies of the proletariat.

10. The political and moral responsibility for the very inception of terrorism within the ranks of the Communist youth falls upon the gravedigger of the party — Stalin.

11. The chief cause that weakens the proletarian vanguard of the USSR in the struggle against Bonapartism is the uninterrupted defeats of the world proletariat.

12. The chief cause for the defeats of the world proletariat is the criminal policies of the Comintern, the blind servant of Stalinist Bonapartism and, at the same time, the best ally and defender of the reformist bureaucracy.

13. The first condition for successes upon the international arena is the liberation of the international proletarian vanguard from the demoralizing influence of Soviet Bonapartism, i.e., from the venal bureaucracy of the so-called Comintern.

14. The struggle for the salvation of the USSR as a socialist state coincides completely with the struggle for the Fourth International.

Postscript

Our opponents — and they are welcome — will seize upon our "self-criticism." So! they will shriek, you have changed your position on the fundamental question of Thermidor; hitherto you spoke only about the danger of Thermidor; now you suddenly declare that Thermidor already lies behind. This will probably be said by Stalinists, who will add for good measure that we have changed our position in order the more easily to provoke military intervention. The Brandlerites and the Lovestoneites, [173] on the one hand, and, on the other hand, certain "ultraleft" wiseacres may express themselves in the same key. These people were never able to point out to us what was erroneous in the analogy with Thermidor; they will shriek all the louder now that we have disclosed the error ourselves.

We have indicated above the position of this error in our general appraisal of the USSR. It is in no case a question of *changing* our principled position as it has been formulated in a number of official documents, but only a question of rendering it more *precise*. Our "self-criticism" extends not to the analysis of the class character of the USSR or to the causes and conditions for its degeneration but only to the historical clarification of these processes by means of establishing analogies with well-known stages of the Great French Revolution. The correction of a partial, even though an important, error not only leaves unshaken the basic position of the Bolshevik-Leninists but also enables us to establish it more precisely and concretely by means of more correct and more realistic analogies. It should also be added that the disclosure of the error was greatly facilitated by the fact that the very processes of the political degeneration, which are under discussion, have in the meantime assumed much more distinct shape.

Our tendency never laid claim to infallibility. We do not receive ready-made truths as a revelation, like the high priests of Stalinism. We study, we discuss, we check our conclusions in the light of existence, we openly correct the admitted mistakes and — we proceed forward. Scientific conscientiousness and personal strictness are the best traditions of Marxism and Leninism. We wish to remain true to our teachers in this respect as well. [174]

"SOVIET DEMOCRACY"[175]

(February 10, 1935)

In order to erect some sort of partial screen to counteract the repulsive impression that has been created by Stalin's man-handling of his political opponents, under the guise of waging a struggle against terrorists, much publicity has been given to a great democratic reform: collective farmers, as members of a socialist society, have been given equal electoral rights with the industrial workers. Upon this score the flunkies have raised a hullabaloo about the entry into the kingdom of gen-uine democracy (but what was there yesterday?).

The inequality in the electoral rights between the workers and peasants had its social reasons. The dictatorship of the proletariat in a peasant country found its necessary and open expression in the electoral privileges of the workers. The *in-equality* of rights presupposed, in any case, *the existence* of rights. The Soviet system provided the toilers with a genuine possibility for determining the fate of the country. The political power was concentrated in the hands of the vanguard party. Through the soviets and the trade unions, the party was al-ways submitted to the pressure of the masses. By means of this pressure, the party kept the Soviet bureaucracy subordi-nate to itself.

It is utter nonsense that the peasantry has seemingly suc-ceeded in reeducating itself socially during the two to three years of collectivization. The antagonism between the city and village still preserves all of its acuteness. Even today the dic-tatorship is inconceivable without the hegemony of the prole-tariat over the peasantry. But the inequality in the electoral rights between the workers and peasants has lost its real con-tent, insofar as the bureaucracy has completely deprived both the former and the latter of political rights. From the stand-point of the mechanics of the Bonapartist regime, the appor-tionment of electoral districts is of absolutely no significance. The bureaucracy might have given the peasant ten times as many votes as the worker—we would obtain the very same result, for each and all possess, in the last analysis, the one and only right: to vote for Stalin.

The secret ballot may at first sight appear to be a genuine concession. But who would dare to counterpose his own candidacy to the official slate? An oppositionist, if elected by "secret ballot," would, indeed, be declared an open class enemy immediately after the elections. Thus the secret ballot cannot effect any real change.

The entire reform represents a Bonapartist masquerade—and nothing more. The very need of such a masquerade is unmistakable testimony to the growing sharpening in the relations between the bureaucracy and the toiling masses. Neither the workers nor the peasants have any need for democratic fictions. So long as Stalin keeps both his hands upon the throat of the proletarian vanguard all constitutional reforms will remain Bonapartist charlatanry.

TO COMRADE SNEEVLIET
ON THE IAG CONFERENCE[176]

(February 26, 1935)

Dear Friend:[177]

I have received your letter of February 21 on the conference of the Amsterdam Bureau. On the same subject, I have also received a fairly extensive report from the Polish comrade V., who attended the conference as a visitor. Aside from that, I have also before me a copy of *Emancipation*, Doriot's paper, which contains an article and the first installment of a report on the conference. Insufficient as all this information may be (the texts of the resolutions adopted have not as yet reached me in their entirety), I nevertheless hasten to convey to you a temporary evaluation of the results of this conference.

1. The Norwegian Labor Party (NAP) was not represented, i.e., it has of its own initiative brought about the break at the precise moment it chose to do so. The NAP was the only real mass party in the IAG. The formlessness of the IAG has always been explained and excused particularly by the need of adaptation to the "great" Norwegian party. Now Tranmael feels he has reached his port, and he says to dear Schwab:[178] the Moor has done his work, the Moor is dismissed. An invaluable lesson for all those who consider unprincipled combinations the highest art in politics.

2. At the same time, Schwab has broken with us in a hostile fashion — precisely because of his inclination toward the great Norwegian party. He has now lost from the right the only real mass party and from the left he has broken off all relations with the ICL, i.e., the one organization that represents a certain amount of ideological capital in the midst of the present chaos throughout the labor movement. And he will not fare any better in the future, for our epoch is merciless towards organizations that are held together by nothing stouter than a string of innocuous formulas.

3. The Swedish party[179] appears to be in a position no

different from that of the NAP. The Swedes are only trailing behind Tranmael in the right course and still need the banner of the IAG, but only for the time being.

4. The fact that the ILP has "conclusively" broken with the Second International while continuing its sterile machinations with the Third, I cannot regard as an advance; it is only another form of the same confusion. If Fenner Brockway[180] had declared for the Fourth International and thereafter returned to the Labour Party, that would have been a real step forward.

5. In 1874, Engels wrote to Sorge[181] about a certain Proudhonist[182] -anarchist conference: "General disagreement on everything that is fundamental, under the cover of no debates, only reports made and listened to." This splendid description fits like a glove on the conference of the IAG. Only such "communities" are even less durable in our times than they were sixty years ago.

6. It is very encouraging to note that Schmidt[183] and you both took such a firm stand for the Fourth International. But that did not shape the character of the conference. Quite the contrary. In the first article on the conference to reach me, Doriot concludes after an outpour of rambling and innocuous phrases, with one lone, concrete, precise remark, namely: "We have not formed a new International. This Trotskyist idea was quite formally condemned by the conference." All the other participants no doubt gave similar reports: general phrases about revival, unity, struggle against war, etc., with a single precise fact: the Fourth International and the Trotskyists were condemned. By this "concrete" result, these gents achieve a certain amount of consolation for the lack of any other achievements. It gives them a sort of moral satisfaction. If you reread the letter I sent you about a month and a half or two months ago, you will find in it a modest prophecy: the gentlemen will wash their hands of the Fourth International, and that will constitute the "positive" content of the conference.

7. The devastating effect of the SAP confusion can be felt almost tangibly in Doriot's editorial. He manages to speak in the same breath of the complete bankruptcy of the Second and Third Internationals and, at the same time, he "formally condemns" the idea of the Fourth International. That is in the tradition of the Walcher school. The Fourth International is to arise in the "process" and Walcher and his conferences appear to have nothing to do with the "process." Perhaps Walcher is of the opinion that it would be of advantage to the process if Walcher were not to interfere with it in matters of the Fourth International. I am becoming more and more convinced that

in that assumption he might not be wrong after all. The whole history of the struggle between Bolsheviks and Mensheviks is dotted with this little word "process." Lenin always formulated tasks and proposed corresponding methods. The Mensheviks agreed with the same "aims" by and large, but left their realization to the historic process. There is nothing new under the sun.

As I have said, I do not yet have before me the resolution of the SAP, but I know the music and also the bandleader. . It is the historical mission of SAP documents to prevent the worst confusionists and centrists from getting a bellyache.

8. An attempt was made to maneuver with the lefts in the Second International. But in vain. And even if they succeeded in this field, it would not have lasted very long. Under the pressure of great events and great dangers, the centrist elements that have been set in motion seek either powerful material support or ideological clarity. Some, mostly skeptics and cynics, seek to find a road to Moscow. Others, the road to us. The banner of the SAP cannot under any circumstances attract for an extended period of time any mass organization or serious tendency.

If we had developed the Declaration of Four, concluded a year and a half ago, patiently and systematically, issued common propaganda documents, made connections under the banner of the Fourth International, then we would make a considerably deeper impression upon the Spanish Socialist youth, the Austrian Schutzbund, etc. The betrayal of the SAP has only served the Stalinist bureaucracy. This betrayal has caused us considerable difficulties, but it could not change our path.

9. An antiwar committee has been created, and the Belgian left has been won for this committee. But, as Comrade V. reports, the Belgian left holds a purely pacifist point of view: "against all wars," "no difference between the USSR and the capitalist states in the war," etc. In a word, sentimental-reactionary, philistine nonsense, which, it appears, was not rejected by the conference. How could it have been? They had enough to do to condemn the Fourth International. And then again, if the pacifist philistines had been confronted with a clear stand, this wonderful antiwar committee would never have been formed. Five simple workers who seriously stand by the Leninist principles of antiwar policy are, in the case of war, a hundred times more important than this kind of committee, which is blown away by the first war breezes like some house of cards.

In any case, the SAP people tried to console the conference or rather themselves — opportunist slogans often lead to revolutionary actions. They are really generous with these crumbs of their Brandlerian wisdom. At any rate, Walcher has to be satisfied for the time being with opportunist slogans: the "process" will have to take care of the "revolutionary actions" for him.

10. The moral of this story was given by Zyromsky, quite correctly in my opinion, when he advised the participants as follows: instead of inviting us into your "labor community," you yourselves should return to the Second and Third Internationals and prepare unification from the inside. That is at least a political idea; if you have no desire or courage to fight for a Fourth International, then return to the old Internationals and reform them or merge them.

11. I have just received the SAP resolution on the Fourth International. This tripe looks just as it should look. There is talk of the *echec* ("defeat") of the two Internationals, and then they leave to Saint Nicholas the historic process, the task of building a new International — God knows on what kind of a foundation. They are forced by the situation itself (and to some extent also by us) to say "something" about this delicate theme, but they take particular pains to say something that does not place any obligations whatsoever upon any tendency whatsoever.

At the same time, I have also received the declaration of Brockway, Kilbom and Kruk, [184] which says that the orientation toward a Fourth International would mean a split in the committee. With this, the physiognomy of the conference has been completely established.

12. What is most important in every political organism is its tendency of development. If we consider the period from August 1933 to February 1935, we cannot ascertain, in spite of the great events that have intervened, any progress whatsoever, either quantitatively or qualitatively. From the NAP some expected to influence the leadership, others expected the creation of a left wing in it, at least the adherence of the Mot Dag; [185] nothing of the sort happened. By the link with Tranmael, criticism was prevented and the latter was actually aided in stifling the opposition. The lesser gains that have been made are outweighed by the departure of the NAP. Ideologically the same confusion prevails, but in the course of time it has become much worse and much more dangerous.

Where can we find the slightest reason to expect that things will improve in the future? Once every year and a half, a few dozen people gather. All of them have long ago completed their political education, and they only need the IAG as a safety valve against their own lefts. The spearhead of the criticism and particularly of their hatred is directed toward the left, against us. There are no binding decisions; there is no organ for discussion. The gatherings and the bulletin only serve, as Engels said, to give reports and to listen to them. Their own members only get some verbiage in the manner of Doriot (not the Fourth International, but the complete unity of the working class). A very deceptive community of interests, without any content, without any perspective, without any future.

Now I come to the practical conclusions. You wrote me, dear friend, that out of consideration for the impending unification with the OSP you cannot publish the critique of the draft resolution of the SAP186 in the organ of the RSP.187 The fusion of the two Dutch organizations is so important that I, for my part, am ready to pay a considerable price for it. I therefore beg you to regard the following, not as a complaint, but only as an analysis of an important symptom.

The SAP is the leading organization of the IAG not because it has any ideas but, on the contrary, because it is helpful to the heterogeneous groups in their disregard for ideas. And it is very easy for the SAP because these gentlemen don't give a snap about ideas. Just because we are very strict with our ideas, they hate us. On the occasion of the entry into the SFIO, this hatred took on the most disgusting expression: yesterday they embraced de Kadt against the "sectarians"; today they align themselves with the hysterical sectarian Bauer against us.

These people are not ashamed of criticizing us in the sharpest forms before and after the conference. In this situation the RSP of Holland feels constrained to refrain in advance from criticizing a draft resolution, and before its fusion with the OSP at that. Really, this small fact illuminates like lightning the whole question of the IAG. We see here also the repetition of a rule that has been observed hundreds of times in the past on a much larger scale; centrists, even left centrists, always respect the opportunists and feel flattered and encouraged when they win their smiles. At the same time, the centrists are terribly outraged when the unbehaved "sectarians" (i.e., Marxists) spoil the pleasure they derive from the smiles of friends at their right by inappropriate criticism. When the centrist makes his big combinations, he always bows low to the right and hisses to the left: shut up! It was this pressure that the RSP must have felt when it refrained, as a sort of advance payment, from publishing a quite reserved, principled and objective criticism. Isn't that symptomatic?

The vote in the Saar188 was a striking confirmation of our analysis of the Second and Third Internationals. No better laboratory experiment could have been asked for to test our new orientation. In France, too, matters are not any different. The French proletariat can be victorious only despite the two official parties. If it should fail, however, it will bury Stalinists as well as Socialists forever. It is these basic historic facts that we must lean on, if we wish to brace ourselves for the long road ahead. In order to draw the most important conclusions from the Saar question alone, we must mercilessly expose before the eyes of the workers the confusion of a Walcher, a Doriot, etc.

For these people, just because they mimic our gestures in order eventually to turn against us, constitute the immediate danger on the road to the Fourth International. To buy the great privilege of an illusory community of ideas with them, through the renunciation or even moderation of our criticism against them, seems to me to be nothing short of a crime. (N. B. And, incidentally, you will have to admit that the entry of our French section into the SFIO had nothing whatsoever to do with such a renunciation of criticism. On the contrary, never have our French friends criticized the opportunists so sharply, so concretely, so effectively as they do now. For combinations with centrist leaderships, behind the backs of the masses, are one thing and work in a mass organization against the centrist leadership is another thing altogether.)

I repeat, the fusion of the two Dutch parties is so important that we are prepared to defray even extra expenses. But under one condition: the ICL must maintain for itself complete freedom of movement and criticism with regard to the Amsterdam Bureau. That we should change our attitude toward the IAG after the Paris conference, I, for one, consider wellnigh impossible. Shall we have to change our minds in the future? The future itself will instruct us as to that.

However, what is to be done at present? A modest but important step in that direction has been taken by the new Workers Party in America.[189] In its constitution we read:

(ARTICLE III: INTERNATIONAL AFFILIATION, p. 26)

"The Party, at its launching, is affiliated with no other group, party, or organization in the United States or elsewhere. Its National Committee is empowered to enter into fraternal relations with groups and parties in other countries and, if they stand on the same fundamental program as its own, to cooperate with them in the elaboration of a complete world program and the speediest possible establishment of the new revolutionary International. Action on any organizational affiliation must be submitted to a National Convention of the Party."

I wish to direct your attention and that of Comrade Schmidt

to this highly important paragraph. Here, it is not a matter of some confused fraternization with Tom, Dick and Harry on the basis of some wishy-washy program for the one lone reason that neither party belongs to the Second or Third Internationals. Not at all, the Americans say; we wish to establish solid relations only with organizations that stand on the same fundamental program as we do, in order to create, together with them, the new revolutionary International. It is, therefore, the first duty of the united Dutch party to turn to the united American party with the proposal to carry on joint, systematic action in the direction of the Fourth International.

The old Declaration of Four, for my part in revised, corrected and improved form, could serve as the point of departure. Together with the International Secretariat of the Bolshevik-Leninists, you could then approach the SAP for the last time: do they or don't they want to participate in our *preparatory work, which does not intend to achieve anything by decree?*

If I have been informed correctly, Comrade Schmidt quite openly and loyally reserved for himself the right to fight for the Fourth International. If, after this, we create a preparatory program commission, which gives its serious and well-founded considerations on the most important questions of the international movement, then this commission, without assuming any administrative rights, will exert a far greater attractive force than the IAG. In no case is it a matter of an ultimatum: with us or with Amsterdam. The Dutch party can, if it finds need for it, continue to remain in the IAG and, at the same time, undertake together with us the preparatory work we have described above. Experience will then have something to teach one of us.

This is a practical proposal that I am communicating through this letter to all members of the plenum. [190] But the practical decision rests in the hands of the leadership of the united Dutch party.

P. S. In spite of the length of this letter, it appears to me that, with regard to the SAP, it is not as thoroughgoing as it should be, and in a twofold sense at that, both theoretically and factually. Therefore here are two important points in addition:

1. I have requested Comrade Adolphe [191] to prepare for the use of our sections a complete report on the Declaration of Four on the basis of authentic documents, i.e., a report of our attempt to collaborate with the SAP. Even for those who now stand on the sidelines, it will then become absolutely clear that the SAP representatives never had a single occa-

sion to speak — let alone to vote — against the desire attributed
to us, to proclaim the Fourth International with one stroke.
The differences were restricted to the question whether it was
necessary to criticize Tranmael and Co. or to tolerate them and
court them.

Nor did we propose even this question in ultimatistic fashion. We always said: that is our opinion; you go right ahead
and have your experience with Tranmael; we shall, however,
reserve for ourselves the right to criticize not only Tranmael
but also your experiences with him. The tone of our criticisms
was always prudent and friendly. Insofar as the several decisions on the Fourth International are concerned, these were
always adopted unanimously. In order to appease the SAP
people, unanimity in decisions was raised to a principle on
our insistence.

But Walcher and the others became frightened by their own
courage after every decision we made. After one step forward,
they made two steps backward. In doing that, they refused
to discuss or even to bring forward a written explanation.
They simply didn't answer the letters and insisted in a huff
in semiprivate conversations that we wanted to improvise the
Fourth International. The real reason was and remains the
fact that they do not dare to approach such a tremendous
task. Their impression, after every contact with us, was the
following: "But these people are taking the thing quite *seriously*; that will never do."

2. The explosion of hatred against us on the occasion of the
crisis in the German section surprised a good many people.
What was the cause of this disgusting spitefulness? Why the
alliance with Bauer? These feelings must have been rooted
deep down in their centrist hearts before they broke into print
in the columns of *Die Neue Front.*

Walcher and consorts hail from Brandler's school. Together
with Brandler-Thalheimer, they slipped on the revolutionary
situation in 1923. They could not summon up the courage
for action. Just as is the case now with the Fourth International, they then too, at the time of the German Revolution, wanted the historic "process" to liberate them from the duty of arriving at great decisions and of assuming responsibility for
them. And that is the very substance of left centrism, whose
most important prototype was the Russian Martov.[192]   In
perspective, he was ready to accept the boldest decisions. But
where it was a matter of taking even the most modest step
along the line of these principles and becoming involved in
their practical realization, he always leaped to the side. He

did, to be sure, invent much wittier explanations for his evasions than Walcher and consorts do for theirs.

In the course of the Chinese Revolution, the Brandlerites, Walcher included, supported the criminal policy of Stalin[193] against us. In the history of the Anglo-Russian Committee, Walcher and his people do not understand to this day what the crime of the Stalin-Tomsky[194] policy, which helped the [British] General Council over the top in a highly critical situation, consisted of. Moreover, the SAP's attitude in the IAG is only a weaker edition of that same policy. In the Russian question also, Walcher went along with Brandler up to 1930, if I am not mistaken. All this could not have been an accident. In 1933 we made a quite honest and straightforward attempt to help these people climb out of the centrist morass. But by their whole manner of acting, they showed that they cannot live and breathe outside of this morass.

I do not mean to imply by this that the whole membership or even leadership is lost forever. The above-mentioned "process" makes its blows felt even on the hardest heads at times. But we do not wish to pursue toward the SAP leaders the same passive policy that they pursue toward their friends from the right. We must *act* in the direction of the Fourth International and by accomplished facts present the SAP with the choice—with us or against us. That is the only correct policy.

Crux [Leon Trotsky]

TO CANNON ON THE NEXT STEPS [195]

(February 1935)

Dear Comrade Cannon: [196]

This is a purely personal letter. In the first place, because your party is not now affiliated to the International Communist League and, in the second place, because I have not been empowered by any group to write to you. This letter will concern itself with the general questions of orientation in order that eventual practical decisions may be prepared. Article III of the Constitution of the Workers Party, which deals with the question of International affiliation, is cited in the copy of the letter [to Sneevliet] enclosed. It is possible that in the next few months the attention of your party will be directed chiefly toward questions of propaganda and organization. Even here, however, you will hardly be able to or wish to escape the question of the new International. It seems to me to be necessary, both from the point of view of the WPUS as well as from that of the International, that certain definite preparatory steps be taken in accordance with your constitutional Article III.

There are certain similarities between the position of your party and that of the united party in Holland, which will come into being in the next few weeks. There is, however, one difference. The OSP, which will form the majority of the membership of the new party, belonged to the IAG before the amalgamation and is now inclined to give its affiliation to this body. Therefore our section of the new party will also come into this organization. At the same time, the leaders of the new party want to arrive at some sort of personal basis of unity with the International Communist League. The idea is that the leaders of both groups, Sneevliet and Schmidt, become members of the International Secretariat.

My opinion of the International Labor Community I need not go into here. I go into the question thoroughly in the attached letter to Sneevliet. It would be absolutely false, however, for us to make withdrawal from the IAG a condition for the establishment of the new party. Further experience will soon show whether the continued affiliation of the Dutch party to this thoroughly confused and centrist organization can be of any good use.

At the February conference of the IAG, our Comrades Schmidt and Sneevliet spoke well and vigorously on the need of the formation of the Fourth International. Our friends in Paris write me with enthusiasm of the position taken by Comrade Schmidt as well as Sneevliet. In spite of its continued affiliation to the IAG, the new Dutch party has reserved to itself the right to do whatever possible for the establishment of the new International. And I believe that the Dutch party and the WPUS are called upon by the existing situation to take practical steps in this direction.

I do not know whether in America the result of the Saar vote has been analyzed in respect to its effects on the international labor movement. Its significance cannot be overestimated. After the miserable capitulation of both parties in Germany, we declared that not only the Second but the Third International as well were historically dead. The establishment of a new International — based on the teachings of the past — was placed on the agenda of history. Many comrades, some of them in our own ranks (Bauer, for example), dissented. They said that the Communist International could still be revived. The Saar vote was a check on these claims and an additional proof of the correctness of our position. If we count the vote of the businessmen friendly to France, the Jewish bourgeois, the pacifist intellectuals (minus perhaps two to three percent), we can credit each of the working-class parties with from three to four percent of the vote, and this under the best conditions of the plebiscite. The workers do not forgive such criminal capitulation. The Saar plebiscite is mathematical proof of the need for systematic preparation for the formation of the Fourth International.

The fact that in France and other democratic countries the parties of the Third and especially the Second Internationals still seem to be organizationally imposing and maintaining a following changes nothing of the lesson of the Saar.

In France the workers can only win if, under the blows of the events of the next period, they forsake both bureaucracies. These events would certainly be seven-mile strides toward the formation of the Fourth International. If fascism conquers in France also, again the two Internationals are exposed. In a word, whether victory or defeat comes, the building of the Fourth International remains on the agenda.

The SAP, in order to hide their despicable cowardice in the face of the tasks of history, accuse us of wanting to "proclaim" the Fourth International at once. We need not go into the utter falsehood of this conception. We are Marxists. We do not play with history. We do not deny the problems it presents. Nor do we consider them solved if they are not in reality. We have said it a hundred times. We only want to put things as they really are.

The important thing is to prove to the working masses again and again the bankruptcy of the two Internationals. Every illusion that the vanguard of the workers loses prepares it for the struggle. That, however, is not enough. We must present our point of view on all important events in the international labor movement. That can only be done in the form of fundamental programmatic documents. In this is the most important preliminary work for the Fourth International.

Certainly we are too weak to "proclaim" the new International. No one has ever proposed such an adventurist step. The thing is to lay the ideological basis for it. The work must continue uninterruptedly, must sometime have an international organ and a committee that will undertake the actual work of preparation.

This committee can, in the first stages, be very cautious, arrogate to itself no administrative functions, concern itself only with the preparation of the basic documents and perhaps issue an international bulletin.

In what way can this work be begun? If the WPUS could reach an agreement with the Dutch party and with the ICL, we could immediately establish an international bureau to begin the work. [197]

In Europe in the next period, great events may transpire, and we may see considerable regroupings in the working-class movement. Revolutionary elements will be forced to look around for a new crystallizing center. That cannot be accomplished at one blow. Preparations must precede it. New splits in the Socialist and Stalinist parties are inevitable as well as in the centrist organizations that are today in the IAG. The international organization that has the correct theoretical and political position and that is deeply impressed with the historical necessity of its cause will conquer. It would be criminal to delay the work of clarification and the gathering of the forces under the banner of the Fourth International.

I do not write this letter to the general secretary of the WP, Muste, [198] not only because I do not know him personally but also because I do not want this letter to be construed in any sense as a formal proposal. If, however, you think it advisable to show this letter to Comrade Muste and to other leading comrades of your party, I would naturally be happy to have you do so.

I hope that I will soon get the reaction of the American comrades to these ideas, which are, by the way, not new ones. We took the initiative in advancing them over a year and a half ago.

With best wishes,
Crux [Leon Trotsky]

CENTRIST COMBINATIONS
AND MARXIST TACTICS[199]

A Letter to the Polish Comrade V.

(February 28, 1935)

I have read your letter about the conference of the organizations of the IAG with great interest and profit, for your report proved to be really revealing. But I must say from the very start that the conclusions you draw from the facts that you so correctly observed appear to me to be one-sided and even false. You are at once an opponent of the entry of the French section into the SFIO and a proponent of the entry of the ICL into the IAG. You are wrong on both counts.

From your own descriptions, it appears that we were confronted at the sessions of the IAG only with diplomatic representatives of various centrist groups and tendencies oriented in various directions, and that every one of these diplomats was particularly interested in not binding himself to anything and was, therefore, inclined to be very liberal toward the others. In other words, the prevailing principle was live and let live, or create confusion and let confusion be created.

The life of the IAG consists of the publication of documents from time to time, which do not mean very much, and of conferences every year and a half or so in order to prove that they are not sectarian, i.e., that, in contradistinction to the cursed Bolshevik-Leninists, they are not at all inclined to inconvenience one another. Thus the IAG becomes an asylum for conservative centrist diplomats who do not wish to risk anything and who prefer to let the omnivorous historical "process" take care of the most burning problems of our times. Should the above-mentioned "process" succeed, perchance, in creating a new, good Fourth International with steady posts for the diplomatic gentlemen, then the latter will most obligingly condescend to recognize the accomplished fact. But up to that time, they would like to leave the door open. Perhaps the Second and Third will merge after all and thus produce from both of these mutually complementary bankruptcies a new and flourishing firm. It will never do to spoil such an opportunity for oneself. Particularly must one avoid being pinned down to distinct principles, because our epoch is much too uncertain and the principle much too inflexible and, on top of that, there are those Leninist hotspurs who are always there to wave under your nose the contradiction between principle and action.

You have observed very well that the people from the SAP, whose spirit dominated the conference, made quite radical speeches in which they advanced our principles quite passably, in order all the better to snap their fingers at these same principles when the time for the adoption of decisions came around. You remark very aptly that this is indeed classical centrism itself. When it is a matter of an honest, naively centrist state of mind of the masses, it is possible, under favorable circumstances and a correct policy, to hold one's own and to push the masses forward. But when one is confronted only with the leaders, and when these leaders are "classical" centrists, i.e., conniving centrist speculators, then very little can be expected from such a labor community, which is neither laboring nor communist. To win five young workers in the SFIO for Marxist ideas is a hundred times more important than to vote on innocuous, i.e., deceptive, resolutions or even to record one's vote against them within the four walls of these conferences.

Such gatherings of solid bureaucrats, particularly when they come from different countries, often make a very imposing impression. It's best "to be there." One is not so "isolated" and, with aid of God, one can gain influence and prestige. — What a naive illusion! One possesses only that power that one conquers, i.e., the power of revolutionists welded together with clear ideas.

What is your objection to our turn in France? You quote from a letter of a representative of the Left Bund (Poland),[200] in which it is quite correctly affirmed that a numerically small group can exert great influence, thanks to its ideological clarity. But from this indisputable fact you also draw the unexpected conclusion that the latest turn of the ICL is harmful to its growing influence and that the unfortunate consequences extend even as far as the Left Bund. How is that to be understood?

The strength of the Bolshevik-Leninists consists, you say together with the representative of the Left Bund, in the clarity of its ideas. Since you maintain that our influence has receded since the turn (which is a hair-raising untruth), it is to be assumed that our ideas had in the meantime lost their clarity. That is indeed the point in question. Has our French section since its entry into the SFIO become less determined, more confused, more opportunistic? Or has it maintained a completely irreconcilable attitude with regard to its fundamental position? That, my dear friend, is what you should decide for yourself, or else your whole judgment rests on a completely lopsided logical basis.

Since, you say, firmness in *principle and ideological clarity* determines the influence of the Bolshevik-Leninists, the change in our *organizational* methods has become fatal for the influence of our organization. That does not rhyme, dear friend. You can, of course, venture the opinion that the change in organizational methods (entry into the SFIO) was a departure from ideological clarity. That is quite possible. The only question is, is that really the case in this instance?

I maintain that none of our sections has as yet had the opportunity to formulate its ideas so sharply and to bring them so directly before the masses as our French section has done since it became a tendency in the Socialist Party. And if one is able to observe, then one must come to the conclusion that the entire life of the Socialist as well as the Communist parties is now determined or at least influenced, directly or indirectly, positively or negatively, by the ideas and slogans of our small French section.

I can very easily conceive that comrades in Poland or some other place who do not read French and cannot keep track of French life may be affected unfavorably by the bare fact of the entrance into the Second International. But in revolutionary policy, it is not the immediate impression that counts but rather the lasting effect. Should the entry into the SFIO prove fruitful for the extension of our influence, then the Polish and other comrades will have to revise their evaluation of the turn we made. The majority of comrades, as a matter of fact, have already done so. It is correct that a small group with clear ideas is more important than one that is, perhaps, large but heterogeneous. But we must not make a fetish of this phrase. For the small group must seek to create the necessary public for its correct ideas. And in doing this, it must adapt itself organizationally to the given circumstances.

You present the whole matter as if Vidal,[201] frightened by the isolation of the French section, artificially invented the turn and imposed it upon the French section to the detriment of the whole movement.

In 1929 Vidal wrote to a Frenchman who accused the Left Opposition of sectarianism, as follows: "You point to individual groups of the Left Opposition and call them 'sectarian.' We ought to come to an agreement on the content of this term.

Among us there are elements who remain satisfied to sit at home and criticize the mistakes of the official party, without setting themselves any broader tasks, without assuming any practical revolutionary obligations, converting the revolutionary opposition into a title, something akin to an Order of the Legion of Honor. There are, in addition, sectarian tendencies that express themselves in splitting every hair into four parts. It is necessary to struggle against this. And I am personally ready to wage a struggle against it, and not to be deterred, if need be, by old friendships, personal ties and so forth and so on."

The letter I quote from, which was written six years ago, then goes on to explain why the Bolshevik-Leninists carried on and had to carry on their work in sectarian form as a propaganda group under the given circumstances, after a series of great international defeats, and ends up with the prognosis that this stage will undoubtedly have to be surmounted — not without a struggle against those who want to deduce from the ideological treasures of our tendency the right to remain immovably conservative, until such time as historic development finally takes notice of them and cordially invites them to be good enough and take over the leadership of the working class. No, dear friend, it is not enough to have correct ideas. It is necessary to know how to apply them. How? There are no universally valid prescriptions for that. It is necessary to investigate the situation concretely in each instance, in order to furnish the power of the correct ideas with the most favorable organizational lever.

At the time of the split with the Brandlerites, a comrade from the Walcher group turned to me to ask my opinion of the prospective entry of the minority into the SAP (I believe it was in 1931). My reply was approximately the following: the entry into this left Social Democratic party cannot in any case be condemned itself. It is necessary to know in the name of what principles and aims you want to bring about this entry. Therefore, it is obligatory, first of all, to elaborate a clear and unequivocal platform of your own.

As you know, Walcher and his people did not proceed in this manner. They have played hide-and-seek with ideas and still do to this day. This is what we condemn them for, not for joining a *certain* Social Democratic organization in a *certain* political situation.

I am informed that a young SAP man declared at the conference of the IAG: The turn of the Bolshevik-Leninists in France is a confirmation of the SAP principles. Serious people can only get a good laugh out of that, because entry in itself proves nothing; the decisive thing is program and action taken in the spirit of this program after the entry. Insofar as they are represented in the SFIO, the SAP produces the effect of formlessness and lukewarm centrism. Our people act in the spirit of Marxist clarity and determination.

But Lenin said it is necessary to break with the reformists, and we are now entering a reformist organization. This manner of counterposing things is completely akin spiritually to that of the Bordigists and their disciple Vereecken,[202] but has nothing in common with Leninism. Lenin proclaimed the necessity of breaking with the reformists after the outbreak of the war, the world war. He pitilessly demanded this of the centrists. At that time there were not in any country outside of the Russian emigration any consistent Bolsheviks. The leftward-turning elements to whom Lenin appealed were centrists, rooted in the Social Democracy not only organizationally but ideologically as well. It was to them that Lenin said: You must break with the reformists. But in order to be able to say that, the Russian Bolsheviks participated zealously in the internal life of the French, Swiss and Scandinavian Social Democracy.

Our great advantage over 1914 consists of the groups and organizations of hardened Bolsheviks that we have almost everywhere, which are internationally aligned and, therefore, subject to international control. They don't have to be convinced of the necessity of breaking with the reformists. They are faced with an altogether different problem: how can and should our small group with its clear ideas best get a hearing among the masses under present conditions? The situation is complicated and involved, so overrun with the remnants of old organizations that, while preserving absolute irreconcilability insofar as our principles are concerned, organizationally we must be very resourceful, very spry, very supple and very enterprising. Otherwise we will decay even with the very best ideas. In his correspondence with Sorge, Engels complains dozens of times that the English and German Marxists in America brought matters to such a pass that they transformed the liveliest theory, Marxism, into a sectarian faith under cover of which to be able to remain passive instead of intervening with all their force and determination in the stream of the living labor movement.

Look at Spain, dear friend. In the midst of all the tremors of revolution around them, the leadership of our section there distinguished itself during the whole period by its doctrinaire passivity. Individually, many of our comrades fought courageously. But the section as a whole distinguished itself more by "objective" criticism than by revolutionary activity. That is undoubtedly the most tragic example in the entire history of the ICL. And observe, it is precisely this section that to the present day remains completely intransigent toward the "opportunistic" turn in France.

In America developments took a different course. Our League has joined with the Muste organization to constitute an independent party. The organization participates eagerly in the actual mass movement and has considerable successes to its credit. And precisely for this reason, it has been able to show a clear understanding for the French turn, despite the difference in conditions and in the methods applied.

As Marxists, we are centralists. We are striving internationally also for the merger of the revolutionary forces. But as Marxists, we cannot be pettifogging doctrinaires, pedants. We always analyze the living stream and adapt ourselves to every new situation without losing our identity. Therein lies the whole secret of revolutionary success. And we must master this secret regardless of the costs.

AGAIN ON THE QUESTION
OF BONAPARTISM[203]

Bourgeois Bonapartism and Soviet Bonapartism

(March 1935)

Some critics complain that we use the term Bonapartism very broadly and very differently. Those critics don't notice that the same holds good for our use of other terms in the vocabulary of politics, such as "democracy" and "dictatorship," not to speak of "state," "society," "governments," etc. We speak of the democracy of the past (based on slavery), democracy of the medieval corporations, bourgeois democracy, proletarian democracy (in the sense of the state), as well as of democracy in the parties, the trade unions, guilds, etc., etc. Marxism cannot renounce such established, economical notions and cannot refuse to apply them to new phenomena; otherwise the transmission of human thought would, in general, be impossible. Marxism has, under pain of error, to define in every case the social content of the notion and the direction of its evolution. Let us recall that Marx and Engels characterized not only the regime of Napoleon III but also that of Bismarck[204] as Bonapartist. On April 12, 1890, Engels wrote to Sorge, "*Every* government today is becoming Bonapartist, *nolens volens.*" That was more or less true for a long period when agriculture was in crisis and industry depressed. The new upsurge of capitalism from about 1895 on weakened the Bonapartist tendencies; the decline of capitalism after the [First World] War strengthened them considerably.

In his *History of the Great Russian Revolution,* Chernov[205] brings forward statements by Lenin and Trotsky describing the Kerensky regime as embryonic Bonapartism and, rejecting this characterization, he notes sententiously, "Bonapartism takes flight with wings of glory." This "flight" of theory is Chernov's manner completely; but Marx and Engels and Lenin defined Bonapartism not by wings but by a specific class relationship.

By Bonapartism we mean a regime in which the economically dominant class, having the qualities necessary for democratic methods of government, finds itself compelled to tolerate — in order to preserve its possessions — the uncontrolled command of a military and police apparatus over it, of a crowned "savior." This kind of situation is created in periods when the class contradictions have become particularly acute; the aim of Bonapartism is to prevent explosions. Bourgeois society has gone through such periods more than once, but these were, so to speak, only rehearsals. The present decline of capitalism not only has definitively undermined democracy but also has disclosed the total inadequacy of Bonapartism of the old type; in its place has come fascism. However, as a bridge between democracy and fascism (in Russia, 1917, as a "bridge" between democracy and Bolshevism), there appears a "personal regime" that rises above democracy and tacks between the two camps — while safeguarding, at the same time, the interests of the ruling class; it is sufficient to give this definition for the term Bonapartism to be fully settled.

In any case, we observe:

1. Not one of our critics has taken the trouble to demonstrate the specific character of prefascist governments: Giolitti and Facta[206] in Italy; Bruening, Papen and Schleicher in Germany; Dollfuss in Austria; and Doumergue and Flandin in France;

2. No one to date has proposed another term. We, for our part, see no need for one; the term employed by Marx, Engels and Lenin is completely satisfactory to us.

Why do we insist on this question? Because it has colossal importance for both theory and policy. It can be said that a prerevolutionary (or prefascist) period officially opens in the country from the moment when the conflict between classes separated into two hostile camps removes the axis of power outside parliament. Therefore, Bonapartism is the characterization of the last period in which the proletarian vanguard can gather its momentum for the conquest of power. Not understanding the nature of a Bonapartist regime, the Stalinists are led to give the following diagnosis: "It is not a *revolutionary situation*"; and they ignore a *pre*revolutionary situation.

Things become complicated when we use the term *Bonapartism* for the Stalin regime and speak of "Soviet Bonapartism." "No," exclaim our critics, "you have too many 'Bonapartisms'; the word is being extended in inadmissible fashion," etc. Usually, objections of this kind — abstract, formal and grammatical — are made when people have nothing to say on the subject.

There is no doubt at all that neither Marx, Engels nor Lenin used the term Bonapartist for a workers' state; there's nothing astonishing about this: they had no occasion to (that Lenin did not hesitate at all to use, with the necessary reservations, for the workers' state terms used for the bourgeois regime is demonstrated, for example, by his expression "capitalism of the Soviet state"). But what are we to do when the good old books do not give the needed indications? Try to manage with one's own head.

What does Stalin's "personal regime" mean and what is its origin? In the last analysis it is the product of a sharp class struggle between the proletariat and the bourgeoisie. With the help of the bureaucratic and police apparatuses, the power of the "savior" of the people and the arbiter of the bureaucracy as the ruling caste rose above *Soviet* democracy, reducing it to a shadow of itself. The objective function of the "savior" is to safeguard the new property forms, by usurping the political functions of the ruling class. Is not this *precise characterization of the socialist regime* at the same time *the scientific sociological definition of Bonapartism?*

The incomparable value of the term is that it allows us immediately to discover extremely instructive historical affinities and to determine what it is that forms their social roots. This comes out: the offensive of plebeian or proletarian forces against the ruling bourgeoisie, like the offensive of bourgeois and petty-bourgeois forces against a ruling proletariat, can end up in political regimes that are completely analogous (symmetrical). This is the incontestable fact that the term Bonapartist best allows us to bring out.

When Engels wrote "*Every* government is becoming Bonapartist, *nolens volens,*" he had in mind, certainly, only the tendency of the development. In this sphere as elsewhere, quantity changes into quality. Every bourgeois democracy bears the features of Bonapartism. One can also discover, with good reasons, elements of Bonapartism in the Soviet regime under Stalin. But the art in scientific thinking is to determine where precisely quantity changes into a new quality. In the era of Lenin, Soviet Bonapartism was a *possibility*; in the era of Stalin, it has become a *reality.*

The term Bonapartism misleads naive thinkers (a la Chernov), because it evokes in the mind the historical model of Napoleon in the same way as the term Caesarism evokes the model of Julius Caesar. In actual fact, these two terms have long been detached from the historical figures who gave them their names. When we speak of *Bonapartism,* without qualification, we have in mind not historical analogies but sociological definition. In the same way, the term chauvinism has a character as general as *nationalism,* although the first word comes from the name of the French bourgeois Chauvin and the second from *nation.*

However, in *certain* cases, speaking of Bonapartism, we have in mind a more concrete historical affinity. Thus, the Stalin regime, which is the translation of Bonapartism in the language of the Soviet state, reveals, at the same time, a certain number of *supplementary* features resembling the regime of the Consulate (or of the empire, but still without a crown); and this is not by chance; these two regimes followed on great revolutions and usurped them.

We see that a correct use, that is to say, a dialectical use, of the term Bonapartism not only does not lead us to schematism — that ulcer of thought — but, on the contrary, allows us to characterize the phenomena that interest us in as concrete a fashion as is necessary, the phenomenon being taken not in isolation as a "thing in itself," but in historical connection with numerous other phenomena connected with it. What more can we ask of a scientific term?

THE BELGIAN DISPUTE AND THE DE MAN PLAN[207]

(March 2, 1935)

To the International Secretariat

Dear Comrades,

I am absolutely in agreement with your appraisal of the dispute in our Belgian section. After studying the documents concerning the crisis, I would like to enlarge a little on my point of view.

On January 15, 1935, Brussels wrote to all the members of the Belgian section: "Our differences merely become intensified. . . . We cannot as revolutionary militants share, even partially, in the responsibilities." This is the language of split. If the attitude of the national and international organization is so bad that it no longer allows "revolutionary militants" to bear even a part of the responsibility, nothing remains but split.

On January 29, Vereecken wrote to the IS: "I am anxious to let you know quite frankly that the 'nonentrist' comrades and myself consider more and more that this radical step is most harmful and the IS must not maintain the slightest illusions regarding an eventual change in our political position. We consider it a political, historical error of the greatest dimensions, and we shall continue, in the interest of the revolutionary movement and the formation of the Fourth International, to fight this tendency with all our strength."

It is the same language. If the Brussels comrades persuade themselves "more and more" that our tactic is most harmful, if we must have no illusions as to an eventual change in the ideas of the Brussels comrades, this can only mean that Comrade Vereecken is busying himself conscientiously and systematically with preparation for a split.

"Our differences merely become intensified." The degeneration of the ICL becomes, for the critics of Brussels, "more and more" obvious. But since the differences have taken on an open and acute character particularly since the discussion on the entry of our French section into the SFIO, we must wait until Comrade Vereecken gives us an analysis of the experience in France since the entry. It is evidently in the light of this experience that he has had to convince himself "more and more" of our decadence. But this is where the enigma begins. In all the documents available to me, I find no analyses by Comrade Vereecken of the activity of our French section. This may appear surprising.

Comrade Vereecken predicted the absolute impossibility of the Bolshevik-Leninists developing their ideas within the Social Democratic party. He predicted the opportunist degeneration and the complete discrediting of our tendency. Does he make any attempt to analyze the real facts? Does he compare his predictions with the living reality? No, not in the least. He was implacable when it was a question of predictions, of discussions, of preliminary questions, but since it has become a reality, Vereecken has lost all interest in the question. This fact characterizes perfectly the abstract manner in which Vereecken approaches ideas and problems.

But we Marxists are interested, above all, in facts. And on the basis of the five months that have passed since the entry, we say: each day and each new fact only give the lie to the purely negative and sterile attitude of Vereecken at the time of the French discussion. And if he is not capable of seeing it and admitting it openly, it is not surprising if he travels farther and farther from Marxism in the direction of Bordigism, that is, of nothing.

Vereecken complains: "The discussion of the youth [was] carried out at a racing speed" and also "the vote was taken in confusion," etc. . . . Vereecken's trouble is that he separates completely the question of the Belgian youth and the question of the French entry and the experience of the French League. For him, political activity is only a series of discussions. The French question was long and bitterly discussed internationally and, above all, in Belgium. In the light of these discussions and, above all, of the experiences that followed them, the question of entry into the Belgian Young Socialist Guard hardly demanded discussion for all Marxists concerned with the facts of reality—but that, unfortunately, was not the case with Vereecken. In turning his back on the French experience, which pitilessly disowns him, he simply wishes to have a new "discussion" and, especially, that it should last, since activity is for him internal discussion.

"Our differences merely become intensified." But what is the

most important point of these differences in Belgium? The
question of the de Man plan, which on its side has reduced
itself to the question of inflation. It is amazing to see the importance that Vereecken attributes to this question. His bulletins are full of demonstrations of the evil intentions of de
Man, who aspires to inflation. Formalist minds frequently
seize upon altogether secondary questions to inflate them out
of all proportion. Are we, for example, knights of the Belgian
franc? Is the saving of the existing currency our way of salvation? One cannot understand the anti-inflation fanaticism
of Vereecken. In this period of social crisis, of economic shocks,
*inflation and deflation are two complementary instruments for
throwing on to the people the cost of decaying capitalism.*
Bourgeois parties organize formidable discussions on the question: is it better to cut the workers' throats with the saw of
inflation or with the simple knife of deflation? Our struggle is
directed with the same energy against the saw and against
the knife.

But Vereecken steels himself, above all, against inflation. To
expose the plan of de Man, he has created a special aphorism:
"nationalization by means of buying back is a kind of inflation." It is the *buying back* that must be countered without
becoming embroiled in questions of financial technique. But
no, Vereecken is intent on showing that de Man is an inflationist. He goes so far as to say that "a campaign in the paper
on this question would have been most significant for our
tendency." But, if I am not mistaken, it is the Theunis[208] government that today starves the people, brandishing, meanwhile,
the fan of the inflationist plan of de Man. That helps in the
best way the knife of deflation. But since all that takes place
in reality and not in discussion, Vereecken remains indifferent.
He demands from the journal a special campaign against not
the deflation of Theunis but the problematic and, in any case,
far distant inflation of de Man. All of Vereecken's mentality
is revealed in this instructive episode.

Vereecken writes: "Since one knows, and one has agreed to
write, that the plan is a deception for the workers, and one
knows besides that shady negotiations are taking place in
order to deliver a treacherous blow against the toiling masses,
Charleroi[209] continues to leave the workers to struggle in total
darkness. One goes so far today as to confound the plan with
socialism in *La Voix.* . . . The editors of *La Voix* can no
longer distinguish between a deception, a delusion, a treason
and socialism."

You can see, comrades, the case is serious. Vereecken accuses *La Voix* not only of identifying deception and treason

with socialism but, moreover, of doing it with full knowledge of the fact. The editors of *La Voix* know that it is a deception, but instead of unmasking it, Lesoil[210] and his friends cover it up, lead the workers into the trap, participate in the treason. And our international organization? Let us read about it in the letter of January 15: "We finish by accusing the IS and Comrade Vidal of covering up the position of Charleroi and we say: to each his responsibility."

You see, the case is serious. The leaders of the Belgian section consciously betray the proletariat, and the international leadership covers them in this work.

But do not hasten to become annoyed. It is not the bad faith of Vereecken that is at stake; it is his anti-Marxist journalist thought that flies from reality and concerns itself with phantoms.

To show that the plan of de Man is a deception, Vereecken builds up a complete Eiffel Tower of demonstrations of the inflationist danger that interests us. De Man is for buying back, and buying back can only be a terrific expense for the people. By what technical process the buying back is effected, that is a question of tenth-degree importance. But, imitating Theunis, Vereecken brandishes the specter of inflation. That is the deception, that is the treason of which Lesoil is the accomplice and the IS the "fence." It would be funny if it were not so tragic, at least for Comrade Vereecken.

The criticism of the plan has been made many times; one can complete it. If we had to present a plan to the Belgian proletariat, this plan would have had an altogether different aspect. Unfortunately, the Belgian proletariat gave this mandate not to us but to the Belgian Labor Party [POB], and the plan reflects two facts: the pressure of the proletariat on the POB and the conservative character of this party.

In what consists the deception of the plan? In the fact that the leadership of the POB, de Man included, does not wish to lead the masses into struggle, and without struggle this plan, inadequate as it is, is completely unrealizable. Then, when we say to the masses that to realize this imperfect plan it is necessary to struggle to the end, we are far from covering up the deception; on the contrary, we are helping the masses to expose it by their own experience.

But you identify the plan with socialism, writes Vereecken. He merely forgets that in the mouth of de Man the word socialism means the same deception as the plan. And for the same reason, the leaders of the POB do not want a struggle. But they are caught in the wheels of the crisis of capitalism and of reformism. They were forced to proclaim the plan and even to make of it the platform of the Belgian proletariat. It is a fact. What is our task? To help the workers to turn the wheels into which the opportunist leaders have been forced to thrust their hands.

Allow me, comrades, to recall a classic example. The Russian Social Revolutionary Party formulated in May 1917 its "plan," that is to say, its agrarian program, basing itself on hundreds of peasant demands. The program contained the expropriation of private landed property, the periodic redistribution of the land among the peasants, the abolition of wage-labor in agriculture, etc. . . . In all, the democratic-revolutionary slogan (expropriation of the landed gentry) was linked to utopian demands, to petty-bourgeois prejudices. The party of Kerensky-Chernov that had launched this "plan" remained in governmental coalition with the gentry and the capitalists.

What was the attitude of the Bolsheviks? They criticized the internal contradictions and inadequacies of the program. But, before all, they recognized that the realization of this program would mean an enormous advantage for the peasants, for the whole people. However, the program could not be realized in collaboration with the exploiters. The Bolsheviks did everything to draw the peasants into the struggle for their plan. They even finished by inscribing the plan into their program of action. They declared to the peasants the faults of your program — we will correct them together with you in the light of common experience, when we have gained power. However, your leaders, Kerensky, Chernov and the others do not want a struggle. Therein lies their deception. Try to draw them into the struggle, and if they are obstinate, drive them out!

This policy was neither trickery nor treason. It was the true policy of Marxist realism. Without this policy, the October Revolution would have been impossible.

The revolutionary task consists in demanding that the POB take power in order to put its own plan into effect. Vereecken replies to this: No! It is necessary to demand a workers' government and not simply a socialist government. We must not forget the Stalinist workers, and besides, the plan is no good — it threatens us with inflation. I, Vereecken, I will propose a better plan. Is this serious? No, it is ridiculous. Vereecken sets himself outside of reality. He constructs in his imagination a united front that does not exist in Belgium. For this imaginary united front he proposes an imaginary program, that is, Vandervelde and Jacquemotte[211] ought to fight together for the perfect plan dreamed up by Vereecken. In this way matters will be splendidly arranged.

Vereecken tries to quote Gourov in favor of his point of

view on the campaign around the plan. This is at least an unfortunate misunderstanding. Gourov's letter[212] recognized the necessity of taking a position on the basis of the campaign, in favor of the socialist party [POB] taking power to carry out its own plan. That's all. Gourov insisted only on the necessity of a sharp criticism of the left socialists. At least nine-tenths of the Gourov letter coincided with the Charleroi position, whereas Vereecken previously was characterizing the de Man plan as an expression of social fascism.

Seizing upon some insufficiently precise formulations in *La Voix,* Vereecken accuses its editors of being subservient to the general staff of the POB and the unions and of renouncing Marxist criticism. This new betrayal is committed as the purchase price for the possibility of entering the POB. Take note of the heinousness of the accusation. The startling disproportion between the facts, that is, the quotations, and the accusation reaches the level of a slander. I take up the issue of *La Voix* that I have just received. I read there: "The victory won by the government on February 4 — and this with the aid of the leaders of the POB and the CS [union federation]." The same article says that the leaders of the POB have reaffirmed with all "the declared enemies of the working class their attachment to the bourgeois regime," and so on and so forth. Really, you do not use such language when you are trying to sell out to the bureaucracy of the POB and the CS. In the same issue there is a criticism of *l'Action Syndicale* [Union Action], which advises the government to bend under the "pressure" of the demonstration. "Those who speak like this to the workers deceive them," says *La Voix*. No, *La Voix* is not vassalized to the union chiefs; it does not deceive the workers, whatever it otherwise does, or whatever errors it sometimes commits. But these mistakes of *La Voix* pale into insignificance alongside the mountains of errors, distortions, unwarranted accusations and complete misconceptions of reality on the part of Comrade Vereecken.

The gravest mistake for which *La Voix* can be reproached — here I am in complete accord with Comrade Martin — is that our Belgian friends identify the revolutionary struggle too much with the general strike. Just as a simple strike has need, above all in this epoch, of a picket line, so a general strike needs a workers' militia, which in the last analysis is nothing else but a generalized picket line. The general strike poses the problem of power, but does not resolve it. What is always involved at bottom is the question of armed force. The fascists penetrate everywhere, in the barracks, through the officers on active duty as well as those in the reserves. The proletarian vanguard should step up their efforts to strengthen their moral ties with their brothers in the barracks. Thus the struggle for power requires not only preparation of the general strike but also education of the will of the vanguard to pass from the defensive to the offensive, to set about creating a workers' militia and to win over the workers in the army. But it is very significant that Vereecken doesn't breathe a word about this. He condemns *La Voix* only when it is perfectly correct.

Vereecken's general attitude resembles that of Bauer, but with a certain time lag. The conservatism of both is offended by the fact that we are passing from the stage of individual propaganda to systematic action among the masses. This transition, which was made inevitable by the logic of things and was foreseen by us a long time ago, seems to them an abnegation of principles, a surrender, a betrayal. If there really has been an abandonment of the most fundamental Marxist principles, it has been by Bauer, by Vereecken, by the unavowed Bordigists and Hennautists. 213

The stage of individual educational propaganda was inevitable. When the centrists accused us of sectarianism, we answered them: without a minimal Marxist cadre, principled action among the masses is impossible. But that is the only reason we form cadres. To one of the French opportunists who often spoke of our sectarianism, the *Biulletin* replied *in June 1929:* Yes, "among us there are elements who remain satisfied to sit at home and criticize the mistakes of the official party, without setting themselves any broader tasks, without assuming any practical revolutionary obligations, converting the revolutionary opposition into a title, something akin to an Order of the Legion of Honor. There are, in addition, sectarian tendencies that express themselves in splitting each hair into four parts. It is necessary to struggle against this. And I am personally ready to wage a struggle against it, and not to be deterred, if need be, by old friendships, personal ties, and so forth and so on." These lines were written, comrades, almost six years ago. It is therefore not at all a question of an unexpected turn, provoked by some exceptional circumstances. It is a case of the growth of our tasks and obligations determined by all of our preceding work. The exceptional circumstances only give an extraordinary sharpness to our new tasks.

In Engels's correspondence with Sorge, which went on for several decades, on almost every page we can find remarkable observations on the question that concerns us here. In England, as in the United States, Marxism remained for too long a time at the level of a propaganda society. Engels never tired of repeating that Marxism is not an academic doctrine or a sectarian profession of faith but an instrument for systematic work among the masses. In 1886, Engels said:

"If they succeed in the Socialist League in educating a nucleus of people who understand things theoretically, a great deal will have been gained for the launching of a real mass movement. . . ."

You see that Engels well understood the importance of a nucleus of theoretically educated people. But this was not for him an end in itself. That same year he wrote about the German Marxists in the United States:

"The Germans have not understood how to use their theory as a lever which could set the American masses in motion; they do not understand the theory themselves for the most part and treat it in a *doctrinaire and dogmatic way as something that has to be learned by heart, which then will satisfy all requirements forthwith. To them it is a credo and not a guide to action"* (emphasis added).

I ask you, isn't this the case with Bauer and Vereecken, who have learned by heart the abstract definitions of reformism and of the Second International, etc., which serve them not to accelerate but, on the contrary, to check our revolutionary activity among the masses?

One month later Engels wrote again about the pseudo-Marxists who in the face of a real mass movement have tried to make of the "not always understood [Marxist] theory a kind of salvationist dogma, and thereby to keep aloof from any movement that did not accept that dogma." Isn't this the case with Vereecken in the face of the mass movement favoring the plan?

In February 1887 Engels wrote: "That great national movement, no matter what its first form, is the real starting point of American working-class development. If the Germans join it, in order to help it or to hasten its development in the right direction, they may do a great deal of good and play a decisive part in it. *If they stand aloof, they will dwindle down into a dogmatic sect and be brushed aside as people who do not understand their own principles"* (emphasis added). Isn't this a mirror created for the Bauers, Vereeckens and others?

Two years later, in April 1891, Engels cited an example in order to draw this conclusion from it: "It demonstrates how very useless a platform that is largely theoretically correct can be, if it does not know how to link itself with the real needs of the masses." Finally, a year before his death, Engels castigated the English and American Marxists "that have managed to reduce the Marxian theory of development to a rigid orthodoxy which the workers . . . have to gulp down . . . as

an article of faith." I could multiply these quotations endlessly.
You will find without difficulty the same ideas adapted to different conditions by Lenin, whose revolutionary intransigence,
we know, had nothing in common with sectarian sterility.

What are our conclusions? Vereecken now represents a *reactionary* tendency in our ranks. His acts of indiscipline may
become very important in and of themselves, but they have
in this situation for us only a secondary importance. We should
unreservedly condemn his false and sterile conceptions, which,
if they won over the leadership, could only reduce our tendency
to the pitiful role of the Bordigists, Hennautists, etc. . . . It
is necessary to declare openly that *we cannot and will not
accept the slightest responsibility for the Bauer-Vereecken tendency.*

Does this exclude common work in the future, even tomorrow, even today? For my part, no. If Bauer, after his unfortunate experience, which has isolated him completely in
Germany as well as in the emigration, should return to our
ranks, he will be welcome. Nobody would impose humiliating
conditions on him in the Stalinist manner. It is not possible
to act without making mistakes. The crime begins when one
refuses to correct mistakes proved by experience.

If Comrade Vereecken knew how to overcome his capricious
and anarchistic individualism, if he will strive to orient himself not in accord with his own texts but in accord with the
reality of the struggle, he has only to reenter the ranks that
he deliberately broke away from. On our part he will find the
most sincere wish to collaborate. Decisive are not the unfortunate episodes of internal struggle but the revolutionary conception and methods. Do we have these in common or not?
That is the question Vereecken should answer if he is to regain
his place in our ranks.

                                        Crux [Leon Trotsky]

FROM A LETTER TO THE CHINESE COMRADES[214]

(March 5, 1935)

Dear Friends,

The role of the Communist International, i.e., of the Stalinist bureaucracy, is thoroughly catastrophic, especially in the East. The latest sessions of the League of Nations show that the Stalinist bureaucracy increasingly abandons the rights of peoples to self-determination. Its main principle is now the "status quo." The consequences of the submission of the Comintern to the conjunctural needs of Soviet diplomacy are not as catastrophic in the East as in the West. The first requisite for the success of the Chinese revolution is the breakaway of the proletarian Chinese vanguard from the national-conservative Soviet bureaucracy.

The greater the crimes the Soviet bureaucracy perpetrates against the international proletariat, the more brutal and odious are the attacks it launches in its struggle with the Bolshevik-Leninists who, with steadily growing success, are its accuser before the court of justice. There is, for example, the failure of the Kirov amalgam, which apparently is credible only to the worst elements of the Comintern. It would, however, be criminally light-minded to believe that the Stalin clique was satisfied with this result. Precisely because the falsification had not the effect intended, the falsifiers must work out a fresh amalgam, which this time will be better prepared. It is not excluded that the wretched piece will be played this time in France. The GPU has sufficient agents in the workers' movement. Where the Stalinist consul was not able to get any letter from the terrorists for Trotsky, the agents of the GPU are well able to prepare a bomb with a Trotskyist visiting card attached. A fresh amalgam is most likely; in other lands too, including China, the provocation against our friends produces a shameful crop. Therefore, vigilance is on the order of the day.

With brotherly greetings,
Crux [Leon Trotsky]

FROM THE CGT'S PLAN
TO THE CONQUEST OF POWER[215]

(Delivered March 18-19, 1935)

Comrades,

The CGT sets as its aim the "intensification of propaganda" in support of the plan.[216] We can only congratulate ourselves on this. The best plan is only a scrap of paper if it does not have the militant masses behind it. It is to be regretted that in the year that has passed since the adoption of the plan, so little has been done to present it to the masses and to win their support.

The notes "for the use of propagandists" that we received from the CGT some months ago stress the necessity for a "vigorous oral propaganda effort to be carried out even to the small, rural centers." I am sure that the departmental unions could mobilize sufficient cadres of loyal propagandists. But for their efforts to be really vigorous and, above all, effective, the unions themselves must have a clear position on this question.

I must, however, acknowledge that the discussions on the plan, even in fairly limited circles, reveal a certain confusion. Perhaps we who come from the provinces are not sufficiently informed. In that case, the center must help us. For my part, I want to take advantage of this session of the CCN to ask some questions, express some doubts, indicate some weaknesses and demand some supplementary clarifications.

Many comrades in this room are too experienced in how the masses respond — certainly, much more than I am — for me to need to stress the idea that propaganda can strike home only when it is clear and concrete. That is why we propagandists ask you for a little more clarity and a little more precision about the plan.

In the different texts of the CGT, we often read that what is involved is a renovation of the national economy, sometimes counterposed to "economic and social reorganization," but sometimes also identified with it.

Comrades, it is very difficult to say to the workers or the peasants, "We want to renovate the national economy," when everybody now uses the same expression: the Patriotic Youth, the Popular Democrats, the Peasant Front,[217] sometimes even the Radicals, but above all M. Flandin — all of them proclaiming and promising the renovation and even the reorganization of the national economy. Our plan must be distinguished from those of the class enemy through the precise definition of its goal. All the renovations and reorganizations that I have just spoken of seek to remain on a capitalist base, that is, to safeguard private property in the means of production. And the CGT's plan? Does it aim to renovate capitalist economy or to replace that economy by another? I confess to not having found an exact reply to this question. Sometimes we read in the same texts that what is involved is not a transformation of the present system but only emergency measures to alleviate the crisis. However, we also find it stated that the emergency measures must open the way to more profound transformations.

Perhaps all that is correct, but we never find the exact definition of the system we want to end up with. What sort of so-called profound transformations should there be? Is it only a question — I am just speaking hypothetically — of transforming a section of private capitalism into state capitalism? Or do we want to replace the whole capitalist system by another social regime? Which one? What is our final goal? It is astonishing, comrades, but all the statements and even the "notes for the use of propagandists" say absolutely nothing about it. Do we want to replace capitalism by socialism, by communism or by anarchy a la Proudhon? Or do we simply want to rejuvenate capitalism by reforming and modernizing it? When I want to travel a distance of one or two stations only, I still must know where the train is going. Even for emergency measures we need a general orientation. What is the social ideal of the CGT? Is it socialism? Yes or no? We must be told — otherwise, as propagandists, we remain completely disarmed before the masses.

The difficulties are increased by the fact that we are only partially acquainted with the CGT doctrine and its program and that the "notes for the use of propagandists" do not indicate to us the literature that could enlighten us. The only doctrinal authority cited in the statements of the CGT is Proudhon, the theoretician of anarchy. It is he who said that the "workshop must replace the government." Do *we* aspire to anarchy? Do we want to replace capitalist anarchy by pure anarchy? It seems not, since the plan speaks of nationalization of the key industries. In practical terms, nationalization signifies statization. Now, if we have recourse to the state to centralize and direct the economy, how can we invoke Proudhon, who demanded only one thing of the state: that it leave him alone! And in truth, modern industry, the trusts, cartels, consortiums, banks, all that totally surpasses the Proudhonist vision of equal exchanges between independent producers. Why, then, invoke Proudhon? That can only increase the confusion.

To the present capitalist system, which has survived for a long time, we can counterpose only socialism. As propagandist for our trade-union organization, I believe I am expressing the idea of many militants in demanding that the plan for economic renewal be renamed the *plan of measures for the transition from capitalism to socialism.*

Then, before taking his place in the railway car, each worker and peasant will know where the CGT train is heading.

Comrades, for our propaganda to be effective, this clarification is absolutely indispensable.

The CGT plan stresses, above all, the fact that credit is the guiding lever of the economy. Comrades, I am far from being a specialist in questions of banking and credit. I mainly want to educate myself in order to be able to explain the issue to the workers. But I confess again that I have not found the clarifications that I need in the documents of the CGT. They speak of "nationalization of credit," and "control of the banks." It's more by way of exception that the same document speaks of "nationalization of the banks." Can you control credit without having nationalized the banks? You can control only what you hold firmly in your hands. Do we want to nationalize the banks or not? I suppose yes. Then it must be said openly and clearly. Unfortunately, instead of this being the case, we find vague formulations, for example: "The bank must be at the service of the economy, and not the economy at the service of the bank" (p. 6 of the statement). A worker asked me to explain that nebulous phrase to him. Seeing my perplexity, he remarked: "But the bank always remains in the service of the economy, like the trusts, the railways, etc. . . . They all serve capitalist economy in robbing the people." This harsh remark seemed to me much more correct than the formulation that I cited above. The capitalist bank serves the capitalist economy. We should say therefore: We now want to seize the bank out of the hands of the capitalist exploiters in order to make it a lever of social transformation, that is, of socialist construction. I would very much like to see this clear formulation in the text of the plan.

The nationalization of the banks could naturally be carried out only to the detriment of high finance. As for small investors, their interests must be not just spared, but protected. We must choose between the interests of the financial sharks and the interests of the middle classes. Our choice is carried out by the expropriation of the former. We will create for the latter conditions much more favorable than at present.

But nationalization of the banks is not enough. After nationalizing the banks, we must proceed to their complete unification. All individual banks must be transformed into branches of the national bank. Only this unification can transform the nationalized banking system into a system of bookkeeping and direction for the national economy.

In the "notes for the use of propagandists," I find some very valuable statistics concerning the organization of the dictatorship of finance capital in our country. Basing themselves on a 1932 investigation, the notes state the following: "In practical terms we can say that ninety persons own and control the economy of our country." *There* is a statement that is precise and overwhelming in its precision. The welfare or misery of a hundred million human beings — for we cannot forget our unfortunate colonies, which the ninety sharks bleed even more than the metropolis — the fate of a hundred million people depends on the wave of the hand of ninety all-powerful magnates. It is they who are making a mess of the national economy to preserve their miserable, bloody privileges and power. Unfortunately neither the text of the plan nor the commentaries on it indicate what must be done with these ninety monarchs who control us. The response should be clear: we must expropriate them, unseat them, to return to the plundered people what belongs to them. This would be a good beginning toward accomplishing the plan. I move, in the name of the departmental union of Isere, to inscribe this measure in the text of the plan. Our propaganda will then become more vigorous and much more effective. [218]

In the text of the plan, we find an important paragraph under the heading "Industrialized Nationalizations." This heading appears very strange. We understand what nationalized industry means, but industrialized nationalization leaves us in a quandary. Permit me to say that such contrived terminology complicates the task of the propagandist by obscuring the most simple things. The "notes for the use of propagandists" don't even mention the nationalization of industry. Perhaps these notes preceded the last editing of the statement. Unfortunately, we seldom find dates on CGT documents, an important weakness that must be overcome if our work is to be facilitated.

We may congratulate ourselves in any case on the fact that

the latest edition of the plan poses the following thesis: *the nationalization of certain key industries is necessary.* However the word "certain" seems superfluous. Naturally we cannot hope to nationalize with one blow all industries, small, middle and big. On the contrary, the regime that we want to establish must show the greatest indulgence toward small manufacturers and artisans, as well as small merchants and peasants. But the text speaks explicitly of the key industries, that is, the powerful trusts and cartels, the combines like the Comite des Forges [Association of Heavy Industries], the Comite des Houilleres [Association of Coal Industries], the Compagnies des Chemin de Fer [railway companies], etc., etc. As key industries, they must all be nationalized, and not only "certain" ones. It even seems to us in Isere that we should add to the plan the list of these key industries with some precise statistics on their capitalization, their dividends, the number of workers they exploit and the number of unemployed they throw on the scrap heap.

To speak to the people, it is necessary to be concrete, to call things by their name and to give exact figures. Otherwise, the worker and even more so the peasant will say, "This is not a plan, but the platonic dream of some bureaucrat."

Under the heading "Conditions of Acquisition," the text of the plan speaks of the conditions for nationalizing the key industries and obviously the banks also. We are accustomed to thinking that nationalization should take place by expropriating the exploiters. However, the plan speaks not of expropriation but of acquisition. Does that mean that the state must simply buy from the capitalists the firms created by the workers' labor? Manifestly so. At what price? The statement replies: the price will be calculated "according to the real value at the time of purchase." We learn later that "the amortization will be calculated over a period of forty or fifty years." There, comrades, is a financial deal that will hardly appeal to the workers or peasants. What is this? We want to transform society, and we begin by total and complete recognition that capitalist property is sacrosanct!

The chairman of the council, M. Flandin, was correct when he said in parliament recently, "Capital is accumulated labor." And all the capitalists in parliament applauded this formulation. Unfortunately, it is not complete. To express the truth, it would be necessary to say: "Capital is the labor of the workers accumulated by their exploiter." Here is the time to cite Proudhon on capitalist property. You are acquainted with the formulation: "Property is theft." In this sense it could be said: "The property of the ninety magnates who control France is accumulated theft." No, we don't want to buy back what has been stolen from the working people; we don't want the new regime to be burdened with debts from its first day when it will have many tasks to resolve and many difficulties to surmount. Capitalism is bankrupt. It has ruined the nation. The capitalists' debts to the people exceed by far the real value of their enterprises. No! No buying back! No new slavery! Expropriation pure and simple or, if you wish, confiscation.

I really hope that in this assembly, which represents the oppressed, the exploited, no one is moved by sympathy for the tycoons threatened with unemployment and poverty. In any case, they are farsighted enough to cover themselves on all sides. And if one of them really found himself without resources, the state would provide him the same pension as retired workers. We have enough of sick and poverty-stricken elderly people and youth, permanent unemployed and women condemned to prostitution. To put an end to all this human misery, we will greatly need the amounts that the plan is all too generously prepared to confer on the exploiters and their descendants over a half century. That provision of the plan, comrades, would have us bringing up two new generations of sluggards! No, that paragraph alone is enough to compromise the entire plan irreparably in the eyes of the starving masses. Comrades, strike out that paragraph as soon as possible. That is another proposal from our departmental union.

The "notes for the use of propagandists" inform us, "Fiscal fraud is raised to an institutional level." Very well said. This is correct and clear. But it is not just fiscal fraud. The Oustric and Stavisky affairs reminded us that the whole capitalist economy is based not just on legalized exploitation but also on general cheating. To hide the cheating from the eyes of the people, there exists a magnificent method called business secrecy — necessary, they claim, for competition. This is a monstrous lie. Flandin's Industrial Agreements Act demonstrates that the capitalists no longer have secrets among themselves. So-called business secrets are nothing but the conspiracy of the big capitalists against the producers and consumers. The abolition of business secrets must be the first demand of the proletariat as it prepares to direct the national economy.

Strictly speaking, the CGT plan is not yet a plan; it contains only general directives and not very precise ones at that. A real economic plan requires concrete statistics, figures, diagrams. Naturally we are very far from that. The first condition for a first outline of the plan consists in setting forth everything that the nation possesses in productive, material

and human forces, in raw materials, etc. We must be acquainted
with the real costs of production like the "incidental expenses"
of capitalist fraud and for that we must abolish once and
for all the fraudulent plot that goes under the name of business secrecy.

The plan speaks, albeit rather briefly, of workers' control
(see "Administrative Council"). In Isere, we are staunch advocates of workers' control. We often meet this objection: "Control is not enough. We want nationalization and workers' management." However we do not in any way counterpose the
two slogans. For the workers to take over the administration
of industry — which is absolutely necessary, and as soon as
possible, for the well-being of civilization — we must immediately
demand workers' control, as well as peasant control over
certain banks, the fertilizer trusts, the milling industry, etc.

For nationalization to operate in a revolutionary way, not
bureaucratically, the workers must participate at every stage.
They must prepare themselves for it, beginning now. They
must intervene, beginning now, in the management of industry and the entire economy in the form of workers' control,
beginning with their factory. The plan envisages this control
in a class-collaborationist form, by subjecting the workers'
representatives to the majority control of the bourgeoisie (see
"Industrial Councils"). Moreover, it stipulates that the delegate
from each category of producers must be nominated by the
"professional organization." We cannot accept that proposition.
Our trade unions, unfortunately, encompass only a twelfth or
a fifteenth of the wage force; the union is not an end in itself;
its mission is, on the contrary, to draw the mass of workers
into the administration of public affairs.

The strike will benefit the workers, organized or not, only
on condition that the trade-union vanguard draws the entire
mass into action. For workers' control to be effective, the same
condition is fundamental. That is why the control committee
in each plant must not be composed only of delegates from
the trade union, that is, from a fifteenth of the workers. No,
it must be elected by all the workers in the plant, under the
leadership of the union. That would be the real beginning of
free and honest workers' democracy, in contrast to bourgeois
democracy, which is corrupt to the core.

The plan calls for the application of the forty-hour week
with no reduction in wages. There can be no debate about
that slogan. But we know only too well that the ruling class
and its state are turning in the other direction, that is, they
want to lower wages without reducing the number of hours
of work. What means, then, can we use to achieve the forty-

hour week? The "notes for the use of propagandists" inform us that "an action has been undertaken for the materialization of an international agreement," and they continue: "It may materialize soon." It may . . . This is not very precise, and, given the international economic and political situation, we are rather more inclined to conclude: it may not. If we are mistaken, our representative at Geneva will correct our pessimism. Until something new happens, the unemployed of Grenoble — and we have some! — don't expect much from the Geneva agreements.

And what is proposed to us, apart from the hope of an early materialization of a diplomatic agreement? The "notes" continue: "Propaganda must be carried out throughout the country to explain the social significance of this workers' demand." Simply to "explain"? But all workers, even the most simple-minded, understand very well the advantage of the forty-hour week with no reduction in wages. What they are waiting for from the CGT is its indication of the means by which this slogan can be implemented. [219] But it is precisely here that the great weakness of the plan begins: it makes proposals; it offers suggestions; it formulates slogans; but it is completely silent on the means of fulfilling them.

However, before passing on to the question of how to fulfill the plan, we must pause on a particularly serious question: the peasant question. Everyone talks about it, everyone proclaims the necessity of improving the situation of the peasants, but there are lots of rogues who would like to prepare an omelet for the peasants without breaking the eggs of big business. This method cannot be ours.

Commenting on the plan, the "notes for the use of propagandists" say: "The peasants must be freed from the dual grip of the fertilizer trusts at the point of production and the consortium of big mills and the milling trade at the distribution end."

It is all very well to say: "The peasants must be freed," but you know very well that the peasant does not like vague and platonic formulations. And he is damned well right. "Must be freed." But how? Here is the only possible reply: We must expropriate and nationalize the fertilizer and milling trusts and put them truly at the service of the farmers and the consumers. The peasants cannot be aided without going counter to the interests of big business.

The plan speaks of the "general reorganization of agricultural production," but it does not specify the direction or the methods of this reorganization. The idea of expropriating the peasants or violently forcing them to take the road of socialist production is so absurd that it is scarcely worth the trouble

of criticizing; no one, moreover, is proposing any such measures. The peasantry itself must choose the road of its salvation. Whatever the peasants decide, the proletariat will promise
its sincere and effective support. The peasant cooperatives are
the most important means to allow the freeing of agricultural
economy from the excessively narrow partitions of the agricultural plot. The commentaries on the plan say: "Peasant
cooperatives for production, stockpiling and sales must be
encouraged and helped." Unfortunately, we are not told by
whom and how they must be encouraged and helped. At every
stage we find the same failing. The demands of the plan often
have the appearance of dead letters.

Who is it who will nationalize the banks and the key industries? Who will come to the aid of the peasants and introduce
the forty-hour week? In one word, who will apply the program
of the CGT? Who and how? This question, comrades, is decisive. If it remains unanswered, the whole plan remains hanging in the air.

In the paragraph on "Industrialized Nationalizations," we
find in passing an indirect and completely astonishing reply
to the question at hand. Here is how the very objective of
the plan is defined in that paragraph: "It is a question of establishing . . . the technical details of a program that can
be applied *independently of the political regime.*" One can't
help rubbing his eyes once or twice on reading this unreal
formulation. So, the plan that is to be directed against the
bankers, the magnates of the trusts, against the ninety dicta-
tors of France and the colonies — the plan that is to save the
workers, peasants, artisans, small businessmen, employees and
civil servants — this plan would be independent of the political
regime? To put it otherwise, the rudder of the state can remain,
as it is presently, in the hands of the exploiters, the oppressors,
those who starve the people — no matter, the CGT presents
this government with its plan of economic renewal? Let us
say it frankly and openly, this supposed independence of the
plan with respect to the political regime totally destroys its
real worth by placing it outside the social reality.

Naturally, at this moment we are not concerned with the
constitutional or bureaucratic forms of the state regime. But
one question dominates all others: which class holds the power? To transform feudal society into capitalist society, the bourgeoisie had to seize the power violently from the hands of the
monarchy, the nobility and the clergy. The Third Estate understood very well that its plan for "economic and social renovation" required an equivalent regime. And just as the conscious
bourgeoisie did not give Louis Capet[220] the task of abolish-

ing the medieval regime, so the proletariat cannot put Flandin or Herriot or other leaders of the bourgeoisie in charge of carrying out the plan that is to lead to the expropriation of the bourgeoisie itself. He who holds the power decides the forms of property, and all reform reduces itself in the last analysis to the abolition of private property and the establishment of collective or socialist property in the means of production. He who believes that the bourgeoisie is capable of expropriating itself is perhaps an excellent poet. But, for my part, I would not entrust him with the funds of the smallest trade union, because he is living in a dream world while we want to remain in the real world.

It must be said in no uncertain terms: only a revolutionary government of the workers and peasants, prepared for implacable struggle against all the exploiters, can apply the plan, complete it, develop it and go beyond it along the socialist road. For the proletariat, that means to conquer power.

Who is the plan addressed to? To the rulers, to soften them up, or to the dispossessed to direct them against their oppression? We propagandists have to know whom we are addressing and in what tone. Neither the plan nor the commentaries teach us anything in this connection. The official statement tells us that the plan launched by the CGT must be "met favorably by the *general public*." I ask you, comrades, and I ask myself: what does that mean, the general public? It is not, I suppose, the public of the great boulevards. In the trade-union movement and the social struggle, we are used to first seeking out classes: the proletariat, the bourgeoisie, the different layers of the petty bourgeoisie. We are certainly hopeful that the proletariat and the lower layers of the petty bourgeoisie will accept the plan favorably, provided it is elaborated carefully, purged of equivocation and presented to the masses as a program of struggle. But the workers and poor peasants are not the general public. Do we mean, for example, that it is the big bourgeoisie who must accept the plan of the CGT? Obviously not, we don't want to make fun of ourselves. Consult *Le Temps*. Some weeks ago, this newspaper, which represents well the ninety business magnates, that is, the ruling oligarchy, was protesting vehemently against any participation of the trade unions in the industrial commissions. I quote you two sentences which speak volumes: "The banning of all workers' associations was the price for obtaining social peace under the *ancien regime*." Behold the big bourgeoisie, its back to the wall, now seeking its inspiration in the *ancien regime!* And then the same article says: "Corporatism [special economic-interest groups] here signifies trade unionism." *Le Temps* is, in this way, demonstrating to us each day that the ruling class is not only not preparing to make concessions along the lines of the CGT plan but, on the contrary, envisages the possibility of crushing the CGT itself.

Jaures rightly said that *Le Temps* is the bourgeoisie in the form of a newspaper. Is collaboration possible with this bourgeoisie that now, taking inspiration from the *ancien regime*, prepares to outlaw any workers' association? To pose this question is to reply to it. Nothing remains but implacable struggle, and to the very end.

The observations, criticisms and suggestions that I am presenting here in the name of our departmental union are already quite extensive, and I am, unfortunately, far from having exhausted even the most important questions. It's all the more necessary, therefore, to indicate the fundamental defect of the plan: its authors wish to place themselves above classes, that is, outside reality. Where they want to win over everyone, they speak of the general public. They want to nationalize the banks, but without prejudice to high finance, and to nationalize the trusts, while luxuriously guaranteeing the big bourgeoisie three more generations of parasitism. They want to come to the aid of the peasants without violating the interests of the landlords, the fertilizer trusts and the big milling companies. They evidently also want to win over all possible political regimes since they state that their plan is neutral with respect to political parties and even regimes. It even seems to me that such labored and incomprehensible expressions as "industrialized nationalizations," etc., are chosen in order not to shock the delicate ears of the magnates of the trusts.

This procedure is not only useless, it is dangerous; it is not only dangerous, it is pernicious. He who seeks to embrace too much grasps poorly or carries away little. We will not win over the bourgeoisie — it has an unshakable class consciousness; it makes fun of our advice; it is preparing to crush us. The more gentle, conciliating and obsequious we are toward the bourgeoisie, the less it respects us and the more intransigent and arrogant it becomes. This lesson, it seems to me, emerges from the entire history of the class struggle.

On the other hand, by running after the supposed general public with our entreaties and by making concession after concession to appease the capitalist idol, we risk displeasing the underprivileged who are already beginning to say to themselves: "These are advisors of the ruling classes and not the leaders of the oppressed classes." We will never win the heart of the class enemy, but we risk losing permanently the confidence of our own class. The misunderstanding of this fundamental rule constitutes the main weakness of the plan. We must reshape it. We must address ourselves directly to the wage earners and the exploited. We must use clear and firm language. We must transform the plan into an action program for the entire proletariat.

The "notes for propagandists" enjoin us to "crystallize all those of goodwill." This is vague. Where are they to be found? We are acquainted with classes and class organizations, but above all we know the bad will of the bourgeoisie. To smash it, we must counterpose the revolutionary will of the working class. As for the middle classes, they will put their confidence in the proletariat only if the latter demonstrates in action its confidence in itself.

It is absurd and even criminal to look for goodwill in the bourgeoisie by breaking down and paralyzing the revolutionary goodwill of the proletariat. The united front of our class is necessary at any cost: unity of action of all the workers, trade-union, political, cooperative, educational and sports organizations and, in the first place, trade-union unity, with a specific goal — the application of the plan for nationalization and socialization through the conquest of power.

We must mobilize all the real worker militants for a vigorous campaign throughout the country. The peasants in the most distant hamlets must be convinced that the proletariat is this time seriously getting ready to overthrow the bourgeoisie, to take the power into its hands to transform our country, to make it habitable at last for the working people.

Either the plan is transformed into a plan for the conquest of power by the proletariat, for the establishment of a workers' and peasants' government, or the people will put it down as null and unworkable. The departmental union of Isere is for revolutionary action. If you call on us in that sense, we will respond: Present! [221]

THE SITUATION IN THE
STOCKHOLM YOUTH BUREAU[220]

(March 23, 1935)

To the International Secretariat
Copies to Members of the Plenum
Copy to Comrade Held[223]

Dear Comrades:

The situation with the Youth Bureau of Stockholm has become absolutely intolerable. The bureau transformed itself in fact into a private affair of the SAP. At the conference of the IAG, the official representative of the Stockholm Bureau attacked Comrades Sneevliet and Schmidt, who defended the slogan of the Fourth International. And this slogan, it must not be forgotten, is at the basis of the youth organization to which we have given our adherence. The people of the SAP continue their usual game. They sign some document in favor of the new International; then they combat the policy that flows from it.[224] In truth, we are the only enemies for the SAP to combat. We do not take it tragically as long as the SAP acts in its own name. But how can we tolerate it when a representative of the Youth Bureau permits himself to attack the qualified representatives of the program of the Fourth International? Is it tolerable that the SAP, which does not represent a great thing either ideologically or politically, should climb on our back to combat us more easily?

The leading position of the SAP in the Stockholm Bureau is explained by the fact that since the youth conference de Kadt, taking advantage of the imprisonment of Comrade Schmidt and usurping the representation of the OSP, supported the SAP against us and assured it a leading post. And in turn, the young man of the SAP had utilized the mandate of de Kadt to attack Schmidt because Schmidt did not want to betray this program.

There are still the Swedish [Socialist] youth. Unfortunately, we know them very little. But what we know of the leading tendency of the party does not inspire us with any confidence. I recall that the leaders of the Swedish youth did not want Held, although a member of the bureau, to reside in Stockholm so that he would not be able to penetrate their organization. Thus, even before the beginning of the collaboration, the leaders of the Swedish youth have shown a ferocious hostility towards our tendency and our ideas. The SAP leans on this hostility. That is natural. But how can we cover up and even support this absolutely rotten combination? Comrade Held is at Oslo, and the young man of the SAP comes to the Paris conference to attack us. I ask myself, what does the SAP and particularly its youth represent? They claim to have 5,000 members in Germany. This cannot be checked. We have contact only with the clique of emigres, who are opportunist maneuverists and not Marxists. In various countries they hang on to bureaucratic cliques and to individuals of the type of de Kadt to combat the program of the Fourth International.

I do not want to make comparison of the ideological forces. As a tendency, we have a tradition, a doctrine, literature and program. The SAP has nothing. Let's take the quantitative side. The unified Dutch party has its 5,000 members, which can be very well checked. As far as I know, the majority of its members are youth.

Our French section has developed great work among the youth. Its exact influence can be measured by exact numbers at the last conference of the "Entente of the Seine"[225] (at this conference the SAP people combated us by getting one-thirtieth of the members).

Our Belgian youth already are developing important work in the JGS. The youth organization of the WPUS represents a considerable force already and is developing successfully. I pass over our youth in Latin America, China, Sweden, Spain, etc. I cite only the facts that can be checked.

And the USSR? If one takes into consideration only the expulsions of the "Trotskyites" for the last couple of months, we have the right to affirm that our numerous forces there, without speaking of the ideological and political traditions, are many times more important than the forces of the SAP and the Swedish youth together.

What interests, then, have we in covering up by our authority the work of the SAP directed against the Fourth International and especially against us as a tendency? I have reproached our youth for being too indulgent and indifferent toward the youth conference. I must state that the supineness still continues. They have created a subbureau in Paris where our youth, which represents something serious, are represented on an equal basis with B. Goldenberg, who represents nothing but Menshevik confusion. They are even getting ready to edit together with Goldenberg a pamphlet on the Second and Third Internationals. The light-mindedness here surpasses all limits. We have already signed a common document with the SAP that it has betrayed and attacked. How can we criticize in a common document the Second and Third Internationals if we are not in agreement on the necessity of a Fourth? By such proceedings one makes ridiculous questions of historic importance. Our youth need tempering, need militancy suitable to our epoch. Where will they get this tempering if they let themselves be terrorized by maneuverists of an insignificant clique? This conduct will end up by compromising us internationally and decomposing the cadres of our own youth.

The vigorous intervention of the International Secretariat and of the plenum seems absolutely imperative. Here are the first measures that seem to be absolutely indispensable:

1. All our youth sections must pronounce themselves clearly and mercilessly on the attitude of the representative of the Stockholm Bureau at the Paris conference; it is necessary to condemn him officially and disavow him formally. The disavowment must be published in all our organs.

2. The Stockholm Bureau must be reorganized. The *minimum* program of the organization demands that the bureau be completed by a representative of the Dutch party and a representative of the French section. The bureau of five must fix its place of residence and name its secretariat.

3. The subbureau of Paris must be liquidated immediately.

If the SAP or the Swedes are not in agreement, the worse for them. We will find our task without august direction.

Given the nefarious work that the SAP is now carrying on in France, it would be absolutely criminal to drag out this affair and to continue the ambiguity. I ask with the greatest insistence that you take up this question as soon as possible.[226]

Crux [Leon Trotsky]

A NEW NOOSE IN THE
STALINIST AMALGAM[227]

(March 31, 1935)

On January 18, 1935, I wrote on the question of the Zinoviev trial: "It would be criminal light-mindedness to think that Stalin has given up trying to frame us up in some new 'case' cooked up by the GPU and its foreign agents. Stalin has no other method of struggle against us."

To be sure, the threat of such a new amalgam is hanging over the heads of our friends in the USSR. Its preparation is filthy and abominable. But that indeed does not hinder it from opening the road to bloody repressions against the Bolsheviks and their relatives.

On March 20, *Pravda* published reports on the expulsion from Leningrad of old nobles, big industrialists, landed proprietors, judges and czarist police officers, in all, 1,074 individuals. The report added: "Part of the exiled are indicted . . . for activity against the state in the interest of foreign nations."

We completely omit here the question of how, eighteen years after October, there could be found in Leningrad more than one thousand dangerous representatives of old czarist Russia. Does this mean that the GPU, while hunting down and exterminating the Leninists, had not noticed the class enemies? Or does it mean that the thousand mentioned above did not previously represent any danger and had raised their heads only now after the Stalinist regime has led to terrorist acts inside the party and to bloody mass repressions against the party youth? In either case, the official information leaves no doubt as to the personalities against whom the Leningrad purging was directed; all the 1,074 individuals belonged unmistakably to strata of the former ruling classes and the czarist bureaucracy.

But five days later, in *Pravda* of March 25, we already find a new version; on the question of the arrests and deportations, it says the following, word for word: "The foul dregs of the

Trotskyists, the Zinovievists, the old princes, counts, gendarmes, *all this refuse*, which acted in concert in an attempt to undermine the foundations of our state."

Thus, among the 1,074 people exiled and indicted, and at their head, were to be found "Trotskyists and Zinovievists" who acted "in concert" with the former ministers and czarist police officers. But why then were the group of Trotskyists and Zinovievists completely omitted from the official report of March 20, which gave a precise enumeration of all those expelled and indicted? It is absolutely clear: the laboratory of amalgams had discovered this belatedly, and it carried a "correction" to the official information several days later; the former police agents, they aver, acted in concert with the Trotskyists and Zinovievists, which they had forgotten, God knows why, five days earlier.

Besides this unexpected "correction," they carry another not unimportant qualification concerning the scope of the crime. The March 20 report says that the nobles and the police officers acted in the "interest (?) of foreign nations." The vagueness of this formula is self-explanatory. The March 25 *Pravda*, referring to the Trotskyists and the nobles who "acted in concert," uses a much more exact formula: they worked, it states, "according to the instructions of foreign information bureaus." Thus, in the span of five days, these miserable falsifiers permit us to see with the naked eye the beginning and the end of the new intrigue, which assuredly is not the last.

Only consummate idiots could think that *Pravda* has merely shown an excess of polemical zeal against the "Trotskyists" by adding lies and calumnies that are superfluous in the account. No, *Pravda* is not *l'Humanite*. Behind *Pravda* is the GPU. The editors of *Pravda* do not write whatever comes into their head; they act on instructions from specific institutions. The March 25 article is direct evidence that in five days it was decided to prepare new bloody repressions against the Oppositionists and since there was no convenient terrorist act at hand, *Pravda* was instructed to link this newest extermination of Bolsheviks to the measures taken against the old proprietors, nobles and police officers.

We speak of new repressions; have they already taken place or do they merely threaten? We do not know that. It is highly possible that the cowardly article in the March 25 *Pravda* might be, after a fashion, an anonymous obituary for Leninists who have already been shot; it is also possible that this is only a preparation for bloody repressions. In any case, it is clear that Stalin is repairing the setback of the Leningrad GPU; the amalgam with the Latvian consul missed fire—so

Stalin substitutes for it an amalgam with nobles and police officers. The technique is different, the aim the same.

The next days and weeks may bring us concrete information of those against whom the Stalinist frame-up was directed this time. But, if the number of new victims is to be reduced to a minimum, it is necessary to begin a campaign to expose a new amalgam and its authors.

NOTES OF A JOURNALIST [228]

(Published April 1935)

How the Stalinists Undermine
the Morale of the Red Army

In recent months the Kremlin has again been busy — and with what furious zeal! — rewriting the history of the Red Army. The aim of the rewriting is to prove that, if not in form, then in essence, Trotsky fought in the camp of the White Guards against the Soviets. We are not at all exaggerating; Trotsky, it turns out, planted in the armies of the Eastern Front "White Guard nests" that would inevitably have destroyed the cause of the revolution if Stalin had not intervened in time and purged the army of Trotsky's agents. At the same time, Trotsky shot Communists fighting bravely in the ranks of the Red Army, and the affair would inevitably have ended in catastrophe had it not again been for the salutary intervention of Stalin who, it seems, had even then decided that Communists were to be shot in peacetime.

These interesting and to some extent "sensational" disclosures evoke some questions.

First: why were the disclosures made so late? Is it because young Soviet scholars have made a series of unexpected discoveries in the archives, or because a new generation has grown up that knows nothing of the past?

Second: what is the relation between the latest disclosures and the preceding ones? From the end of 1923, Trotsky was accused of "underestimating the peasantry" and of a passion for "permanent revolution." It now turns out that from 1917 Trotsky was in reality an agent of the Whites in the Red Army, which was created by Stalin. What then was the point in confusing the mind of the whole of humanity for many years with "underestimation of the peasantry" and other trifles when, in fact, all along it was a matter not of a revolutionary but of a counterrevolutionary?

Third: why did the Bolshevik Party for seven years (1918-25) keep at the head of the Red Army a man who was destroying it? Why did it not appoint Stalin, who created it? This cannot be explained only by Stalin's universally known modesty, for it was a matter of the life and death of the revolution. Nor can we consider that the party was uninformed; surely Stalin knew what he was doing when he was purging the Red Army of the counterrevolutionary nests planted by Trotsky and putting a stop to the shooting of Communists, reserving this task for himself alone. But since Stalin never acted except on the orders of the Political Bureau, that means the higher institutions of the party must also have been aware of what was going on.

True, the Political Bureau at that time consisted largely of counterrevolutionaries or apprentice counterrevolutionaries (Trotsky, Zinoviev, Kamenev). But Lenin? Let us suppose he was a poor judge of events and people (his "Testament" allows such a conclusion to be drawn). But Stalin himself? Why did he not present the Central Committee and the party with the question of Trotsky's deadly work in the Red Army during the civil war?

A literate, intelligent Red Army man, looking at old books or newspapers would have to say to himself: "For seven years Trotsky was at the head of the Red Army and the Red Fleet. He was appointed organizer and leader of the forces of the Soviet Republic. Trotsky took the oaths made by the Red Army men. It turns out that he was a traitor. His criminal acts caused hundreds of thousands of needless sacrifices. That means we were deceived. But who deceived us? The Political Bureau headed by Lenin. That means there were traitors and people covering up for betrayal in the Political Bureau.

"Now they tell me that the real creators and leaders of the Red Army were Stalin and Voroshilov.[229] But can it be that I am being deceived again? They didn't tell me about Trotsky's betrayal till ten years after his removal. And when will they tell me about the betrayals of Stalin and Voroshilov? Whom can you trust at all?"

So speaks the thinking young Red Army man. The old soldier, who knows from experience how things went, will draw more or less the following conclusion: "When they accused Trotsky of 'underestimating the peasantry,' I thought that that may well have been true; it is a complicated question, and it is difficult to figure out. But when they tell me that Trotsky planted White Guard nests in the Red Army, I say straight out: the present leaders are lying! And if they lie so barefacedly about the civil war, then probably they are lying about the underestimation of the peasantry too."

There can be only one result to the new campaign of sensa-

tional disclosures: damage to trust in the leadership, old or
new, any leadership.

You have to ask yourself: why does the Stalin clique consider
it necessary now—in 1935!—to engage in such two-edged
disclosures, which are at least 50 percent *self*-disclosures? Trotskyism was destroyed in 1925, then destroyed again in 1927,
irrevocably destroyed in 1928 (Trotsky exiled to Alma-Ata)
and the "last remnants" of the "miserable fragments" again and
again subjected to extermination after Trotsky's exile abroad,
where he finally "revealed himself" as an agent of imperialism.
It would seem to be time to get back to business. But no, the
ruling gentry cannot sit calmly in their places; they find it
necessary to worry; they sweat from the effort of thought;
can't something more be thought up, something a little stronger,
a little harder, a little more venomous, that will really and
truly destroy this already seven-times destroyed Trotskyism?

Radek Writes Well

In Gogol's time the "gentry from Kursk" wrote well. In our
time, when there are no more gentry, Radek writes well. But
since Radek is a foreigner in all languages, it would be unfair
to attack him from that side. He is neither profound nor grammatical but, all the same, the truth is apparent. Betrayal peers
through every word. One cannot be mistaken: even if he's not
one of the Kursk gentry he does not spare his life for the
leader.

"Nikolaev's shot," writes Radek, "most clearly illuminated
the counterrevolutionary rot concealed in the ranks of our
party" (*Bolshevik*, No. 3, p. 61). Here every word strikes
home: it was precisely *rot;* it was precisely *concealed;* it was
precisely in the *party.* And as for the shot, it precisely "most
clearly illuminated" all this rot. And, most amazing of all,
Radek himself unexpectedly fell under the light of this most
clear illumination—as a moralist, of course, and not as *rot.*
For who would allow a rotten publicist on to the pages of
Bolshevik? Yaroslavsky, true, was removed from the editor-
ship after years of service, but even the vigilant Stetsky[230]
will do.

In any case, Radek himself—this is precisely the aim of
his article—proves in twenty pages of closely-packed text that,
as far as he himself is concerned, his high revolutionary morals
stand above all suspicion. And who should know better than
Radek? Trotsky "openly crossed to the camp of counterrevolution." Zinoviev and Kamenev had recourse to "two-faced confession." But he, Radek, has confessed with all the four per-
fections. Whip him, boil him in oil—he, like Vas'ka Shibanov,

will praise his master. But—*homo sum*—Radek prefers, of course, to arrange the truth-test without the oil. Some ill-wishers even assert that it is Radek's inclination to a peaceful way of life and his revulsion from boiling oil in all its forms that have produced in him such an intense feeling of truth to the leader, the leader's house porter and even the leader's dog (we apologize for the shadow of Molchalin that peeps through).

Such purely *psychological* hypotheses, however, are unconvincing. Radek's truthfulness has a *sociological* basis. A good part of the twenty pages is filled with quotations from Stalin, proving that *any* opposition is *always* bourgeois and *always* leads to counterrevolution. In the scriptures, it is put simply: "There is no power, except from the Lord." In the language of Radek and the other theoretical lackeys of the bureaucracy, the same thought is expressed in more contemporary terms: "Everything to the right or left of Stalin is bourgeois counterrevolution; the meridian of the proletariat passes through the bridge of the leader's nose."

While Radek remains on the heights of general sociology (we mean the sociology of bureaucratic lackeys), his positions are almost inaccessible. Things become rather worse when Radek has to give answers to lower and more concrete questions, such as about the trial of Zinoviev and Kamenev. In the government communique as well as in numerous articles in *Pravda* there was, as is well known, the direct and categorical assertion that Zinoviev and Kamenev *had as their goal the restoration of capitalism and military intervention.* We not only doubted this but even called the whole assertion a mixture of baseness, stupidity and caddishness. "The question is not," says Radek in defense of the leader, "whether capitalism is the ideal of Messrs. Trotsky and Zinoviev but whether the construction of socialism is possible in our country," etc. In a word, Radek blurts out that Zinoviev and Kamenev started no conspiracies to restore capitalism — contrary to what the official communique shamelessly asserted — but completely rejected the theory of socialism in one country, the very national-reformist theory that Stalin himself was still rejecting in 1924 and that Radek accepted only in the severe climate of Siberia in 1929. Q. E. D.

With the exception of such slips, it must be admitted that Radek writes very well, with a tremble in his pen. But for some reason, while reading his article you cannot help thinking, surely I've read this article a hundred times already. And for some reason, there even rises from the paper on which it is written a strange odor, like that of an old fur on which the house cat has brought up several generations of kittens.

Where Has Manuilsky Gone?

The proletarian masses of both hemispheres have suffered
a cruel blow in recent months: a leader of international revolution is missing! Very recently, in the full flower of his strength
and talents, he was still giving directives to sixty nations on
the subject of the simultaneous passing through of periods
(it was then, as it happens, precisely the unforgettable "third
period"), writing florid articles, which, it is true, nobody read,
and in his free time telling the other leaders anecdotes about
national life, which met with great success. And suddenly he
is missing! Missing so completely you cannot find a trace.
But since it is a case not of a needle but of a leader of the
Comintern, his sudden disappearance threatens to evoke a
whole series of cosmic consequences. But it was said long
ago: *le roi est mort, vive Bela Kun!* [the king is dead, long
live Bela Kun!].

All the same, minor consequences could not be avoided. Some
sections were thrown into confusion by the lightning change
of leaders. Some said: But wasn't Bela Kun killed on the Hungarian barricades? Others, on the basis of his name, asserted
that this time a leader from the female sex had been appointed.
But everything quickly turned to everyone's advantage. "One
priest is as good as another," said the Spaniards. "This one
won't be worse than Manuilsky," added the Italians. "Lozovsky
seems to have disappeared too," observed the British with a
sigh of relief. Nobody even remembered Kuusinen. So the
history of humanity entered its fourth period. Meanwhile the
earth continued to turn on its axis as if nothing special had
happened.

THE SITUATION IN FRANCE AND THE TASKS OF THE BOLSHEVIK-LENINIST GROUP OF THE SFIO[231]

(April 15, 1935)

The bombshell of the law on two-year conscription and the consequent reintroduction of conscription in Germany have put France in an atmosphere of fevered preparation for war. The only "chance of peace" now lies in the uncertainty of the result of an armed conflict, which still prevails on both sides.

It is at this moment that military circles are contemplating with anticipation the possibility of a preventive strike. The Bonapartist and fascist reaction is whipping up the chauvinist passions of the Paris petty bourgeoisie with a very vigorous campaign and using systematic blackmail to force the government on to the path of militarization of the nation (the law on passive resistance, the Pernot proposals) and of merciless repression of any attempt at protest by the workers (persecution of the leaders of the Socialist and Communist youth leagues, persecution of *l'Humanite,* prohibition of demonstrations by leftist veterans against the two-year service period).

Premier Flandin, who recently confirmed his intention of "punishing" both the "enemies of the country" and the agitators of the right, yesterday delivered proof of his Bonapartist character by moving sharply to the right under the "chastisements" of the royalists and fascists. He first of all promised to free the year's conscripts still in service, on grounds of "honor," but did not hesitate to take an opposite decision, when *L'Echo de Paris* and *Jour* put out some strong articles, and to prolong by three months the period of military service for the contingent due for release. The result of this was vigorous resistance in the barracks. The passivity of the workers' parties, however, made it impossible to use this to the advantage of the revolutionary cause.

In the economic field, the massive orders for war material produced a sudden revival in the production of the industries concerned. For precisely this reason there was an observable fall in the unemployment-weekly-growth curve (the statistics show 28,000 less unemployed for the last week). This, however, shows nothing but a momentary assuagement, which is, moreover, limited to a single industry and cannot be interpreted as an indication of a general rise in overall production. It is, nevertheless, enough for the bourgeoisie again to see war as the only way out of the crisis. The state had to make additional expenditure of several billion, while its budget was already showing a deficit. Thus when the chambers meet, they will be faced in all its sharpness with the problem of working out what to do about this expenditure, in other words, what means to use to bleed the workers again: inflation or deflation.

The news of the devaluation of the Belgian franc brought panic into the hearts of the Bourse [French stock exchange], which immediately sacrificed fixed-interest stocks. To bring back calm, the government promised quickly to circulate gold coins, but in such a small ratio that it is clear that it is only a platonic satisfaction for the zealous supporters of gold currency, and not at all an attempt to forestall devaluation. What means will the Flandin government choose to get its billions, which it cannot possibly get in an ordinary way?

The easiest way is certainly inflation, which would have the support of exporter and speculator circles. The experience of the world war also shows that all layers of the bourgeoisie come together in the long run when that final way out comes into question. But since it also brings with it sacrifices for amassed wealth, it is only used when the situation is utterly desperate, i.e., when there is no longer any chance of getting sacrifices from the toiling masses by a direct and brutal amputation. For this reason French big industry has not yet been won over for inflation. One of their spokesmen, de Wendel, owner of one of the biggest fortunes in the country, emphasizes that he prefers a continuation of the policy of deflation, i.e., of sacrifices demanded from the creditors of the state (rentiers, civil servants and pensioners). This is also the opinion of the "Comite de salut economique" ("Committee of economic welfare") of the fascist Nicolle. The present finance minister Germain-Martin, the faithful officeholder of big capital, also seems to incline in this direction.

It therefore looks as if before the leap into inflation the bourgeoisie still wants to attempt with a last wild effort to squeeze the last drop out of the exploited. But this makes it necessary to strengthen the state apparatus still more, and means for Flandin the compulsion to move still farther right or else, after a new *coup de main* [surprise attack] like that of February 6, to yield his place to a Doumergue or a Tardieu. The latter, who at the moment is undergoing a decontamination cure at the seaside, declared in an interview he gave *Jour* that an "active minority" would have to open the country's eyes, and that it would not come to power "under the conditions of the present ill-starred and irreparable (*nefaste et imperfectible*) parliament," but only through "a useful action."

At the same time, Flandin is upbraided and publicly provoked by the fascist and reactionary bands who, in the matter of the two-year conscription, very ably held him above water "like the rope holds the hanged man." With this they all make preparations, by organizing mobilization exercises (4,000 "Croix de Feu"[232] in Reims) and the like, and especially by nocturnal demolitions of the premises of the Socialist Party (rue Feydeau). The Socialist youth groups originally wanted on their own initiative to take on the protection of these premises. The Socialist leaders of the CAP [the SFIO National Council], however, forbade this on the pretext that the building did not belong to the party. Furthermore, in the countryside one can observe symptoms of the growing fascist influence at the expense of the traditional democratic parties. The peasant agitator Dorgeres[233] gained a considerable number of votes from the Radicals at an election in Chautemps's district.

What attitude do the workers' parties, the united front, take in this situation of a course for war, of strengthening the repressive apparatus and of raging fascist agitation? No serious action was undertaken against the two-year conscription. The Socialist leaders Blum, Paul Faure and in fact all the parliamentarians have already given the assurance that they are ready for the holy alliance "in the event of a decided attack from Hitler Germany." Blum declared this in the Chamber in the name of the Socialists and Communists, without the latter making any denial. The SFIO and the CP support the same international policy: assistance pacts, defense. *L'Humanite* is waging a campaign against the "traitors" in the camp of the bourgeoisie, i.e., the French fascists who want to "talk with Hitler." The poet Vaillant-Couturier[234] is showing, more and more, the ambition to follow the tradition of Deroulede[235] and is hurrying "to the aid of French culture." Cachin is preparing to play the same role as in 1914.

The manifesto signed by the various "Communist" Parties of the West declares without any reservation: "In the case of a counterrevolutionary war against the fatherland of socialism, we shall support the Red Army of the Soviet Union and fight for the defeat of German imperialism and its allies and for the defeat of any power that wages war on the Soviet Union. We shall further by every means, even at the cost of our lives, the victory of the Soviet Union in its struggle against all who attack that country of socialism" (*l'Humanite*, April 18, 1935). The CP manifesto for the local elections of May 1935 takes up the same theme in the same terms and calls on "the community (union) of all Frenchmen."

A no-less-criminal pacifism can be discerned in the fight of both leaderships against fascism, in which both continue to demand of Flandin *the dissolution of the fascist leagues*. The Stalinists openly reject the idea of the [workers'] militia itself. In the course of a discussion meeting between the responsible Stalinists for the Paris area and one of our comrades in the Paris fifteenth *arrondissement* on the topic "militia or self-defense of the masses," the responsible Stalinists declared that the slogan of the militia was a sectarian error and that no special organization was necessary to ensure physical defense, that the example of the Vienna Schutzbund clearly showed the danger of such an organization.

Our conclusion is that *the multiplication of the two leaderships can produce only defeat unless the third factor gains the upper hand in the selection process of the struggle, that is, the vanguard that is forming around our Bolshevik-Leninist tendency.*

Today no one can deny that the favorable environment for the formation of this vanguard, as far as France is concerned, is constituted by the Socialist left. It is here that the revolutionary slogans are coming from now. One need only read the articles of Marceau Pivert, the leader of the left. On the question of war and the question of the militia, he combats both the standpoints of the Social Democrats and those of the Stalinists and supports our slogans. He is not just a man of goodwill, but the representative of the leadership of a thoroughly active tendency that is developing strongly toward our positions. The main question is whether this vanguard will be capable of setting up, at the right time, the close link with the masses, freeing them of the poison of Stalinism, centrism and reformism and sweeping them along on to the revolutionary path, the path of the conquest of power. Our Bolshevik-Leninist Group has hitherto had to carry on internal propaganda work within the SFIO. From now on, it will turn its efforts with doubled intensity toward developing and separating out the vanguard more and more clearly.

The tendency in the SFIO that is followed by sound elements must serve as a lever to get into motion the unorganized mass that contains very militant elements, which, however, as a result of the inactive attitude of the workers' parties are full of mistrust. This poses for us a very big task, not only in political respects but also in respect to material effort. *La Verite* as a weekly organ will no longer suffice for this. From the moment when the link with the masses is achieved, when we have brought the mass and the best elements of the SFIO and the CP to the consciousness that they can find a leadership in our direction, the movement may take on a very accelerated character and present us with great and immediate opportunities. All Bolshevik-Leninists in the world must understand this situation and double their efforts to display their practical and political solidarity with our French section.

P. S. The question of organic unity is at present being discussed by the leaderships in a unification commission. The CP — which originally declined to take part in the work of this commission, which also includes the PUPists — has changed its mind and has taken part in the last session. This is a matter of agreement on the principles of a united party. The old reactionary Lebas (SFIO) is leading the dance. From all the things one has heard of these secret negotiations behind the scenes, it looks very much as if the CP is determined to give up the last vestiges of Leninism in order to provide proof of its desire for a reconciliation with the social reformists and patriots.

The Bolshevik-Leninists had asked for meetings between the Socialist sections and the Communist branches in order to discuss unity, not because they are for the watchwords "organic unity" but because, in the course of these discussions, there existed the possibility of setting forth the principles of a truly revolutionary party. If organic unity comes about, we will organize on the basis of this organic unity to carry on our propaganda and to create the vanguard through a process of continuous differentiation. It is correctly said that organic unity among the masses is progressive because for us it means a lasting contact with the elements making up the base of the CP. But it must also be seen that it can have catastrophic results among the masses because (and it does this in large numbers) it means the merging of the Social Democracy and Stalinism. Without fighting against organic unity — which, in the absence of a revolutionary party, presents the most favorable milieu for its formation — the Bolshevik-Leninists point out that what is needed most is not organic unity but a revolutionary policy carried out by a revolutionary vanguard.

ON THE SOUTH AFRICAN THESES 236

To the South African Section

(April 20, 1935)

The theses are clearly written on the basis of a serious study of both the economic and political conditions of South Africa, as well as of the literature of Marxism and Leninism, particularly that of the Bolshevik-Leninists. A serious scientific approach to all questions is one of the most important conditions for the success of a revolutionary organization.

The example of our South African friends again confirms the fact that in the present epoch only the Bolshevik-Leninists, that is, the consistent proletarian revolutionaries, take a serious attitude to theory, analyze the realities and are learning themselves before they teach others. The Stalinist bureaucracy has long ago substituted a combination of ignorance and impudence for Marxism.

In the following lines I wish to make certain remarks in regard to the draft theses that will serve as a program for the Workers Party of South Africa. Under no circumstances do I make these remarks in opposition to the text of the theses. I am too insufficiently acquainted with the South African conditions to pretend to a full, conclusive opinion on a series of practical questions.

Only in certain places am I obliged to express my disagreement with certain aspects of the draft theses. But here also, insofar as I can judge from afar, we have *no differences in principles* with the authors of the theses. It is rather a matter of certain polemical *exaggerations* arising from the struggle with the pernicious national policy of Stalinism.

But it is in the interest of the cause not to smooth over even slight inaccuracies in presentation but, on the contrary, to expose them for open deliberations in order to arrive at the most clear and blameless text. Such is the aim of the following lines dictated by the desire to give some assistance to our South

African Bolshevik-Leninists in this great and responsible work to which they have set themselves.

The South African possessions of Great Britain form a dominion only from the point of view of the white minority. From the point of the black majority, South Africa is a slave colony.

No social upheaval (in the first instance, an agrarian revolution) is thinkable with the retention of British imperialism in the South African dominion. The overthrow of British imperialism in South Africa is just as indispensable for the triumph of socialism in South Africa as it is for Great Britain itself.

If, as it is possible to assume, the revolution will start first in Great Britain, the less support the British bourgeoisie will find in the colonies and dominions, including so important a possession as South Africa, the quicker will be their defeat at home. The struggle for the expulsion of British imperialism, its tools and agents thus enters as an indispensable part of the program of the South African proletarian party.

The overthrow of the hegemony of British imperialism in South Africa can come about as the result of a military defeat of Great Britain and the disintegration of the empire. In this case, the South African whites could still, for a certain period — hardly a considerable one — retain their domination over the blacks.

Another possibility, which in practice could be connected with the first, is a revolution in Great Britain and her possessions. Three-quarters of the population of South Africa (almost six million of the almost eight million total) is composed of non-Europeans. A victorious revolution is unthinkable without the awakening of the native masses. In its turn, that will give them what they are so lacking today — confidence in their strength, a heightened personal consciousness, a cultural growth.

Under these conditions, the South African republic will emerge first of all as a "black" republic; this does not exclude, of course, either full equality for the whites or brotherly relations between the two races — depending mainly on the conduct of the whites. But it is entirely obvious that the predominant majority of the population, liberated from slavish dependence, will put a certain imprint on the state.

Insofar as a victorious revolution will radically change the relation not only between the classes but also between the races and will assure to the blacks that place in the state that corresponds to their numbers, thus far will the *social* revolution in South Africa also have a *national* character.

We have not the slightest reason to close our eyes to this

side of the question or to diminish its significance. On the
contrary, the proletarian party should in words and in deeds
openly and boldly take the solution of the national (racial)
problem in its hands.

Nevertheless, the proletarian party can and must solve the
national problem by *its own* methods.

The historical weapon of national liberation can be only
the *class struggle.* The Comintern, beginning in 1924, transformed the program of national liberation of colonial people
into an empty democratic abstraction that is elevated above
the reality of class relations. In the struggle against national
oppression, different classes liberate themselves (temporarily)
from material interests and become simple "anti-imperialist"
forces.

In order that these spiritual "forces" bravely fulfill the task
assigned to them by the Comintern, they are promised, as
a reward, a spiritual "national-democratic" state — with the unavoidable reference to Lenin's formula: "democratic dictatorship of the proletariat and the peasantry."

The theses point out that in 1917 Lenin openly and once
and for all discarded the formula of "democratic dictatorship
of the proletariat and the peasantry" as a necessary condition
for the solution of the agrarian question. [237] This is entirely
correct.

But to avoid misunderstanding, it should be added: (*a*) Lenin
always spoke about a revolutionary *bourgeois* democratic
dictatorship and not about a spiritual "people's" state; (*b*) in
the struggle for a *bourgeois* democratic dictatorship, he did
not offer a bloc of all "anticzarist forces" but carried out an
independent class policy of the proletariat.

An "anticzarist" bloc was the idea of the Russian Social Revolutionaries and the Left Cadets, that is, the parties of the
petty and middle bourgeoisie. Against these parties the Bolsheviks always waged an irreconcilable struggle.

When the theses say that the slogan of a "black republic"
is *equally* harmful for the revolutionary cause as is the slogan
of a "South Africa for the whites," then we cannot agree with
the form of the statement. Whereas in the latter there is the
case of supporting complete oppression, in the former there
is the case of taking the first steps toward liberation.

We must accept decisively and without any reservations the
complete and unconditional right of the blacks to independence. Only on the basis of a mutual struggle against the
domination of the white exploiters can the solidarity of black
and white toilers be cultivated and strengthened.

It is possible that *after victory* the blacks will find it unnecessary to form a separate black state in South Africa. Certainly we will not *force them* to establish a separate state. But let them make this decision freely, on the basis of their own experience, and not forced by the *sjambok* [whip] of the white oppressors. The proletarian revolutionaries must never forget the right of the oppressed nationalities to self-determination, including full separation, and the duty of the proletariat of the oppressing nation to defend this right with arms in hand, if necessary.

The theses quite correctly underline the fact that the solution to the national question in Russia was brought about by the October Revolution. National democratic movements by themselves were powerless to cope with the national oppression of czarism. Only because of the fact that the movement of the oppressed nationalities, as well as the agrarian movement of the peasantry, gave the proletariat the possibility of seizing power and establishing its dictatorship did the national question as well as the agrarian find a bold and decisive solution.

But the very conjuncture of the national movements with the struggle of the proletariat for power was made politically possible only thanks to the fact that the Bolsheviks during the whole of their history carried on an irreconcilable struggle with the Great Russian oppressors, supporting always and without reservations the right of the oppressed nations to self-determination, including separation from Russia.

The policy of Lenin in regard to the oppressed nations did not, however, have anything in common with the policy of the epigones. The Bolshevik Party defended the right of the oppressed nations to self-determination *with the methods of proletarian class struggle,* entirely rejecting the charlatan "anti-imperialist" blocs with the numerous petty-bourgeois "national" parties of czarist Russia (the Polish Socialist Party [PPS — the party of Pilsudski in czarist Poland], Dashnaki in Armenia, the Ukrainian nationalists, the Jewish Zionists, etc., etc.).

The Bolsheviks have always mercilessly unmasked these parties, as well as the Russian Social Revolutionaries, their vacillations and adventurism, but especially their ideological lie of being above the class struggle. Lenin did not stop his intransigent criticism even when circumstances forced upon him this or that episodic, strictly practical, agreement with them.

There could be no question of any permanent alliance with them under the banner of "anticzarism." Only thanks to this *irreconcilable* class policy was Bolshevism able to succeed in the time of the revolution to throw aside the Mensheviks,

the Social Revolutionaries, the national petty-bourgeois parties and gather around the proletariat the masses of the peasantry and the oppressed nationalities.

"We must not," say the theses, "compete with the African
National Congress[238] in nationalist slogans in order to win
the native masses." The idea is in itself correct, but it requires
concrete amplification. Being insufficiently acquainted with the
activities of the National Congress, I can only outline our
policy concerning it on the basis of analogies, stating beforehand my readiness to supplement my recommendations with
all the necessary modifications.

1. The Bolshevik-Leninists put themselves in defense of the
Congress, as it is, in all cases when it is being attacked by
the white oppressors and their chauvinistic agents in the ranks
of the workers' organizations.

2. The Bolshevik-Leninists place the progressive over the
reactionary tendencies in the program of the Congress.

3. The Bolshevik-Leninists unmask before the native masses
the inability of the Congress to achieve the realization of even
its own demands, because of its superficial, conciliatory policy. In contradistinction to the Congress, the Bolshevik-Leninists develop a program of revolutionary class struggle.

4. Separate episodic agreements with the Congress, if they
are forced by circumstances, are permissible only within the
framework of strictly defined practical tasks, with the retention
of full and complete independence of our own organization
and freedom of political criticism.

The theses bring out as the main political slogan not a
"national democratic state" but a South African "October." The
theses prove, and prove convincingly:

a. that the national and agrarian questions in South Africa
coincide in their bases;

b. that both these questions can be solved only in a revolutionary way;

c. that the revolutionary solution of these questions leads
inevitably to the dictatorship of the proletariat, which guides
the native peasant masses; and,

d. that the dictatorship of the proletariat will open an era
of a soviet regime and socialist reconstruction. This conclusion is the cornerstone of the whole structure of the program.
Here we are in complete agreement.

But the masses must be brought to this general "strategic"
formula through the medium of a series of tactical slogans.
It is possible to work out these slogans, at every given stage,
only on the basis of an analysis of the concrete circumstances
of the life and struggle of the proletariat and the peasantry

and the whole internal and international situation. Without going deeply into this matter, I would like briefly to deal with the mutual relations of the national and agrarian slogans.

The theses several times underline that the agrarian and not the national demands must be put in the first place. This is a very important question that deserves serious attention. To push aside or to weaken the national slogans with the object of not antagonizing the white chauvinists in the ranks of the working class would be, of course, criminal opportunism, which is absolutely alien to the authors and supporters of the theses. This flows quite clearly from the text of the theses, which is permeated with the spirit of revolutionary internationalism.

The theses admirably say of those "socialists" who are fighting for the privileges of the whites that "we must recognize them as the greatest enemies of the revolution." Thus we must seek for another explanation, which is briefly indicated in the text itself: the backward native peasant masses directly feel the agrarian oppression much more than they do the national oppression.

It is quite possible. The majority of the natives are peasants; the bulk of the land is in the hands of a white minority. The Russian peasants during their struggle for land put their faith in the czar for a long time and stubbornly refused to draw political conclusions.

From the revolutionary intelligentsia's traditional slogan, "Land and Liberty," the peasant for a long time only accepted the first part. It required decades of agrarian unrest and the influence and action of the town workers to enable the peasantry to connect both slogans.

The poor enslaved Bantu hardly entertains more hope in the British king or in MacDonald.[239] But this extreme political backwardness is also expressed in his lack of national self-consciousness. At the same time, he feels very sharply the land and fiscal bondage. Given these conditions, propaganda can and must first of all flow from the slogans of the agrarian revolution, in order that, step by step, on the basis of the experience of the struggle, the peasantry may be brought to the necessary *political and national* conclusions.

If these hypothetical considerations are correct, then we are concerned not with the program itself but rather with the ways and means of carrying the program to the consciousness of the native masses.

Considering the small numbers of the revolutionary cadres and the extreme diffusion of the peasantry, it will be possible to influence the peasantry, at least in the immediate future, mainly, if not exclusively, *through the medium of the advanced workers.* Therefore, it is of the utmost importance to train advanced workers in the spirit of a clear understanding of the significance of the agrarian revolution for the historical fate of South Africa.

The proletariat of the country consists of backward black pariahs and a privileged, arrogant caste of whites. In this lies the greatest difficulty of the whole situation. As the theses correctly state, the economic convulsions of rotting capitalism must strongly shake the old barriers and facilitate the work of revolutionary coalescence.

In any case, the worst crime on the part of the revolutionaries would be to give the smallest concessions to the privileges and prejudices of the whites. Whoever gives his little finger to the devil of chauvinism is lost.

The revolutionary party must put before every white worker the following alternative: either with British imperialism and with the white bourgeoisie of South Africa or with the black workers and peasants against the white feudalists and slave owners and their agents in the ranks of the working class.

The overthrow of the British domination over the black population of South Africa will not, of course, mean an economic and cultural break with the previous mother country, if the latter will liberate itself from the oppression of its imperialist plunderers. A Soviet England will be able to exercise a powerful economic and cultural influence on South Africa through the medium of those whites who in deed, in actual struggle, have bound up their fate with that of the present colonial slaves. This influence will be based not on domination but on proletarian mutual cooperation.

But more important in all probability will be the influence that a Soviet South Africa will exercise over the whole of the black continent. To help the Negroes catch up with the white race, in order to ascend hand in hand with them to new cultural heights, this will be one of the grand and noble tasks of a victorious socialism.

In conclusion, I want to say a few words on the question of a legal and illegal organization, concerning the constitution of the party.

The theses correctly underline the inseparable connection between organization and revolutionary tasks, supplementing the legal apparatus with an illegal one. Nobody, of course, is proposing to create an illegal apparatus for such functions as in the given conditions can be executed by legal ones.

But in the conditions of an approaching political crisis, there must be created special illegal nuclei of the party apparatus, which will develop as need arises. A certain part and, by the way, a very important part of the work cannot under any circumstances be carried out openly, that is, before the eyes of the class enemies.

Nevertheless, for the given period, the most important form of the illegal or semilegal work of revolutionaries is the work in mass organizations, particularly in the trade unions. The leaders of the trade unions are the unofficial police of capitalism; they conduct a merciless struggle against revolutionaries.

We must have the ability to work in mass organizations and avoid falling under the blows of the reactionary apparatus. This is a very important—for the given period, the most important—part of the illegal work. A revolutionary group in a trade union that has learned in practice all the necessary rules of conspiracy will be able to transform its work to an illegal status when circumstances require this.

CENTRIST ALCHEMY OR MARXISM?[240]

(April 24, 1935)

Internal Groupings in Germany
and International Questions

Political life in Germany is so crushed and the consequences of the defeat are so acutely felt by the masses that the diverse groupings within the working class are still deprived of the opportunity to develop in scope and in depth and to disclose the tendencies lodged in them. During such periods, of utmost importance for the training of the advanced workers are: first, political emigration; secondly, the international problems. What has been said is not intended to minimize the importance of the internal organizations and the internal problems of the German working-class movements. The primacy and continuity of revolutionary thought and revolutionary training during even the very dullest periods is a great boon, which subsequently bears its fruits a hundredfold in the periods of the revolutionary upsurge.

It is precisely now, in the steel tentacles of the dictatorship of the Nazis, that the cadres of steeled fighters are being trained who will set their seal upon the fate of Germany. I wish only to underscore as sharply as possible the idea that our German comrades must review, today more than ever, their internal relations and groupings — not taken by themselves but in connection with the life of those countries where the revolutionary problems are posed in a more developed and clearer form. For example, it is quite self-evident that a major success of the Bolshevik-Leninists in one of the nonfascist countries of Europe would immediately have a very vigorous reaction upon the fate of our section in Germany. Nor should we forget also that the political questions in the nonfascist countries are for Germany questions relating not only to the past but also in large measure to the future; the German proletariat will have to begin all over again in many things and to repeat others anew, only within incommensurably shorter periods of time.

What has been said applies, with the necessary changes, of course, also to other organizations. With no perspectives, with no clear slogans, the Communist Party of Germany is nevertheless carrying on considerable illegal work; this fact is evidence of how numerically large is the stratum of revolutionary workers who refuse to capitulate despite everything; knowing no other banner, they group themselves under the banner of the German Communist Party. To this we should also add the financial "factor." Money by itself, of course, does not guarantee victory. But it can maintain the existence of an organization for a fairly long period of time, even if the latter is doomed to the junk heap.

On the other hand, the general suppression of political life in Germany and the extremely narrow limits of the working-class movement prevent the CP from revealing and drawing to a conclusion its false tendencies. The organization, the agitation, as well as the mistakes, still remain in an undeveloped form. But the CP does not stand by itself; all the pieces on the European chessboard are now linked together more closely than ever before. There is much reason to think that the fatal and criminal policy of the French Communist Party will deal the German CP a cruel blow even before the latter succeeds in undermining its own illegal organization. Today, there is even less reason to believe in the regeneration of the Comintern than a year or two ago.

It does not follow from all this, however, that it is presumably necessary to turn our backs upon the illegal organizations of the German CP. On the contrary, one must rather say that our German friends have devoted much too little attention to this organization, incomparably less, in any case, than they have to the small SAP. Were they correct?

An answer to this question is inconceivable without precise criteria. What did our comrades seek from the SAP? Was it an *arena* for their activity? Obviously not; the SAP, which numbers a couple of thousand members, is much too narrow to serve as an arena. The CP could sooner serve as an "arena," not to mention the young generation of workers that is stirring for the first time to political life under the lash of Hitler. There remains another possibility: the SAP as an *ally,* as a *co-thinker.* Naturally, the merger of both organizations would result in absolutely self-evident benefits for future revolutionary work. But merger requires agreement — not on partial and second-rate questions but on the *fundamental ones.* Does it exist?

The leaders of the SAP often say that "in essence" their views are the same as ours, but that they are able to defend our views better, more realistically and more "wisely." If that were the case, then a split would have been sheerest insanity; within the framework of a single organization, the leaders of the SAP would have taught us how to develop our common views much more ably and successfully. But, unfortunately, such is not the case. The leaders of the SAP calumniate themselves. If after long vacillation they shied away from unity within the national framework, if subsequently they broke off the international connections with us, then there must have been very serious causes for it, and there are such. We are separated not by nuances of tactic but by *fundamental questions.* It would be absurd and unworthy to shut one's eyes to this after the experiences we have passed through. The differences between us and the SAP fall entirely into the framework of the contradictions between *Marxism* and *centrism.*

In the following lines I do not undertake to say anything new. I wish only to draw the balance sheet of the experience of the entire political period, particularly for the last year and a half. Nothing is more beneficial for political training than to check *principles* in the light of *facts* that had been evaluated in time or even forecast beforehand. If I ask the readers of this article to pay strict attention to the detailed analysis of the political nature of the SAP, it is not at all for the sake of initiating periods of new negotiations but rather in order to attempt to bring them to a close. The leaders of the SAP are not our followers nor our allies but our opponents. The attempts to draw closer to them have been exhausted for the period immediately ahead, at any rate. Naturally, it is impossible, particularly from the outside, to express oneself categorically against this or that joint action in Germany itself. But our German followers, it seems to me, must establish their interrelationship with the SAP not only with regard to a greater or lesser correspondence of views in the sphere of the undeveloped internal German questions of the Hitler underground (in the twilight of fascism, all cats appear to be gray) but also with regard to the role that the SAP plays or attempts to play upon the international arena.

It might perhaps appear strange that we should devote comparatively so large a labor to such a small organization. But the gist of the matter lies in the fact that *the question revolving around the SAP is much greater than the SAP itself.* Involved here, in the last analysis, is the question of correct policy towards the centrist tendencies that now play with all the colors of the rainbow within the field of the working-class movement. The conservative centrist apparatuses inherited from the past must be prevented from checking the revolutionary development of the proletarian vanguard; that is the task!

The Balance Sheet of the IAG Conference

After an interval of a year and a half, a conference of the IAG was held in Paris. What were the results of this conference? Up to this moment, no one has told us anything essential upon the subject. It is true that in the report of the SAP (*Die Neue Front,* March 1935) there can be found not at all bad sketches of certain participants in the conference, but it is utterly impossible to find there any answer to the questions: why was the conference called and what results did it bring? The *report of the conference* is presented not in a Marxist manner, i.e., not with the aim of disclosing all the existing tendencies and contradictions, but in the centrist manner, with the aim of glossing over the differences and presenting a picture that all is well.

The academic theses on the *world situation* were accepted "unanimously." As a matter of fact, what harm is there in repeating once again the general formulas about the collapse of capitalism and so on? It smacks of radicalism but puts no one under any obligation whatever. Such formulas have become a very cheap commodity during the years of the world crisis. But did the resolution on "the world situation" attempt to give voice to that tiny truth that the NAP,[241] having obtained 45 percent of the votes and, consequently, having behind it the indubitable majority of the population, could, if it so desired, have transformed Norway into a working-class stronghold, could have instilled by its example revolutionary courage into the masses of Scandinavia and could have become an important factor in the development of Europe? For the NAP is still a member of the IAG! Despite this — no, precisely on this account — the conference evaded the issue of the NAP and busied itself with "higher" questions. How could Kilbom, this future "statesman," permit tactless and sectarian criticism of his neighbors? Never! And Schwab, how could he grieve Kilbom? No! Better talk about the collapse of capitalism "in general." Such is the spirit that pervaded this conference. And such is the spirit pervading the SAP report.

The resolution of the conference on *war,* passed after the report by the hoary centrist, Fenner Brockway, the leader of the ILP, rings very radical. But we have known for a long time that on the question of war the most extreme opportunists are inclined to extreme radicalism, particularly those in small

organizations or in "neutral" and small countries that are not
involved in the actual struggle. Naturally, there can also be
genuine revolutionists in small organizations and in "neutral"
countries; but in order to differentiate between them and the
opportunists, we must take into account their *day-to-day policies* and not a holiday resolution on (somebody else's) war.
Kilbom's vote for the general strike and for an insurrection
against war are rendered absolutely worthless by the opportunistic policy of this same Kilbom in Sweden. And were circumstances to draw Sweden into war, then Kilbom would
surely draw his practical conclusions not from the academic
resolution of the IAG but from his own opportunistic policy.
Have we not seen such examples by the hundred?! Yet, not a
single one of the resolutions, of course, has a word to say
about the opportunistic policy of the Swedish party, the largest
organization after the NAP in the IAG.

What weight has Doriot's signature to a radical resolution
on war if Doriot, "in the interests of peace," advises the diplomats of his country to "negotiate with Hitler"! Not an alliance
with the USSR but an agreement with Hitler — that is Doriot's
program. As we shall soon see, when the SAP itself passed from
an academic resolution on war "in general" to the question of
the "struggle for peace" under the present conditions, all the
high-sounding phrases went flying to the devil; the SAP presented to the conference a second, "practical" resolution, which is
permeated through and through with the spirit of pacifist
philistinism.

For this reason it is impossible to read without revulsion
the verbiage in *Die Neue Front* about how "Leninist theory and
practice [!] on the question of war found its sole [!] and genuine [!!] defenders in the parties of the IAG." To Lenin the
task of a resolution of any kind was to put the opportunists
to the test, leaving them no loopholes, bringing them out into
the open and catching them up on the contradictions between
their words and their actions. A "revolutionary" resolution for
which the opportunists could also vote was deemed by Lenin
to be not a success but a fraud and a crime. To him, the task
of all conferences consisted not in presenting a "respectable"
resolution but in effecting the selection of militants and organizations that would not betray the proletariat in the hours of
stress and storm. *The methods of the SAP leadership are directly opposed to the methods of Lenin.*

The SAP delegation placed before the conference a draft of
a *principled resolution*. Like all SAP documents, the draft
is a collection of general, "radical" postulates, together with
a diligent evasion of the most acute questions. Nevertheless,

this document impinges much more closely upon the current work of the party than do the academic theses on the world situation.

What fate befell this draft of the SAP? We read: "The draft of the *principled resolution* presented at the conference could not be put to a vote because of lack of time [!!] and [?] because some [?] parties did not have the previous opportunity [!!] to consider it." To Marxists, this single sentence is worth more than whole volumes. The conference was postponed for month after month; it convened after an interval of one year and a half, during which time events occurred of colossal importance; the disoriented vanguard of the working class demands clear answers. . . . So what? So, the conference was unable to find the time [!!] to pass on a principled resolution.

The second argument ("and") is no whit better: some parties (what parties?) did not have the opportunity (why not?) to ponder over those principles that must serve to direct the working-class movement in our epoch. Then what, in general, are these "same parties" preoccupied with? The IAG has now existed for three years. On what principled foundation? Nobody knows. "Some" parties do not find it necessary to waste time on principled questions. The conference also cannot find the time to occupy itself with this. Is it possible to conceive a more crushing, a more deadly and more vile pauper's plea?

As a matter of fact, the wretched balance sheet of the conference is to be explained not by lack of time but by the *heterogeneity* of its composition, with its preponderance of right-centrist combinationists. The very same heterogeneity distinguishes "some" of the parties that adhere to the IAG. Hence flows the internal need for not touching upon the most acute, i.e., the most important and undeferrable questions. *The sole principle of the IAG is to keep mum about principles.*

Let us recall that the international plenum of the Bolshevik-Leninists in its resolution of September 13, 1933,[242] made the following evaluation of the previous IAG conference held in August 1933: "There cannot be even talk, of course, that the new International can be built by organizations that proceed from profoundly different and even antagonistic bases. . . . As regards the decisions that were passed by the variegated majority of the conference and that are utterly pervaded with the seal of this variegated assortment, the plenum of the Bolshevik-Leninists deems it impossible to assume any political responsibility for these decisions." Whoever cherishes no illusions does not have to lose them subsequently!

"The Profound Problem" of Centrism

The conference rejected the resolution presented by the Dutch delegates, Comrades Sneevliet and Schmidt, in favor of the Fourth International. Let us view a little closer the muddled explanations given by *Die Neue Front.*

It appears that the delegates of the SAP were ready to sign the Dutch resolution, *provided* it was not put to a vote, but would remain only the expressed "desire of the undersigned organizations." But desire presupposes a *will.* Whoever expresses a desire seeks to realize his will. At a conference, this is achieved by means of a poll. One should imagine that the delegates of the SAP would have welcomed the opportunity to force all those to vote against the resolution who are in essence opposed to the Fourth International. But no. Schwab refuses to vote for the resolution, not because *he* himself is against it but because *others* are against it. Incidentally, the majority does not vote against it either . . . but resorts cravenly to abstention. This does not prevent Doriot, who himself abstained, from writing that the conference "condemned the Trotskyist idea of the Fourth International." Can you make head or tail out of all this? But wait, this is only the beginning.

The Dutch resolution, it seems, is distinguished by a "complete abstraction from the present actual situation" and by a lack of understanding "of the profound problem involved in the task." Granted. Then why did the delegation of the SAP agree to sign so wretched a resolution? Schwab, obviously, does not place a very high value on his signature (incidentally, he had already demonstrated this in 1933!). But still, what is the position of the SAP in substance? "The proclamation of the new International," we read, "despite the need for it objectively, is in the meantime rendered impossible by subjective causes." In the first place, we find here confounded consciously, that is to say, unscrupulously, the "proclamation of a new International" and the proclamation of the need to struggle for the Fourth International. We demand the latter, and not the former.

However, wherein does the "profound problem" involved in this question lie? Observe, *objectively* the new International is necessary, but *subjectively* it is impossible. In simpler terms, without the new International the proletariat will be crushed, but the masses do not understand this as yet. And what else is the task of the Marxists if not to raise the subjective factor to the level of the objective and to bring the consciousness of the masses closer to the understanding of the historical necessity — in simpler terms, to explain to the masses their own interests, which they do not yet understand? The "profound problem" of the centrists is profound cowardice in the face of a great and undeferrable task. The leaders of the SAP do not understand the importance of *class-conscious revolutionary activity in history.*

Die Neue Front adduces for our edification Doriot's argument: it is impossible "to ignore the present condition of the masses." Then why did Doriot himself break with the Communist Party, which has behind it incomparably greater masses than has Doriot, at any rate? The abstract and hollow argument about unknown "masses" is a wretched piece of sophistry to screen the incapacity of the leaders that lurks behind it. The nonparty, i.e., the numerically strongest, "masses" stand outside of any International. The party "masses" in their overwhelming majority remain in the Second and Third Internationals, and not at all behind the IAG; it is not without good cause that Zyromsky demands that the organizations of the IAG return to their old pastures, to the "masses." Behind the IAG there are no masses whatever. The question lies not in what the masses think *today* but in what spirit and direction Messrs. Leaders are preparing to educate the masses.

As a matter of fact, in the parties of the IAG not the masses but the leaders are opposed to the Fourth International. Why? For the very same reason that they are opposed to the principled resolution. They don't want anything that would restrict their centrist liberty to vacillate. They want to be independent from Marxism. For reasons very easily understood, they label Marxism as the "Trotskyist idea of the Fourth International."

The SAP leaders were able to find a common language with everybody except the Dutch. In the report, there is to be found a polemic *only* against Sneevliet and Schmidt. Not a word of criticism against the opportunists who composed the majority at the conference! Is it not evident from this alone that Schwab and Co. are centrists who have turned their backs to the Marxists and their faces to the opportunists?

"Disarmament" or . . . Castration?

In addition to all its other achievements, the conference has inaugurated a "struggle" for peace. By what methods? By old German methods: it created . . . a *Verein* (union), a *Verein* of the Friends of Peace. This *"Verein"* consists as yet of the representatives of three (as many as three!) parties and is called the "Initiative Committee."* This Initiative Committee has for its task the creation of a new *"Verein"* which is to be

---

* As usual, we are not told *which parties.* 243

called — mind you! — the International Committee for the Struggle for Peace. Why, the name alone will make the imperialists shiver in their boots. As *Die Neue Front* reports, the task of the International Committee for the Struggle for Peace is "the inauguration and fulfillment of a world-embracing mass movement for a genuine [my! my!] disarmament and for peace." As is its custom, the SAP introduced a special resolution "for spreading the international struggle for peace." As usual, the conference was in no condition to accept this resolution either (obviously for lack of time). But since a committee of as many as three people had been established, the most important thing has been achieved. Schwab is right; the conference has "achieved all it was possible to achieve in the given situation." We are ready to subscribe to this melancholy remark.

The SAP resolution "For the Struggle for Peace," which was not adopted by the conference, was — to give it its due — the most pathetic piece of opportunistic thinking that we have had the occasion to meet during the recent period. For its authors, there exists neither the history of Marxism nor the age-long struggle of tendencies within the working class nor the fresh experience of wars and revolutions. These alchemists have newly discovered their philosopher's stone.

As we have already learned from *Die Neue Front*, the central slogan of the future "world-embracing" struggle is "genuine disarmament." Litvinov's slogan is "correct." The only fault with Litvinov is that he turns with his slogan "only to the government." Thus, our alchemists, without suspecting it, overthrow in passing all the conquests of revolutionary experience and of Marxist theory. Whoever said that the slogan of disarmament was correct? The Kautsky of the decline,[244] Leon Blum, Litvinov, Otto Bauer and Bela Kun "himself." But how did Marx, Engels, Lenin and the Third International, in its period of bloom, view this question? We do not hear a single word about this. Yet, Engels counterposed to the program of disarmament the program of a people's militia, and he demanded — horror of horrors! — the military training of the student youth. Lenin irreconcilably denounced the slightest concession to the idea of "disarmament." In 1916, in a special article written for the youth, Lenin explained that so long as oppression and exploitation continue to exist, weapons will remain a necessary factor in the relation between classes, as well as between states. Today, the bourgeoisie militarizes the youth. Wrote Lenin: "Tomorrow, it may perhaps resort to the militarization of women; to this, we must say, so much the better . . . so much the nearer to the armed insurrection against capitalism." Are we to curse war and to demand disarmament? The women of the revolutionary class will never reconcile themselves to such an ignoble role. They will say to their sons: ". . . you will be given weapons. Take your gun and learn well the art of war. This science is necessary for proletarians. . . ."[245] Lenin goes on to explain, "An oppressed class that does not strive to learn how to handle weapons and to possess guns, such an oppressed class would only merit being treated as slaves." (Slaves of the Communist International, take note!) At this same period, Lenin jotted down in his notebook, in German: "Disarmament — is castration. Disarmament — is a reactionary, Christian jeremiad. Disarmament implies not the struggle *against* imperialist reality but an escape *from* it into the entrancing future, which will follow *after* the victorious socialist revolution."

Consequently, there is no harm in the fact that Soviet diplomacy has proposed disarmament to capitalist governments. The harm and the crime lie in the fact that the Communist International and, today, the SAP have transformed this proposal into a slogan for the proletariat. Indeed, it is necessary to utilize the experiment of Soviet diplomacy in order to expose and explain the unrealness, the falseness and the illusion of both bourgeois and socialist pacifism.

Even if, by dint of a given historical correlation of circumstances, this or that capitalist government were compelled to effect "disarmament" in one shape or another, then this military-diplomatic "reform" would in no measure at all guarantee peace. The theses of the Bolshevik-Leninists, *War and the Fourth International,* state, among other things, the following: "Disarmament is not a measure against war for, as we have seen from the experience of Germany itself, episodic disarmament is only a stage on the road to new armament. The possibility of a new and, moreover, a very rapid arming is lodged in the modern, industrial technology. 'Universal' disarmament, even if it could be realized, would imply only the strengthening of the military preponderance of the more powerful industrial countries. . . . To advance disarmament as the 'sole, real method of preventing war' implies fooling the workers for the sake of achieving a common front with petty-bourgeois pacifists."[246] This point is aimed directly at the Stalinists, but it applies wholly to the SAP as well.*

---

* When the Bolshevik-Leninists formulated their position on the war question in their draft theses (*War and the Fourth International*), they submitted, in good time, the manuscript of the draft to the leaders of the SAP and invited them to participate in discussing it. A promise was given, but no *reply* was *forthcoming*. The leaders of

Let us allow that Marx, Engels, Lenin and their pupils, the Bolshevik-Leninists, were mistaken. But why didn't the theoreticians of the SAP so much as take the trouble to explain to us precisely where the mistake of our teachers lies? Our innovators, without any commentaries, simply stepped over the revolutionary traditions of Marxism in one of the most important questions. How explain this astonishing fact? Very simply. Our alchemists are interested neither in theory nor in historical experience nor in tradition. They operate by making estimates by means of their eyes, their olfactory organs and their sound horse sense. They wish to discover the philosopher's stone for every particular case.

In addition, it must be said that the demand that the capitalist governments disarm in order to escape war lies on the same political plane as the demand that the fascist leagues be disarmed [by the capitalist government] in order to escape the physical phase of the class struggle. Both these "demands" flow from petty-bourgeois cowardice and serve not to disarm the bourgeoisie but to demoralize the proletariat.

"The Struggle for Peace"

Thus, in the very center of the SAP resolution, there are lodged, to use Lenin's words, "nice, humane and almost-left phrases about peace, disarmament, etc." The very committee that will be created by means of the committee already created at the conference of the IAG will have as its duty to develop "a large-scale struggle for peace." *A large-scale struggle!* . . .

From the sectarian conception of the class struggle, the resolution passes over to an appeal to "the opponents [!] of war the whole world over." The Marxist vocabulary does not contain, as yet, the political meaning of "the opponents of war." The professional "opponents of war" are the Quakers, the Tolstoyans, the Gandhists; and then too, there are the parlor pacifists, the democratic windbags, the acrobats and the charlatans. The Marxists are the class enemies of the bourgeoisie and of imperialist wars, but they are the supporters of national-liberationist and revolutionary wars, both defensive and offensive. Have the leaders of the SAP really heard nothing at all on this score? Or have they succeeded in refuting these antiquated views? If so, in what books and what articles?

---

the SAP obviously "didn't have the time." They never have time for problems of the revolution, and besides what would Tranmael say? What would Kilbom say? . . . From this instance, the reader can see for himself that we have passed through a serious experience with the SAP.

The section of the resolution that is devoted to the description of the future activity of the future "world-embracing" committee is an entirely unsurpassed blob of phrasemongering. To counteract the preparation for war, the committee will have to "draw in specialists [!] and in this [!] sense gather together all of the effective forces for joint and planned labor who even today remain still [!] outside any organizational ties." The "specialists" and the "forces," which remain anonymous, are to utilize the "yearning for peace that imbues millions and millions of people as a lever to set in motion a world-embracing antiwar movement borne by the national masses of all countries. . . ." And so forth and so on.

The governments that would attempt to crush the world-embracing movement for peace will be "morally condemned and branded" — an extremely tangible weapon against Hitler, Mussolini and the others. The liberal governments will, in all probability, receive laudatory diplomas. And besides, the SAP has in reserve the "universal economic boycott" to be used against especially vicious governments. In order that the boycott be really "universal," the International Peace Committee will evidently have to enter into an alliance with pacifist banks and trusts and, on the other hand, "condemn" those capitalists who reap profits from war. But even this does not exhaust the entire arsenal of the SAP. The resolution recommends taking the example of "the experiment tried in England by the pacifists," i.e., arranging for demonstrative "national polls." One need only add petitions addressed to the general staffs; then peace would really find itself encircled!

"Democratic Control"

The SAP "committee" will wage a struggle for "international democratic control over war preparations," and to this end — hark! hark! — it will create in every country "special commissions." After that, there will be nothing left for Hitler to do except drown himself in the bucket of water that he could easily squeeze out of the SAP resolution.

"Democratic [!] control [!] over war preparations." Even Henderson[247] himself could not have put it more eloquently. This strikes a particularly fine note coming, at the present time, from the pen of a *German* Socialist. Where, oh where, are the beautiful days of Weimar?[248] Their shades have come to life again in the headquarters of the SAP.

During the last war, there existed in England the *"Verein* of Democratic Control" (that was actually its name: *the Union of Democratic Control*), under the leadership of the well-known left-liberal Morel.[249] In 1916, Lenin wrote upon this occasion:

"Only the immaturity of political relations and the absence of political freedom in Germany hinders the formation there as rapidly and as easily as in England of a bourgeois League for Peace and Disarmament, with Kautsky's program." The SAP evidently deems that the political relations in Germany today are sufficiently "mature" for the creation of a democratic *Verein* with the program of Morel-Kautsky-Schwab.

But we are in favor of democratic slogans! the author of the resolution may perhaps attempt to object, who snitched some things from the Bolshevik-Leninists that he understood badly. Yes, revolutionists defend even the sorriest remnants of democratic liberties, so long as they are unable to pass to the offensive for the seizure of power. But revolutionists never promise to transform these sorry remnants into a world-embracing sovereignty of democratic control by means of "special commissions," consisting of nobody knows whom. It is one thing to defend the *real* democratic trenches of the working class in the revolutionary struggle; it is something entirely different to build democratic castles in Spain after losing all the democratic trenches. It is precisely along this point that there passes the line of demarcation between revolutionary realism and illusory pacifism.

The SAP resolution is not at all original; as a matter of fact, it is merely a counterfeit of the Communist International. Why create this world-embracing committee when it has already been created? Its name is the Amsterdam-Pleyel Committee! It unifies all the specialists and all the "forces": Barbusse, the world-embracing Muenzenberg,[250] Hindu liberals, petty demagogues, colossal windbags, English lords and American widows, in short, "all the forces" suffering from the disease that is called the "yearning for peace. . . ." This committee manufactures much more beautiful documents than does the SAP, because at Muenzenberg's disposal there are the very best specialists. . . . The great plan of Schwab and Co. is a provincial handmade forgery of the bureaucratic adventurism of the Stalinists. Aided by ringing coin, the Stalinists at least arrange pompous parades (they arranged them *yesterday*; they will hardly arrange them *tomorrow*), while the IAG could not even do as much. No new committee will come out of its present committee. Peace, perhaps, will not even notice that it has been surrounded on all sides.

It is no accident that in the policy of the Comintern, as well as that of the reformists, purely negative formulations predominate, like *anti-imperialism, antifascism, antiwar* struggle, with-

out any class delimitations and without a revolutionary program of action. Such formulations are absolutely necessary for
the policies of masquerade blocs (the Anti-Imperialist League,
the Amsterdam-Pleyel Committee Against War and Fascism
and so on). All these blocs and congresses and committees
have as their task to screen the passivity, the cowardice and
the incapacity to solve those tasks that compose the very
essence of the class struggle of the proletariat. Following in
the footsteps of the Stalinists and the reformists, the IAG has
taken to the same road. The very same leaders sit down on
different stools in the hope that the masses will fail to recognize them and will come flocking to them. This self-abnegation
is a voluntary confession of one's own worthlessness.

A New "Zimmerwald"?

Some comrades reason as follows: The leaders of the SAP
are, of course, not Marxists, but the Third International did
not spring up spontaneously either; it was preceded by conferences in Zimmerwald and Kienthal,[251] in which Lenin participated side by side with the centrists. But is the IAG a new
"Zimmerwald"? In this argument, there are no less than four
fundamental mistakes.

First, Zimmerwald took place *during the war.* The overwhelming majority of the centrists who during peacetime spoke
about the struggle for peace and disarmament went over to
the camp of nationalism in the very first days of the war. Only
an insignificant minority of prewar centrists, isolated individuals, evinced their readiness to confer with the "enemies" of
their country. Thus the composition of Zimmerwald was subjected to the ruthless selection under war conditions.

In the second place, outside of Russia and partly Germany
(R. Luxemburg, K. Liebknecht[252]), in no country were there
at that time real revolutionists who understood the tasks of
the struggle to their ultimate conclusion. The Social Democrats,
who were drawn into the struggle against war (not a *future*
war, not war in *general,* but a *given, actual war*), were then
passing through the centrist stage almost in their entirety.
There were no other political partners to be found to take the
first steps.

In the third place, under war conditions when entry into
relations with working-class organizations of enemy countries
was punished as a crime, the very fact of an international
conference, convoked illegally, was a political event and a
revolutionary signal, independent of even what decisions it
reached.

In the fourth place, Lenin participated in the conference not to reach conciliation with the centrists, not to present hollow "resolutions," but to struggle for the principles of Bolshevism. No sooner did the "Zimmerwald Left" consolidate itself than Lenin, despite its extreme weakness (it was incomparably weaker than the present international organization of the Bolshevik-Leninists), posed the question of a break with Zimmerwald. The break lagged *against* the wish of Lenin who, however, was not mistaken in his estimate; the majority of the participants at Zimmerwald soon took their place in the ranks of the Second International.

Our present situation is fundamentally different from that of the past. There is no war as yet. Ninety-nine percent of the reformists and centrists who are now harping on the pacifist phrases ("against war," "for disarmament") will turn out on the side ot their governments in the event of a new war. Today, in times of peace, a doubly strict revolutionary selection is necessary. The criteria for this selection are clarity in theory and a practice corresponding to theory. Leaders, who en route to an "international" conference, forget to take along their "principles" (these are not cigarette cases or matches!) do not give the slightest guarantees for revolutionary conduct in times of war.

Moreover, the year 1935 is not the year 1915. We have behind us the experiences of the last war and of Zimmerwald. The Schwabs and the Kilboms, Doriot and the others are no children. They are not even youth. They were leading participants in the Communist International. If from the experience of the last two decades they have drawn not revolutionary but centrist and pacifist conclusions, then we must seek for other allies.

Finally, we must not forget also the fact that we have already participated once before in the "Zimmerwald" of peace times; in August 1933 we participated in the conference of the IAG, which refused even to put to a vote our resolution on the Fourth International. The pretext was that "the participants were not sufficiently acquainted with it." A year and a half has elapsed. The attempt of Sneevliet and Schmidt produced the same result. Isn't it at last time to draw the necessary conclusions?

In all countries there now exist genuine revolutionary organizations and groups that took form in the struggle against reformism and Stalinism. Their numbers and strength are growing. The vicious persecution and calumny of the enemies steel them. Their ideological equipment has been tested in colossal historical events. All this was entirely lacking during the last war. The Bolsheviks have no reason for uniting with the centrist leaders (*"unity"* . . . once every year and a half at a conference!). Hollow international parades are of no use to us. Revolutionists do not flirt with centrists at conferences but carry on tireless day-to-day work against them in their own countries, and they participate at their own revolutionary international conferences, where they do not blow soap bubbles but discuss and decide the questions of the class struggle.

Some Facts from the History of the Formation of the SAP Leadership

In order to estimate correctly the political physiognomy of a given group, we must know its past. The leadership of the SAP emerged from the ranks of the Right Opposition of the German Communist Party (Brandler, Thalheimer, Walcher and others). In 1923, this group led the Communist Party, and, under the conditions of the greatest revolutionary crisis connected with the occupation of the Ruhr district, it revealed its utter incapacity. The blame for letting slip the revolutionary situation falls not upon the "masses," as the opportunistic leaders asserted, but upon the Brandler-Walcher faction, which vacillated, let time slip during the most critical months and shifted the revolutionary obligations upon "the historical process." After the revolutionary situation had turned into a counterrevolutionary situation, the leadership, as usual, evinced a false optimism ("the revolution is approaching"!), and by its entire subsequent policies it generally demonstrated that it had completely failed to understand its "mistake" of 1923, which became a colossal signpost in the history of the triumph of German fascism.

The entire opportunistic policy of the Communist International (the strategy of the Chinese Revolution, the "workers' and peasants' parties" in the Orient, the Anglo-Russian Committee, the "Peasant International," placing all stakes on the kulak in the USSR, the struggle against Marxism under the guise of a struggle against "Trotskyism") occurred with the participation or with the direct support of the Brandler-Walcher faction. Involved here is not the question of minor tactical episodes but the question of the strategy of the proletariat during events on a colossal historical scale.

We do not at all mean to say that a group carrying upon its shoulders such a heavy burden of opportunistic crimes against the revolution is doomed once and for all; there are not a few instances in history where revolutionists turned opportunists and opportunists became revolutionists. But in any case the passage to the road of revolutionary policy could have only implied for the representatives of the Brandler-Thalheimer school a profound internal crisis, a revaluation of values and a break with their own past. The split of the Walcher group, in connection with its entry to the SAP,* from the Brandler group, which continued obediently and assiduously to pin hopes upon the mercy of the Stalinist bureaucracy, created the most favorable conditions for the review of their own past by Walcher and the others. The tragic annihilation of the German proletariat made such a review necessary and undeferrable, and, as a matter of fact, the Walcher group, which assumed the leading posts in the SAP, did sway to the left on the eve of emigration.

It is precisely to this period that date back the attempts of Bolshevik-Leninists to impel the leadership of the SAP to review, in the light of new events, the experience of 1923 in Germany, of the Chinese Revolution, of the Anglo-Russian Committee, etc. The leaders of the SAP evinced the minimum of interest in all these questions. Our theoretical insistence appeared to them to be sectarian "hairsplitting." They indicted the Communist International, at any rate up to its latest ultraopportunist turn, for one single sin: *ultraleftism*. They could not at all digest the definition *bureaucratic centrism*. Generally speaking the term *centrism* has a bad effect on their nerves. Nevertheless, under the fresh impression of the bankruptcy of the Second and Third Internationals in Germany, the Walcher group went so far as to admit the need for beginning to build *the Fourth International*.

In August 1933 the SAP leadership signed jointly with us the well-known *Declaration of Four*. The leaders of the SAP proclaimed, together with us, that "in full realization of the great historical responsibility that devolves upon them, the undersigned . . . obligate themselves to direct all their forces to the formation in the shortest possible time of this [Fourth] International on the firm foundation of the theoretic and strategic principles of Marx and Lenin."

This resolution was the extreme left point to which the leadership of the SAP was able to oscillate under the blows of events. After this, the pendulum of centrism began its downward swing to the right. Without openly removing their signatures from the resolution, the leaders of the SAP opened an undercover,

---

* Incidentally, one of the leaders of the group asked me by mail for my opinion on the entry into the SAP. My reply was that one could not say anything *in principle* against such an entry, the whole point in question being under what banner and for what aims the entry was made.

an equivocal and a disloyal struggle against the idea of the Fourth International. On what grounds? On the ground that "the Trotskyists want to proclaim the new International *immediately.*" Foreseeing the possibility of such insinuations on the part of the centrist slowpokes, a special declaration of the Bolshevik-Leninists was presented at the conference of the IAG in August 1933, declaring that: "The course towards the new International is dictated by the entire course of development. This does not mean to say, however, that we propose *to proclaim the new International immediately.* . . . The creation of the new International depends not only upon the objective course of events but also upon *our own efforts.*"

Isn't this manifestly clear enough? One should imagine that the precise written declaration would leave no room for stupid insinuations and calumnies. And finally, if someone *else* were proposing an incorrect, hasty and adventuristic road, how could that change the content of *my own task?*

As a matter of fact, the leadership of the SAP had the same superficial, trifling, verbal attitude toward the declaration for the Fourth International as centrists generally have toward theoretical principles. While signing the declaration, they had the following idea in back of their heads: "We shall sign this very unpleasant document in order to preserve the harmonious cover of our left wing; but we shall continue to do what Seydewitz and we ourselves have been doing up to now, i.e., to seek allies *from the right.*" It goes without saying that this was a remarkable plan. It fell through because the Leninists refused to play the role of an honorary revolutionary guard at opportunist deals. Hence, the split.

The Experience with the NAP

The situation received its most brilliant clarification on the question of the NAP. Without in any way overestimating the international role of the SAP, we, however, pointed insistently to the fact that its bloc with the NAP, through the medium of the IAG, aided the opportunist leadership of the NAP to tame its own left-wing opposition. It is precisely for this, and only for this, reason that the leaders of the NAP kept up their "compromising" connections with the left. We forecast that Tranmael would unceremoniously break with the IAG as soon as he has reached the harbor: *"Der Mohr hat seine Schuldigkeit getan* . . ." [The Moor has done his duty]. We advised the leaders of the SAP to ponder over the experience of the Anglo-Russian Committee, which in 1925-27 literally broke the neck of the very promising opposition movement in the British trade unions (the Minority Movement). How smugly did the leaders of the SAP wave our arguments aside! "Masses . . . masses . . . masses . . . historical process . . ." We were not astonished: if centrists were able to understand the interrelationships between the "masses" and the vanguard, between the vanguard and the leadership, between "the historical process" and the initiative of the minority, then they would not be centrists.

The actual course of events developed even more clearly and convincingly than we had forecast. Directly and immediately from the ranks of the IAG, the leaders of the NAP transplanted themselves to the government benches and, as their first act, they passed the king's civil list. "The historical process" can play dirty tricks! Yet, it is an incontestable fact that the leaders of the SAP broke with the grouping for the Fourth International precisely in order to be able to maintain, without any hindrance, their friendship with the leaders of the NAP and their like.

Observe that we bitter-end "sectarians" did not put any ultimata to Schwab and Co. We said to our temporary centrist semiallies: "You say that the experience of the Anglo-Russian Committee is insufficient *for you?* Very well, go on with *your* experience with Tranmael; we will patiently wait for the results, reserving to ourselves only the full freedom to criticize." But it is precisely this that the leaders of the SAP could not tolerate. The policies of centrist combinationism demand a diplomatic backstage; to think their own thoughts out to their conclusion and to say openly what is implies nipping the centrist delusions in the bud. It is true that in order to "disarm" us they also "criticized" Tranmael, but just enough so as *not* to expose before their readers the rottenness and falseness of their alliance with Tranmael; they roared angrily like lovesick doves.

Much more important is the fact that for the Norwegian workers there existed only the alliance between the NAP and a whole number of "revolutionary" foreign parties standing outside the Second International; under the banner of this alliance, the "leaders" of the NAP were able to perform their business excellently. And since it was much too uncomfortable for the leaders of the SAP to admit to their own followers that they broke a semialliance with revolutionists for the sake of an alliance with opportunists, they put in circulation a stupid piece of gossip that "the Trotskyists want to proclaim the Fourth International next Thursday," whereas the SAP, as a rational cautious body alien to any kind of adventurism, wants to . . . incidentally, what does it want? To marry the "historical process." The address of this famous and rich bridegroom is well known to old and experienced centrist marriage brokers.

At the present moment, the SAP leaders are most concerned with *getting the workers to forget* the entire story of the affair with the NAP. Why bring up old questions? Tranmael is going away from us anyway . . . fortunately without any undue noise. We have on hand many German affairs . . . Hitler . . . the war danger . . . and so forth and so on. No, we *shall not permit* these wiseacres to hide under the table the ignominious collapse of their ignominious policy with the NAP. We will compel them to give an accounting to the workers. We will call the advanced workers to study thoroughly the question as to who was correct, we or the SAP?

The Bolshevik-Leninists in Germany are all the more bound to carry on an energetic campaign on this question since this new scandalous experience has taught the smug strategists of the SAP nothing. On the contrary, they have swung still further to the *right,* into confusion, into the morass. In their innermost thoughts, they consider that they repelled Tranmael by their unbridled leftism (under the insidious influence of the "Trotskyists"). Ah, but now they will conduct themselves differently. They will not permit Kilbom to escape from their embraces, no matter what he does. But what hinders these people from learning from their own mistakes? Their firmly ossified, their thoroughly conservative centrist political psychology.

The Fatal Role of the SAP in the Stockholm Youth Bureau

In the sphere of the youth movement, the grouping took shape—at any rate up to the present—somewhat differently than it did in the IAG, but the policies of the SAP leaders bear here, too, the very same, that is to say, an unprincipled and horse-trading character, especially harmful in the midst of the revolutionary youth. The Stockholm Bureau in its present composition was created by means of fictitious magnitudes, by means of the great phantom of the NAP[253] and the minute clique of de Kadt that "represented" the OSP (Holland). The SAP united with the shadow of the NAP and with the all-too-real petty-bourgeois philistine de Kadt (against the Bolsheviks, all alliances are good!) in order to seize the leadership of the Stockholm Bureau into its hands. It is necessary to state the truth; the young Leninists evinced an impermissible submissiveness at the conference. They were insufficiently imbued with the understanding of the most important trait of centrism: its eternal readiness to put its foot in the way of revolutionists or to strike them a blow in the back in order to retain the favor of the opportunists.

At the last conference of the IAG, the representative of the

Stockholm Youth Bureau accused Comrades Sneevliet and
Schmidt of sectarianism and, in order to give them a lesson
in "realism," this young combinationist voted for two resolutions at once: for the Dutch resolution in favor of the Fourth International — and for the SAP resolution against the Fourth
International. To tolerate such mockery of principles is to
trample underfoot the elementary requirements of revolutionary
hygiene!

The French *Bulletin* issued by the Stockholm Bureau (No. 1,
April 1935) represents a new political scandal. The editorial
article seems to have been specially written with a view to
confuse, to mislead and to fool the readers. The summary of
the participating organizations in the article is based upon
equivocations; the opportunist wing is monstrously exaggerated,
while all the organizations of the Bolshevik-Leninist youth except for the American Spartacus Youth League are consciously
skipped over in silence. Messrs. Centrists are always *embar-
rassed* to appear in "respectable" (i.e., opportunist) society alongside revolutionary allies!

The task of the Stockholm Bureau is set forth in a purely
negative manner: "Its task does not lie in preparing a new
split." To this Zyromsky correctly replies: but the very fact
that the bureau exists is a split, for the grouping of the youth
must henceforth proceed along not two but three axes. One
should and one must propose a new "axis" only in case the old
axis is worthless, whereas the new is trustworthy, solid and able
to meet its historical purpose. The misfortune lies, however,
in the fact that centrism has and can have no axis *of its own.*

The editorial suddenly states the following: "Together with
the Socialist youth of Spain, the Stockholm Bureau demands
[!] a new International." But don't rush to rejoice. Having
blown a kiss to the Spaniards, our diplomatist reminds himself of Doriot, the PUPists, Zyromsky and all the prophets
of "complete unity," and he immediately adds: "its [the Stockholm Bureau's] task is to overcome the split . . . in order to
obtain the one and only genuine International." Ergo, not a
new International but the merger of the two old Internationals.
Ergo, the SAP expresses itself in principle for unity with reformists and patriots, entirely after the manner of its teacher,
Miles.

But what about Lenin, to whom *Die Neue Front* so inap-
propriately refers, who taught that "unity with opportunists
is the alliance of the workers with 'their' national bourgeoisie
and the split of the international working class." What will the
leaders of the SAP say on this score? Naturally, a *temporary*
organizational tie-up with opportunists, under specific concrete

conditions, may be forced by the circumstances*. But to turn
it into a principle is a betrayal! It is, first of all, the renunciation of the international unity of the proletariat, for in time
of war the opportunists will once again destroy that fiction
that they call the International and that they keep up during
peacetimes to soothe the centrist boobies. "Universal," "complete" unity implies the worst possible split under the most
difficult conditions.

A few lines further down we read: "This International will
be the result of the *historic process,* and it will be able to take
form only through the *actions of the masses.*" Very well! But
why then do *you* butt into somebody else's business; you
haven't been given the power of attorney for this either by the
"historic process" or by the "masses," have you? . . . The author
of the article is the accomplished pupil of Russian Mensheviks
who were in the good old days the virtuosos in the field of
correlating "revolutionary" formulas with the practice of fatalism and prostration. But how much crasser, weaker and more
impotent, indeed, is this pupil from the SAP than such classical
figures of left centrism as the deceased Martov!

The task at present is to prepare the cadres of Leninist youth,
to raise them to the level of the tasks of our epoch. In this
sphere, the requirements are special theoretical clarity, ideological honesty and an irreconcilability to opportunism and to
diplomacy. The policies of the SAP in the Stockholm Bureau
are a downright mockery of the fundamental demands of the
revolutionary education of our successors! This cannot be
tolerated.

The Two-and-a-Half International?

Those optimists who pin hopes upon the "evolution of the
IAG" must answer for themselves the following question: how
and why must this evolution proceed to the left and not to
the right? The initial positions of the participants in the IAG
are far removed from Marxism. Kilbom, Doriot, the PUPists,
Maurin (a petty-bourgeois Catalan nationalist) are the *open*

---

* Let us recall that after the war, the French adherents of the Third
International, during a considerable period of time, participated,
together with the SFIO, in the Berne (Two-and-a-Half) International.
On this score an instructive polemic broke out between Lenin and
Martov. Here is what we read in Lenin: "Martov has somewhere
written, 'You Bolsheviks inveigh against the Berne International,
but "your" own friend Loriot belongs to it.' *This is the argument
of a swindler. For, as everyone knows, Loriot is fighting for the
Third International, openly, honestly and heroically.*" We trust that
Lenin's argument requires no commentaries.

enemies of Leninism. In their current work, these parties do not exert the least influence upon one another. Once every year and a half, their delegates come together in order to reveal "the lack of time" for discussing principled questions. How then, ultimately, is the "regeneration of the working-class movement" to take place and, first of all, the regeneration of the members of the IAG itself? The only answer reads: by dint of the "historical process."

But the historical process "engenders" everything, Bolshevism as well as centrism as well as reformism as well as fascism. "Mass actions" are also of diverse kinds: there are the pilgrimages to Lourdes, the Nazi plebiscites, the reformist polls, the patriotic demonstrations, the strikes under the leadership of traitors and, finally, the revolutionary battles doomed to defeat because of centrist leadership (Austria, Spain). And, in the interim, an entirely different question is posed before us, namely, *what content does the small propagandist organization called the SAP prepare to bring into the "historical process" and into the future "activities of the masses"?* How absurd to pin behind oneself a pompous peacock's tail of *future* (!) mass activities in order to distract attention from the absence of clear ideas in one's head. The past of the leading group of the SAP (1923!) is not at all of such a kind as to enable us to *take its word for it* that it is capable of leading the revolutionary masses. In any case, at the given preparatory stage, the leaders of the SAP must prove their right to leadership by a correct theoretical position, by the clarity and consistency of their revolutionary line. Alas, there is not even a sign of such qualities among them!

Having no axis of their own, they attempt to "combine" somebody else's axes, which extend in different and even in opposite directions. The NAP is, in essence, a party of the Second International; the ILP hesitantly gravitates towards the Third; the Dutch party stands firmly for the Fourth; Doriot and the PUPists stand for "complete unity"; whereas the alchemists from the SAP assure the German workers that out of such diversified elements there will be distilled just what is needed.

Theoretically speaking, a second inception of the Two-and-a-Half International[254] is, of course, not excluded. But in view of the existence of the pathetic initial experience of this sort, and particularly in view of the extreme sharpening of the class struggle, the second experiment could only prove much weaker and much more insignificant than was the first. This prognosis already finds sufficient confirmation in the brief history of the IAG, the centrifugal forces of which have shown themselves up to now to be more powerful than all the centrist formulas. Let us once again recall several fresh facts.

The NAP is a serious opportunist party; the bourgeoisie even entrusts it with the management of its state. That is why the NAP broke with the SAP. The Bolshevik-Leninists are a serious revolutionary organization; they have their own tradition and their own principles. That is why the SAP broke with the Bolsheviks. The de Kadt clique (in the OSP) upon which Schwab leaned, left the revolutionary ranks at the very first serious test. Schwab cannot find a common language with the leading group of Schmidt, which really stands for the Fourth International. Schwab and his friends considered the American Workers Party (Muste) almost as their "own" organization; yet, the AWP merged with our section. Schwab almost succeeded in luring the Belgian, Spaak,[255] into the IAG. But Spaak suddenly became the minister of His Majesty. And things will proceed similarly in the future. The centrist diplomatists of the ILP will not save their party from further disintegration. An internal differentiation is inevitable within the Swedish party (Kilbom). In order to entrench oneself in the working-class movement, one must have, today more than ever before, clear principles and a distinct banner, one easily to be distinguished from afar.

Worthless Pilots in Stormy Weather

In France, the leaders of the SAP support centrists of the type of Zyromsky and Doriot *against* the Bolshevik-Leninists. While so doing, they whisper in their ears about our "sectarianism," our intolerance, our tendency to split each hair into four parts and so forth and so on. ("Please, for God's sake, don't think we are like those fanatics — far from it. . . .") They shut their eyes to a single fact: the Bolshevik-Leninists are the only group that made a timely and correct analysis of the situation and of the tendencies of its development, that drew from its analysis all the necessary practical conclusions and that actually does fight irreconcilably against the epidemic of light-mindedness on the part of the "leaders," against their irresponsibility and against their faith in miracles. The difference is not at all that Zyromsky and Doriot are "kinder," "more broad-minded," more "realistic" than the Bolsheviks. No, the difference, or rather the misfortune, is that they, Zyromsky, Doriot and the like, do not understand the character of the situation, that they dare not open their eyes as Marxists do and that they lack the resolution to draw the necessary revolutionary conclusions. In other words, Zyromsky and Doriot are passing through the very same political phase as did Brandler, Walcher and Co. in 1923. Under these conditions, the influence of the leaders of the SAP is all the more dangerous because in the struggle against revolutionary policies they exploit not unskillfully the Marxist vocabulary and even utilize the ready-made formulas of the Bolshevik-Leninists.

This new and most important stage of the struggle of the leaders of the SAP against the Bolshevik-Leninists must be attentively and seriously plumbed to its very conclusion; this time the stakes are much too great.

In all those countries where fascism is just beginning to assume the offensive, the chief danger lies not at all in the "passivity" of the masses but in the fact that the reformists and centrists of various shades continue to put a brake on the mobilization of the proletariat. "Objectively," to use the language of *Die Neue Front,* revolutionary resistance is necessary. "Subjectively," it is impossible . . . to the extent that the centrists, fearing a break with the reformists and among themselves, dare not take to the revolutionary road and in their own justification invoke the "masses." While so doing, the centrists wage a struggle against the Leninists. We have here the very same groupings, the very same interrelations and even the very same arguments as in the question of the Fourth International. This is no accident; *these are only the two sides of one and the same question.* When the matter in question happens to be the building of the International, the centrists from the SAP — and it is precisely they and not we — think abstractly, abstracting themselves from historical reality: somehow, sometime the work will be done, the working-class movement will be "renovated." It seems to them that they have an unlimited credit as to time. But when the question is posed of fascism or of war, it is more difficult to hoodwink oneself and others, for the perspective is not distant and amorphous but very close and distinct. Fascism is now assuming the offensive, and it assumes the offensive at its own tempo, independently of centrist calculations. It is necessary to resist by revolutionary methods, *right now, immediately.* It is necessary not to adapt oneself to the subjective condition of the neighbors on the right who invoke the argument about the "masses" but to explain openly to the masses the objective acuteness of the danger. Whoever actually fulfills this labor thereby prepares the Fourth International; he does not have and he cannot have any reasons for hiding his banner. These are the two sides of one and the same labor.

As regards the leaders of the SAP, insofar as they have any influence, let us say in France, they direct it everywhere and always in the support of centrists, who stand marking time, and against the Bolsheviks, who say what is, i.e., disclose the demands of the *objective* condition of things. The reactionary character of the work of the leaders of the SAP in this case stands revealed with special clarity because involved here is the question of the *objective* danger that is drawing closer on heels of steel. The leaders of the SAP repeat, under new conditions, the very same fatal blunder that resulted in and that brought defeat to their ill-fated policies in Germany in 1923: they lack the resolution to draw the practical revolutionary conclusions when the objective situation pressingly demands this.

The aim of the present article consists, first of all, precisely in dispelling any illusions whatever as regards the fitness of the SAP leaders to lead the *revolutionary* movement of the masses. This is not because they are *personally* incapable people. No, in this group there are to be found smart, serious and worthy activists, sincerely devoted to the interests of the proletariat. They are capable of giving advice that is not at all bad on the trade-union movement or an election campaign during a comparatively peaceful period. But, by habit of mind, they remain on the surface of events. They seek for the line of least resistance. They shut their eyes to real obstacles. They are absolutely incapable of seizing upon the logic of the struggle in the period of revolutionary — or counterrevolutionary — swirl-tide. They tragically proved it in 1923; since that time they have learned nothing, as demonstrated by their entire conduct in the years of emigration. Inveterate centrists, politicians of the golden mean and combinationists, they become hopelessly lost in difficult and responsible situations; they lose their positive traits and play a negative role. Our warning reduces itself to a brief formula: with all their incontestable merits, *the leaders of the SAP are absolutely worthless pilots in stormy weather.* And Europe today stands under the sign of storms.

The Bolshevik-Leninists
and the Fourth International

The only organization that has developed during the past years is our organization, the Bolshevik-Leninists. Both Internationals know only of defeats, decline and shambles; in the sphere of theory, they have fallen below zero. A few years ago, side by side with them there stood a very influential organization of the Communist Right Opposition (Brandler-Thalheimer-Walcher). Today only chips of this organization remain; the cadres of the SAP are one of these chips.

The international organization of the Bolshevik-Leninists

came into being only in the spring of 1930, on a foundation
that was still weak and unstable. The brief history of the work
of the Leninists was, at the same time, the history of an internal
ideological struggle. A whole number of individuals and
groups, seeking a haven among us from the vicissitudes of life,
have succeeded, fortunately, in leaving our ranks. At this very
moment, the Belgian section is passing through an acute crisis.
Undoubtedly, there will be crises in the future too. Philistines
and snobs, who are ignorant of how a revolutionary organization takes shape, shrugged their shoulders ironically over
our "splits" and "cleavages." Yet, upon the whole, our organization has grown numerically; it has established sections in most
countries; it has become steeled ideologically; and it has ma-
tured politically. During that period, the Revolutionary Socialist
Party of Holland (Sneevliet) joined our ranks. The Dutch
OSP, after purging itself of the de Kadt clique (the staunch
ally of Schwab against us), merged with the RSP on a Marxist
program. In America, the AWP (Muste) merged with our American section on rigidly principled bases. The French Bolshevik-
Leninists who have completed a very bold organizational step
(entry into the Socialist Party) now stand with their slogans
in the center of the proletarian vanguard of France. It is impossible not to point out also the new wild campaign against
the "Trotskyists" in the USSR, where the underground work
of the Bolsheviks is immeasurably more difficult than even
in Italy or Germany. Tens, if not hundreds, of thousands
of expulsions from the party, mass arrests and exile testify
that the Stalinist bureaucracy lives under the constant fear
of the sympathies to our banner it has been unable to uproot.
At the first revolutionary successes in the West, we shall reap
at once a rich harvest in the USSR.

The Bolshevik-Leninists are far from being self-satisfied; our
internal discussions are sufficient evidence of this. We are ready
to learn from all those who have anything at all to teach.
Our numerous publications in all parts of the world are evidence that our sections learn diligently and successfully. The
viability of our international organization, its capacity for
development, its readiness to surmount its own weaknesses and
ills have been proved to the hilt.

Our Dutch friends (the majority of the party) still apparently
deem it necessary to remain in the IAG. Let them pass through
this experience! We have no qualms as to the conclusions they
will draw on the morrow. But it would be a mistake to postpone, even for a single additional day, the work for the further building of the Fourth International. If the revolutionary
Marxists of all countries, together, of course, with our Dutch

friends, will establish at once an international joint body under their own banner, they will speed the inevitable disintegration of the IAG, as well as of the two old Internationals, and they will become the center of attraction for all the genuinely revolutionary groupings in the proletariat.

"Personal Influences" and Personal . . . Insinuations

As happens often, attempts are made to invest a personal struggle with a principled character. But sometimes the contrary happens: when one cannot very well wage a principled struggle, then it is screened by personal motivations. Schwab has dozens of explanations why he and his friends are able to work with opportunists but cannot work with the Bolsheviks: among us, you see, *"personal* influences" are much too strong; there is too little *"counterbalance"* and so on and so forth. We shall try to overcome our revulsion and to pause on this argument.

The *excessive* personal influence of X or Y, if it actually exists, can be (and should be) scaled down by the one and only method: by counterposing to the false or inadequately conceived views of X or Y other views that are more correct and better formulated. This road is open to everyone; we have no censorship, no bureaucracy, no GPU and no treasury to employ for corruption. The question of "personal influences" can thus be solved only en route, as a result of political collaboration, the clash of opinions, checking them by experience, etc. Whoever poses the question of "personal influences" as an *independent* question that must be solved by some special measures, apart from the ideological struggle and political checks, will find in his arsenal no other weapons except . . . gossip and intrigues.

Consequently, it is not difficult to understand that the raising of the bogey of "personal influence" is the product of the centrist incapacity to give battle on the plane of principles and methods. A particular "personal influence" is hateful and inimical to us when it stands at the service of ideas *inimical* to us. All the revolutionary teachers of the proletariat, both great and small, were accused of wielding excessive personal influence by those who did not share their views. All centrists, all muddleheads who run away from clear, open, bold and honest ideological struggle always seek for an indirect, an accidental and a personal psychological justification for the not-at-all accidental fact that they themselves happen to be in an alliance with opportunists against the revolutionists.

As a matter of fact, no other organization discusses ques-

tions so openly and democratically, in full view of friends and
foes, as we do. We are able to permit this only because we
do not substitute horse trading and diplomacy for the analysis of facts and ideas. To put it in simpler language, we do
not hoodwink the workers. But it is precisely our principle
of *saying what is* that is most hateful to the leaders of the
SAP, for the policy of centrism is inconceivable without mouth-
fuls of water, tricks and . . . personal insinuations.

Conclusion

For a long period of time, we tried the experiment of drawing closer to the leadership of the SAP; we did it loyally and
patiently, but the results are nil. Thanks precisely to the me-
thodical character of our experience, we obtained the possibility of plumbing the full depth of the centrist conservatism
of this group. In our criticism, we have dealt only with a
part of the controversial questions involved. But we trust that
what has been said will suffice to refute utterly the naive or
hypocritical assertions that the differences between us and the
SAP seemingly only touch upon partial tactical or "personal"
questions. No, the differences cover *the fundamental questions
of theory, strategy, tactics and organization:* and, moreover,
during the most recent period, after the temporary leftward
vacillations of Schwab and his friends, these differences have
increased enormously and have broken into the open.

*The leadership of the SAP represents the classic type of con-
servative centrism.*

1. It is capable neither of understanding a revolutionary
situation nor of utilizing it (1923 in Germany, the present
policies in Western Europe).

2. It has failed to master the ABC of Leninist revolutionary
strategy in the Orient (events in China in 1925-27).

3. Instead of waging a struggle for the masses, it chases
after the opportunistic leaders, supporting the latter against
the revolutionary section of the mass (Anglo-Russian Committee, the NAP).

4. It substitutes lifeless automatism and fatalism (faith in
the "historical process") for revolutionary dialectics.

5. It has the scorn of inveterate empiricists for theory and
principles, placing diplomacy and horse trading first and fore-
most.

6. It has acquired its conceptions of the role of the party
and of the revolutionary leadership not from the Bolsheviks
but from the "left" Social Democrats, the Mensheviks.

7. It presents academic "left" resolutions in order to untie
its own as well as other hands for opportunistic work; the

contradiction between thought and words, between words and deeds, the chief canker of centrism, rots away the entire policy of the SAP.

8. Despite the enormous flood of centrist tendencies in the present critical epoch, the leadership of the SAP ignores the very concept of *centrism,* shielding from criticism, in this manner, its own allies and, first of all, itself.

9. It flirts with the right-wingers and carries on a disloyal struggle against the left, putting a brake upon the process of the emancipation of the proletarian vanguard from the influences of reformism and Stalinism.

10. In countries where fascism is advancing with seven-league boots, the leadership of the SAP aids the centrists in lulling the proletariat by the struggle it wages against the only consistently revolutionary organization.

11. In the burning question of war, it has completely substituted pacifism ("disarmament," "the offensive for peace," "democratic control," etc.) for Leninism.

12. It signed the programmatic resolution for the Fourth International in order to carry on a struggle against it in action.

13. In the IAG, which it leads, it is steering a course toward the Two-and-a-Half International.

It is clear that the work of fusing the revolutionary forces under the banner of the Fourth International must proceed apart from the SAP and against the SAP.

STALINIST TREASON IN L'HUMANITE [256]

(Published April 26, 1935)

The working masses are searching for the political line that will prevent war or, if the war breaks out in spite of the efforts of the proletariat, that will accomplish the overthrow of the capitalist regime, which is responsible for war, and substitute the socialist regime for it.

We wish to show merely by quotations from *l'Humanite,* the daily paper of the Communist Party of France, which can easily be verified by anyone, what the real political line of the Communist International is toward war.

The international line of the Third International is thus defined in the sixth condition of admission:

"All parties desiring to affiliate with the Third International must denounce not only social patriotism but social pacifism with its falseness and hypocrisy as well; they must systematically reveal to the working class that without the revolutionary overthrow of capitalism no international tribune of arbitration, no debate on the reduction of armaments, no democratic reorganization by the League of Nations can preserve humanity from imperialist war."

That was the line of yesterday.

Today, since the Comintern has been reconstructed (after the expulsion of the Leninists) on the dogma of "socialism in one country," that is to say, independently of the world revolution, the international line of the Third International is the following:

Defense of the peace policy of the USSR, consisting of proposals to disarm addressed to the imperialist nations, and mutual assistance pacts against "any aggressor."

The political line is based on the following premise: there are imperialist nations interested in peace and others interested in war.

"We must know," says Peri[257] in *l'Humanite,* April 11, 1935, "if the powers who are not interested in war will assure peace through promises of mutual assistance or if they will fall into line with the plans for a new division of Europe conceived by A. Hitler."

From this flows the whole line of the Comintern. Take Peri again in *l'Humanite,* April 16, 1935:

"What formula alone can make warlike enterprise most difficult under the present system? The best formula, it is evident, would be the general or partial disarmament proposed and defended by the USSR but opposed by all the other powers. Failing a general reduction of armaments, *which the USSR has no intention of renouncing,* the Soviet government and the proletariat of all European countries with it believe a system of pacts whereby the signatories agree to boycott an aggressor nation would place the greatest obstacles in the way of war. We must see things as they are and realize that any other contractual formula is vain or dangerous."

Under these conditions what is the task of the Comintern? To join Soviet diplomacy in an attempt to convince the various imperialisms "that are interested in peace" of the necessity of mutual assistance pacts.

The following shows how the organ of the French CP goes about the task (*l'Humanite,* April 2, 1935):

"But what then does the National Union government of France think of the attitude of the National Union government of Britain? It is no longer a secret that Laval [258] is lending his ear to Hitler's propositions. Does he believe that an accord with the Nazis against the Soviet Union would benefit French imperialism? Is he forgetting that the mass movement against war and for the defense of the Soviet Union is much stronger in France than in England?

"Has he already forgotten the time, not so distant, when the French imperialist government was able to pacify the mass movement of the workers and soldiers for the dictatorship of the proletariat only by stopping immediately the war against the Soviets?"

In other words, if French imperialism wishes to survive the war, let it lend an ear to the advice of the pupils of Stalin, let it conclude a pact with the Soviet Union.

To help Laval "understand," Peri becomes positively lively and pressing:

"In the name of the Franco-British Entente, Pierre Laval has lent himself to those criminal evasions that we have so often denounced here and that we must denounce today more vigorously than ever.

"Everything indicates that Laval has given up the Eastern Pact[259] and mutual assistance. The minister of foreign affairs has deliberately renounced the only formula capable of preserving peace and putting a stop to armament. His deplorable attitude earned him the felicitations of *Der Voelkische Beobachter*260 yesterday. But it will rouse against him the anger of all those who sincerely wish to conquer war" (*l'Humanite,* April 4).

Blum rates Pertinax, of *L'Echo de Paris,* among the "awkward" friends of the USSR (*Le Populaire,* April 21) because, bourgeois realist that he is, he considers the question of an alliance with the USSR from the point of view of relative force, without attaching any importance to vague promises. Pertinax is solely concerned with "French" interests. If he were solely concerned with "Russian" interests, he would no doubt write as Peri, true friend of the USSR, writes:

"Others believe that M. Laval together with John Simon261 would be disposed to replace the project of an Eastern Pact by an Air Alliance open to all the signatories of the Locarno Pact,262 the USSR and the Little Entente. They boast of having obtained the support of Poland and of Germany for this system.

"Well, without a second thought we can say, this system has nothing to do with peace. Those who support it would precipitate the very rule of cannons that the masses wish to avert at any cost.

"Aggression will not be discouraged if the sole risk to the aggressor is the risk of not being actively assisted. Passivity by itself is an encouragement to adventures.

"In the concrete case under consideration, the system invented by M. Laval would limit itself to an agreement that Germany might carry on its Eastern projects, that France would lend no assistance but, at the same time, would offer no opposition" (*l'Humanite,* April 4).

Peri and the CP of France, from the point of view of the national interests of the Soviet bureaucracy, and Pertinax, from the point of view of the national interests of the bourgeoisie, advance, in fact, the same political line.

If, as Thorez has informed us since July 1934, it is the Communists who love their country well, it follows that those who do not love their country, the bourgeoisie, are "the traitors."

This is just what Cachin informs us in an article of April 10, in which he concludes:

"We shall tear off the masks of the exploiters of the country, the worst enemies of the French people, without failing in our duty to defend the peace and bread of their victims."

Cachin, who is a past master when it comes to traitors, is not fully understood by the true patriots, as appears from his denunciation of Taittinger:263

"Taittinger, the fascist, divulges with impunity official diplomatic and military communications that he receives in his
official positions on the various committees in parliament.
Thus he furnishes Hitler with new arguments for rearmament
and carries coals to the fires of fascism across the Rhine. A
'patriot' who conducts himself in such a treasonable manner,
at the same time, advocates repression against the antifascists!"

From which we conclude that the country, at present under
the leadership of the bourgeoisie, does not understand where
its real interests lie.

P. Vaillant-Couturier, moreover, makes no effort to conceal
it from the country; he undertakes a crusade "to the rescue
of French culture."

"If the proletariat, according to Marx, 'has no fatherland,'
they have now as internationalists something to defend: that
is the cultural patrimony of France, the spiritual wealth, the
works of its artisans, its workers, its artists and its thinkers"
(*l'Humanite,* April 13).

In other words, if the proletariat has no fatherland, nevertheless for *l'Humanite* it has had one for some time — the
French patrimony. "Conquer the country" for Cachin and P.
Vaillant-Couturier[264] means to reconquer, by means of brain-
storms in *l'Humanite, their positions of 1914.*

From such equivocations can come nothing but treason.
Happily for the proletariat, the Comintern and its various
sections have just advertised their treason without any equivocation or shame.

The duty of the proletariat in case of war is outlined in the
following appeal of the European CPs of April 18:

"We salute the progress made in the military field by the
only workers' land, the progress in reinforcing the Red Army
of workers and peasants, a true guarantee of peace; we salute
every strengthening of the frontiers of the socialist fatherland;
we will support, in case of counterrevolutionary war against
the socialist fatherland, the Red Army of the Soviet Union by
every means, and we will struggle for the defeat of *German
imperialism and its allies,* for the defeat of every power that
engages in war against the Soviet Union.

"We will aid by every means, even by the sacrifice of our
lives, the victory of the Soviet Socialist Union in its war against
all those who attack the land of socialism."

The proletariat is no longer to struggle for the defeat of its
own imperialist government, but for the defeat of "German
imperialism and its allies."

In other words, the French proletariat will go to war hand
in hand with its own bourgeoisie against German imperialism

for the defeat of the latter. *That is what is known as national defense.*

The appeal of the French CP on the occasion of the municipal elections confirms us (*l'Humanite,* April 21):

"The most sacred duty of the proletarians of the entire world is the defeat of aggressors against the Soviet Union and the defeat of all the aggressors' allies.

"The Communists want the *unification of all Frenchmen* who work in the factories, docks, offices, stores, laboratories, schools, universities and the workers of all nationalities and races who share the same suffering and the same hopes."

There we are, twice warned. Blind are the workers who do not immediately draw the correct lessons and the consequences thereof.

STALIN HAS SIGNED
THE DEATH CERTIFICATE
OF THE THIRD INTERNATIONAL[265]

An Open Letter to the World Proletariat

(Published May 25, 1935)

Stalin together with the renegade Laval has signed the death certificate of the Third International. Today, there is not a single worker, even the most politically backward, who is unaware that the Soviet bureaucrats have just publicly, decisively betrayed the international proletariat. For the first time, Stalin has openly said what is, i.e., in full view of the entire world, he has repudiated revolutionary internationalism and passed over to the platform of social patriotism. He has informed his lackeys in France of his open betrayal through the medium of a bourgeois minister, who is himself a traitor to the working class in his own country. The hired bureaucrats of French Stalinism have immediately drawn from it all the necessary conclusions, and Vaillant-Couturier in his article adds ignominy to betrayal.

While the proletarian masses mobilize themselves on the revolutionary road, while the peasant strata are seething and are vigorously intervening in the political struggle, while the petty bourgeoisie, directly hit by the economic crisis that is steadily deepening, is becoming radicalized as a whole, this bureaucrat has the audacity to write that there is no longer any room for the independent activity of the proletariat in its revolutionary struggle against its own bourgeoisie, that all efforts are to no avail and that to stave off the invasion of the USSR nothing remains except to place faith in French imperialism. Crawling on his belly, he consummates the betrayal of his master.

In the eyes of everyone, the Third International has become the diplomatic agent of Stalinism, loaded down with blunders and crimes, which has just openly taken the decisive step on the road to civil peace.

Let us review the facts.

The Stalin-Laval pact rests on the same plane as the Brest-Litovsk peace.[266] The Soviet government enters into a military alliance with an imperialist government not at its own whim but in order not to be annihilated. In any case, that is its only justification. The Brest-Litovsk peace was a defeat, but the Franco-Russian pact has been proclaimed, for all those who care to listen, a great victory for the USSR. It is unnecessary to attempt a comparison between the relation of forces in 1918 and at the present time. The facts speak for themselves. Whatever the differences in the world situation and in the relationship of forces, the Franco-Soviet treaty from the standpoint of principles and politics rests entirely upon the same plane as the treaty of Brest-Litovsk. *Should, then, the Communists and Socialists vote in parliament for the ratification of the Franco-Soviet agreement?* And this, too, regardless of the question of whether or not Soviet diplomacy was really forced to sign the treaty?

Let us recall the historic example of Brest-Litovsk. The German Social Democrats voted in the Reichstag for ratifying it, claiming that since the Bolsheviks had accepted it there was no reason whatever for their opposing it. The Bolsheviks replied to them, "You swine. We are objectively compelled to negotiate in order not to be annihilated, but as for you — you are politically free to vote for or against, and your vote implies whether or not you place confidence in your own bourgeoisie."

If we allowed that the Soviet government is really compelled to conclude a military alliance with French imperialism, the proletariat of the latter country does not at all have to do so. By their votes in parliament, the Socialist and Communist deputies are called upon to express themselves not upon the reason and motives for the action of the Soviet government *but solely upon the reasons and motives of the Flandin-Laval government.* If they vote confidence in it, they are the same swine as the German Social Democrats of 1918.

Only yesterday, Thorez and Co. swore that "We love our country, but we cannot countenance national defense under the capitalist regime." If this formula has any meaning, it implies that we cannot confide to the hands of our bourgeoisie the task of defending "our country" (which, besides, is not "ours"). Today we are told, "with throbbing hearts we shall make common cause with our bourgeoisie in the defense of the USSR." We want to know, "how is it that the French bourgeoisie, which is not good enough to defend 'our deeply loved country,' proves itself good enough for the defense of the USSR"? This is the nub of the question. There can be no middle of the road. The very same people will be obliged to proclaim, "with throbbing hearts we shall make common cause with our bourgeoisie to defend our people against the barbarism of Hitler, because the French people has the right to call for the same sacrifices on the part of its heroes as the Russian people."

There is nothing new in the new position of the Communist Party. It is social patriotism.

"But the immediate danger comes from German fascism," it will be said, "so it is necessary to make a bloc against it." Such an argument suffices for this or that diplomatic combination of the Moscow government. But this conception has nothing in common with Marxism. We have always maintained that the danger of war is the inevitable product of world imperialist antagonisms. German fascism as well as the dangers of war are the products of the colossal productive forces of German capitalism that seek for outlets and that must seek for outlets, whatever the political regime of the country. The most progressive capitalist regimes of Europe are stifling within the framework of the national state. France is marching hand in hand with fascist Italy and with quasi-democratic England against fascist Germany.

Have we forgotten that revolutionary activity during the last war consisted precisely in denouncing the propaganda of the allies who spoke in the name of democracy against the Prussian junkers and the Hohenzollerns? The old catchwords are being refurbished to camouflage imperialist antagonisms by means of sham conflicts between political systems.

On this road one quickly arrives at the idealization of French democracy as such, counterposed to Hitler Germany.

Here again, there is no middle of the road. We repeat: "It is the policy of social patriotism."

The conception of the "aggressor" is very handy for the fiendish work of diplomacy, but it is fatal for the orientation of the proletariat. To checkmate the alleged aggressor, France protects Mussolini, allowing him a free field for action in Abyssinia, 267 and also as regards Austria. And it is precisely the tightening grip of Italy on Austria that may fan to white heat German nationalism and lead to the outbreak of the war. Involved here are the permanent antagonisms that are deepening and sharpening. Their inevitable explosion and the preventive measures of the capitalist states can and must cause the catastrophe.

We will be told in answer, "All this may, perhaps, be true, but isn't it necessary all the same to save ourselves from the most immediate danger, which is the very same Hitler Germany?" Let us observe, first of all, that only yesterday the Comintern advanced in Germany the slogan of "national liberation," which is impossible without a war. Today the Communist International wants to defend the Versailles status quo in order to escape war. He is lost who abandons the position of class struggle and of international revolution and who begins to seek safety outside of the revolutionary struggle against one's own government within one's own country. Today the betrayal will be covered by the plea of the need to "save peace"; tomorrow when war breaks out, nevertheless, the betrayal will be perpetuated in order to save democracy or to save the USSR. But neither peace nor democracy nor the USSR can be saved by the surrender of the French proletariat.

If, after Germany has been annihilated for the second time, France, Italy and England turn against their temporary ally, does anyone believe that it will be possible on the spur of the moment to sever at a single stroke the proletariat from the bourgeoisie that, with the aid of the working-class parties, will have succeeded in raising itself as the master of the nation and that has gagged and demoralized the working class through civil peace?

To fritter away the only capital we possess, the revolutionary independence of the proletariat, in return for precarious, equivocal and unstable diplomatic combinations would be tantamount to walling up the avenue to the revolutionary future. The basic crime of reformism lies precisely in the fact that, chasing after the shadows of reforms, it castrated the proletariat by class collaboration. This policy is ten times, one hundred times, a thousand times more criminal at a time when it is a question not of a peaceful period of parliamentary combinations but of a war that concentrates all the instruments of oppression and destruction in the hands of the bourgeoisie and leaves the proletariat its one and only weapon: its political independence, its hatred of the bourgeoisie, its revolutionary will.

Moreover, who has the right to declare that the docile submissiveness of the French proletariat to its own bourgeoisie must inevitably frighten German fascism and force it to retreat? This indeed would be a gratuitous assertion; just the opposite result would occur in the long run.

Hitler has not yet morally crushed the German proletariat. In order to succeed in this, his propaganda revolves around the weighty argument, "we are encircled, we are hated, they seek our destruction." It is a question of the race struggle. Already the fact that the workers' state was compelled to fraternize with the French bourgeoisie against Germany has strengthened the position of the Nazis against the German working class. Should the French proletariat deliberately participate in this alliance by surrendering its class independence, the theory of the race struggle will make great headway in Germany to the detriment of the theory of the class struggle. Driven by the irresistible national spirit that he has himself incited, Hitler may be compelled to unleash the war.

On the other hand, the open, irresistible, thunderous opposition of the French proletariat to its own imperialism will be a disavowal of racism and will give a powerful impetus to the German revolution.

The USSR participated actively at Geneva in the elaboration of measures against terrorism and terrorists. The assassination of the king of Yugoslavia was the reason for this incident. We Marxists have always been the opponents of individual terrorism, but we have also assumed the defense of national terrorists against imperialist oppression. This elementary tradition has now been abandoned; the USSR has taken its place in the sphere of national struggles as the pillar of the established order and of the status quo.

In the light of the Stalin-Laval communique, the international working class is beginning to gain a better understanding of why Stalin undertook a new persecution of the Bolshevik-Leninists and of the Zinoviev group. Before finally delivering the Kremlin to the bourgeoisie, he found it necessary to overwhelm and exterminate all those who might raise their voices in protest.

The enemy is Stalinism! But the point in question is not to forget or overlook reformism. The treacherous policy of the Stalinists provides them with tremendous support. From now on Blum and Paul Faure openly spread the idea of the defense of the "national soil" because these philistines themselves, likewise, do not approve of "unconditional" defense. This stupidity of wishing to "condition" the defense of the national bourgeoisie or of the proletarian state is clear to everyone. If our country, as it is, is worthy of being defended, it must be defended no matter what the origin of the war may be: it would be absurd to punish "our country" for the idiocy of Laval and his colleagues. *To us, it is the class character that is decisive* and not the policy of the government. We are committed to oppose the war budgets of the most democratic governments of the bourgeois states, and we are pledged to defend the USSR despite and against Stalin and his infamy.

But the absurdity of the "conditional" defense of the bourgeois state bears, nevertheless, a grave political meaning. Were Blum to render to the bourgeoisie all that the latter demands, he would be unable to differentiate himself from Herriot or even from Louis Marin.[268] He would lose the confidence of the working class and become a cipher. By resorting to pacifism right up to the outbreak of the war, he retains the possibility of rendering a double service to the bourgeoisie during the war; a large section of the working class will say to itself: "If this tried-and-true pacifist now joins the ranks of 'civil peace,' it is because the war has been foisted upon us, it is because the defense is just." In order to be able to achieve this mission, Blum must reject as invalid the orders of Stalin. This perfidious game is enormously facilitated by the social-patriotic turn of the Stalinists.

Leon Blum and Co. lament that the communique does not sufficiently conform to the statutes of the League. Yet the CAP [National Council of the SFIO] as early as January elaborated its famous program that proclaims the necessity of destroying the bourgeois state and of opposing to it the interests of the working people, including the interests of the country. What is the League of Nations? It is also the mechanism of the bourgeois state or of several bourgeois states acting jointly and, at the same time, antagonistic to one another. If the mechanism of the bourgeois state deserves only to be destroyed, how can anyone stake the hopes for a better future upon the League of Nations, which is the by-product of this very same mechanism?

It is the doctrine of Jauresism[269] that democracy or the democratic state ("the bourgeois mechanism") envisages constant improvement of its fate and advances slowly but surely toward socialism. Viewed in this perspective, the League of Nations must naturally have its place to regulate the international relations of the democrats.

Today not only Pivert and Zyromsky but also Blum and Paul Faure are obliged to recognize the necessity of overthrowing and destroying the mechanism of the bourgeois state. *Under these conditions, how can they maintain their faith in the League of Nations?*

The same question presents itself on the subject of disarmament. Zyromsky expresses his regrets at the sight of his newly acquired friend Litvinov abandoning the slogans of disarmament in favor of collective security. The very same Zyromsky refuted, in his previous article, "social pacifism" in domestic policies, i.e., the hope of settling the social question amicably. Zyromsky is unable to understand that external social pacifism is the reverse side of the coin of internal social pacifism. If the bourgeoisie allows itself to be disarmed in order to secure peace, it will be, at the same time, disarmed in the struggle against the proletariat. We find here the same contradiction as in the question concerning the League of Nations. We have at least the verbal recognition of the need for the proletariat to arm itself and to gain powerful strongholds in the bourgeois army in order to lead to the victory of the internal class struggle. At the same time, one busies oneself with securing peace under the capitalist regime through general disarmament. Why then make a revolution against a humanitarian bourgeoisie that will be disarmed through a covenant of the League of Nations?

The solution of this enigma is quite simple. These people haven't the slightest confidence either in a revolution or in the destruction of the mechanism of the bourgeois army. Moreover, they demonstrate this by reiterating the slogan, "disarm the fascist leagues." Zyromsky is unaware that this famous revolutionary demand is the most stupid incarnation of social pacifism.

In refutation it will be said, "Yet you Bolshevik-Leninists yourselves recognize the right of the Soviet government to conclude alliances with imperialist states for its immediate safety. Is it, then, not our duty as French workers to support these alliances insofar as they are useful to the workers' government?"

No, never! We have already pointed out why the German Socialists were duty bound to fight against the Brest-Litovsk peace, although it was absolutely necessary for the continued existence of the Soviets at the given moment.

Let us take this very same question more concretely and more practically. Revolutionary defeatism doesn't at all imply the sabotage of the sham national defense by an active minority. It would be absurd to attribute to revolutionary workers the idea of blowing up bridges and railroads, etc., etc. . . . in case of war. The revolutionary workers, *insofar as they are the minority*, participate in the war as the slaves of imperialism who are conscious of their enslavement. At the same time, they prepare through agitation the transformation of the imperialist war into a civil war.

Should the USSR succeed in securing the military assistance of the French bourgeoisie in the event of aggression on the part of German imperialism (which is, by the way, by no means certain), this assistance supplied by the bourgeoisie in power will in no way be hindered by the fact that the revolutionary minority will continue to fulfill its duty in incessantly preparing for the overthrow of the bourgeoisie, whatever may be the military assistance of the imperialist general staff (and it will always be precarious, equivocal and perfidious).

The revolutionary repercussions that will be engendered in Germany by the revolutionary movement in France will provide another sort of effective assistance for the salvation of the USSR, as well as for the development of the world revolution.

Should the revolutionary movement in France, in the event of war, gain such force as to directly threaten the military machine of the bourgeoisie and imperil its alliance with the

USSR, it would imply that the French proletariat is capable
of seizing power at the height of the struggle. Should they
perhaps be restrained in such a situation? Let them say it.
Will we run the risk of defeat? Obviously. Revolution, like
war, carries risk with it since danger is the essential element
in it. But only wretched philistines would wish to emerge from
an international situation that is brimful of mortal dangers
without incurring any risks whatever.

Thus revolutionary defeatism does not prevent the Soviet
government on its own responsibility from profiting by such
and such a pact or this and that imperialist military assistance.
But these fleeting transactions cannot and must not in any
way commit the French and the world proletariat whose task
is, above all during the time of war, to prepare for the liquidation of imperialism through the victorious revolution.

The pact indicates weakness and not strength on the part
of the USSR. This new treaty is the product of the defeats
in China, in Germany, in Austria and in Spain.

*Since the world revolutionary factor has been weakened, the
government of the USSR has found itself forced to adapt to
the imperialist factor.* That is the only correct formula for the
Franco-Soviet treaty.

The Kremlin bureaucrats, who see only the strengthening
of the USSR, thereby posit the independence of the workers'
state from the world working-class movement; the more defeats
the latter suffers, the stronger becomes the international position of the USSR. These are the statements of charlatans — they
must be nailed to the pillory.

But if, because of annihilation of the proletariat in a number
of countries, the Soviet government is compelled to fraternize
temporarily with the oppressors of the French working class,
this cannot be the ground for further weakening the latter by
demoralizing it and thus still further worsening the international situation, forcing the revolution to retreat and consequently placing the USSR directly in danger.

When events of worldwide importance are at stake, the revolutionary party has no right to permit itself to be motivated
by secondary, episodic, conjunctural and always problematic
considerations. It is necessary to be farsighted, preserving and
accumulating the revolutionary strength of the class; it is in
this manner that one can also best exert influence on all secondary questions; revolutionary policy is always the most
practical. *The enemy is Stalinism!* It weakened the USSR because it delivered the Chinese workers and peasants to the
bureaucracy of the Kuomintang, the English workers to the
bureaucracy of the trade unions, etc. . . . Frightened by the

consequences, it sought to play the card of adventurism, "third period." The results proved themselves even more fatal. Today Stalin and Co. have lost all confidence in the revolutionary forces. They resort to pure diplomacy, that is to say, to the filthiest sort. They refuse to see anything except combinations with this or that imperialism against some other. They are, above all, afraid lest the French workers compromise their combinations. Thorez and Co. subscribe to this disgraceful attitude. They also deem the revolutionary movement to be an obstacle to the safety of the USSR. They accept the order to penalize and hamstring the revolution.

They openly become the Stalinist police over the French proletariat, and, what is more, the Stalinist police become, at the same time, the police of French imperialism.

When we, the Bolshevik-Leninists, began our struggle against the theory of socialism in one country, it may have seemed that only an academic question was under discussion. Today the historical function of this formula may be clearly seen: its task is the severing of the fate of the USSR from the fate of the world proletariat. It has created a national base for the Soviet bureaucracy that allowed it to concentrate all the power in its own hands. The new law that extends capital punishment to children twelve years old reveals with fearful eloquence not only that the USSR is still a considerable distance from socialism but also that under the domination of the omnipotent bureaucracy the social decomposition of wide strata of workers and peasants has attained formidable proportions despite all the technological conquests bought so dearly by the workers and peasants. And it is precisely at the moment when the war danger threatens the state founded by the October Revolution that the government of the USSR draws the final conclusions from the theory of socialism in one country, prostituting the ABC of Marxism and degrading the Comintern to the role played by Scheidemann, Noske, Renaudel, Vandervelde and Co.[270]

When, after the capitulation of the Communist International before Hitler, we proclaimed: it is the "August 4" of the Third International, we met with not a few protests. "August 4," we were told, was a conscious betrayal, while the capitulation before Hitler was the inevitable consequence of false policy. Today we see how superficial are such purely psychological evaluations. The capitulation was the expression of the internal degeneration, a consequence of accumulated blunders and crimes. This degeneration implied in its turn the capitulation to imperialist war and a prelude to the capitulation before the imperialist bourgeoisie, which is preparing for war. That is why the "August 4" of the Third International was already lodged in the capitulation to Hitler. It is the great merit of the Bolshevik-Leninists that they stated this in time.

Leninism is betrayed and vilified by Stalinism.

The urgent task of the hour is to reconstitute the ranks of the vanguard of the international proletariat. For this a banner and a program are necessary, and they can only be the banner and the program of the Fourth International.

The Third International is dead. Long live the Fourth International!

TO THE STUDENTS OF
EDINBURGH UNIVERSITY[271]

(June 7, 1935)

Dear Sirs,

I am indebted to you for your so unexpected and flattering proposal: to put me up as candidate for the rectorate of your university. The freedom from any nationalist considerations that you show is a great tribute to the spirit of the students of Edinburgh.

I appreciate your confidence all the more since you, as you yourselves say, are uninfluenced by the refusal of the British government to grant me a visa. Nevertheless, I do not feel that I have the right to accept your proposal. The elections to the rectorate, you write, are conducted on a *nonpolitical* basis and your letter itself is signed by representatives of every political tendency. But I myself occupy too definite a political position; all my activity has been and remains devoted to the revolutionary liberation of the proletariat from the yoke of capital. I have no other right to responsible posts. I would therefore consider it a crime toward the working class and a disloyalty toward you to appear on no matter what public tribune not under the Bolshevik banner. You will find, I have no doubt, a candidate much more in conformity with the traditions of your university.

I wish you with all my heart the greatest success in your work.

Sincerely yours,
L. Trotsky

THE SEVENTH CONGRESS
OF THE COMINTERN[272]

(June 7, 1935)

It seems the Seventh Congress is to be convened after all (that is the news at any rate from the Paris White Russian press), after an interval of seven years.

It can be said with complete safety: had our organization not existed, had the banner of the Fourth International not been unfurled and had our French friends not met with fresh successes, the Third International would still have had to wait for its Seventh Congress.

Like the latest French congress, the Seventh Congress of the Comintern will also revolve essentially, if not solely, around the question of the Bolshevik-Leninists and the Fourth International.

After Hitler's victory, we declared the Third International politically bankrupt. The example of the Second International is there to prove that where there are political organizations with a mass base, their death — in the sense that it develops progressively — is far from being synonymous with the death of the self-preserving autocracy. Despite its shameful failure, the Third International still has immense reserves in the bureaucracy and this by itself assures it of great possibilities for continuing to vegetate and also to commit many more crimes against the world proletariat. The whole question is whether the Soviet bureaucracy still needs the Third International.

From this point of view, the Soviet bureaucracy is gripped in the vise of flagrant contradictions. Its present policies — particularly its international policy with its increasingly preponderant role — make the Comintern more of a hindrance than a help. But if the Comintern were to disappear and its place taken immediately by its adversary, the Fourth International — and that would mean the complete ideological failure of Stalin and his clique — it would be the shattering downfall of the entirely false constructions on which the general line is built. Stalin could not but shudder at this unless he is prepared to show himself as a future Bonaparte, that is, to break openly with the October tradition and clap a crown on his head. However advantageous the "ideological" and political conditions for an openly Bonapartist coup d'etat, it would be risking too much to commit himself to this road. The Soviet proletariat is, in fact, a much more definite and stable factor than was the French petty bourgeoisie at the beginning of the last century and, consequently, the Bolshevik tradition has much more weight at present than the Jacobin tradition had then. Stalin must hang on to the appearance of Bolshevism, and that is why, in view of the present danger represented by the Fourth International, he is compelled to convene the Seventh Congress.

War will obviously be the main question on the agenda. We must expect a tactic of retreat. Stalin certainly did not expect the extremely unfavorable reactions to his famous declaration. The leaders of the French party went to Moscow in a state of near panic. Leon Blum gave them a good lesson: We mustn't use all our patriotic powder right now or we shall find ourselves disarmed morally and physically when the war does start. The Stalinists have already refused to vote the war credits in parliament. And the reason? The officers are fascist; the imperialist army should be democratic, that is, should express "People's Front"[273] principles (let us recall that Noske's speeches in the Reichstag on the Hohenzollern declaration of war [in 1914] were dressed in the same language). The resolutions of the Seventh Congress will be drawn up in approximately this way. The resolutions will say roughly the following: right now we must not openly support the imperialisms of France, Czechoslovakia, etc., but rather prepare the workers progressively and with caution to support imperialism when the war does come. In other words, the defeatist strategy that conforms to the most elementary teachings of Marxism is, for a time, replaced by the strategy of exhaustion. However, were Stalin to go on and do as he wants in the way expressed in the news, we could only be grateful to him. But that would really be too good — for the proletariat as for us.

We can be certain that not one of the hireling "leaders" summoned to the congress will have the courage to raise a question about Zinoviev's fate. Of the six congresses in the history of the Comintern to date, Zinoviev was president of five. Now he is in prison, ostensibly for having wanted to restore capitalism by a terrorist act against the Soviet bureaucracy. In his personal fate is expressed the unheard-of about-face executed by the Soviet bureaucracy. But can a Cachin or Pieck[274] be troubled by that? As long as they preserve their positions and salaries, it is all the same to them whether Zinoviev is president of a revolutionary world congress or finds himself in prison as a counterrevolutionary.

Who will make the main speeches and draft the main resolutions this time? Bela Kun, perhaps? He is the man who suits, especially if we recall Lenin's famous speech to the plenum of the Executive Committee on the eve of the Third Congress; the speech was devoted almost exclusively to Bela Kun and for its leitmotiv had the excellent theme, "The Stupidities of Bela Kun." It wasn't by chance that he attacked Bela Kun.

Another candidate is Dimitrov.[275] The only reason for his sudden and very unexpected advance to the forefront was his bearing before the Nazi court. We all applauded it—especially when we compared his bearing to that of the chairman of the Stalinist parliamentary fraction, Torgler.[276] But we mustn't exaggerate things. The Russian revolutionaries, not only the Bolsheviks but also, for example, the Social Revolutionary terrorists, in general always behaved with dignity and courage before the courts of the czar. That was the rule, not the exception. There was contempt for anyone who behaved like a coward, but there never was veneration for anyone who behaved like a man. That Dimitrov has been made a demigod because of his courageous bearing before the court is now very characteristic of the moral level of the bureaucracy of the Communist International. However, Dimitrov never found nor sought the opportunity to express himself as a Marxist, a Bolshevik, in opposition to the Stalinist general line. He took a part in all the scandalous policies of the epigones, in all its stages, and he bears full responsibility for them.

In due course we shall state our positions on the congress resolutions. These lines are no more than preliminary remarks.

AN OPEN LETTER TO THE
WORKERS OF FRANCE[277]

Stalin's Treachery and World Revolution

(June 10, 1935)

Dear Comrades:

I leave France today, and this circumstance enables me, at last, to put my case openly before you; so long as I remained on French soil, I was condemned to silence.

Two years ago, the "left" government of Daladier, in its honeymoon weeks, gave me permission to settle in France, presumably with the same rights as other foreigners. As a matter of fact, I was forbidden to live in Paris, and I found myself immediately under the strict surveillance of the police. Shortly after February 6, 1934, the minister of internal affairs, Albert Sarraut, after a wild campaign in the press, signed a decree deporting me from France. No foreign government, however, could be found willing to accept me. This is the sole reason why the deportation order was not put into effect until now. I was instructed through the Surete Nationale [police] to live in a certain department, in a tiny village under the strict surveillance of the police. Thus, during my last year's sojourn in France I was cut off from the outside world more than when I lived on the island of Prinkipo, in Turkey, under the surveillance of the police of Kemal Pasha. Thus, the visa of a Radical government turned into a trap, after its own fashion.

Furthest from my mind is any intention to complain about the government of the Third Republic. The most "democratic" ministers, just as the most reactionary ones, have as their task to *preserve* capitalist slavery. I am a member of the revolutionary party that sets as its goal the *overthrow* of capitalism. Out of this irreconcilable contradiction there inevitably flows the struggle, with all its consequences. There is no cause here for complaint!

If, however, I took the liberty to call your attention to so minor a question as my living conditions in France, it was only because this episode is most intimately bound up with the policies of the Communist International, which has today become the principal obstacle on the historic road of the working class.

Two years ago, *l'Humanite* used to harp daily: "The fascist Daladier has called the social fascist Trotsky to France in order to organize, with his assistance, a military intervention against the USSR." There were to be found quite a number of honest but naive and ignorant people who believed in this canard, just as, in the spring of 1917, millions of Russian peasants, soldiers and even workers believed Kerensky that Lenin and Trotsky were the "agents of Kaiser Wilhelm." One should not accuse uneducated and duped people—one must, instead, enlighten them. But one can and one must accuse the enlightened scoundrels who consciously broadcast lies and slanders in order to fool the toilers. Such enlightened scoundrels are the leaders of the so-called Communist (?!) Party: Cachin, Thorez, Vaillant-Couturier, Duclos and Co.

Today, as everybody knows, these gentlemen have made an antifascist "People's Front" with the "fascist" Daladier. The Stalinists, who call themselves Communists, have stopped talking altogether about the intervention of French imperialism into the USSR. On the contrary, at present they perceive the guarantee of peace in the military alliance between French capital and the Soviet bureaucracy. Upon Stalin's order, Cachin, Thorez and Co. are summoning the French workers today to support their national militarism, i.e., the instrument of class oppression and of colonial enslavement. These calumniators have exposed themselves quickly and mercilessly. Yesterday they branded me as the ally of Daladier and the agent of the French bourgeoisie, but today they themselves have actually concluded an alliance with Daladier-Herriot and Laval and have harnessed themselves to the chariot of French imperialism.

Right now, Messrs. Calumniators are beginning to say (see, for example, the paper of the Belgian Stalinists) that the policy of Trotsky and of the Bolshevik-Leninists performs a service not to Herriot and Daladier but to Hitler, i.e., not to French but to German imperialism. This new calumny, however, has the ring of much too old and familiar a melody. During the imperialist war, because I maintained the position of revolutionary internationalism, Messrs. Social Patriots—Renaudel, Vandervelde, Severac[278] and Marcel Cachin—accused me of "supporting" German militarism against the French democracy. It is precisely for this reason that the government of Briand-Malvy[279] deported me from France in 1916. And the valiant Marcel Cachin, during this very same period, "in the interest of French democracy" and on the instructions of the imperialist government, fetched the money for Mussolini for propaganda in favor of Italy's participation in the war. All these facts have been frequently attested to in the press and may be easily verified and proved. Cachin, incidentally, has never even attempted to deny them.

At the present moment, Marcel Cachin is resuming the very same social-patriotic labors that so dishonored him during the imperialist war. Cachin is followed by all the other leaders of the French Communist (?!) Party. These are not revolutionists but functionaries. They carry out whatever their superiors order them to do. Andre Marty[280] alone gave proof in his time of the qualities of a genuine revolutionist; his past deserves respect. But the environment of the Communist International has managed to demoralize him as well.

To justify their social-patriotic turn, these gentlemen invoke the necessity to "defend the USSR." This argument is utterly false. As is very well known, even the idea of "national defense" is only a mask by means of which the exploiters cover up their predatory appetites and bloody brawls for booty, turning, besides, their own nation into mere cannon fodder. But if we Marxists have always maintained that the imperialist bourgeoisie never can and never will defend the actual interests of its own people, how, then, can we suddenly believe that it is capable of defending the genuine interests of the USSR? Can anyone for a moment doubt that at the first favorable opportunity, French imperialism will set in motion all its forces in order to overthrow socialized property in the USSR and restore private property there? And if that is the case, then only traitors to the working class are capable of painting up their own militarism, giving direct or indirect, open or masked support to the French bourgeoisie and its diplomacy. Stalin and his French flunkeys are precisely such traitors.

To mask their betrayal they invoke, naturally, Lenin — with the same rights as Lebas, Paul Faure, Longuet[281] and other opportunists invoke Marx. Almost daily *l'Humanite* quotes Lenin's letter to the American workers, in which the story is told of how Lenin at the beginning of 1918 received a French royalist officer in order to use his services against the Germans, who had launched a new offensive against us. The aim of this unexpected argument is not to elucidate the question but, on the contrary, to throw dust into the eyes of the workers. We shall establish this immediately beyond the shadow of a doubt.

It would be absurd, of course, to deny the Soviet government the right to utilize the antagonisms in the camp of the imperialists or, if need be, to make this or that concession to the imperialists. The workers on strike also make use of the compe-

tition between capitalist enterprises and make concessions to
the capitalists, even capitulate to them, when they are unable
to gain victory. But does there follow from this the right of
the trade-union leaders to cooperate amicably with the capitalists, to paint them up and to turn into their hirelings? No one
will label as traitors the strikers who are forced to surrender.
But Jouhaux, who paralyzes the class struggle of the proletariat in the name of peace and amity with the capitalists, we
have not only the right but the duty to proclaim as a traitor
to the working class. Between the Brest-Litovsk policy of Lenin
and the Franco-Soviet policy of Stalin, there is the same difference as between the policy of a revolutionary trade unionist,
who after a partial defeat is compelled to make concessions
to the class enemy, and the policy of the opportunist, who
voluntarily becomes the ally and flunkey of the class enemy.

Lenin received the reactionary French officer. During those
same days, I also received him with the very same object in
mind: Lubersac undertook to blow up bridges in the path of
our retreat so that our military supplies would not fall into
the hands of the Germans. Only some utterly hairbrained an-
archist will view such a "transaction" as a betrayal. During
those same days, the official agents of France paid me visits
and offered assistance on a wider scale—artillery and food-
stuffs. We very well understood that their aim was to embroil
us again in a war with Germany. But the German armies
were actually waging an offensive against us, and we were
weak. Did we have the right to accept the "assistance" of the
French general staff under these conditions? Unconditionally,
yes! I introduced precisely such a motion in the Central Executive Committee of the party on February 22, 1918. The text
of this motion has been published in the official minutes of
the Central Executive Committee, issued in Moscow in 1929.
Here is the motion.

"As the party of the socialist proletariat in power and waging
war against Germany, we, *through the state organs,* take all
measures in order best to arm and equip our revolutionary
army with all the necessary means and, with this in view,
to obtain them wherever possible and, consequently, from capitalist governments as well. While so doing [our] *party preserves the complete independence of its foreign policy,* does
not commit itself politically with any capitalist government
and in every given instance takes their proposals under consideration from the standpoint of expediency."

Lenin was not present at this session of the CEC. He sent
a note. Here is its authentic text: "Please add my vote *for* accepting potatoes and arms from the brigands of Anglo-French

imperialism" (Minutes, p. 246). This is how the then Bolshevik CEC reacted toward the utilization of capitalist antagonisms: *practical agreements* with imperialists ("accept the potatoes") are entirely permissible, but absolutely impermissible is *political solidarity* with the "brigands of imperialism."

Stalin's crime does not lie in his entering into this or that practical agreement with the class enemy; these agreements may be correct or wrong, but they cannot be rejected on principle. His crime lies in the fact that Stalin has approved the policy of the imperialist government that keeps guard over the rapacious and predatory Versailles peace. Stalin has not yet taken any sort of "potatoes" from the brigands of imperialism, but he has already *solidarized politically* with them.

The French bourgeoisie is, of course, able to strengthen its army, which oppresses sixty million colonial slaves without Stalin's approval. If it required his approval, it was only in order to weaken and demoralize the class struggle of the French proletariat. By signing the *cum laude* to French imperialism, Stalin behaved not like a striker who is compelled to make temporary concessions to the capitalist but like a strikebreaker who paralyzed the struggle of the workers.

The betrayal of Stalin and of the leadership of the Communist International is explained by the character of the present ruling stratum in the USSR; it is a privileged and an uncontrolled bureaucracy, which has raised itself above the people and which oppresses the people. Marxism teaches us that *existence determines consciousness.* The Soviet bureaucracy, above all, fears criticism, movement and risk; it is conservative; it greedily defends its own privileges. Having strangled the working class in the USSR, it has long since lost faith in the world revolution. It promises to build "socialism in one country," if the toilers shut up, endure and obey.

To defend the USSR, the bureaucracy pins its hopes upon its political agility, upon Litvinov's diplomacy, the military alliance with France and Czechoslovakia, but not upon the revolutionary proletariat. On the contrary, it is afraid lest the French or Czech workers frighten the new allies by their careless actions. It sets as its task to put a brake upon the class struggle of the proletariat in the "allied" countries. Thus, the source of Stalin's betrayal is the national conservatism of the Soviet bureaucracy, its outright hostility to the world proletarian revolution.

The consequences of Stalin's betrayal manifested themselves immediately in the cynical change in the policy of the French Communist Party, which is led not by the leaders elected by the workers but by agents of Stalin. Yesterday these gentle-

men babbled about "revolutionary defeatism" in event of war.
Today they have assumed the standpoint of "national defense"
. . . in the interests of securing peace. They repeat word for
word the formulas of capitalist diplomacy. The imperialist
vultures, of course, have always stood for "peace"; they all
conclude alliances, increase armies, manufacture poison gases,
cultivate bacteria — only and solely "in the interests of peace."
He who says that "the Franco-Soviet pact is the guarantee
of peace" assumes the responsibility not only for the Soviet
government but also for the French stock market, its general
staff and the gases and bacteria of this staff.

L'Humanite writes that the French government will find itself
"under the *control* of the French workers." But that is only
a hollow phrase of miserable demagogues. Where and when
has an oppressed proletariat "controlled" the foreign policy
of the bourgeoisie and the activities of its army? How can
it achieve this when the entire power is in the hands of the
bourgeoisie? In order to lead the army, it is necessary to overthrow the bourgeoisie and seize power. There is no other road.
But the new policy of the Communist International implies
the renunciation of this only road.

When a working-class party proclaims that in the event of
war it is prepared to "control" (i.e., to support) its national
militarism and not to overthrow it, it transforms itself by this
very thing into the domestic beast of capital. There is not
the slightest ground for fearing such a party; it is not a revolutionary tiger but a trained donkey. It may be kept in star-
vation, flogged, spat upon — it will nevertheless carry the cargo
of patriotism. Perhaps only from time to time it will piteously
bray: "For God's sake, disarm the fascist leagues." In reply
to its braying, it will receive an additional blow of the whip.
And deservedly so!

The Communist International has depicted the entry of the
USSR into the League of Nations and the signing of the
Franco-Russian pact as the greatest victory of the proletariat
and of peace. But what is the actual content of this victory?

The program of the Comintern, accepted in 1928, states that
the "*chief aim* [of the League of Nations] is to put a halt to
the impetuous growth of the revolutionary crisis and to strangle
the USSR by means of blockade or war." Naturally enough,
under such conditions, the representatives of the USSR could
not enter the League of Nations, i.e., the general staff of the
world imperialist counterrevolution.

But what has changed since that time? Why has the USSR
found it necessary to enter the League of Nations? Whose
victory have we here? The leaders of the Comintern dupe the

workers on this question as well. The French bourgeoisie would never have made an agreement with the USSR if it had continued to see in the latter a revolutionary factor. Only the extreme feebleness of the world revolution has made possible the inclusion of the USSR into the system of the warring camps of imperialism.

Assuredly, if Soviet industry had not achieved serious successes, if there were no Soviet tanks and Soviet aviation, no one would have reckoned with the USSR. But there are ways and ways of reckoning. Had the USSR remained the citadel of international revolution, had the Comintern waged a victorious offensive, then the ruling classes of France, England and Italy, without any vacillation, would have empowered Hitler to wage war against the USSR. But, at the present moment, after the annihilation of the revolution in China, Germany, Austria and Spain, after the successes of European fascism, after the collapse of the Comintern and the national degeneration of the Soviet bureaucracy, the bourgeoisie of France, England and Italy replies to Hitler: "Why run the risk of a crusade against the USSR? Even without it Stalin is successfully strangling the revolution. It is necessary to attempt to arrive at an understanding with him."

The Franco-Soviet pact is not a guarantee of peace — what brazen nonsense! — but a *deal in event of war*. The benefits of this deal for the USSR are problematic, to say the least. France is "bound" to come to the aid of the USSR only in the event that its cosignatories in Locarno agree to it, i.e., England and Italy. This means that in case French imperialism finds it more advantageous to reach an agreement with Hitler at the last moment at the expense of the USSR, then England and Italy will always assist in legalizing this "betrayal." *L'Humanite* maintains strict silence on this restrictive clause in the pact. Yet everything hinges on it. The pact binds the USSR, but it does not bind France!

Let us allow, however, that the Soviet bureaucracy, after all its mistakes and crimes, really had nothing left except to conclude this equivocal and unreliable military alliance with France. In that case, the Soviets could have no recourse other than to ratify the Stalin-Laval pact. But matters are entirely different insofar as France is concerned. The French proletariat must not permit its bourgeoisie to hide behind the backs of the Soviet bureaucracy. The aims of the French imperialists after signing the pact with the Soviets remain unchanged: to set a seal upon the old pillages, to prepare for new ones, to facilitate a new mobilization of the French people, to utilize the blood of the Soviet proletariat. Should the Communist and

Socialist deputies vote in parliament in favor of the Franco-Russian alliance, they would only give another proof thereby of their betrayal of the proletariat!

The struggle against war is unthinkable without struggle against one's own imperialism. The struggle against imperialism is unthinkable without the struggle against its agents and allies, the reformists and the Stalinists. It is necessary ruthlessly to purge the working-class organizations, both political and trade union, of the social-patriotic traitors to the working class, whatever be their names: Leon Blum or Thorez, Jouhaux or Monmousseau.

In France there is only a single group that defends honestly, consistently and courageously the principles of the proletarian revolution: the Bolshevik-Leninist Group. Its organ is the weekly newspaper, *La Verite.* Every thinking worker is duty bound to become acquainted with this newspaper.

The Bolshevik-Leninists have defined clearly and precisely the tasks of the proletariat in the struggle against war in a special pamphlet, *War and the Fourth International.* Firsthand knowledge of this pamphlet and a scrupulous discussion of the questions advanced in it are likewise the duty of every advanced proletarian, both as regards himself and his class.

The betrayal of the Stalinists, adjoined to the old betrayal of the reformists, demands a complete renovation of all proletarian organizations. A new revolutionary party is necessary! A new, a Fourth International is necessary! Service to this historic task is the content of the activity pursued by the international organization of the Bolshevik-Leninists.

The betrayal of Stalin did not catch us by surprise. We forecast it since 1924 when the Soviet bureaucracy forsook the theory of Marx and Lenin in favor of the theory of "socialism in one country." Shysters and philistines said our struggle against Stalin was a "personal" struggle. Now even the blind can ascertain that this struggle is being waged for the basic principles of internationalism and revolution.

During the last few years, we have said hundreds of times: "Scratch a Stalinist and you will find an opportunist." Today there is no need even to scratch. The Stalinists actually stand at the extreme right wing of the working-class movement, and to the extent that they continue to drape themselves with the authority of the October Revolution, they are immeasurably more harmful than the old, traditional opportunists.

The hatred of the Stalinists toward the Bolshevik-Leninists (the "Trotskyists") is the hatred of the conservative bureaucrats toward genuine revolutionists. In the struggle against the Bolshevik-Leninists, nothing is too low and vile for the bureaucracy, trembling for its power and income.

Prior to executing his latest open betrayal, Stalin carried out a new pogrom — for the hundredth time — against the left wing in the USSR. He initiated a number of fraudulent trials of oppositionists, hiding their real views and ascribing to them acts that they never committed. Thus, the former chairman of the Communist International, Zinoviev, was condemned to ten years' imprisonment solely because, after a number of vacillations and recantations, he was compelled to admit the fatal character of Stalin's policies.

The Soviet bureaucracy made an attempt to implicate me, through a provocateur, in the trial of the terrorists who assassinated Kirov. In the beginning of this year, Stalin arrested my son, a young scientist, a loyal Soviet worker, in no way involved in the political struggle.[282] The aim of this arrest is to wage a relentless terror not only against the Bolshevik-Leninists but also against the members of their families. The bureaucracy knows no pity in sight of the impending threat to its domination and its privileges. In this sphere the Stalinists find constant support on the part of the capitalist police of the entire world.

Only recently, in the month of April, Stalin sent the leaders of the Russian Young Communist League to Paris to urge the French revolutionary youth to go over to the patriotic position.[283] These young bureaucrats organized within the Socialist Party a special Stalinist faction whose main slogan is: "Expel the Trotskyists!" Needless to add that for this disruptive work the Stalinist clique did not and does not spare monetary resources; poor as it may be in ideas, it has no lack of currency.

But revolutionists do not capitulate in the face of terror. Just the contrary. They reply by redoubling the offensive. *Stalinism is today the chief plague of the world working-class movement.* This plague must be extirpated, excised, burned out with a hot iron. Once again the proletariat must be united under the banner of Marx and Lenin!

Dear Comrades!

I have far from said everything I wanted to say to you nor at all as I wanted to say it. But I am forced to hurry; at any moment the police official is scheduled to arrive who is to escort me and my wife, the faithful companion in my struggle and my wanderings, beyond the frontiers of France. I depart with a burning love for the French people and with an unwavering faith in the great future of the French proletariat but with an equal hatred toward the hypocrisy, greed and cruelty of French imperialism.

I firmly believe that the toiling people will sooner or later offer me that hospitality that the bourgeoisie today refuses. I would consider it the greatest boon if in the near future the French proletariat were to offer me the opportunity to participate in its decisive struggles. Workingmen and working women of France, so long as I am physically able, I am ready at any moment by word and action to answer your revolutionary call!

Allow me, then, to shake your hands warmly as a comrade and to close this letter with that cry that in the course of some forty years has guided my thoughts and actions:

Long live the world proletarian revolution!

L. Trotsky

A NEW TURN IS NECESSARY[284]

(June 10, 1935)

To the International Secretariat

Dear Comrades:

We are obviously entering a new period. Two events determine it: the development of our section in France and the definite turn of the Comintern.

1. The correctness of our entry into the SFIO is now proved by objective facts. Our section, thanks to the entry, has changed from a propaganda group into a revolutionary factor of the first order. No one will dare to assert that our group, in adapting itself to the new environment, has become softer, more moderate, opportunist. Quite the contrary. We can correctly say that the Bolshevik-Leninist Group in France at the present moment surpasses all our other sections by the revolutionary precision of its slogans and by the offensive character of its entire political activity. The comrades who were opposed to our entry ought now to recognize that they were wrong. The danger of such a move is incontestable, but no less incontestable is the manner in which the facts have demonstrated that, thanks to the tempered character of our cadres and thanks to the control of our international organization, we can and we must resort to very daring moves to get out of our isolation and penetrate the masses. Vereecken and others who violently opposed the entry have demonstrated by their very position that they have not sufficiently understood the inestimable advantages of our Bolshevik education and of our centralized organization. Should they continue now, after the experience, to repeat their abstract arguments, they would only make themselves ridiculous. The best advice we can give them, if they can still be saved, is that they take cognizance of their mistakes and reenter our ranks.

2. The decisive betrayal of Stalin and of his Comintern crew opens to us great possibilities not only within the Comintern

but also within all the working-class organizations, especially
in the trade unions. Up to quite recently, every stage of the
radicalization of the masses implied inevitably a new flow
towards the Stalinists. This was precisely the cause for our
isolation and for our weakness. Going to the left meant going
to Moscow, and we were looked upon as an obstacle on this
road. Today, Moscow has taken on an aspect which means
the obligation to support the imperialism of France, Czechoslovakia, etc. For us it is no longer a question of propounding
the subtleties of the theory of socialism in one country and of
the permanent revolution but of putting squarely the question:
Are we the willing slaves of our own imperialism or its mortal
enemies? Even if the differentiation within the framework of
the Communist Party does not take place quite rapidly (although we may also expect catastrophic upheavals, above all
if we know how to intervene), the elementary flow of the masses
toward the CP must inevitably slacken and even stop.

The latest electoral successes of the French CP in no way
invalidate this assertion. The masses have not had the necessary time to assimilate the Stalinist betrayal, even in its most
general aspect. Yesterday's inertia is still in effect, but Stalinism today is corroding on all sides. It must fall to pieces.
Tomorrow or the day after we will appear to the masses as
the only revolutionary possibility. The slogan for the Fourth
International assumes under these conditions an exceptional
importance.

3. The same circumstances demonstrate the necessity for the
implacable struggle against the SAP that we have undertaken
after two years of negotiations, attempts at rapprochement,
hesitations, etc. The SAP gentry have revealed themselves to
be irreconcilable and perfidious enemies. They prowl around
us, pilfer our ideas, our slogans, dulling their revolutionary
edge and spreading insinuations about us that we are sectarians, bunglers, diehards; one can have nothing to do with us,
despite the seeming correctness of our ideas. The fact that
Bauer went over to their side has supplied them with a telling
argument, all the more so since our German section is not
quite intransigent enough towards the SAP gentry. The more
flexible, many-sided and, above all, daring our policy of pene-
tration into the mass organizations, all the more intransigent
must be our general policy, all the more aggressive must it
be against all centrist ideologies, both those already hardened
and those crystallizing. The banner of the Fourth International
must be immutably opposed to all other banners.

4. The preparation for the Mulhouse Congress (which has
opened today, at the moment these lines are being written)

was a remarkable schooling not only for our French section but also for our entire international organization.

The struggle centered around three motions: the right, the centrist and ours. In all the districts in which our comrades, numerically weak as they are, have counterposed unswervingly our resolution to the others, they have gained votes and sympathizers; and, at the same time, they have compelled the centrists to draw away a little further from the right, in order not to lose their entire influence. And, on the other hand, in the few cases in which our comrades committed the grave error of entering into a combination with the centrists, they gained nothing for our tendency and, at the same time, pushed the centrists to the right.

These experiences provide us with the key for our entire policy in this period; to enter into combinations with the leaders of the SAP, of the IAG (London-Amsterdam Bureau) and so forth would imply losing our own identity, compromising the banner of the Fourth International and arresting the development of the diverse centrist currents on the road of the revolution. As regards our French section itself, the Mulhouse Congress implies, or should imply, the beginning of a new period. Not only is the SFIO not a revolutionary party but it is not even a proletarian party. It is petty bourgeois, not only in its policies but also in its social composition. This party opened to us certain possibilities, and it was correct to have formulated and utilized them. But these possibilities are limited. The Mulhouse Congress, together with the repercussions that will follow it, should more or less materially limit these possibilities. The prestige gained by the Bolshevik-Leninist Group must transform itself by flooding light upon the workers. But the workers are primarily outside of the SP: in the CP, in the trade-union organizations and among the unorganized. The Bolshevik-Leninist Group *must know how to effect a new turn,* which is the logical development of the previous stage. Without, of course, making the slightest concessions, it is necessary to concentrate nine-tenths of the efforts upon the denunciation of the Stalinist betrayal.

5. The struggle of the different tendencies against us coincides today almost entirely with the ideological indoctrination for the new imperialist war. Opposition to the war must coincide to an ever-increasing degree with sympathy for the Fourth International. The condition for success is ruthless struggle against the slightest concession to the theory of national defense. The inevitable regroupment in the different working-class organizations (Communist Party, trade unions, etc.) must open for us an outlet to the working-class masses. It is nec-

essary to orient ourselves in this direction with all the required independence. This regroupment can result in *the creation of a revolutionary party* within a set and quite close period of time.

6. It is absolutely essential to speed up the preparatory work for the Fourth International. The revolutionary elements that will separate themselves during the general regroupment inside the working class must have the possibility of directly joining an international organization that bases itself on the entire experience of the revolutionary struggles.

Crux [Leon Trotsky]

DISCIPLINE MUST BE RESTORED[285]

(June 13, 1935)

To the International Secretariat

Dear Comrades:

The question of the relations between our French section and the group of Comrade Naville has become quite acute. I do not wish to dwell upon the past, even the most recent. I mention only the absolutely abnormal and intolerable fact: the "independent" document with the signatures of Naville and three comrades of our section that was circulated at the time of the Mulhouse Congress. This fact alone demonstrates that we cannot continue any longer in an equivocal state.

Upon the plane of political principles there are no differences. The protest against the bad regime as an argument for perpetuating a regime ten times worse is absurd. In any case, as an international organization, we cannot at all tolerate the fact that a group that declares itself in agreement on principles demands from us ultimatistically that we "improve" the regime of our section so that it may be able to join. The regime must be improved through joint collaboration. We value quite highly the qualities of several comrades who compose the group of Comrade Naville, but we cannot tolerate a prolongation of the equivocal condition.

What is to be done? In my opinion the answer is indicated by the whole situation. The International Secretariat might perhaps call together the representatives of our section and of the Naville group and arrive at an agreement with them upon the manner and the set period for fusion. It would be dangerous to set an interval that is too long, for example, more than three or four weeks. The decision must be categorical and obligatory. The International Secretariat should itself control its execution. It is to be hoped that the exceptional responsibilities weighing on us and the enormous possibilities opening before us will impose upon all Bolshevik-Leninists the necessary discipline.

Crux [Leon Trotsky]

NOTES AND ACKNOWLEDGMENTS

1. "The Foreign Policy of the Soviet Union." *The Militant,* June 16, 1934. *The Militant* was then the paper of the Communist League of America (CLA), section of the International Communist League (ICL). The undated article was signed "Sympathizer," but it is not known if this was an editorial addition or Trotsky's; around the same time this article was circulated in England under the signature "G." It was written between President Franklin D. Roosevelt's diplomatic recognition of the Soviet Union (November 1933 — seventeen years after the Russian Bolshevik Revolution) and the Soviet Union's admission into the League of Nations (September 1934). Both these events were stimulated by the Nazi assumption of power in Germany in 1933, which Trotsky had been warning for years would inevitably lead to a German war against the Soviet Union. Trotsky's aim in this article was to alert his movement to signs that a deep rightward turn in Soviet foreign policy was being prepared. Its full significance became plain to the whole world in May 1935, when the Soviet Union and France signed a nonaggression pact and Stalin personally expressed approval for the rearmament program of the French capitalist government. This policy, then called "collective security," was the precursor of "peaceful coexistence." The Soviet government followed this policy of supporting good, democratic, imperialist governments against bad, fascist, imperialist governments until August 1939, when it signed another nonaggression pact — with Hitler.

2. The Third International (or Communist International; Comintern) was organized under Lenin's leadership as the revolutionary successor to the Second International. In Lenin's time, world congresses were held around once a year — the First in 1919, the Second in 1920, the Third in 1921, the Fourth in 1922 — despite the civil war and the insecurity of the Soviet Union. Trotsky regarded the theses of the Comintern's first four congresses as the programmatic cornerstone of the Left Opposition and later of the Fourth International. The Fifth Congress of the Comintern, where Stalin's machine was in control, was held in 1924, the Sixth not until 1928 and the Seventh not until 1935. Trotsky called the Seventh the "liquidation congress" of the Comintern (see *Writings 35-36*), and it was in fact the last before Stalin announced its dissolution in 1943 as a gesture to his imperialist allies.

3. Alexander A. Troyanovsky (1882-1955) was a member of the Central Committee of the Menshevik Party and an opponent of the Bolshevik Revolution in 1917. At the Constituent Assembly in 1918, he was still denouncing Lenin and Trotsky as German agents. He became reconciled to the Soviet government after the civil war of 1918-20 and rose to prominence as a diplomat only after the Stalin faction took over the Soviet Communist Party and the Soviet state.

4. The Second International (or Labor and Socialist International) was organized in 1889 as the successor to the First International (or International Workingmen's Association), which existed from 1864 to 1876 and was led by Karl Marx. The Second International was a loose association of national Social Democratic and labor parties, uniting both revolutionary and reformist elements, whose strongest and most authoritative section was the German Social Democracy. Its progressive role had ended by 1914, when its major sections violated the most elementary socialist principles and supported their own imperialist governments in World War I. It fell apart during the war, but was revived as a completely reformist organization in 1923.

5. The Little Entente was the French-dominated alliance of Romania, Czechoslovakia and Yugoslavia. The Entente was the World War I alliance of Great Britain, France, Russia, Belgium and later Italy.

6. Maxim Litvinov (1876-1951), an Old Bolshevik, was people's commissar for foreign affairs, 1930-39, ambassador to the United States, 1941-43, and deputy commissar for foreign affairs, 1943-46. Stalin used him to personify "collective security" when he sought alliances with the democratic imperialists and shelved him during the Stalin-Hitler pact period and the cold war.

7. *Pravda* (Truth) was the official organ of the Central Committee of the Bolshevik Party from April 1912; it became a daily in March 1917.

8. Japan withdrew from the League of Nations in March 1933, Germany in October 1933.

9. Karl Radek (1885-1939) was a left-winger in the Polish, German and Swiss sections of the Second International before World War I, a leading propagandist of the Comintern in Lenin's time, and a member of the Russian Left Opposition against Stalinism until 1929, when Trotsky was deported to Turkey. Then he capitulated to Stalin, was readmitted to the Communist Party and served as an abject apologist for the Kremlin, especially its foreign policy. He was indicted and convicted in the 1937 Moscow purge trial.

10. "Socialism in one country" was the theory proclaimed by Stalin in 1924 and later incorporated into the program and tactics of the Comintern. It became the ideological cover for the abandonment of revolutionary internationalism in favor of narrow nationalism and was used to justify converting the Communist Parties throughout the world into docile pawns of the Kremlin's foreign policy. For a critique by Trotsky, see his 1928 book, *The Third International After Lenin*.

11. Since the French government was engaged in behind-the-scenes negotiations with Moscow at the time this article was written — negotiations that culminated in the Franco-Soviet pact in May 1935 —

the suspicion that the French government's harassment of Trotsky beginning in April 1934 was connected with those negotiations is not at all farfetched.

12. The disarmament conference referred to was another in a long and futile series sponsored by the League of Nations during the 1930s. The British government's attitude to Nazi Germany at this time was not unfriendly; in 1935 they were to agree on a naval expansion program.

13. The Fourth International (World Party of Socialist Revolution). The political movement led by Trotsky during his third exile was called the International Left Opposition (Bolshevik-Leninists) until 1935. It then discontinued its original policy of working for the reform of the Comintern, proclaimed the need for a new International, changed its name to the International Communist League (Bolshevik-Leninists) and set to work gathering forces for revolutionary parties throughout the world. Trotsky proposed that the Fourth International be founded at an ICL conference held at Geneva in July 1936, but the conference disagreed and instead established the Movement for the Fourth International. The founding conference of the Fourth International was held in France in September 1938. One more conference was held during Trotsky's lifetime — an emergency conference in the Western Hemisphere in May 1940, which adopted a manifesto on World War II written by Trotsky (see *Writings 39-40*).

14. "A Program of Action for France." *La Verite,* June 1934; *Fourth International,* October 1942. *La Verite* (The Truth) was the paper of the Communist League of France, section of the ICL. The main ideas in this document, published in the name of the League, came from Trotsky, parts being dictated to secretaries during the hectic weeks when he was trying to find a place to live, and the whole being edited by him. This program was a response to the prerevolutionary situation that developed after February 6, 1934, when fascist and reactionary groups staged an armed demonstration against the Daladier government at the Chamber of Deputies. The French workers answered on February 12 with a one-day general strike and demonstrations throughout the country. France rapidly became polarized, and the government shifted to the right, Doumergue replacing Daladier as premier and promising to provide a "strong" government. The idea of a united front against fascism, which had been the Communist League's agitational strong point for some time, now began to gain acceptance in the mass working-class parties and unions. "A Program of Action" was designed to provide the political content and goals of the proposed united front. It can also be read as an early version of the Transitional Program adopted by the founding conference of the Fourth International in 1938 (see *The Death Agony of Capitalism and the Tasks of the Fourth International* by Leon Trotsky [Pathfinder Press, 1970]), although the latter, of course, is of international scope and not restricted to a single country.

15. The Austrian proletariat fought heroically in armed struggle against the Dollfuss regime in February 1934, but was defeated.

16. Albert Oustric was a French banker whose speculations wiped out many banks and led to the downfall of the Tardieu cabinet in

1930. Serge Alexandre Stavisky was another financier whose shady operations involved widespread payoffs to police and bourgeois politicians. His mysterious "suicide" in January 1934 was so embarrassing to his friends in the Chautemps government that it fell; this scandal also figured in the right-wing agitation leading to the attempted coup d'etat of February 6, 1934.

17. Alsace-Lorraine is a frontier region between France, Germany, Belgium and Switzerland, which Germany grabbed in 1871 after defeating France in the Franco-Prussian War. When Germany was defeated in World War I, the area was awarded to France under the Versailles Treaty. On neither occasion were the inhabitants even consulted.

18. The Saar, a western region of Germany, is one of the richest coal basins in Europe. It was a part of France in the eighteenth century and then was divided between Prussia and Bavaria by the 1815 Treaty of Paris. The Versailles Treaty took the Saar from Germany, putting its administration under the League of Nations and its coal mines under the control of France. In March 1935, the overwhelming majority of the population voted in a plebiscite to be reunited with Germany, despite the fact that the Nazis then controlled Germany.

19. Jean Louis Barthou (1862-1934) was minister of foreign affairs in the Doumergue regime. He and King Alexander I of Yugoslavia were assassinated in Marseilles in October 1934 after Barthou, a leading French advocate of "collective security," had arranged the Soviet Union's admission into the League of Nations. Andre Tardieu (1876-1945) was the reactionary politician who had the assignment in the Doumergue regime of preparing amendments to the French constitution that would strengthen the state, that is, curtail democratic rights. Edouard Herriot (1872-1957) was the leader of the bourgeois Radical Party who was most prominently identified with the policy of seeking alliances with the Socialist Party in the 1920s — an early form of the People's Front. Trotsky wrote a pamphlet about him, *Edouard Herriot, Politician of the Golden Mean* (see *Writings 35-36*).

20. The General Federation of Labor (CGT) was the major union federation in France, dominated by a reformist leadership. A split in 1921 resulted in the formation of a more radical but smaller rival, the Unitary General Federation of Labor (CGTU), which lasted until the two were reunified in 1936.

21. Bonapartism was a central concept in Trotsky's writings during the 1930s. A concise explanation of what he meant by bourgeois Bonapartism will be found in this volume in the article, "Bonapartism and Fascism." His analysis of Soviet Bonapartism will be found in this volume in the article, "The Workers' State, Thermidor and Bonapartism."

22. The Third Republic of France, extending from the downfall of Louis Napoleon in 1870 to the French defeat by Germany in 1940, was viewed by revolutionaries as the epitome of bourgeois corruption and hypocrisy. It is contrasted here with 1793, when the French bourgeoisie was still revolutionary.

23. SFIO stands for the French Section of the Labor (Socialist) International, the formal name of the Socialist Party. The Communist Party's formal name was the French Section of the Communist International (SFIC), but the initials used for it in this volume are CP.

24. February 12, 1934, was the day of the general strike protesting the fascist demonstration of February 6.

25. "The League Faced with a Turn." *Internal Bulletin,* Communist League of America, Number 16, September 1934. This was translated from a French League internal bulletin, but no copy could be found to supply the date, which was probably July 1934. It was signed "Vidal," a pen name Trotsky had used in the past, and was circulated along with articles by members of the French League debating the proposal that they join the SFIO and its youth group. At this time, in the summer of 1934, the French Social Democracy was in ferment. A right wing, the Neos or Neo-Socialists, had left the SFIO at the end of 1933; left-wing groups in the party were gaining influence, especially among the youth; and even the traditional leadership around Leon Blum was making unusually radical statements. Unlike the Communist Party, the SFIO permitted members to form factions that could present their views to the party ranks and even publish public newspapers and magazines. At its May 1934 congress in Toulouse, leftward moving groups that had quit or been expelled before the Neo split were invited to return. The SFIO membership was around 120,000, while the CP had, according to some estimates, between 20,000 and 30,000, and, according to others, no more than 12,000. The SP-influenced CGT had over a million members; the CP-led CGTU around 70,000. Trotsky thought the League members could make substantial gains if they would join the SFIO promptly and work there in a disciplined manner to spread their ideas. On July 2 the SFIO and CP leaders held a joint meeting to explore the possibility of united action; by the end of the month they were to sign a pact pledging common action against fascism and repression. This at once opened speculation about the possibility of "organic unity," that is, the merger of the two parties. Trotsky saw in these developments added reason for immediate entry into the SFIO, because every tendency outside of the united front or the merged parties would be more isolated than ever, and the CP leaders would do everything they could to keep the League members on the outside. The leaders of the League, however, were divided over the entry proposal; some, like Pierre Naville, were strongly opposed. These are factors that explain the "tone" of Trotsky's articles in this discussion. But his criticisms of the League were not new. In September 1933, shortly after he arrived in France and had an opportunity to observe how the French leadership responded to the decision to work for a new International, he wrote a criticism of the League's "organization, discipline and leadership" that in many ways paralleled the one he made now in July 1934 (see "It Is Time to Stop," *Writings 33-34*).

26. The theory of "social fascism," a brainchild of Stalin, held that Social Democracy and fascism were not antipodes but twins. Since the Social Democrats were only a variety of fascism, and since just about everyone but the Stalinists was some kind of fascist (a liberal-fascist or a labor-fascist or a Trotsky-fascist), then it was impermissible for the Stalinists to engage in united fronts with any other tendency against the plain ordinary fascists. No theory was or could have been more helpful to Hitler in the years leading up to his winning power in Germany. The Stalinists finally dropped

the theory late one night in 1934 without the decency of an explanation and soon were wooing not only the Social Democrats but also capitalist politicians like Roosevelt and Daladier whom they were still calling fascists early in 1934.

27. George Plekhanov (1856-1918) broke with the Russian Narodniks (Populists) to become the founder of the Russian Marxist movement and the teacher of people like Lenin and Trotsky. Later he degenerated, supported the czarist government in World War I and opposed the Bolshevik Revolution in 1917. Despite this, Lenin highly recommended Plekhanov's early writings, especially in philosophy.

28. See V. I. Lenin's *"Left-Wing" Communism: An Infantile Disorder.*

29. The Socialist Workers Party (SAP) of Germany was formed in October 1931, after the Social Democrats expelled several left-wingers headed by Max Seydewitz. In the spring of 1932, a split occurred in the German Communist Right Opposition (KPO, the Brandlerites), and a group of 800 led by Jakob Walcher entered the SAP. When Seydewitz and other founders withdrew, the ex-Brandlerites assumed the leadership of the SAP, which then claimed 14,000 members; its numbers were greatly reduced after Hitler came to power. In August 1933, at a conference in Paris sponsored by the IAG (International Labor Community), the SAP joined the International Left Opposition in signing the Declaration of Four, proclaiming the necessity to work for a new International. Trotsky urged a merger of the German section of the ILO and the SAP, but the SAP leaders thought that such a step would hamper their efforts to win over the Norwegian Labor Party (NAP) and declined. Later the SAP became an active opponent of the movement for the Fourth International.

30. The Independent Socialist Party (OSP) of Holland was another signer of the Declaration of Four in 1933. After a split by a right wing, the OSP merged with the Revolutionary Socialist Party to form the Revolutionary Socialist Workers Party of Holland in 1935. The point Trotsky was making about the SAP and OSP was that it is permissible to work inside the same organization with tendencies that are not in full agreement with you, and often necessary to do so.

31. The Independent Labour Party (ILP), founded in 1893, played an influential part in the creation of the British Labour Party, to which it was affiliated and in which it usually occupied a position on the left. Expelled from the Labour Party in 1931, the ILP for some years was attracted by Stalinism. Its actual affiliation in the mid-1930s was to the centrist International Labor Community (IAG). It later returned to the Labour Party.

32. The 1920 congress of the SFIO was held in Tours, where a majority of the delegates voted to affiliate to the Third International, thus giving birth to the French Communist Party. A minority of the delegates, led by Leon Blum and Paul Faure, split away and continued functioning as the SFIO.

33. *Le Populaire* (The Populace) was the SFIO's daily paper, *l'Humanite* (Humanity) the CP's. For short they were sometimes called *Popu* and *l'Huma.*

34. "The League Faced with a Decisive Turn." *Internal Bulletin,* Communist League of America, Number 17, October 1934. Signed

"Vidal." Like the previous article, it was written for members of the French League.

35. Reformism is the theory and practice of gradual, peaceful and parliamentary change (as opposed to revolution) as the best or only means of proceeding from capitalism to socialism. The reformists therefore strive to soften the class struggle and promote class collaboration. The logic of their position leads them to side with the capitalists against workers and colonial peoples attempting to make a revolution.

36. Jacques Doriot (1898-1945), a leader of the French CP and mayor of Saint-Denis, a radical industrial suburb, became an advocate of a united front against fascism early in 1934, before Moscow did. When the CP would not discuss his proposals, he made them publicly. He resigned his mayoral post, but was reelected. Expelled from the CP in June when he refused to go to Moscow for "discussion," he retained the support of the large CP organization in Saint-Denis. For a while he toyed with the centrist elements connected with the IAG, then swung to the right and formed a fascist party in 1935.

37. Bolshevism and Menshevism were the two major tendencies in the Russian Social Democratic Labor Party, section of the Second International, following its Second Congress in 1903. The Bolsheviks, led by Lenin, and the Mensheviks, led by Julius Martov, eventually became separate parties, ending up on different sides of the barricades in 1917.

38. Jakob Walcher (1887-   ), a member of the Spartakusbund and a founder of the German Communist Party, was expelled from the Comintern in 1929 as a supporter of the Brandlerite Communist Right Opposition (KPO). He left the KPO in 1932 and became a leader of the SAP. After World War II, he returned to Stalinism, accepting a minor government post in East Germany.

39. *Action Socialiste* (Socialist Action) was the publication of a left tendency in the SFIO, the Comite d'Action Socialiste et Revolutionnaire, whose leaders included Claude Just.

40. Leon Blum (1872-1950) was the top SFIO leader in the 1930s and premier of the first People's Front government in 1936.

41. The Central Committee was the Communist League's highest executive body. The Political Bureau (Politburo) was a subcommittee of the Central Committee. The International Secretariat was a committee of the ICL, elected by the plenum.

42. *The New International,* in whose first issue (July 1934) Trotsky's greetings appeared, was the monthly magazine of the Communist League of America, and later of the Workers Party of the United States and of the Socialist Workers Party. Its editor was Max Shachtman, one of the founders of the American Left Opposition and editor of several of Trotsky's books. In 1939, after the Stalin-Hitler pact and the outbreak of World War II, Shachtman, along with James Burnham, led a factional struggle to revise basic principles of the SWP and the Fourth International. Defeated at an SWP convention in April 1940, the Shachtman-Burnham group split from the SWP, founded the Workers Party and utilized their technical control of *The New International* to proclaim it their own magazine. The *NI* was published until 1958, when the Shachtmanites joined

the Socialist Party, where most of them became members of its right wing. Trotsky's views on the questions disputed in the 1939-40 struggle, and on the seizure of the *NI*, are collected in the book *In Defense of Marxism.* The SWP responded to the loss of the *NI* by starting the publication in May 1940 of *Fourth International,* whose name was later changed to *International Socialist Review.*

43. "The Evolution of the SFIO." *The New International,* September-October 1934, where it was joined together with another article under the title "Bolshevik-Leninists and the SFIO" and signed "V."

44. Kurt von Schleicher (1882-1934), the German "social" general who preceded Hitler as chancellor, tried to prolong his stay in office by seeking a coalition with both the trade unions and a dissident wing of the Nazi Party. He was murdered by the Nazis during the "blood purge" of June 1934. His role and that of his predecessors, Heinrich Bruening and Franz von Papen, are examined at length in the Trotsky collection, *The Struggle Against Fascism in Germany* (Pathfinder Press, 1971).

45. Adrien Marquet (1884-1955), mayor of Bordeaux, a Neo-Socialist, became minister of labor in Doumergue's 1934 National Union government. Later he left the Neos and moved further to the right. Gaston Doumergue (1863-1937), Radical deputy and minister, president of the republic in 1924, retired in 1931. In February 1934, following the attempted fascist coup, he replaced Daladier as premier, promising a "strong" government and a constitutional reform that would restrict democratic liberties. When he lost the confidence of the Radicals, his government fell in November 1934. Leon Jouhaux (1870-1954) was the general secretary of the CGT, the chief labor federation in France, which had about one million members in 1934. He was a reformist, social patriot and practitioner of class collaboration.

46. Roger Langeron (1882-1966) was appointed prefect of police in Paris by the Doumergue government in 1934 and was retained in this post by People's Front governments.

47. Louis August Blanqui (1805-1881) was a participant in several nineteenth-century uprisings and spent thirty-three of his seventy-six years in prison. "Blanquism," as used by Marxists, refers to the theory of armed insurrection by small groups of selected and trained conspirators, as counterposed to revolution based on mass action and organization. As used by reformists, it is often an epithet directed against revolutionaries; Lenin and Trotsky, for example, were dubbed Blanquists by the Mensheviks because they were serious about making the revolution.

48. Marceau Pivert (1895-1958) was a member of the Bataille Socialiste tendency in the SFIO and organizer of the Gauche Revolutionnaire group in 1935. He served as an aide of Blum in 1936, but after his group was ordered dissolved in 1937, he left the SFIO and founded the Workers and Peasants Socialist Party (PSOP) in 1938. After World War II, he returned to the SFIO. Claude Just was a leader of the left SFIO tendency, Comite d'Action Socialiste et Revolutionnaire, and a member in the 1930s of the SFIO's National Council (Commission Administrative Permanente, or CAP). After World War II, he joined the French section of the Fourth International.

49. Centrism is the term used by Trotsky for tendencies in the radical movement that stand or oscillate between reformism, which is the position of the labor bureaucracy and the labor aristocracy, and Marxism, which represents the historic interests of the working class. Since a centrist tendency has no independent social base, it must be evaluated in terms of its origin, its internal dynamic and the direction it is taking or being pushed in by events. Until around 1935, Trotsky saw Stalinism as a special variety — bureaucratic centrism; thereafter he felt this term was inadequate to describe what the Soviet bureaucracy was becoming. In a letter to James P. Cannon on October 10, 1937, he wrote: "Some comrades continue to characterize Stalinism as 'bureaucratic centrism.' This characterization is now totally out of date. On the international arena, Stalinism is no longer centrism, but the crudest form of opportunism and social patriotism. See Spain!"

50. Jean Zyromsky (1890-   ), founder of the Bataille Socialiste tendency in the SFIO, was a party functionary with pro-Stalinist leanings. An advocate of "organic unity" in the mid-1930s, he joined the Communist Party after World War II.

51. "Bonapartism and Fascism." *The New International,* August 1934. Unsigned.

52. Trotsky had no doubt that the Italian duce Benito Mussolini and the Polish marshal and chief of state Joseph Pilsudski were fascists, but he felt, for various reasons, that it was wrong to use that term for the Spanish dictator Miguel Primo de Rivera, the Chinese Nationalist military dictator Chiang Kai-shek, the liberal president of Czechoslovakia Thomas Masaryk, the conservative Catholic chancellor of Germany Heinrich Bruening, the dictatorial Christian Socialist chancellor of Austria Engelbert Dollfuss, the monarch of Yugoslavia Alexander I, the Social Democratic minister of the interior for Prussia Carl Severing, or the British reformist Ramsay MacDonald.

53. Dmitri Manuilsky (1883-1952) was, along with Trotsky, a member of the independent Marxist organization, the Mezhrayontzi (Inter-City Group), which fused with the Bolshevik Party in 1917. In the 1920s he supported the Stalin faction and was secretary of the Comintern from 1931 to 1943. Otto Kuusinen (1881-1964) was a Finnish Social Democrat who fled to the Soviet Union after the collapse of the Finnish Revolution in April 1918. He became a Stalinist spokesman and was a secretary of the Comintern from 1922 to 1931.

54. In the "blood purge" of June 30, 1934, Hitler slaughtered unreliable Nazi leaders as well as non-Nazi political figures.

55. Giovanni Giolitti (1842-1928) was Mussolini's predecessor as Italian premier.

56. Isaac Deutscher was in 1934 one of the Polish Bolshevik-Leninists who had such differences. Decades later, in a footnote in *The Prophet Outcast,* page 276, he wrote: "Trotsky was, in his time, the only political theorist to produce a precise definition of fascism. Yet on some occasions he applied it rather imprecisely. He saw the imminence of fascism in France; and he insisted on labelling Pilsudski's pseudo-Bonapartist dictatorship over Poland as fascist, although Pilsudski did not rule in a totalitarian fashion and had to put up

with the existence of a multi-party system. On the other hand, Trotsky described, rather unconvincingly, the ephemeral governments of Schleicher and Papen, and also Doumergue's feeble government of 1934, as Bonapartist. (Only in 1940 did he at last describe the Petain regime as pseudo-Bonapartist rather than fascist.) I argued on these points with Trotsky in the nineteen-thirties; but the issue is perhaps of too little historical significance and too involved to be taken up here." Whatever argument Deutscher had on Pilsudski, Trotsky's position on that question is clearly presented here. Deutscher's parenthetical sentence is confusing in at least two respects: since the Petain regime came into being only in 1940, it is difficult to see how Trotsky could have characterized it before 1940. And his characterization of it as "a senile form of Bonapartism in the epoch of imperialist decline" and not "fascism in the real sense of the term" (see "Bonapartism, Fascism and War" in *Writings 39-40*) was completely in accord with his reasoning on this question throughout the 1930s rather than, as Deutscher seems to imply, a departure from it.

57. "Summary of the Discussion." *Internal Bulletin,* Communist League of America, Number 17, October 1934. Signed "Vidal." Like the two previous "Vidal" articles, this was meant for members of the League and the ICL only, and was intended to influence the voting for delegates elected to the third national conference of the League, to be held at the end of August, where the "entry" question was to be decided.

58. Pierre Naville (1904-   ) was a founder of the French League and a member of the International Secretariat of the ICL. He opposed the "entry" proposal, although he and his group later joined the SFIO after the majority of the League had done so. He left the Fourth Internationalist movement during World War II. He is the author of many scientific books and of a memoir, *Trotsky Vivant,* published in 1958.

59. Pierre Renaudel (1871-1935) was a leader of the SFIO right wing and of the "Neo" group that was expelled at the end of 1933.

60. Eugene Bauer, a member of the International Secretariat and signer as the ICL's representative of the 1933 Declaration of Four, was so strongly against the entry proposal that he broke from the ICL in October 1934 and became a member of the SAP.

61. The Anglo-Russian Trade Union Unity Committee was formed by Soviet and British union representatives in May 1925. The British used it as a cheap device to demonstrate their "progressivism" and to shield themselves against criticism from the left, especially useful at that time, not long before the British general strike of 1926. The committee folded when the British members, no longer needing it, walked out in 1927.

62. Martin Tranmael (1879-1967) was the leader of the Norwegian Labor Party (NAP).

63. NAP, the Norwegian Labor Party, was the major working-class party in its country, claiming 200,000 members in affiliated unions in 1933. It broke with the Second International and affiliated with the Comintern in 1919, then left the latter in 1923. It united with the Norwegian Social Democrats, but did not return to the Second International. It was one of the sponsors in 1932 of the IAG,

the International Labor Community, and attended the IAG Paris conference in August 1933, where it opposed the creation of a new International. In 1934 it resumed collaboration with the Scandinavian Social Democratic parties, which prepared the way later for the NAP's return to the Second International. In 1935 it became the governing party of Norway and granted asylum to Trotsky. A year later, under Soviet pressure following the first Moscow trial, the Norwegian Labor government interned and silenced Trotsky for four months, after which it sent him to Mexico (see *Writings 35-36*).

64. Amadeo Bordiga (1889-1970), a founder of the Italian Communist Party, was expelled from the Comintern on charges of "Trotskyism" in 1929. The Left Opposition tried to work with the Bordigists but failed because of the latter's inveterate sectarianism. *Bilan* (Balance) was the French-language magazine of the Bordigists.

65. This concerned the nature of the public statement the League members should make if they decided in favor of entry.

66. As Trotsky notes here, the turn he was proposing for the French section was identical to the one he had proposed for the British section in 1933, when he had urged it to enter the Independent Labour Party. If his critics had been more alert, they could have started their fight against the tactic a year earlier, in which case it might have been remembered as the "British turn."

67. The French entry, although approved by a majority of the League and of the ICL, did result in splits, not only in France but also in other countries where entry into Social Democratic parties was later proposed, such as Belgium, Spain and the United States.

68. "The Task of Revolutionary Teachers." From Trotsky's *Le Mouvement Communiste en France*, edited by Pierre Broué, 1967, from which this note is adapted. Unsigned. Translated for this volume by Walter Blumenthal. On August 8, 1934, Trotsky secretly met in Noyarey with Maurice Dommanget, Jean Aulas and Gilbert Serret, leaders of the Federation Unitaire, the teachers union affiliated with the CGTU. Trotsky hoped to persuade them to join the SFIO and to take a more positive attitude toward negotiations, then going on, for merger of the Federation Unitaire with the Syndicat National, the teachers union affiliated with the CGT. He did not make much headway with them on either of these issues. This letter to Dommanget, two days later, which was transmitted by a mutual friend rather than through the mail, was not signed for security reasons, which also explain why Trotsky uses "we" to designate teachers. Trotsky's efforts to continue the discussion met no response from Dommanget or the others.

69. Gaston Monmousseau (1883-1960), a former revolutionary syndicalist, became a leader of the CP, the CGTU and the unified CGT.

70. The Radical Party, or Radical Socialists, neither radical nor socialist, was the principal capitalist party of France between World Wars I and II, comparable to the Democratic Party in the United States.

71. Maurice Thorez (1900-1964) had sympathized with the ideas of the Left Opposition in the mid-1920s but later became the chief Stalinist in France, defender of all the zigzags of the Comintern and, after World War II, a minister in de Gaulle's government.

72. Bela Kun (1886-1939?), leader of the defeated Hungarian Revolution of 1919, became a Comintern functionary after moving to Moscow. He was reportedly shot during the purges of Communist exiles in the late 1930s.

73. The recently-held Montpellier congress of the Federation Unitaire had received a proposal from the Syndicat National for immediate merger .of the two groups. At Montpellier this proposal received only 37 votes, while 390 voted in favor of merger only if it took place on the basis of union independence, freedom of expression, recognition of minority representation and recognition of the class struggle. Monmousseau, representing the CGTU leadership, sided with the majority at Montpellier, that is, against immediate merger.

74. Andre Delmas (b.1899), a Socialist, was general secretary of the Syndicat National and a strong supporter of merger.

75. Paul Faure (1878-1960) was elected general secretary of the SFIO minority that opposed affiliation to the Comintern in 1920 and headed its apparatus until World War II. In 1944 he was expelled from the SFIO for having collaborated with Vichy during the war.

76. Marcel Cachin (1869-1958), an ardent social patriot during World War I, moved into the CP with the SFIO majority in 1920, became a Stalinist and, with World War II, again became an ardent social patriot.

77. "To the Bolshevik Leninists in the USSR." *The Militant*, September 8, 1934. This open letter was signed "Foreign Representatives of the Russian Bolshevik-Leninists." In February 1934 Christian Rakovsky (see note 78), the best-known Oppositionist still inside the Soviet Union, had finally capitulated to Stalin after six years of deportation, illness, medical neglect and isolation. He and Trotsky had been close friends for a long time, but with his capitulation Trotsky broke off all political and personal relations. Only in his diary, in an entry dated March 25, 1935, did he make a comment on what this break meant personally: "Rakovsky was virtually my last contact with the old revolutionary generation. After his capitulation there is nobody left. Even though my correspondence with Rakovsky stopped, for reasons of censorship, at the time of my deportation, nevertheless the image of Rakovsky has remained a symbolic link with my old comrades-in-arms. Now nobody remains. For a long time now I have not been able to satisfy my need to exchange ideas and discuss problems with someone else."

78. Christian Rakovsky (1873-1941) was a leading figure in the Balkan revolutionary movement before the Russian Revolution. In 1918 he became chairman of the Ukrainian Soviet and later served as ambassador to London and Paris. An early leader of the Russian Left Opposition, he was deported to Siberia in 1928; in 1934 he capitulated. In 1938 he was one of the major defendants in the third Moscow trial, where he was sentenced to twenty years' imprisonment.

79. Ernst Thaelmann (1886-1945) was the leader of the German Communist Party, its presidential candidate and a supporter of the Kremlin policies that led to Hitler's victory. Arrested by the Nazis in 1933, he was executed at Buchenwald in 1945.

80. Lev Semyanovich Sosnovsky (1886-1937), an outstanding So-

viet journalist, was, like Rakovsky, among the early supporters of the Left Opposition and one of the last to capitulate.

81. Ossip Piatnitsky (1882-1939), an Old Bolshevik, was a secretary of the Comintern, 1922-31, and headed its Organizing Bureau, whose aim was to control the practical everyday work of the various Communist Parties. Solomon Lozovsky (1878-1952) was in charge of the Profintern, the Red Trade Union International, and the ultraleft tactics it imposed on Stalinist trade-union work throughout the world in the "third period." The Profintern was organized in 1921 as a rival to the reformist international federation whose headquarters were in Amsterdam (the "Amsterdam International").

82. "If America Should Go Communist." *Liberty,* March 23, 1935. This article was written for a broad American audience during the Great Depression, when millions were becoming radicalized and interested in learning what Marxism was and what a socialist revolution would mean in the United States. This was in the middle of the second year of the New Deal regime headed by Franklin D. Roosevelt, when the labor movement was beginning to stir, but before the organization of the Committee for Industrial Organization (CIO). An editorial caption in *Liberty* said: "Don't believe a word of this! Read the reply of former Secretary of Labor Davis next week."

83. "Technocracy" was an American program and movement that achieved a great vogue in the early years of the depression, particularly in the middle class. It proposed to overcome the depression and bring about full employment by rationalizing the U. S. economy and monetary system under the control of engineers and technical experts — all without class struggle or revolution. The movement eventually split into a left and right wing, with the latter developing fascist tendencies.

84. Herbert Hoover (1874-1964), Roosevelt's Republican predecessor, was the thirty-first president of the United States.

85. The National Recovery Administration (NRA) was set up in 1933 as a New Deal agency for preparing and enforcing codes of fair practices for business and industry. While it established a minimum wage and maximum hours and supported the right of workers to join a union, it was primarily an aid to business in that it allowed member firms to set standards of quality and establish the lowest prices that could be charged for goods. The NRA's symbol was a blue eagle. The U. S. Supreme Court ruled the NRA unconstitutional in May 1935.

86. The "Brain Trust" was the popular name for Roosevelt's advisers in the White House.

87. From 1920 to 1933, the United States was formally "dry," that is, the sale of alcoholic liquor was prohibited by constitutional amendment. In 1933 this amendment was repealed, making the country "wet" again.

88. "The burning of Darwin's works" refers to state laws that prohibited the teaching of theories of evolution in the public schools. The Scopes trial of 1925 in Dayton, Tennessee, was the most dramatic of the legal contests over these repressive laws.

89. "The Way Out." *La Verite,* September 1934, where it was signed "CC"; *The New International,* September-October 1934, where it was

combined with the earlier "The Evolution of the SFIO," and signed
"V." Written for the public, it was not printed until after August 29,
when the League's national conference voted to enter the SFIO. The
issue of *La Verite* in which it appeared described itself as the paper
of the Bolshevik-Leninist Group (GBL) in the SFIO. Besides explain-
ing the reason for the entry, Trotsky's article warned that the conclusions reached with respect to the Social Democracy in France
should not be mechanically applied to other countries; each national
situation had to be examined concretely. At the same time, his implication was that an entry tactic need not be restricted to France. Later
that year, he was to favor entry into the Belgian and Spanish Socialist parties, and he agreed with the decision of the Communist
League of America to merge with the American Workers Party into
the Workers Party of the United States, founded in December 1934.
It was not until more than a year later, early in 1936, that the WPUS
decided to join the American Socialist Party.

90. The "third period," according to the schema proclaimed by the
Stalinists in 1928, was the final period of capitalism, the period of
its immediately pending demise and replacement by soviets. Following
from this, the Comintern's tactics during the next six years were
marked by ultraleftism, adventurism, sectarian "red" unions and opposition to the united front. In 1934 the theory and practice of the
"third period" were discarded and replaced by those of the People's
Front (1935-39), but the latter period was not given a number. The
"first period" was 1917-24 (capitalist crisis and revolutionary upsurge); the "second period" was 1925-28 (capitalist stabilization).

91. "'Amsterdamian' parades" refers to the activities of various
"front" organizations of Stalinism (world committee against war,
world committee against fascism, etc.), often initiated or headquartered
in Amsterdam. Their two principal international congresses were at
Amsterdam in August 1932 and at the Pleyel hall in Paris in June
1933. A typical affiliate was the American League Against War and
Fascism, renamed in the People's Front period as the "more positive"
League for Peace and Democracy.

92. Otto Wels (1873-1939) and Carl Severing (1875-1952) were
leading German Social Democratic Party functionaries. As military
commander of Berlin, Wels crushed the Spartacist uprising of 1919;
later he led the SPD delegation in the Reichstag. Severing was minister of the interior in Prussia until removed by Papen in July 1932.

93. Epigones are disciples who corrupt the doctrines of their teacher.
Trotsky used the term for the Stalinists, who claim to be Leninists.

94. A considerable number of CP members and supporters did
fight alongside the fascists and royalists in the February 6, 1934,
demonstration, some of them under the banner of a CP-led veterans
organization. This was reminiscent of the so-called red referendum
in August 1931, when the German Stalinists joined the Nazis in an
effort to vote out the Social Democratic government of Prussia.

95. The PUP (Party of Proletarian Unity) was a short-lived centrist group formed by expelled CP and former SFIO members.

96. "On the Theses 'Unity and the Youth.'" From an undated and
unnumbered internal bulletin of the Workers Party of the United
States, 1935. Signed "Crux." This was Trotsky's intervention in a discussion going on among the French Bolshevik-Leninists in the sum-

mer of 1934 over the position they should take toward the possible merger ("organic unity") of the Communist Party and the SFIO.

97. Louis-Olivier Frossard (1889-1946) was one of the leaders of the SFIO supporting its affiliation to the Comintern at the Tours Congress of 1920, and then the general secretary of the new CP. He resigned from the CP in 1923 and later rejoined the SFIO. He came close to the Neos in 1933, although he remained in the SFIO until 1935, when he resigned to become minister of labor. He later was a minister in various People's Front cabinets and in the first Petain regime.

98. Jean-Baptiste Lebas (1878-1944) was an SFIO functionary.

99. Yvan Craipeau (1912-   ) was a Bolshevik-Leninist leader in the French Socialist youth and a Fourth Internationalist during World War II. He left in 1946 to join various centrist groups.

100. "An Advocate Takes Up a Position on the French Situation." *De Nieuwe Weg,* October 1934. *De Nieuwe Weg* (The New Road) was published by the Dutch RSP. Signed "Crux." Translated for this volume by John Fairlie. It is unlikely that this was Trotsky's title. This article was written less than a month after the members of the French Communist League had joined the SFIO, where they constituted themselves as the Bolshevik-Leninist Group (GBL). Members of the League minority had also begun to enter the SFIO.

101. J. de Kadt was a leader of the Dutch OSP right wing, hostile to the ICL and Trotsky. He and his wing resigned in the summer of 1934, strengthening the OSP forces who wanted to work with the ICL. (See *Writings 33-34* for Trotsky's March 1934 criticism of de Kadt.)

102. The Belgian Labor Party (POB) was the Belgian section of the Second International.

103. The Young Socialist Guard (JGS) was the youth section of the Belgian Labor Party. In August 1934 the JGS, the Belgian Young Communist League and the Young Leninist League signed a united-front pact, one of whose clauses pledged them to common action "for the right of asylum in all capitalist countries for all the victims of international capitalist reaction and, above all, for Trotsky." This was a hard pill for the Stalinists to swallow, but they did it because of their eagerness to influence the JGS, which then had 35,000 members and major prestige among radical youth. Soon after Moscow sent orders for the YCL to withdraw from the pact. Almost 40 percent of the YCL Charleroi district voted against withdrawing.

104. "To the Ukrainian Comrades in Canada." *Robitnichi Visti,* December 1, 1934. *Robitnichi Visti* (Workers News) was a Ukrainian-language periodical published in Toronto from 1933 to 1938 by the Canadian section of the ICL. Translated for this volume by Robert Vernon. Trotsky's later thinking on the Soviet Ukraine will be found in *Writings 39-40.*

105. Trotsky himself was born and raised in the Ukraine.

106. Taras Shevchenko (1814-1861) was a Ukrainian poet who became known as the father of Ukrainian nationalist literature. He founded an organization to promote social equality, abolition of slavery, etc.

107. "Austria, Spain, Belgium and the Turn." From an undated and unnumbered internal bulletin of the Communist League of America, 1934. Signed "Crux."

108. The Schutzbund was the Republican Defense Corps founded by the Social Democracy in response to the growth of fascism in Austria. Its members fought a heroic struggle against the dictatorial Dollfuss government in February 1934, but they were crushed, thanks in part to the vacillations of their leaders. The Schutzbund conference of June 1934 was held in exile. Otto Bauer (1882-1939), leader of the Austrian Social Democracy and founder, with Friedrich Adler, of the Two-and-a-Half International (1921-23), was the chief theoretician of Austro-Marxism. Julius Deutsch (1884-1968) was a leader of the Austrian Social Democracy and of the Schutzbund.

109. Austro-Marxism refers to the brand of reformism practiced by the Socialist Party of Austria.

110. Kurt Landau was for a short time a member of the Left Opposition in Austria. He was assassinated by the Stalinists during the civil war in Spain.

111. An insurrection against the government of Spain, led by the Socialist Party, had just been crushed.

112. The leaders of the Izquierda Comunista, Spanish Bolshevik-Leninists, were opposed to entering the Socialist Party. Headed by Andres Nin, they were soon to break with the ICL and then to merge with the Workers and Peasants Bloc, led by Joaquin Maurin, to form the Workers Party of Marxist Unification (POUM).

113. This *Action Socialiste* (Socialist Action), not to be confused with the French SFIO periodical of the same name, was the publication of the Belgian POB left wing, headed by Paul-Henri Spaak.

114. "On Bonapartism (Marxism Is Superior)." *La Verite*, December 1, 1934. Unsigned. Translated for this volume by Fred Buchman.

115. Heinrich Bruening (1885-1970) was the leader of the Catholic Center Party. Appointed German chancellor by Hindenburg in March 1930, he ruled by decree from July 1930 to his dismissal in May 1932. Franz von Papen (1879-1969) was appointed chancellor by Hindenburg in June 1932 and greased the way for Hitler by dissolving the Social Democratic government of Prussia. He was replaced by Schleicher in December 1932. He became Hitler's vice-chancellor in January 1933. Engelbert Dollfuss (1892-1934), chancellor of Austria, crushed the workers of Vienna when they resisted his dictatorial attacks on their rights in February 1934. Favorable to the Italian Fascists and hostile to the German fascists, he was assassinated by the Nazis in July 1934.

116. Pierre-Etienne Flandin (1889-1958), a leader of the Left Republicans, succeeded Doumergue as premier in November 1934, serving until May 1935. Hendrik Colijn (1869-1944) was premier of the Netherlands in 1925-26 and 1933-39.

117. August Thalheimer (1884-1952), a founder of the German Communist Party, was expelled with Heinrich Brandler in 1929. Together they organized the Communist Party Opposition (KPO), also called the Right Opposition. Heinrich Brandler (1881-1967), the leader of the German Communist Party during the early 1920s, was made the scapegoat by Moscow for the revolutionary situation

that was bungled in 1923 and was expelled in 1929, when the Comintern had entered its "third period" and a left zigzag. The policies of the KPO paralleled those of the Bukharin-Rykov tendency in the Soviet Union and the Lovestone group in the United States during the 1930s.

118. The Comite de Vigilance des Intellectuels Antifascistes was founded March 5, 1934, by the physicist Paul Langevin, the ethnologist Paul Rivet and the philosopher Alain. It was an association of intellectuals, scholars, writers and artists who became alarmed by the fascist demonstration on February 6 and saw the need for left-wing unity and action. Members of the committee included Pablo Picasso, Andre Gide, Julian Benda and Irene Joliot-Curie. This committee subsequently participated in the gigantic demonstration on July 14, 1935, which coincided with the launching of the People's Front movement in France.

119. Louis Napoleon Bonaparte (1808-1873), Napoleon III, was the subject of Karl Marx's book, *The Eighteenth Brumaire of Louis Napoleon.*

120. "On the SAP's Proposals." *Unser Wort,* February 1935. *Unser Wort* (Our Word) was the publication of the ICL's German section. Signed "Crux." Translated for this volume by Fred Buchman. The German SAP had signed the Declaration of Four for a new International at the Paris conference in August 1933; at the same time it signed a vague resolution on internationalism along with the NAP and other centrist groups. In the following year, the SAP dragged its feet on implementing the Declaration of Four while courting the NAP, which, Trotsky and the ICL warned, was turning to the right and heading back toward the Second International. In August 1934, at a Northern Workers Conference held in Stockholm, the NAP openly began to move to the right, much to the distress of the SAP leadership. In the autumn of 1934, in preparation for a conference of the IAG to be held in Paris in February 1935, the SAP wrote a document, "Wesen und Aufgaben der IAG" (The Character and Tasks of the IAG), which sought, among other things, to maintain ties with the NAP. Trotsky's letter is an analysis of the SAP's theses.

121. IAG were the German initials for the International Labor Community, also known as the London-Amsterdam Bureau and, beginning in 1935, as the International Bureau for Revolutionary Socialist Unity. It was set up in Berlin in May 1932 at the initiative of the Norwegian Labor Party (NAP) and the British Independent Labour Party in collaboration with the SAP and the left wing of the Dutch Social Democracy, which later became the OSP. Participants in its August 1933 conference in Paris included, besides the NAP, ILP, SAP and OSP, the Independent Communist Party of Sweden, led by Karl Kilbom (which later changed its name to the Socialist Party of Sweden), the French Party of Proletarian Unity (PUP), the Catalan (or Iberian) Federation led by Joaquin Maurin, the Dutch Revolutionary Socialist Party led by Henricus Sneevliet, the Italian Maximalists, the German Leninbund and the International Left Opposition.

122. Hendrik de Man (1885-1953) was a leader of the Belgian Labor Party's right wing and author in 1933 of a "labor plan" to

end the depression and promote production. (See *Writings 33-34* for Trotsky's comments.) The reformists in the French CGT, headed by Jouhaux, soon came up with a similar plan.

123. "The Stalinist Bureaucracy and the Assassination of Kirov." From the pamphlet *The Kirov Assassination,* Pioneer Publishers, February 1935, in which a note reported that it had been written in response to a request from a group of Americans. Translated by John G. Wright. At the end of 1934 Trotsky had been exiled from the Soviet Union for almost six years. Moscow had announced several times that "Trotskyism" had been completely annihilated in the USSR. Along with these announcements, there went a continuous campaign to slander the Left Opposition and to suppress any other voices of dissent, in or out of the Communist Party. The assassination of Sergei M. Kirov, Stalin's loyal lieutenant in Leningrad, on December 1, 1934, evidently resulted from bungling on the part of the Soviet secret police during an effort to manufacture a plot that could be used to smear Trotsky as a terrorist. Many of the details are still unknown to the public, despite the fact that Nikita Khrushchev exposed the official version as a frame-up in his famous speech at the Twentieth Congress of the Soviet CP in 1956. Stalin used the Kirov case as the opening move in a series of public trials and party purges in the next four years that wiped out virtually the entire remaining leadership of the Russian Revolution and completed the CP's transformation into a submissive agency of the bureaucracy.

124. "Amalgam" was the term frequently used by Trotsky to designate the Kremlin's practice of lumping together different or opposing political opponents and accusing them of common crimes or sins.

125. White Guards (also known as "Whites") was the general designation for Russian counterrevolutionary forces following the October Revolution.

126. GPU was one of the abbreviated names for the Soviet political police department; other names were Cheka, NKVD, MVD, KGB, etc., but GPU is often used in their place.

127. The Wrangel army, led by Pyotr Wrangel, was one of the counterrevolutionary forces defeated during the civil war.

128. The "sealed" train was the train that carried Lenin and twenty-nine other Russian emigres from Switzerland through Germany en route to Russia in March 1917. The emigres had previously tried to make other arrangements to travel to Russia, following the February Revolution, but when these efforts proved unsuccessful, they negotiated the conditions for passage through Germany, which was then at war with Russia. The emigres demanded that there be no supervision of the passengers on the train, nor of their passports and baggage. In exchange, the emigres agreed to insist upon the release from Russia of a corresponding number of German and Austro-Hungarian civil prisoners. Many counterrevolutionaries later charged that this trip through Germany was evidence of the revolutionaries' collaboration with the reactionary German government.

129. William Green (1873-1952) was the conservative president of the conservative American Federation of Labor.

130. See *The Class Nature of the Soviet State,* October 1, 1933, (originally published in the United States under the title *The Soviet Union and the Fourth International*), reprinted in *Writings 33-34.*

131. Smolny was the CP's headquarters in Leningrad.

132. The "two-class workers' and peasants' parties" was a formula used by the Stalinists in the 1920s to justify support for the Kuomintang and other bourgeois parties in the Orient. Trotsky's critique will be found in *The Third International After Lenin.*

133. The Peasant International (Krestintern), formed by the Comintern in 1923, was an experiment that did not meet much success. It disappeared without publicity sometime in the late 1920s or early 1930s.

134. The theory of "national liberation" referred to the efforts by the German Stalinists to compete with the Nazis as champions of German nationalism in opposition to the oppressive Versailles Treaty. Only the Nazis benefited from this competition.

135. The Communist League of America played a leading role in the Minneapolis teamsters' strikes of 1934. In December it merged with the left-centrist American Workers Party, led by A. J. Muste, to create the Workers Party of the United States (WPUS).

136. *Le Temps* (The Times) was the unofficial voice of the French government in the 1930s.

137. Henry Yagoda (d.1938) was the head of the secret police in 1934. In 1937, he who had supervised the organization of the 1936 Moscow trial was himself made a defendant and executed. Emelyan Yaroslavsky (1878-1943) was the Stalinist author of falsified Soviet histories who fell from favor when he failed to keep up with the political gyrations of the Kremlin.

138. Albert Treint (b.1889) was a prominent leader of the French Communist Party who expressed support for the Left Opposition and was expelled in 1927. After a few years he left the Opposition.

139. Samuel Gompers (1850-1924) was president of the American Federation of Labor from 1886 until his death.

140. Nadezhda K. Krupskaya (1869-1939) was a leader of the Bolshevik Party and the companion of Lenin.

141. "The Indictment." *New Militant,* January 19, 1935, and also the pamphlet, *The Kirov Assassination. New Militant* was the paper of the Workers Party of the United States (1934-36). In this article Trotsky was able, ahead of anyone outside of the Soviet Union, to deduce that the Soviet secret police had financed Nikolaev — a deduction that was confirmed less than a month later.

142. Jacques Duclos (1896-   ) was a Stalinist deputy and a member of the Political Bureau of the French Communist Party.

143. The "consul of a foreign power" was the Latvian consul named Bisseneks, an obvious agent of the GPU, who quickly left the country after being identified. More details will be found in Trotsky's March 17, 1938, letter to the *New York Times,* reprinted in *Writings 37-38.*

144. "Wrangel officer." See the third paragraph of "The Stalinist Bureaucracy and the Assassination of Kirov."

145. Jacob Blumkin (1899-1929) was a left Social Revolutionary terrorist who became a Communist. As a supporter of the Left Opposition, he was the first Russian to visit Trotsky in exile in Turkey. Bringing back a letter from Trotsky to the Opposition, he was betrayed to the GPU and was shot in December 1929.

146. *Biulletin Oppozitsii* (Bulletin of the Opposition) was the Russian-language magazine founded by Trotsky shortly after his exile

to Turkey in 1929. A total of sixty-five issues was published before it was discontinued in 1941. Trotsky was the actual editor until his death in 1940, and his son, Leon Sedov, was in effect its managing editor until his death in 1938. The *Biulletin* was printed in Paris from 1929 to 1931, in Berlin from 1931 to 1932, in Paris from 1933 to 1934, in Zurich from 1934 to 1935, in Paris from 1935 to 1939 and, with war imminent in Europe, in New York from 1939 to 1941. It was one of the first publications banned by the Nazis when they came to power in Germany in 1933. The *Biulletin* contained many of Trotsky's most important pamphlets and articles during his last exile, documents of the Left Opposition, International Communist League and Fourth International, and articles by other members of those organizations.

147. "Statement to the Press." *La Voix Communiste* (The Communist Voice), January 6, 1935. This was the paper of the Belgian Bolshevik-Leninists. Translated for this volume by Fred Buchman. Trotsky elsewhere noted bitterly that while Stalin's lies were reproduced without criticism by the French press, this brief statement was not printed in a single bourgeois paper in France. The "special pamphlet" referred to in the last sentence consisted of the two previous selections in this volume, dated December 28 and 30, 1934.

148. "Some Results of the Stalin Amalgam." *New Militant,* February 9, 1935, where it was entitled "Late Episodes in Kirov Assassination Analyzed by Trotsky."
149. The 1926 platform of the Opposition was first printed in the United States in *The Real Situation in Russia,* 1928.
150. Pavel Miliukov (1859-1943), leader of the Cadet Party, was minister of foreign affairs in the Russian Provisional Government, March-May 1917, and an outstanding enemy of the Bolshevik Revolution. Alexander Kerensky (1882-1970) was a member of the Russian Social Revolutionary Party and head of the government overthrown by the Bolsheviks in 1917.
151. YCLers were members of the Young Communist League (Komsomols in Russian).
152. Lazar Kaganovich (1893-   ) was a crony of Stalin and an undeviating Stalinist in various Soviet party and governmental posts. He was removed from all his posts as an "antiparty" element when Khrushchev took over the Soviet leadership following the CP's Twentieth Congress.

153. "The Case of Zinoviev, Kamenev and Others." *Biulletin Oppozitsii,* Number 42, February 1935. Translated for this volume by Fred Buchman.
154. Cheka was the abbreviated name of the first Soviet political police department established after the 1917 revolution.
155. Nikolai Bukharin (1888-1938) was an Old Bolshevik and the second president of the Comintern (after Zinoviev), 1926-29. He joined with Stalin against the Left Opposition, but they split in 1928 and Bukharin formed a Right Opposition before he was expelled in 1929. He capitulated, but was convicted and executed in the 1938 Moscow trial.
156. See section 1, "A Grandiose Amalgam" in "The Stalinist Bu-

reaucracy and the Assassination of Kirov."

157. See note 156.

158. M. N. Riutin was a leading Soviet propagandist in the early 1930s. He was close to several intellectuals of Bukharin's tendency and, together with them, drew up a program of reform for the country and the party that was an indictment of Stalin's policies. He was arrested at the end of 1932, was expelled from the party and was sentenced to death.

159. See note 156.

160. "Everything Gradually Falls into Place." *Biulletin Oppozitsii,* Number 42, February 1935. Translated for this volume by Fred Buchman.

161. Bela Kun's name may be included in the reference to the "latest policy" of the Stalinists (using the united front as a stepping-stone to the class-collaborationist People's Front) as an ironic reminder that Kun had been an opponent of the Leninist policy of the united front when it was being developed by the Comintern in 1921.

162. "Where Is the Stalin Bureaucracy Leading the USSR?" *The New International,* March 1935. Unsigned.

163. The Kuomintang (People's Party) of China was the bourgeois-nationalist party founded by Sun Yat-sen in 1911 and led after 1926 by Chiang Kai-shek, butcher of the Chinese Revolution of 1925-27 and ruler of the country until overthrown by the Chinese Revolution of 1949.

164. NEP was the New Economic Policy initiated in 1921 to replace the policy of "military communism," which prevailed during the civil war and which led to conflict between the workers and the peasants as industrial production declined drastically and grain was requisitioned and confiscated from the peasants. To revive the economy after the civil war, the NEP was adopted as a temporary measure allowing a limited revival of free trade inside the Soviet Union and foreign concessions alongside the nationalized and state-controlled sections of the economy. The NEPmen, who benefited from this policy, were viewed as a potential base for the restoration of capitalism. Trotsky uses the term Neo-NEP here to describe certain developments in the Soviet economy, but he did not continue to use it.

165. Alexander Petrovich Smirnov (1877-1938), an Old Bolshevik, was deputy people's commissar for internal affairs and deputy people's commissar for food after the October Revolution. In January 1933, he and two other Old Bolsheviks, Eismont and Tolmachev, were charged with forming an antiparty group designed to remove Stalin. There was opposition within the Central Committee to having these oppositionists shot; instead Eismont and Tolmachev were expelled from the party and jailed subsequently; and Smirnov was expelled first from the Central Committee and later (December 1934) from the party.

166. "The Workers' State, Thermidor and Bonapartism." *The New International,* July 1935. There was no precedent for the Russian Revolution — it was the first successful workers' revolution in history. But the Bolsheviks were eager to learn from other revolutions,

even bourgeois revolutions, anything that might be useful as they
entered uncharted territory after 1917. That was why they were so
interested in the Great French Revolution at the end of the eighteenth
century, and especially in what happened to bring about the downfall of the revolutionary Jacobins, headed by Robespierre, in 1794,
and in the succeeding shifts of power in the Convention (revolutionary parliament) that led first to the government of the Directory, then
to the rule of Napoleon Bonaparte, initially as first consul and finally
as emperor. (The day on which Robespierre fell was called Ninth
Thermidor [July 27, 1794] in the new calendar; the day on which the
first Bonaparte seized power was Eighteenth Brumaire [November 9,
1799].) The Russian Revolution was anticapitalist while the French
Revolution was antifeudal, but Trotsky and other Bolsheviks saw valid though partial analogies between the Russian 1920s and the French
1790s and often debated their significance. In the present essay — an
outstanding example of Marxist self-criticism and self-correction —
Trotsky reviewed the debate and changed his position on certain
important aspects of the Thermidorean analogy.

167. "The old organic course" refers to the course followed by
the Stalin-Bukharin faction of the Comintern from 1925 to 1928.

168. See V. I. Lenin's *The State and Revolution.*

169. Alexander V. Kolchak (1874-1920) commanded one of the
Eastern counterrevolutionary fronts during the Russian civil war.

170. Bessedovsky, Dimitrievsky and Agabekov were Soviet diplomats who defected to the capitalist world.

171. Walter Duranty and Louis Fischer were American journalists
whom Trotsky denounced as apologists for Stalinism.

172. Romanov was the name of the last Russian czar.

173. Lovestoneites were named after Jay Lovestone, a leader of the
American Communist Party in the 1920s who was expelled in 1929
shortly after the downfall of his international ally, Bukharin. The
Lovestoneites maintained an organization until World War II, when
they dissolved. Lovestone later became cold-war adviser on foreign
affairs for AFL-CIO president George Meany.

174. The major criticism of this essay appears in Isaac Deutscher's 1963 book, *The Prophet Outcast.* Deutscher held that the
whole Thermidor analogy was confusing and harmful and that
Trotsky's 1935 correction represented no improvement. He denied
that the defeat of the Left Opposition in 1923 was "in any sense an
event comparable to the collapse and dissolution of the Jacobin party;
it corresponded rather to the defeat of the left Jacobins which had
taken place well before Thermidor. . . . What the early nineteen-
twenties had in common with the Thermidorian period was the ebb-
ing away of the popular revolutionary energies and the disillusionment and apathy of the masses. It was against such a background
that Robespierre had sought to keep the rump of the Jacobin Party
in power and failed; and that Stalin struggled to preserve the dictatorship of the Bolshevik rump (i.e. of his own faction) and succeeded" (p. 316). If Robespierre was to be compared to anyone,
in Deutscher's opinion, it was Stalin, not Trotsky. Relevant or ir-
relevant, it is plain that for both Trotsky and Deutscher the lessons
of Thermidor were connected, if only in a supporting way, to their
perspectives for the Soviet Union — Trotsky's that a political revolution was needed, Deutscher's (in the 1950s) that the need was for

reform and not revolution and (in the 1960s) that Trotsky's advocacy of political revolution would have to be judged by a historian of the next generation.

175. "'Soviet Democracy.'" *New Militant,* March 30, 1935. Signed "L. T."

176. "To Comrade Sneevliet on the IAG Conference." *International Information Bulletin,* Workers Party of the United States, Number 1, 1935. Signed "Crux." This letter was written shortly after the conference of the IAG (Amsterdam Bureau) in Paris, which had been attended by Henricus Sneevliet, representing the RSP of Holland, and Peter J. Schmidt, representing the OSP of Holland. Trotsky's letter was in reply to one by Sneevliet, dated February 22, 1935, and printed in the same bulletin. Sneevliet thought that the conference's resolutions on the world situation and the war question contained nothing "that we would have to combat especially," except that they were silent about the need for a new International. He also thought that the ICL had made "a big mistake" by not participating in the conference and that it should consider sending its larger sections into the IAG.

177. Henricus Sneevliet (1883-1942) was a founder of the Marxist movement in Indonesia and of the Communist Party in Holland. While imprisoned for defending "mutinous" sailors, he was elected to the Dutch parliament in 1933. He signed the Declaration of Four in 1933 and his party, the RSP, adhered to the ICL. He left the Fourth Internationalist movement in 1938 and was executed by the Nazis during World War II.

178. Jacob Schwab was a leader of the SAP.

179. "The Swedish party," formerly the Independent Communist Party of Sweden, led by Kilbom, was now called the Socialist Party of Sweden.

180. Fenner Brockway (1890-   ) was a leader of the Independent Labour Party, an opponent of the Fourth International and later secretary of the London-Amsterdam Bureau. Trotsky thought in 1935 that the ILP should enter and work in the larger Labour Party, rather than remain isolated from its ranks.

181. Friedrich Sorge (1828-1906), friend and comrade of Marx and Engels, was secretary of the First International.

182. Pierre Joseph Proudhon (1809-1865) was one of the first theoreticians of anarchism.

183. Peter J. Schmidt was the leader of the Dutch OSP.

184. Dr. Joseph Kruk was the representative of a small group, the Independent Labor Party of Poland.

185. Mot Dag was a Norwegian centrist group.

186. The reference is to Trotsky's critique, "On the SAP's Proposals."

187. The RSP of Holland (Revolutionary Socialist Party) was the group headed by Henricus Sneevliet that joined in the call for a new International in 1933 and became the ICL's Dutch section. A few days after this letter, the OSP and RSP merged to form the RSAP. The latter voted to maintain ties with both the ICL and the IAG.

188. The Saar plebiscite, held on January 13, 1935, resulted in an overwhelming victory for the Nazis and the return of the Saar to Germany. For Trotsky it was further evidence of the continuing

bankruptcy and impotence of Stalinism and Social Democracy two years after Hitler came to power.

189. As a concession to the American Workers Party, the Communist League of America had not insisted on affiliation to the ICL as a condition for their merger.

190. A plenum is a full and formal meeting of a committee. This reference is to a full meeting of the International Executive Committee of the ICL.

191. "Adolphe" was a pen name of Rudolf Klement, a member of the International Secretariat, who was murdered by the GPU in Paris shortly before the founding conference of the Fourth International in 1938 (see *Writings 38-39*).

192. Julius Martov (1872-1923) was a close associate of Lenin in the leadership of the Russian Social Democracy until 1903, when he became the leader of the Mensheviks. He emigrated to Berlin in 1920.

193. The "criminal policy" of Stalin in the Chinese Revolution is discussed in Trotsky's *The Third International After Lenin, Problems of the Chinese Revolution* and *The Chinese Revolution: Problems and Perspectives.*

194. Mikhail Tomsky (1886-1936), an Old Bolshevik, was always in the right wing of the party and opposed the Bolshevik insurrection. He was head of the Soviet trade unions and a member of the Political Bureau until he joined the right-wing fight against Stalin led by Bukharin and Rykov. He committed suicide during the first Moscow trial in 1936.

195. "To Cannon on the Next Steps." *International Information Bulletin,* Workers Party of the United States, Number 1, 1935. Signed "Crux."

196. James P. Cannon (1890-   ) was an IWW organizer, a leader of the left wing in the Debsian Socialist Party and a founder of the American Communist Party. Expelled from the CP in 1928 for expressing solidarity with Trotsky, he led in the formation of the Left Opposition and later the Socialist Workers Party and the Fourth International.

197. Efforts along these lines resulted a few months later in the publication of an "Open Letter for the Fourth International," signed among others by the leaders of the Dutch RSAP, the WPUS and the ICL. The signers also established a Provisional Contact Committee, with an address in Amsterdam, which was entrusted with the tasks of publishing an information bulletin and coordinating the "collective working out of the fundamental programmatic and tactical documents of the Fourth International" (see *Writings 35-36*).

198. A. J. Muste (1885-1967), a Protestant minister and pacifist, became involved with the labor movement during World War I. In 1929 he helped found the Conference for Progressive Labor Action (CPLA), which promoted militancy, union democracy and industrial unionism inside the AFL and helped to organize the unemployed when the depression began. In 1933 the CPLA organized the American Workers Party, whose members were active in important strikes and unemployed struggles. In 1934 the AWP, moving leftward, merged with the Communist League of America to form the Workers Party of the United States, of which Muste was secretary. In 1936,

after the WPUS had voted to enter the Socialist Party, Muste broke with Marxism and returned to pacifism and the church. In the 1950s he was one of the few to defend victims of the witch-hunt and helped form the American Forum for Socialist Education to encourage systematic exchange of radical views. In the 1960s he played a leading role in building the antiwar movement.

199. "Centrist Combinations and Marxist Tactics." *International Information Bulletin,* Workers Party of the United States, Number 1, 1935. Signed "Crux." A report on the IAG conference by V. appeared in the same bulletin.

200. The Jewish Bund (the General Jewish Workers Union of Lithuania, Poland and Russia) was part of the Russian Social Democratic Party until 1903, when it opposed Lenin's concept of a multinational, democratically centralized party. When the Social Democratic congress rejected its demand for a federated party structure, in which the Bund would be in charge of relations with Jewish workers, the Bund split and became an independent organization. In 1917 it sided with the Mensheviks against the Bolshevik Revolution.

201. "Vidal" was one of Trotsky's pen names.

202. George Vereecken was a representative of a sectarian tendency in the Belgian section of the ICL.

203. "Again on the Question of Bonapartism." *Quatrieme Internationale,* February 1937. *Quatrieme Internationale* (Fourth International) was a French-language magazine published by the International Secretariat. Translated for this volume by A. L. Preston.

204. Otto von Bismarck (1815-1898) was the reactionary head of the Prussian government, 1862-71, and chancellor of the German Empire, 1871-90. He organized the unification of Germany through the Seven-Weeks' War against Austria and the Franco-Prussian War.

205. Viktor Chernov (1876-1952) was a founder and leader of the Russian Social Revolutionary Party. He participated in the Zimmerwald conference, served as minister of agriculture in the Kerensky government and opposed the Bolshevik Revolution.

206. Luigi Facta (1861-1930) was premier of Italy in 1922 and a senator in 1924.

207. "The Belgian Dispute and the De Man Plan." The first part was translated in an undated, unnumbered bulletin of the Workers Party of the United States, 1935; the second part has been translated for this volume by George Novack from a bulletin of the Belgian section of the ICL, April 1935. Signed "Crux." The Belgian section held a national conference on March 10, 1935, to discuss perspectives and see if it was possible to avert a split by a minority, centered in Brussels and led by George Vereecken, which was opposed, among other things, to the French turn and its application in Belgium. Trotsky's letter, written in support of the position taken by the International Secretariat and its delegate to the conference, Martin, was discussed by the delegates there. A resolution introduced by the Charleroi branch, approving entry into the Belgian Labor Party (POB) but not setting a date for entry, was adopted by the conference. The split was not averted. In the fourth paragraph from the end, beginning "Two years later, in April 1891," it appears that

either this date was a typographical error or a preceding citation from Engels was omitted inadvertently.

208. Georges Theunis (1873-1966) was Belgian minister of finance and prime minister, 1921-25, minister of national defense in 1932, and prime minister, 1934-35.

209. "Charleroi" refers to the leadership of the Belgian section, whose paper was *La Voix Communiste.*

210. Leon Lesoil (d. 1942) was one of the founders of the Belgian CP and one of its leaders who was expelled in 1928 for opposing the repression of the Soviet Opposition. He helped to organize the Belgian section of the Opposition and remained a leader for the rest of his life. Arrested by the Gestapo in June 1941, he died in a concentration camp the following year.

211. Vandervelde and Jacquemotte were leaders of the POB and the CP respectively.

212. The Gourov letter, dated January 9, 1934, appears under the title "Revisionism and Planning" in *Writings 33-34.*

213. The Hennautists was a tendency that had split from the Belgian section, with whom it negotiated unsuccessfully for reunification in 1933.

214. "From a Letter to the Chinese Comrades." Bulletin of the German section of the ICL, Number 2, June 1935. Signed "Crux." Translated for this volume by Fred Buchman.

215. "From the CGT's Plan to the Conquest of Power." From Trotsky's *Le Mouvement Communiste en France,* edited by Pierre Broue, 1967; notes have also been adapted from that book. Translated for this volume by J. R. Fidler. Although it was printed in *La Verite,* April 5, 1935, and as a pamphlet (*La Breche Syndicale,* 1935), this document never appeared under the signature of its real author until 1967. It is a speech to the CGT's National Confederal Committee (CCN), delivered March 18-19, 1935, by Alexis Bardin, a delegate to the CCN from the departmental union of the CGT unions of Isere. Bardin was a young member of the Bolshevik-Leninist Group in the SFIO, living not far from Trotsky, and Trotsky prepared the entire speech. In addition to the fact that many of the problems it deals with are still relevant, this document is valuable for showing how Trotsky thought a revolutionary member of a reformist union could and should intervene even at a meeting of reformist bureaucrats in order to spread revolutionary ideas.

216. After the Belgian Labor Party adopted Hendrik de Man's plan in 1933, the French union leaders followed suit. At Leon Jouhaux's initiative, the CGT set up a "plan" study center in May 1934, whose draft of a plan was adopted by the CCN in October 1934. In a pamphlet completed March 28, 1935, Trotsky wrote, "Neither de Man nor Jouhaux are the inventors of their 'plans.' They merely took fundamental demands from the *Marxist program of the transition period* — the nationalization of the banks and key industries — threw overboard the class struggle and, in place of the revolutionary expropriation of the expropriators, substituted the financial operation of *purchasing* [that is, buying out the capitalists]." Trotsky charged that the goal of the plan was "to disguise the final *collapse of reformism* and to instill new hopes in the proletariat, in order to sidetrack

it away from revolution." But he also thought that the plan, "which was projected to sidetrack the workers away from 'evil thoughts,' can become the banner of a revolutionary movement" (*Whither France?*, Pathfinder Press, 1968, pp. 96-97).

217. The Patriotic Youth and the Peasant Front were organizations of the ultraright, collaborating with the French fascists. The Popular Democrats were a more traditional bourgeois organization, something like the Radical Party.

218. The question of nationalization came up later in 1935, when the People's Front program was being formulated, and was omitted from the program at the insistence of the Communist Party. Maurice Thorez reported in *l'Humanite,* July 13, 1936: "The comrades of the Socialist Party wanted to introduce nationalizations into the program. We were unwilling to sow illusions. We took a stand. We were right."

219. The Forty Hours Act was adopted by parliament in June 1936 under the pressure of a gigantic wave of strikes and factory occupations preceding the formation of the People's Front government headed by Blum.

220. Louis XVI (Capet) was the head of the old feudal monarchy (*ancien regime*) overthrown by the French Revolution in 1792.

221. The CGT leaders had no intention of encouraging anybody to engage in any kind of revolutionary action. At the CCN meeting where Bardin spoke, Jouhaux retreated from his own plan and stifled all efforts to further popularize or extend it. Trotsky put the blame for Jouhaux's ability to do this on the leaders of the Communist and Socialist parties (*Whither France?*, pp. 97-98).

222. "The Situation in the Stockholm Youth Bureau." *International Information Bulletin,* Spartacus Youth League of America, undated, 1935. Signed "Crux." The International Bureau of Revolutionary Youth Organizations was founded in February 1934 at a conference begun in Holland and completed in Belgium, with its goal "to work for the creation of a new international youth organization." Its main organizations were the youth affiliates of the ICL and of various IAG groups. It set up a Youth Bureau in Stockholm, which soon became paralyzed because of differences over perspective, particularly as the SAP tendency and its allies in the Youth Bureau hardened in their opposition to the need to proclaim the Fourth International. The Youth Bureau sent a delegate to the IAG conference in Paris in February 1935, who denounced the Dutch delegates supporting the Fourth International, Sneevliet and Schmidt. This delegate, who was also a member of the SAP, later became better known as the Social Democratic chancellor of West Germany; his name was Willy Brandt.

223. Walter Held (d. 1941), German emigre and ICL delegate to the Youth Bureau, later served as a secretary for Trotsky in Norway. Shortly before the Nazis invaded Norway, he went to Sweden and secured papers to enter the United States. In the spring of 1941, he undertook to travel there via the USSR and Turkey, for both of which countries he had been granted the necessary transit papers. He was taken off the train by Soviet secret police and executed in Saratov.

224. At the Paris conference in August 1933, the SAP signed the Declaration of Four, calling for a new International. The SAP and the

OSP also signed a resolution associating themselves with five other groups opposed to a new International.

225. At a congress of the Socialist youth's Entente of the Seine at the end of February 1935, a "Trotskyist motion" got 236 votes, while its opponents tallied 408.

226. Despite protests from a number of Youth Bureau affiliates, Brandt and his allies went further to the right, and in August 1935 they expelled Held. The Youth Bureau folded up soon after.

227. "A New Noose in the Stalinist Amalgam." *New Militant,* May 4, 1935 (where it had the title "Bolshevik-Leninists in USSR Face New Frame-Up").

228. "Notes of a Journalist." *Biulleten Oppozitsii,* Number 43, April 1935. Signed "Alpha." Translated for this volume by John Fairlie. The first part appeared in another translation in *New Militant,* June 15, 1935.

229. Kliment Voroshilov (1881-1969), an early supporter of Stalin, was a member of the Political Bureau from 1926 and president of the revolutionary military council and people's commissar of defense, 1925-40. He became president of the USSR, 1953-60.

230. A. I. Stetsky was a follower of Bukharin who later temporarily replaced him as theoretician in Stalin's circle. He was arrested in 1938.

231. "The Situation in France and the Tasks of the Bolshevik-Leninist Group of the SFIO." Bulletin of the German section of the ICL, Number 2, June 1935. Unsigned. Translated for this volume by John Fairlie. Although the article is dated April 15, 1935, the quotation from *l'Humanite* of April 18 indicates it was actually not completed until later.

232. Croix de Feu was a paramilitary fascist organization headed by Colonel Casimir de la Rocque. From the February 6, 1934, events in which it played a leading role, until around 1936, it was the strongest fascist movement in France.

233. Henry Dorgeres (b.1897) was the profascist leader of the Peasant Front.

234. Paul Vaillant-Couturier (1892-1937), French Stalinist leader and editor of *l'Humanite,* was a leading exponent of social patriotism.

235. Paul Deroulede (1846-1914) was a French politician and author of patriotic verse.

236. "On the South African Theses." *Workers' Voice* (South Africa), November 1944; *International Socialist Review,* Fall 1966. The Workers Party of South Africa had submitted a programmatic document for discussion; Trotsky's reply stated his position on the national question in that country, then still a semicolony of Britain.

237. Before 1917 Lenin thought that the next Russian revolution would be based on an alliance between the workers and the peasants within the framework of a bourgeois democracy. In 1917 he replaced that with the perspective of a dictatorship of the proletariat (workers' state) supported by the peasantry. The evolution of Lenin's thinking on the question of the "democratic dictatorship of the proletariat and the peasantry" is traced by Trotsky in *The. Permanent Revolution*

and in the essay "The Three Conceptions of the Russian Revolution" in *Writings 38-39.*

238. The African National Congress, formed in 1913, was the first South African organization to formulate a program based on Bantu unity, political, economic and social equality between black and white in state and church, guaranteed land rights for Africans, abolition of the color bar and other racial discrimination against non-Europeans. The ANC became a favorite haunt of the Stalinists in the 1930s. It was banned following the Sharpeville massacre in 1960.

239. Ramsay MacDonald (1866-1937) became prime minister in the first British Labour government (1924) and bolted the Labour Party during his second term as prime minister (1929-31) to form a "national unity" cabinet with the Tories (1931-35).

240. "Centrist Alchemy or Marxism?" *The New International,* July 1935. Unsigned. The SAP's long and bitter reply was translated and published under the title "A Necessary Discussion" in the November 1935 issue of *New International Bulletin,* published by the League for a Revolutionary Workers Party, headed by B.J. Field.

241. Between the IAG conference in February 1935 and the writing of this article, the NAP had become the governing party of Norway.

242. See *Writings 33-34* for this resolution, written by Trotsky.

243. The three parties represented on the "Initiative Committee" were the SAP, Doriot's group in France and the Spanish group led by Joaquin Maurin.

244. Karl Kautsky (1854-1938) was, after Engels, the most respected figure in the Second International until he abandoned internationalism during World War I and opposed the Russian Revolution—that is, until he became "the Kautsky of the decline."

245. See V. I. Lenin, "The 'Disarmament' Slogan," October 1916, in *Collected Works,* volume 23, page 94.

246. Thesis 36, *War and the Fourth International* (see *Writings 33-34*).

247. Arthur Henderson (1863-1935), one-time secretary of the British Labour Party and president of the Second International, was an outstanding social patriot during World War I and a member of the British cabinet on several occasions.

248. Weimar was the small town where the government of the German Republic was organized in 1919. The Weimar Republic lasted until Hitler assumed full power in 1933.

249. The Union of Democratic Control was a pacifist organization, supported by liberal and radical intellectuals and socialists, which grew rapidly during the war. Eugene Dene Morel (1873-1924), a writer and journalist, was a member of the ILP and a Labour member of the House of Commons at the time of his death. He is known for his work in Africa, particularly in forming the Congo Reform Association in 1904, which exposed and forced the cessation of the horrors on the rubber plantations in the Congo.

250. Henri Barbusse (1873-1935) was a pacifist novelist who joined the French Communist Party, wrote biographies of Stalin and Christ and sponsored amorphous antiwar and antifascist congresses used by the Stalinists as showcase substitutes for genuine struggle. Willi Muenzenberg (1889-1940), an organizer of the Young Communist

International, masterminded many propaganda enterprises for the German CP and the Kremlin. He broke with the Stalinists in 1937 and was found dead in France at the time of Germany's invasion.

251. Zimmerwald, Switzerland, was the site of a conference in September 1915 to reassemble the antiwar and internationalist currents that had survived the debacle of the Second International. Although most of the participants were centrists, it proved to be a step in the direction of a new International. Kienthal, Switzerland, was the site of a second international conference, held in April 1916, which attempted to continue and go beyond the positions taken at the Zimmerwald conference.

252. Rosa Luxemburg (1871-1919) was one of the outstanding leaders in the history of the Marxist movement and a prominent opponent of revisionism and opportunism before World War I. Jailed in 1915, she helped to found the Spartakusbund and the German Communist Party. She and Karl Liebknecht were assassinated in January 1919 by order of Gustav Noske, Social Democratic minister of war in the Ebert-Scheidemann government. Karl Liebknecht (1871-1919) at first followed Social Democratic discipline in voting for war credits in the Reichstag on August 4, 1914. But then he broke discipline, publicly opposed the war and organized opposition to it.

253. Trotsky was in error here. The Stockholm Youth Bureau was created not with the NAP but with the Mot Dag group of Norway.

254. The Two-and-a-Half International (or International Association of Socialist Parties) was formed in February 1921 by centrist parties and groups that had left the Second International under pressure from the revolutionary masses. While criticizing the Second International, its leaders did not have a basically different orientation, and their main function was to act as a counterbalance to growing Communist influence among the workers. In May 1923 the Two-and-a-Half International reunited with the Second International.

255. Paul-Henri Spaak (1899-   ) was briefly a left-winger in the Belgian Labor Party and editor of *Action Socialiste* in 1934. When Trotsky arrived in France in 1933, Spaak visited him for advice. But he followed other advice, becoming a minister in the Belgian cabinet in 1935 and secretary-general of the North Atlantic Treaty Organization (NATO) in the 1950s.

256. "Stalinist Treason in *l'Humanite.*" *New Militant*, May 12, 1935. Unsigned.

257. Gabriel Peri (1902-1941) was a CP leader and *l'Humanite* editor. He was executed by the Nazis in World War II.

258. Pierre Laval (1883-1945), a Socialist in his youth, was minister of foreign affairs, 1934-35, and negotiated the Franco-Soviet pact. He was premier, 1935-36, and again in 1942, when he pursued a policy of collaboration with Germany. He was executed for treason.

259. On December 6, 1934, a Franco-Soviet protocol pledging mutual support to an Eastern European agreement to keep the peace was signed. This was the "Eastern Pact" Peri said Minister of Foreign Affairs Laval was giving up. How wrong Peri was became clear less than a month after his article.

260. *Der Voelkische Beobachter* (The People's Observer) was the leading Nazi paper.

261. John Simon (1873-1954) was a Conservative leader who held many cabinet posts including foreign secretary, 1931-35, home secretary, 1935-37, chancellor of the exchequer, 1937-40, and lord chancellor, 1940-45.

262. The Locarno Pact was a series of five treaties and arbitration conventions signed in December 1925 by Germany, Belgium, France, Italy, Great Britain, Czechoslovakia and Poland, "guaranteeing" the continuation of peace and existing territorial boundaries.

263. Pierre Taittinger (1887-1965) was the founder of one of the many French fascist organizations prominent in the mid-thirties, the Jeunesse Patriotes (Patriotic Youth).

264. Both Cachin and Vaillant-Couturier supported the French imperialist government in World War I.

265. "Stalin Has Signed the Death Certificate of the Third International." *New Militant*, June 8, 1935. Signed "International Secretariat of the International Communist League." On May 2, 1935, the announcement of a Franco-Soviet nonaggression pact was made in Moscow. A final communique at the end of Laval's conferences with Stalin, Litvinov and Molotov on May 15 stated: "They were wholly in agreement about recognizing, in the present state of the international situation, the obligations that force themselves upon the governments sincerely dedicated to safeguarding the peace and which have clearly demonstrated this desire for peace by their participation in every search for mutual guarantees, precisely in the interest of preserving peace. Duty first of all obligates them not to weaken in any way their means of national defense. In this respect Mr. Stalin understands and fully approves of the policy of national defense made by France in order to keep its armed strength at the level of security."

266. Brest-Litovsk was a town on the Russo-Polish border where a treaty ending hostilities between Russia and Germany was signed by the Soviet delegation on March 3, 1918. The terms were exceedingly unfavorable for Soviet interests, but the new Soviet government felt it had to sign because it was unable at that time to fight back. Later, the November 1918 Revolution in Germany and the German defeat in the war restored to the Soviet government most of the territory lost through the Brest-Litovsk treaty.

267. Fascist Italy at this time was preparing the invasion of Ethiopia (Abyssinia), which took place in the autumn of 1935. Mussolini had the tacit approval of French imperialism for this invasion.

268. Louis Marin (1871-1960) was an extreme right-wing deputy in the French parliament.

269. Jean Jaures (1859-1914), an outstanding French Socialist orator, was a pacifist, assassinated at the start of World War, I.

270. Philipp Scheidemann (1865-1939) and Gustav Noske (1868-1946) were leaders of the German Social Democratic right wing and members of the cabinet that crushed the November 1918 Revolution. Emile Vandervelde (1866-1938) was a Belgian Social Democratic reformist who served as president of the Second International, 1929-36.

271. "To the Students of Edinburgh University." *New Militant*, June 29, 1935. Another translation was used in *Trotsky's Diary in Exile, 1935.*

272. "The Seventh Congress of the Comintern." *Biulletin Oppozitsii,* Number 44, July 1935. Unsigned. Translated for this volume by Fred Buchman. Another translation appeared in *New Militant,* July 27, 1935.

273. The People's Front (or Popular Front) was the name given in 1935 to the coalition of the French workers' parties (Communist and Socialist) with the bourgeois-democratic Radical Party (or Radical Socialist Party). The Radical and Socialist parties had formed such a coalition in the 1920s, called the Cartel des Gauches (Left Bloc), which the Communist International bitterly condemned as class collaboration. What was new in 1935, in addition to the name, was the Communist Party's endorsement of and active participation in class collaboration. People's frontism became the official policy of the Comintern at its Seventh Congress in 1935 and remained the policy of all Stalinist parties until 1939, when the Stalin-Hitler pact was signed. It was revived under various names (antimonopoly coalition, etc.) after World War II.

274. Wilhelm Pieck (1876-1960) was a member of the Spartacus League and an official of the German Communist Party from its founding. He spent World War II in Moscow and then returned to East Germany, where he headed the Socialist Unity Party.

275. Georgi Dimitrov (1882-1949), a Bulgarian Communist who had moved to Germany, attracted world attention in 1933 when the Nazis imprisoned and tried him and others on charges of having set the Reichstag on fire. He defended himself courageously at the trial and was acquitted. He became a Soviet citizen and served as executive secretary of the Comintern from 1934 to 1943. In 1945 he returned to Bulgaria, where he became premier, 1946-49.

276. Ernst Torgler (1893-1963) joined the German Communist Party in 1920 and was a member of the Reichstag from 1924. He was arrested after the burning of the Reichstag in 1933, but was acquitted. He was confined to a Nazi concentration camp and resumed activity in West German politics in 1945.

277. "An Open Letter to the Workers of France." *The New International,* August 1935. Trotsky had been informed at the end of May 1935 that the Norwegian government had decided to grant him a visa, and he left Domene for Paris the day this open letter was completed, which was three days after the formation of a new French cabinet, headed by Pierre Laval.

278. Jean-Baptiste Severac (1879-1951) was a reformist official of the SFIO.

279. Aristide Briand (1862-1932) was a former Socialist, and Louis Malvy (1875-1949) was a Radical.

280. Andre Marty (1886-1956) was leader of a sailors' mutiny in 1919 and a leader of the French CP until 1952, when he was expelled for alleged indiscipline.

281. Jean Longuet (1876-1938), grandson of Karl Marx, was a right-wing French Socialist and founder and editor of *Le Populaire.*

282. Sergei Sedov (1908-1937?), Trotsky's younger son, was arrested in Siberia, according to the Soviet press, and died in a concentration camp after refusing to "confess" to crimes implicating his father.

283. One of these leaders, Chemodanov, secretary of the Young

Communist International, told the French Socialist youth, "If war occurs against the USSR and you make your revolution, you will be traitors" (*New Militant*, July 13, 1935).

284. "A New Turn Is Necessary." *International Information Bulletin*, Workers Party of the United States, Number 2, September 7, 1935; excerpts also appear in *Le Mouvement Communiste en France*. Signed "Crux." On June 9, 1935, the night before this letter was written, the SFIO opened its thirty-second national congress at Mulhouse, the first held since the entry of the Bolshevik-Leninists. The letter shows that Trotsky viewed the French turn as having completed its usefulness. What he foresaw now was a regroupment for the construction of an independent revolutionary party able to take full advantage of the Comintern's latest drastic swing to the right. This was not an opinion shared by all of the GBL leaders, some of whom thought in terms of an indefinitely protracted stay inside the SFIO. They were shaken in that belief by what happened at the Mulhouse Congress, at which there were 2,025 mandates for a majority (reformist) motion, 777 for a Bataille Socialiste (centrist) motion, 105 for a Bolshevik-Leninist motion. Firmly in control, the reformist leaders soon began to expel left-wingers in the SFIO and the Socialist youth. Trotsky's position, motivated in this letter, was taken before the repressions.

285. "Discipline Must Be Restored." *International Information Bulletin*, Workers Party of the United States, Number 2, September 7, 1935. Signed "Crux." This letter was written on the day Trotsky left France for the last time, on his way to Norway by way of Belgium.

OTHER WRITINGS OF 1934-35

In addition to the material in the present volume, the following writings of Trotsky during the period covered here have been published:

La Vie de Lenine: Jeunesse. 1936. The first volume in Trotsky's projected biography of Lenin, published at the time only in France. An English translation has been announced by Doubleday for publication in 1972.

Trotsky's Diary in Exile, 1935. 1958. Contains entries from the French period between February 7 and June 9, 1935.

Whither France? 1936. This collection includes two pamphlets— *Whither France* (October 1934) and *Once Again, Whither France?* (March 28, 1935)—published anonymously while Trotsky was in France.

The second English edition of *Terrorism and Communism* contains a new introduction by Trotsky dated January 10, 1935.

INDEX

BOOKS AND PAMPHLETS
BY LEON TROTSKY
PUBLISHED IN THE UNITED STATES
AND IN PRINT AS OF 1971

* The Age of Permanent Revolution
* The Basic Writings of Trotsky
  The Case of Leon Trotsky
  The Chinese Revolution: Problems and Perspectives
  The Death Agony of Capitalism and the Tasks of the Fourth International
  Fascism: What It Is and How to Fight It
* The History of the Russian Revolution (3 volumes)
  In Defense of Marxism
* Lenin: Notes for a Biography
* Literature and Revolution
  Marxism in Our Time
  Military Writings
  My Life
  On Black Nationalism and Self-Determination
  On Engels and Kautsky
  On the Jewish Question
  On the Labor Party in the U. S.
  On Literature and Art
  On the Paris Commune
  On the Suppressed Testament of Lenin
  On the Trade Unions
  The Permanent Revolution/Results and Prospects
* Problems of the Chinese Revolution
  Problems of Civil War
  The Revolution Betrayed
* Stalin
  The Stalin School of Falsification
  Stalinism and Bolshevism
  Stalin's Frame-up System and the Moscow Trials
  The Struggle Against Fascism in Germany
* Terrorism and Communism
  Their Morals and Ours
  The Third International After Lenin
* Trotsky's Diary in Exile, 1935

Whither France?
Women and the Family
Writings of Leon Trotsky 1939-40
                             1938-39
                             1937-38
                             1935-36
                             1934-35

In preparation:
Leon Trotsky Speaks
The Spanish Revolution, 1931-39
 Problems of Everyday Life and Other Writings on Culture and
   Science
 (Reprinting of) The First Five Years of the Communist Interna-
   tional (2 volumes)
 Six volumes of Writings of Leon Trotsky, from 1929 to 1934
* The Young Lenin (Doubleday)
* 1905 (Random House)

* Distributed but not published by Pathfinder Press

For a free catalog, write

PATHFINDER PRESS
410 West Street
New York, N. Y. 10014